FIFTY YEARS OF ATTACK
AND CONTROVERSY

Fifty Years of Attack and Controversy

The Consequences Among Disciples of Christ

By

STEPHEN J. COREY

1368

Thirty-Six Illustrations in Facsimile

Published by

The Committee on Publication of the Corey Manuscript

Printed in the United States of America

By The

Christian Board of Publication

St. Louis, Missouri

FOREWORD

This book was written to represent the facts, dispassionately and objectively, concerning the major controversial issues over which the Disciples of Christ have struggled for more than fifty years. Repeated attacks on the organized and cooperative agencies and leaders of the brotherhood, led by certain periodicals, have disrupted the harmony and thought of this indigenous American Protestant body.

The numerous quotations are thoroughly documented from brotherhood periodicals, official documents, reports, and other publications. In addition, official minutes of agencies are cited and pages of periodicals, letters, and documents are reproduced in facsimile from the originals. Thus, the pages are a challenge to a fair examination of the actual record.

Dr. Stephen J. Corey, the author, is one of our most respected and beloved leaders. He served most of his many years of significant ministry among us in a secretarial or presidential capacity with brotherhood organizations. They were the New York Christian Missionary Society (1903-1905), the Foreign Christian Missionary Society (1905-1919), The United Christian Missionary Society (1919-1938), and The College of the Bible (1938-1945). Now eighty years old, he is retired and president-emeritus of the seminary. Dr. Corey is the author of seven other religious books.

Time and again during the fifty years, Dr. Corey suffered from attacks launched against him personally or the policies and actions of the agencies which he served in our behalf. Yet he writes in the pages of this suspense-filled narrative with a spirit of kindly, Christian brotherliness. There is no name-calling of his brethren, which is in keeping with the record of the organized and cooperative forces of the Disciples across the years.

v

30105

Because of the significance of this volume, copies are being made available on a complimentary basis to all of the ministers, cooperative and non-cooperative, who serve our brotherhood congregations. This number includes the young preachers studying in Bible colleges and seminaries. The complimentary distribution is mainly made possible by the voluntary subsidy of a group of concerned Christian churches. Most of the churches endorsed the project by official action of their boards. In addition, some interested friends, upon learning of the project, shared in it. Such gifts paid for publication and distribution. Names of the churches and their ministers (those marked by an asterisk * had recently resigned) follow:

Amarillo, Tex., First Church, Newton J. Robison
Ashland, Ky., First Church, Joseph S. Faulconer
Atlanta, Ga., Peachtree Church, Robert W. Burns
Austin, Tex., Central Church, John Barclay
Bartlesville, Okla., First Church, George G. Beazley, Jr.
Beckley, W. Va., First Church, A. H. Wilson
Birmingham, Ala., First Church, J. Wayne Drash
Boulder, Colo., First Church, Millard L. Riley
Bowling Green, Ky., First Church, Jean Stuart Wake
Cedar Rapids, Ia., First Church, Galen Lee Rose
Champaign, Ill., University Place Church, W. J. Jarman
Chicago, Ill., University Church, Irvin E. Lunger
Chicago Heights, Ill., Christian Church, C. H. Wilhelm
Cincinnati, O., Walnut Hills Church, Edward S. Moreland
Colorado Springs, Colo., First Church, Gerald Berneking
Columbus, O., Fourth Ave. Church, Kermit Traylor
Corbin, Ky., Christian Church, John S. Chambers
Covington, Ky., Madison Ave. Church, Barton A. Johnson
Dallas, Tex., East Dallas Church, W. A. Welsh
Denver, Colo., South Broadway Church, W. Reid Ferguson
Des Moines, Ia., Central Church, B. C. Bobbitt
Des Moines, Ia., Highland Park Church, William A. Knight
Des Moines, Ia., University Church, Warner Muir
Detroit, Mich., Central Woodward Church, Perry Epler
    Gresham*
Elkhart, Ind., Central Church, Glenn L. Tudor
Enid, Okla., Central Church, Ray E. Snodgrass

Eureka, Ill., Christian Church, Hilton A. Windley
Fort Worth, Tex., First Church, L. D. Anderson
Fullerton, Calif., First Church, Carlton C. Buck
Glendale, Calif., Central Church, Ira L. Ketcham
Hannibal, Mo., First Church, Kenneth A. Kuntz
Harrodsburg, Ky., Christian Church, Claud E. Stinson
Hopkinsville, Ky., Ninth St. Church, LeRoy S. Hulan
Indianapolis, Ind., Central Church, W. A. Shullenberger
Indianapolis, Ind., Downey Avenue Church, F. W. Wiegmann
Indianapolis, Ind., Third Church, A. C. Brooks
Indianapolis, Ind., University Park Church, Lewis H. McAdow
Jackson, Miss., First Church, Lee C. Pierce
Kalamazoo, Mich., Central Church, Kenneth B. Seeley
Kankakee, Ill., Central Church, William Harold Edds
Kansas City, Mo., Country Club Church, Warren Grafton*
Lexington, Ky., Central Church, Leslie R. Smith
Little Rock, Ark., First Church, Eulis H. Hill
Louisville, Ky., Douglass Blvd. Church, Thomas M. Giltner
Lubbock, Tex., First Church, Travis White*
Macon, Ga., First Church, Ernest E. Thompson
Mayfield, Ky., First Church, J. Howard Baxter
Memphis, Tenn., Lindenwood Church, Howard Thomas Wood
Mexico, Mo., First Church, Philip Byron Carlisle
Minneapolis, Minn., Portland Ave. Church, Forrest L. Richeson
Mt. Carmel, Ill., First Church, Allen S. Estill
Mt. Sterling, Ky., Christian Church, John C. Chenault
Nashville, Tenn., Vine Street Church, G. Curtis Jones
Ponca City, Okla., First Church, Loyal S. Northcott
Portland, Ore., First Church, Myron C. Cole
Richmond, Va., Hanover Ave. Church, H. Myron Kauffman
Richmond, Va., Seventh St. Church, Wayne H. Bell
St. Louis, Mo., Union Ave. Church, Hampton Adams
Santa Monica, Calif., First Church, Wales E. Smith
Seattle, Wash., University Church, John Paul Pack
Shaker Heights, O., Heights Church, Waymon Parsons
Sherman, Tex., Central Church, Robert L. Badgett
Springfield, Ill., First Church, Harry M. Davis
Topeka, Kan., First Church, Lowell C. Bryant
Tulsa, Okla., First Church, Hallie G. Gantz
Warren, O., Second Church, John B. Bridwell

Whittier, Calif., First Church, Rush M. Deskins
Yakima, Wash., First Church, Orval D. Peterson

This book is presented, therefore, with the confident hope that its reading may provide new awareness of the truth that sets men free, and thus become an increasing blessing.

COMMITTEE ON PUBLICATION

Ben C. Bobbitt, Chairman
Riley B. Montgomery, Treasurer
Hallie G. Gantz
Edward S. Moreland
Forrest L. Richeson
W. A. Welsh

ACKNOWLEDGMENTS

As can be readily seen, the writing of this volume has not been an easy task. I have depended largely on documentary material. This meant the review and careful study of numerous editorials, articles, and news reports in the *Christian Standard* of the last fifty years, as well as the reading of a large amount of additional source material. Having lived through these fifty years and being acquainted rather intimately with what has occurred, I have drawn on my own memory to a considerable degree. I have checked those recollections, however, with many of my living contemporaries among the Disciples of Christ as well as against the original records.

I wish to acknowledge much valuable help received. This was of real assistance in preparing the volume for publication, a task that went on for several years. I am greatly indebted to J. Edward Moseley of Indianapolis, Indiana, for painstaking editorial work on the manuscript on two time-consuming occasions. He carefully checked all references and quotations against the primary source materials. He discovered many new items of real interest and weight. Also, he wrote the last helpful chapter on the present status of the cooperative work of the Disciples of Christ.

In addition, I wish to express my appreciation of the work of Miss Arris Hayes of The College of the Bible staff in Lexington, Kentucky, for her help in much copying and typing; and to Professors George V. Moore and Howard E. Short of The College of the Bible for their useful suggestions about the manuscript. A number of other friends and former colleagues, too numerous to list here, offered valuable suggestions, time and again.

I am grateful, also, to the following:

The Disciples Divinity House of The University of Chicago for making available its files of the *Christian Standard* covering the years 1866-1894 and from 1904 to date.

The School of Religion of Butler University, Indianapolis, for granting the frequent use of its adequate library of historical materials of the Disciples of Christ, particularly rich in periodicals, including early numbers of the *Christian Standard* on microfilm, and a rare, complete file of the *Restoration Herald*.

The Disciples of Christ Historical Society, whose increasingly valuable archives were recently moved from Culver-Stockton College, Canton, Missouri, to the Joint University Library, Nashville, Tennessee, and whose curator, Claude E. Spencer, assisted frequently in checking the accuracy of many quotations and was of real help, too, in preparation of the Index.

The Library of The United Christian Missionary Society in Missions Building, Indianapolis, and its unselfish librarian, Mrs. Ada M. Mosher, always willing to search for records, minutes, reports, pamphlets, and other data such as the rare copies of *The Touchstone*.

The Library of the Midway (Ky.) Junior College for the use of the *Christian Standard* files of earlier years.

I cannot mention all of the numerous friends who were so kind as to read the manuscript carefully and who offered helpful criticisms and suggestions for revision, for all of which I am extremely grateful.

STEPHEN J. COREY

Santa Monica, California
October 2, 1953

CONTENTS

xi

  9. THE LOGICAL OUTCOME 241
     The Use of Labels 250
     Two Alternatives for Disciples 257

 10. THE COOPERATIVE WORK CONTINUES TO GROW 261
     Other Representative Brotherhood Agencies 267

     Epilogue 276
     Christian Unity 276
     Interchurch Cooperation 277
     Church Organization and Work 278
     Church Membership 279
     Ministerial Education 279

     Bibliography 281

     Index 287

ILLUSTRATIONS IN FACSIMILE

INTRODUCTION

The controversy discussed in this volume has been a development in antagonism to the regular and ordered life of the Disciples of Christ through a period of approximately fifty years, growing more and more inclusive and more and more caustic. It has finally resulted in separatism and distrust. The survey of these many years reveals a sad and divisive movement striking at the heart of the spirit of brotherhood and understanding.

This schism now expresses itself in separate conventions, separate youth meetings, separate missionaries, separate missionary support, a separate group of schools, distinctive periodicals, and a separate doctrinal plea. In the latter, the almost total emphasis is not so much on Christian unity, either among the other Christian forces of the world or among ourselves. Rather, it is on the "Restoration" of primitive Christianity.

The *Christian Standard,* a weekly periodical issued by the Standard Publishing Company of Cincinnati, Ohio, has led this movement of opposition. Consequently, a host of earnest Christian people and many churches look upon those who are connected with the organized and cooperative life of our fellowship as apostates, no longer adhering to the faith and to the position of our fathers. Again and again these accusations have been made until many groups of the younger generation have come to feel that the cooperative life of our brotherhood is built on an erroneous basis.

During this period of fifty years, the *Christian Standard* has changed from a notable family and church newspaper. Originally, inspired by the broad and progressive ideals of its great, first editor, Isaac Errett, it was widely read by a cooperative constituency. Today it is a paper found less and less in the homes of our church leaders who support the cooperative agencies of the Disciples through state or national conventions.

The change of the *Christian Standard* from the high, positive level and cooperative leadership of Isaac Errett, its founder, is strikingly evident when one compares the editorials and statements of the last fifty years with those of its first editor. He was the one, more than any other, who fought against dogmatism, narrowness, and separatism. Along with his battle, first against close communion and then against the anti-organ movement, as tests of fellowship, he was the enthusiastic supporter of united and cooperative effort in missionary work. He was the great progressive champion of his day. Writing in the *Standard* of June 20, 1868 (p. 196), on "The True Basis of Union," he said:

Let the bond of union among the baptized be *Christian character* in place of *orthodoxy*—right doing in place of *exact thinking;* and outside of plain precepts, let all acknowledge the liberty of all, nor seek to impose limitations on their brethren, other than those of the law of love.

Early in his editorship of the *Christian Standard* (March 2, 1867, p. 68), Mr. Errett declared:

The *Standard* is the only weekly paper among us now, that advocates Missionary Societies; and we want the brethren to know this fact. Where there is a great end to be accomplished—a scriptural end,—and the Word of God does not shut us up to any special routine of operations, we go for the best expedients that the united wisdom of the brethren in a given District, State or Nation, may suggest. . . . But we have no idolatrous attachment to the General Missionary Society. If it can do the work proposed, we will encourage it. If it fails to command sufficient confidence and sympathy to enable it to do its work wisely and well, we shall go in for whatever form of associated effort the general wisdom of the brotherhood may approve. But we record our deliberate convictions here, that if the attacks on our General Missionary Society prevail to its destruction, and we are left to rely simply on what individual churches may see fit to do, we will throw back our cause at least half a century, and devolve on a coming generation at least tenfold labor to recover lost ground. We mean to do what we can to save our brethren from this folly.

In the third issue of the *Standard* (April 21, 1866, p. 20), the leading editorial by Isaac Errett was on missionary work among Disciples of Christ. He wrote:

We note with regret that, at a time when, above all others, we need united counsels and action, efforts are being made to weaken, or destroy our missionary societies—not by practical exemplification of a better way, but by newly broached theories, or by old theories revamped, and by uncharitable and unjust constructions of the proceedings of the societies.

This statement is most apropos to the present situation as well as that of the last thirty years.

In the *Standard* of October 1, 1870 (p. 316), Mr. Errett wrote on "Our Wants," as follows:

It is impossible to form a familiar acquaintance with our churches and not be painfully impressed with the fact that immense resources are unemployed, and even undeveloped. . . . With us, however, it looks as if we were content to gather up fragments, *and lose all the rest.* . . . We have been, for forty or fifty years, carrying on a revolutionary movement, in some of its aspects more *de*structive than *con*structive; and there has been but little time to attend to the organization of the forces we have captured. . . . This state of things can not continue. We must come under system. We must learn clear and definite ideas of church-life and church-work, as well as of personal consecration to the service of God, . . . The individualism of past times must subordinate itself largely to congregationalism; and—what is more difficult to accept— congregationalism must enlarge its sphere of activity and develop into systematic cooperation for all the grand purposes that enter into the aggressive work of the church.

It is interesting to note the spirit of courtesy and fairness which Isaac Errett carried into his editorship of the *Christian Standard.* C. C. Smith, an outstanding missionary leader of his day, wrote in the paper of September 11, 1909 (p. 1590), as follows:

I wish to speak also of his relation to our missionary enterprises; not his official relation, for that is a part of our history. We knew he threw the power of his great life into all our missionary enterprises. He helped to organize and backed them without stint. The American Christian Missionary Society, the Christian Woman's Board of Missions and the Foreign Christian Missionary Society—all owe a great debt to him. . . . I read the lives of all the world's great missionaries, yet I wish here to record the fact that I owe more to the influence of Isaac Errett for my own conception of an interest in missions than to any other one influence.

Earlier, in this tribute to Mr. Errett, Mr. Smith wrote that, "All his controversies were dignified and were sweetened by a splendid courtesy."

When the Foreign Christian Missionary Society was formed in 1875 at Louisville, Kentucky, Isaac Errett was elected president and served continuously in that capacity until his death on December 19, 1888. He ardently supported its work and that of the Christian Woman's Board of Missions, which was established in 1874 at Cincinnati, Ohio. One of his famous editorials concerning the C. W. B. M., was entitled, "Help Those Women" (*Standard,* July 11, 1874, p. 220).

Compare his spirit and attitude, as stated above, with editorial statements of the *Christian Standard* in recent years concerning the United Christian Missionary Society, the successor of the societies which Isaac Errett espoused and enthusiastically supported, and other cooperative brotherhood organizations:

Now, apparently, we are back where the movement started, and it becomes necessary to choose between abandoning the vested interests of the "Disciples" denomination or abandoning undenominational Christianity. (From "The Merry-Go-Round," *Christian Standard,* April 5, 1947, p. 242.)

Let us look at the record of the 7,800 churches listed in the current Year Book. Approximately 5,600 have shown themselves too lethargic to care much for the cause or anything else outside their own narrow interests. They are content to keep their own doors open and to live and die in their own selfishness. The "organized" forces claim to have support from one-fourth of the churches. We will be liberal and say that their support comes from 2,000 churches. This leaves approximately 200 congregations which, in their zeal for New Testament Christianity, and in their love for the cause, support as many missionaries and evangelists, sponsor as many missionary training schools which educate as many preachers as is done by ten times their number of churches tied to a cold, institutional, pseudo denominationalism. (From "The Local Church and Vested Interests," *Christian Standard,* September 13, 1947, p. 626.)

We have called it "A Crusade for $14,000,000," but that is only the first objective. It is a "Crusade for Control," a campaign of desperation to completely denominationalize the "Disciples" once and for all, and to insure the smooth and constant flow of funds from the captive churches into the denominational treasuries. (From "An Insidious Invasion," *Christian Standard,* February 14, 1948, p. 107.)

. . . there is the United Christian Missionary Society, a political organization gathering missionary funds from the churches and using the greater part of them for its own political and promotional benefit. . . .

Through the Department of Home Missions, the U.C.M.S. has regimented and controlled the "State Secretaries" who have learned that they must "produce results" or seek other employment. (From "Evidences of 'Disciples' Denominationalism," *Christian Standard,* August 21, 1948, p. 552.)

What has happened in the last twenty-four years is now history, a sorry and disgraceful history that has completely vindicated the judgment of Russell Errett. The clear-cut nature of the division that exists between those who hold to the faith once for all delivered, and its enemies, would have been made plain to the rank and file if men in places of leadership had placed right ahead of might, truth ahead of personal advantage, and the cause ahead of vested interests. (From "Prophecy Fulfilled," *Christian Standard,* October 16, 1948, p. 686.)

. . . the "International Convention," with its misrepresentations, its spurious claims to monopoly in all matters pertaining to the brotherhood, rather than being "an evidence of . . . solidarity and stability" has itself become a source of confusion and division within the brotherhood, an embarrassment to all who preach the plea that made us a brotherhood, and a stumblingblock to many who might be attracted by that plea.

Apparently, Mr. [Gaines M.] Cook [executive secretary of the International Convention] and his associates subscribe to the Hitlerian doctrine that if a falsehood is repeated often enough the people will come to accept it as the truth. (From "The Same Old Fiction," *Christian Standard,* October 23, 1948, p. 706.)

Today, timid little preachers, alerted by the cracking of the co-operative whip, are forced to bleed from their congregations $14,000,000 in taxes under the high sounding "Crusade for a Christian World." (From "The Camel Speaks," *Christian Standard,* May 14, 1949, p. 314.)

Fifty years ago, such schools as College of the Bible, Hiram, Eureka, and Drake were graduating ministers who knew and revered the Word of God. Great men of God, such as J. W. McGarvey, B. J. Radford, D. R. Dungan, made these institutions centers of power and influence for the simple gospel message.

The next chapter is a dark one, with which our older readers are familiar, as "modernism," or infidelity in a new and subtle guise, stole nearly all the established Bible colleges or Bible departments. (From "A Chapter in the History of Christian Education," *Christian Standard,* May 21, 1949, p. 328.)

Many will contribute [during the Week of Compassion appeal] in response to such heart-tugging appeals without understanding the heartless scheme on the part of ecclesiastical bureaucrats to siphon off the greater part of the money. (From "Be Sure to Read the Fine Print," *Christian Standard,* March 4, 1950, p. 138.)

The Christian Restoration Association, incorporated legal successor to the Sidney S. Clarke Fund (*Restoration Herald,* October, 1939, p. 8), was set up with the support of the *Christian Standard* in 1925. The *Standard* of July 18, 1925 (p. 1001), claimed that the Christian Restoration Association was "nothing more or less than the Clarke Fund under a new name, a new charter, and an enlarged personnel."

Afterwards, the *Christian Standard* withdrew its support from the Christian Restoration Association because of alleged irregularities of Leon L. Myers, then president. In an editorial, "Inadequate Trusteeship" (February 5, 1938, p. 124), the *Standard* stated, "Inasmuch as we formerly gave support to the Christian Restoration Association, and some brethren may have been influenced thereby to give it their support, we feel that they should know that we can not any longer endorse the Association" (See also, "Plain Talk," four letters, in the *Christian Standard,* September 17, 1938, p. 918). Yet an article in the *Restoration Herald* (October, 1950, cover page) lists Burris Butler, present editor of the *Christian Standard,* as a trustee of the Christian Restoration Association.

This Christian Restoration Association publishes the monthly magazine, the *Restoration Herald.* Editorial comment appears therein frequently under the title, "UCMS Octopus." Referring to the United Christian Missionary Society of Disciples of Christ under that title, the paper of March, 1951 (p. 5), characterized the Society as a "monstrous ecclesiastical machine, with its centralized government, its secretarial dynasty, its provincial bureaus, its regimentation of the clergy, its taxgatherers and carpet-baggers, its vicious appropriation and monopoly of the inalienable rights of the free churches of our Lord Jesus Christ." The comment concluded, "In a later number, we shall consider other arms of this octopus, which arms, as Webster would say, 'are provided with 2 rows of suckers by means of which they cling to prey.'"

The October, 1950, issue (p. 10) of the *Restoration Herald,* referring to the United Society, stated, "The secretaries have moved with the craft of the Jesuit, and with the cunning of the serpent."

In extreme contrast, one recalls the words of Isaac Errett as he became editor of the *Christian Standard* in 1866 and wrote concerning Alexander Campbell, who had just died. On page one of the first issue, April 7, 1866, referring to Mr. Campbell, the editor said: "Seldom, however, even in the hottest of the strife, were sentences written unworthy of the dignity and benevolence of the religion of Jesus."

The editor of the *Restoration Herald,* Robert E. Elmore, is the same man whom the Standard Publishing Company engaged to edit its *Touchstone* of 1925-27. The latter publication continuously attacked the United Christian Missionary Society, enthusiastically organized in 1919 during the regular International Convention of Disciples of Christ. The trend of that attack persisted in the *Christian Standard* during subsequent years. In *The Touchstone,* Mr. Elmore, under supervision of the Standard Publishing Company, laid the pattern and sowed the seed. The *Christian Standard* followed that pattern and now the inevitable harvest is being reaped in a shameful schism.

One would hesitate to repeat to the Christian public these continuous attacks against a significant cooperative movement, initiated and directed by a vast body of devoted, Christian people, were it not for the fact that this is what is being indoctrinated into the minds of a large group of earnest, young preachers. These men are being trained in the schools that are usually given editorial support and publicity by the *Christian Standard.* Many of these young persons, so influenced, are being called into churches and are in turn indoctrinating these congregations with this same divisive suspicion.

Many of these devoted, young ministers and workers go out enthusiastically, feeling that they are called to help save a great fellowship from "apostasy." When they can turn churches from their long connection with the organized and cooperative work of Disciples of Christ, and enlist such churches in "independent" brotherhood work, they are convinced that they are serving the cause of Christ.

The following documentation will reveal how a great and noble paper, first edited by Isaac Errett, the champion of cooperative and organized work among Disciples of Christ, has attacked virtually every larger cooperative move of our people for nearly half a century. I say "documentation" for this is not so much an answer to the attacks as it is a record of the accusations speaking for themselves.

The departure has not been alone from the precept and advocacy of Isaac Errett, but from the real genius of our people in their stand for Christian liberty and progress.

It is indeed ironical that the ecumenical outlook, which was so evident in the minds of Thomas Campbell and Barton W. Stone, two of the most irenic of the movement's early leaders, has been so changed by certain groups in our history. This change has resulted in parallel movements that are anti-ecumenical, legalistic, and backward-looking. The first movement of this kind, largely led by Benjamin Franklin, resulted in the early non-cooperative separation that was centered in opposition to instrumental music in church worship and the right to organize and use missionary societies. The second, which we are now experiencing, is led by the *Christian Standard* in its attacks on biblical scholarship and its revival of opposition to missionary organizations and has developed a new division among Disciples of Christ.

This later schism repudiates the whole cooperative organization of our fellowship and sets itself against the International Convention of Disciples of Christ and all organizations affiliated with it. This includes all missionary societies, state and national, and the Board of Higher Education with its member educational agencies and institutions. This divisive movement also divorces itself entirely from the present-day approach to cooperation and unity in the National Council of Churches and the World Council of Churches, though a former editor of the *Christian Standard,* the late Edwin R. Errett, was a delegate from the International Convention to the 1937 World Faith and Order Conference in Edinburgh, Scotland. That assembly took action to join in forming the World Council and Mr. Errett accepted a place on the Faith and Order Continuation Committee. On the platform of "Restorationism" as a means towards an end, this later schism has subordinated the great goal, or end, of Christian unity to that means.

Thus, there are two streams of thought and development among Disciples of Christ. The one, advocating the unity of all Christians, has been creative, inclusive, and experimental. It has endeavored to keep itself open to changing conditions and the adaptation to circumstances which would not contradict the genius and spirit of early Christianity, but enable it to recognize change and the possibility of new approaches. This has been a movement of the spirit and its advocates have felt that such was the essential principle working in early Christianity.

The other stream of thought and development has been backward-looking, static in its demand that all come to its point of view before there can be any possible unity. It has refused to acknowledge or cooperate with any of the longings and the changes of outlook toward Christian unity emerging in world Protestant Christianity. The emphasis has been largely one of conformity, rather than cooperation and unity, and it has been essentially legalistic.

Fortunately, the main body of the movement designated as Disciples of Christ has followed the first stream of thought. Simultaneously, the *Christian Standard* of more recent times, together with those who have continuously supported it, has followed the second stream.

So it has developed that we, for the second time in our history, are at the crossroads of decision as a movement for unity among the followers of Christ. The course of Disciples of Christ depends upon the outcome of the conflict between that which would resolve itself into a literalistic sect and that of an universal, creative, and flexible, spiritual movement, such as early Christianity proved itself to be.

As early as 1834, in the *Millennial Harbinger* (p. 315), Alexander Campbell wrote:

The primitive congregations communicated jointly and co-operated in everything that was beyond the power of a single congregation—in prayers, in counsel, in labor, in giving and receiving. There can be no Christian co-operation in one of these that does not suppose a co-operation in all.

In 1842, in the *Millennial Harbinger* (pp. 59 ff.), Mr. Campbell also wrote:

I cannot conceive of a kingdom without a constitution, an organization, a joint and common interest, and a constant co-operation in reference to its self-preservation and comfortable existence. If Christ have a kingdom on this earth, it must be a community organized, united in common interests, in harmonious concert, and conservative of its own integrity and prosperity. . . .

But the New Testament itself teaches both by precept and example the necessity of united and concentrated action in the advancement of the kingdom. . . .

It allows not persons to send themselves or to ordain themselves to office; but every where intimates the necessity of choice, selection, mission, and ordination. . . .

I lay it down as a maxim not to be questioned, that where there is a Christian communion of any sort, special or common, there must be an amenability of the participants to some common tribunal, and a mutual responsibility to watch over, and nourish, and comfort one another. . . .

But is it so amongst us!

During the last fifty years, aside from the leadership of the chief owner of the *Christian Standard* (Russell Errett, son of Isaac Errett, who succeeded his father in the management of the periodical at the father's death in 1888), there have been six editors of the weekly magazine. The first was J. A. Lord, serving for most of the first ten years, until 1909; the second, S. S. Lappin, 1909-16; the third, George P. Rutledge, 1917-22. Willard Mohorter (son of J. H. Mohorter, for many years the secretary of the National Benevolent Association), became associate editor in 1917, then editor in 1922 and served until 1929 when he was made secretary of the Standard Publishing Company, which position he continues to hold. He was succeeded in 1929 by Edwin R. Errett (a nephew of Russell Errett) who served until his death on January 29, 1944. Since that time Burris Butler has been editor of the magazine (*Christian Standard*, April 6, 1946, p. 215).

It is not difficult to divide the attacks of the *Christian Standard* upon the cooperative work of our brotherhood into periods. I shall start with the beginning period early in 1900, previous to which time the paper had observed a sympathetic and positive attitude toward the developing cooperative work, representing it well in its news reports and editorials.

Following the death of his father, Isaac Errett, in 1888, and up to the beginning of the century, 1900, Russell Errett had kept up the early, sympathetic attitude toward the missionary work. In fact, A. McLean, president of the Foreign Christian Missionary Society, wrote favorably concerning Mr. Errett's attitude during those years before 1900. For several years Russell Errett had served as auditor of the Annual Report of the Foreign Christian Missionary Society. Mr. McLean made the following statement (p. 442) in the section, "The Period of

Foreign Missions," that he wrote for *The Reformation of the Nineteenth Century*, edited by J. H. Garrison and published in 1901:

> One man to whom the [Foreign Christian Missionary] society owes as much as to any other is one who has never had a prominent place in any of our conventions. He has been a steadfast and generous friend of the society since its organization. He has planned and wrought unseen for the enlargement of the work. Comparatively few know his face and fewer still the value of his services. Not more than a score are aware of what he has done for this cause. Russell Errett has been in a position where he could help; he has quietly and persistently and joyfully done what he could to send the gospel to those who are sitting in darkness and in the shadow of death.

The launching of direct opposition and the campaign of propaganda against our organized life began shortly after 1900 and by 1910 was in full swing.

I will endeavor to chronicle the history of this development through the fifty-year period. I have been moved to undertake the task for several reasons. This very real and harmful division has developed among Disciples of Christ and has definitely separated the churches from each other, causing distrust and disfellowship. At the same time great numbers of our people, especially of the younger generation, do not know the reason for this sad state of affairs and are confused when the reality of this schism confronts them. The time has fully come when the course of events for the last fifty years should be recorded and the issue made clear. Having been in intimate touch with the cooperative life of the Disciples of Christ through this whole period and realizing what was taking place, I felt moved to set the facts down in a narrative record. The task was not a pleasant one. Not only was I definitely connected with the brotherhood's cooperative organizations that have been attacked, but many times I was at the center of attack. I have endeavored to be objective and fair in what I have written. There has been much sadness, but no bitterness in my heart and no malice in my purpose. The reader will find, as I have, many things to sadden his heart and bring deep regret that such controversy could exist in a body of Christians.

I have been very hesitant to believe that an actual division of rather widespread proportions has developed among us, but the *Christian Standard* has had no such hesitancy. In editorials of recent date, it has heralded its announcement of division as far as the paper is concerned, in no uncertain terms.

An editorial in the *Christian Standard* of October 12, 1946 (p. 714), on "The Brotherhood," stated:

> We do not share the fear, based on sectarian pride, of "splitting the brotherhood," because we recognize that "contending earnestly for the faith" draws the brotherhood of believers closer together as the borderline between belief and unbelief is more closely defined.
>
> We further maintain that when any man by his public utterances proves himself to be no longer a believer in Christ, he has separated himself from the brotherhood and has placed himself beyond the pale of the conference table of brethren in Christ.

Three weeks later (November 2, 1946, p. 771) in an editorial entitled "On 'Splitting the Brotherhood' " the *Christian Standard* stated: "We contend that our fundamental danger today is not one of 'splitting the brotherhood.' It is the danger of a 'lost brotherhood.' "

In the issue of June 3, 1950 (p. 346), in an editorial, "Of, By, and For the Restoration Movement," the *Christian Standard* stated:

> This is one serious indictment of the United Christian Missionary Society, the various state societies, the colleges, in fact, the whole coterie of institutions associated in and with the "International Convention of Disciples of Christ." They may have started out to implement the Restoration ideal, but the very nature of their claims forced them to forsake that ideal and settle down to wall-building. Now after many years, they are used, ironically, as instruments to oppose the restoration of New Testament Christianity, both in principle and in practice.
>
> This is the fundamental issue in regard to support or nonsupport of these institutions on the part of men and women and congregations committed to the Restoration plea. It is not that they are inefficient, or wasteful, or present a wrong method of doing things—it is that they have abandoned the plea and forsaken the movement. They are no longer of the Restoration movement. . . .
>
> In the matter of objectives, these agencies look in a different direction than do those persons and agencies committed to unity of all believers and the consequent salvation of men by means of the restoration of primitive Christianity. They are committed to "ecumenicity" rather than restoration, to a federation of sects rather than the destruction of sectarianism, to a World Council of Churches rather than the "whole

counsel of God," to comity rather than the open field, to compromise rather than conviction. If one scratches a little beneath the surface he finds that this difference in objectives rests on a fundamental contradiction in theology and philosophy.

A week later, in another editorial, "Champions of This Plea," (June 10, 1950, p. 362), referring to the "old agencies," the periodical declared:

So much for the old agencies. Long ago we gave them up as impossible of reformation from their apostasy. We do not trouble to name names in this brief editorial. We have named names and cited instances and sounded warnings through the years. And if we had never uttered a word these agencies and their policy-makers stand self-condemned by their own pronouncements and their own policies. They have set themselves to destroy the plea that ostensibly they were meant to forward and defend.

One is reminded that the term "apostasy" means, according to Webster, a total desertion of the principles of faith!

A significant editorial statement appeared on the cover (p. 465) of the July 29, 1950, issue of the *Christian Standard*. It was entitled, "A Program on Which All Can Unite," and stated, in part:

AREN'T WE ALL TIRED OF FIGHTING AND CONTROVERSY OVER ISSUES THAT WON'T MATTER ANYWAY ONE HUNDRED YEARS FROM NOW!

. . . By this time, we ought to know that there are many things on which we will never all agree—like which convention is best to attend, which missionary is most deserving of support, which school is best in which to be educated, . . .

FROM NOW ON

The CHRISTIAN STANDARD IS PLEDGED TO DO EVERYTHING IN ITS POWER TO PROMOTE NEW TESTAMENT EVANGELISM IN OUR PAGES.

Since the publication of this front-page statement, one may search in vain through the columns of the *Christian Standard* for the customary denunciations of the cooperative forces of the Disciples of Christ. The periodical has, in effect, ignored this large segment of the brotherhood.

In the pages which follow, I will attempt to show how this division in our fellowship developed through the years.

Chapter 1

THE BEGINNING OF THE CONTROVERSY, 1900-1910

This fifty-year period of controversy began shortly after 1900 with a running attack upon federation by the *Christian Standard*. The issue did not have any direct connection with the Disciples of Christ except that our American Christian Missionary Society, in some home fields where surveys had been made, favored federated undertakings. This was especially true in new industrial areas of the United States where an attempt was made to coordinate Christian work. These plans were projected by the Home Missions Council of North America. The American Christian Missionary Society had, in a few instances, given its support to the starting of this sort of a community, federated program.

The National Federation of Churches and Christian Workers was established by representatives of local churches on February 6, 1901. E. B. Sanford, secretary of the new organization, delivered an address on the principles of federation at the Omaha (Neb.) National Convention of Disciples of Christ in October, 1902. Afterwards, at this convention, J. H. Garrison, editor of *The Christian-Evangelist,* presented a resolution of approval for federation. This recommendation expressed "our cordial approval of the effort to bring the Churches of this country into closer cooperation and to give truer expression to the degree of unity which already exists" (*A Comprehensive History of the Disciples of Christ* by W. T. Moore, p. 704). J. A. Lord, editor of the *Christian Standard*, spoke against it, inquiring if such action would not be "recognizing the denominations." The resolution was adopted, amid much confusion, and with some opposition.

Following the Omaha Convention, the *Standard* published editorials and articles strongly opposing the idea of federation. The purpose of federation was expressed by Mr. Sanford in an article in *The Christian-Evangelist* (December 4, 1902, p. 851). The article was sent to the religious press as a general release, for the *Christian Standard* of the same week (December 6, 1902, p. 1692) also quoted the federation executive from this article, as follows:

The object of these federations as generally stated is "the promotion of acquaintance, fellowship, and effective co-operation among the several churches of all denominations in order that their essential unity may be manifested."

In its editorial, the *Standard* then added:

Here is the basis of federation, and hence no disciple of Christ, at once intelligent and loyal to the divine plea, can take any part in it. To say that denominational churches and churches simply Christian have "essential unity" is to say that the plea of the Campbells and Stone was much ado about nothing.

For years *The Christian-Evangelist* supported the idea of federation as a necessary step in the right direction. An editorial in that periodical on "Compromise Christian Union" (June 21, 1894, p. 386) stated:

There is no good reason why we should wait until such full, organic unity is possible, before we recognize each other as Christian bodies, holding the vital truths and the essential faith, in spite of more or less error in doctrine and practice, and co-operate, as far as practicable, in missionary and benevolent work, and in all moral reforms. This degree of union is called federation. We have often expressed ourselves in favor of it.

The *Christian Standard* consistently opposed any form of federation. The paper's thesis was expressed editorially on February 17, 1906 (p. 251), thus: "Federation is not a union in Christ, but union in denominationalism, union in an order of things which Christ and his apostles condemn as carnal and as an enemy to Christian union or the union in Christ." In other words, the paper contended that Methodists, Baptists, Presbyterians, and other Christians cannot be recognized as parts of the true church of Christ as we, ourselves, are. Any form of alliance with other Christian bodies was opposed. The paper seemed determined that the Disciples should remain apart from any of the larger movements in the Christian world until the other churches accepted our position, or, as some persons put it, "joined us." Such Christian cooperation was indeed viewed by the *Christian Standard* as being a concession to "denominationalism" or "recognizing the denominations."

The federation movement resulted in plans for the organization of a Federal Council of Churches at a New York City Interchurch Conference on Federation in November, 1905. Thirty or more leading Disciples of Christ took part in the meeting. The controversy in our religious press over whether the Disciples should become a part of the new Federal Council or remain out was long and tedious. —

The issue was resolved for Disciples of Christ at a called special mass meeting held in October, 1907, at the time of our National Convention at Norfolk, Virginia. A committee to make recommendations was chosen the previous March at a meeting in Cincinnati. F. D. Power, pastor in Washington, D. C., was the chairman. The report of the committee endorsed the idea of federation and approved the appointment of delegates to the Federal Council. The report was adopted almost unanimously. Disciples of Christ thus became identified with the new Council, now a part of the National Council of Churches, from its organization. Through the years an increasing number of Disciples, both individually and through their local congregations, came to share in the support, financially and otherwise, of such Christian work.

The Campbell Institute

During this period, early in the century, J. W. McGarvey, president of The College of the Bible of Lexington, Kentucky, was a regular contributor to the *Christian Standard*. He conducted a department of biblical criticism. He was a recognized scholar and an outstanding teacher, but was very conservative in his personal views. He became quite vitriolic in the recurring attacks on this regular weekly page of his in the *Christian Standard* with anyone disagreeing in the least with the more conservative view in theology. President McGarvey was opposed to instrumental music in the churches, as were many of the earlier leaders of our churches, but did not make this view a point of contention. He had left the Broadway Christian Church of Lexington, Kentucky, when the organ was introduced in the church worship and had joined the Chestnut Street Church of that city (*"Brother McGarvey"* by W. C. Morro, p. 223).

During this period, President McGarvey and the *Christian Standard* discovered that there was an organization of ministers among the Disciples of Christ called the "Campbell Institute." This was a small group of young men who had gone beyond the college course and the biblical training provided for Disciples and had taken university graduate and seminary studies. At that time our Bible colleges did not offer what is now termed graduate work. That is, the ministerial course was combined with college instruction. There was no plan to take students beyond college graduation into studies for graduate degrees like the Master of Arts or the Bachelor of Divinity. Therefore, quite a number of Disciples, feeling the need of further training, availed themselves of graduate studies in other ministerial training centers, such as Yale, Harvard, Union, Rochester, Chicago, and Princeton, where a three-year seminary course was offered.

There was quite a group of these men in the early years. The number included Henry Lawrence Atkinson, Edward Scribner Ames, Miner Lee Bates, Levi S. Batman, Jesse C. Caldwell, Hall L. Calhoun, George A. Campbell, A. L. Chapman, Stephen J. Corey, Edgar F. Daugherty, G. D. Edwards, James Egbert, Edwin R. Errett, John Ray Ewers, A. W. Fortune, Charles A. Freer, W. E. Garrison, John Paris Givens, J. H. Goldner, T. J. Golightly, F. F. Grim, Edward A. Henry, Austin Hunter, Burris Jenkins, Frederick D. Kershner, Clinton Lockhart, Levi Marshall, George A. Miller, Raphael H. Miller, Herbert Moninger, E. E. Moorman, W. C. Morro, William Oeschger, Wallace C. Payne, Allan B. Philputt, James M. Philputt, Perry O. Powell, H. O. Pritchard, Perry J. Rice, Henry Barton Robison, W. F. Rothenburger, Carlos C. Rowlison, Joseph A. Serena, Harry D. Smith, E. E. Snoddy, Alva W. Taylor, Hiram Van Kirk,

Baxter Waters, Charles M. Watson, L. N. D. Wells, Herbert L. Willett, Charles A. Young, and many others later on.

A small group had been formed for mutual help, extension of reading, and fellowship. That was in 1896 at Springfield, Illinois. The group of fourteen charter members, two of whom are still living, was named the Campbell Institute. It was a free assembly where the members felt unconstrained. Intellectual and theological issues were discussed with complete freedom. It was a helpful society of mutual understanding. Some of the men were quite liberal in their views, others were very conservative. This made no difference in the fellowship of the group. The Campbell Institute meetings were as free as the air in their open discussion.

In an issue of the *Christian Standard* (November 10, 1906, p. 1697), President McGarvey wrote an attack on the Campbell Institute and its monthly magazine called *The Scroll* (successor to *The Quarterly Bulletin of the Campbell Institute*), published by the Institute, beginning in September, 1906. In the attack, on his page of "Biblical Criticism," he said that writers of *The Scroll* were "inspired by the three evil spirits of evolution, higher criticism and the new theology." Adverse discussion of evolution and higher criticism was quite popular then.

An interesting incident occurred in connection with this attack by President McGarvey. Aside from his page of "Biblical Criticism," with numerous attacks on the Institute, the *Christian Standard* had editorials excoriating this so-called "high-brow" group. Before publishing one of Mr. McGarvey's denunciations (November 24, 1906, p. 1775) the *Christian Standard* sent the column proof to the members of the Campbell Institute whose names it had secured. In this connection, a covering letter from Russell Errett for the *Standard* stated that if any members of the Institute at that time wished to resign from the group, the magazine would not mention their names in the list which it was about to publish.

I became a member of the Campbell Institute in 1904 (*The Quarterly Bulletin of the Campbell Institute,* January 1, 1905, p. 6), following my graduation from the theological seminary of Rochester, New York. Along with the other members, I received the surprising note from the *Standard*. One can imagine the reaction that this produced. It was a serious matter for some of the members.

It happened that Herbert Moninger, who was employed by the Standard Publishing Company for several years as its leading Sunday school authority (he began work for the Standard Publishing Company on July 1, 1905, and remained in its employ until his death, shortly after he was 35 years old, on June 21, 1911—see *Christian Standard,* July 1, 1911, p. 1052 and July 15, 1911, p. 1124) was one of the most devoted members of this group (see membership roster in *The Quarterly Bulletin of the Campbell Institute,* October 1, 1903, p. 7; also, October 1, 1905, p. 11). He was requested to resign. He regretted this very much and in a private conversation with me made the statement that he thought the storm would soon blow over and when it did he would be glad to have fellowship with the helpful group again.

The attack upon the Campbell Institute not only continued with unabated zeal, for some time, but curiously enough, many times through the nearly fifty years since, it has been held up to view by the *Christian Standard* as one of the main reasons for division among Disciples of Christ. The paper has constantly claimed that the members have attempted to dominate our missionary organizations, colleges, International Convention, and all the cooperative work that we have. The often reiterated claim that the Campbell Institute has tried to divert our brotherhood from its main genius apparently has been an obsession with this periodical. Of course, the Campbell Institute flourished under this sort of opposition and a large number of our leaders joined its ranks. Indeed, the present membership is around six hundred.

The Rockefeller Gifts

Up to 1907, even though the *Christian Standard* became very negative in its attitude toward some of the development in our brotherhood life, still it was a paper of great influence. Men hesitated to differ from it in writing or in public address. It had experienced so long a history under the progressive leadership of its founder, Isaac Errett, and had become so embedded in the home life of our people that many looked upon it as next to the Bible in the realm of authority. However, its constant criticism made an increasing number of Disciples skeptical of its usefulness and strongly opposed to its trend.

In 1907 the *Standard* entered into a controversy which proved to be a great breaking point in its influence. It happened that the Foreign Christian Missionary Society, of which Archibald McLean was the president, and F. M. Rains and Stephen J. Corey, the secretaries, had received a series of gifts from John D. Rockefeller, Sr. He had become interested in the Society and its work in mission fields. Although Mr. Rockefeller was a Baptist and contributed largely to the Baptist missionary program every year, yet on solicitation by Mr. Rains, he began to send annual checks to the Foreign Christian Missionary Society. These totaled $25,000 for 1905, 1906, and 1907. There were no strings to the contributions, no suggestions as to how they should be used. They were given for the work that was being conducted in mission lands. Mr. Rockefeller had even indicated that his interest in the Foreign Society's program was growing and that he proposed to increase these gifts as the years went by.

Early in the century there had been a press attack upon Mr. Rockefeller and the Standard Oil Company. Ida Tarbell had written a series of exposure articles in *McClure's Magazine*, published in New York. Undoubtedly, there was a great deal of truth in her attack and the business procedures of those days were far from being above question. However, the officers of the Foreign Christian Missionary Society felt that this money was as good as any money, since there were no conditions attached to it, and that to use it for a great cause need not be any commendation of Mr. Rockefeller's principles.

On learning that Mr. Rockefeller had given money to the Foreign Christian Missionary Society, the *Christian Standard*, through its editor, J. A. Lord, launched a strong attack upon the organization and demanded that the money be returned. It happened that Thomas W. Phillips, one of the leading laymen among our people, residing at New Castle, Pennsylvania, who was likewise a wealthy oil man, was exceedingly critical in his attitude toward Mr. Rockefeller. No doubt Mr. Phillips had some valid reasons for his feelings in his contacts with the Standard Oil Company and its methods. The *Christian Standard* secured his services to write a series of articles (*Christian Standard,* July 13, August 17 and 31, September 14, 21 and 28, 1907) against receiving money from Mr. Rockefeller. Paralleling his articles, during that year of 1907, Mr. Lord, the editor, ran a series of editorials that grew increasingly caustic. The demand was repeatedly and strongly made that this "tainted" money should be returned and not used for Christian work.

These *Standard* editorials finally became personal, especially against A. McLean. The temper and the inconsistency of the editorials aroused Mr. McLean until he felt that an answer should be made to the accusations. He was a very vigorous writer. He was a Scot and a man who had been the secretary or the president of the Foreign Christian Missionary Society for more than thirty years. He had been all over the brotherhood, in thousands of churches, and was beloved on every hand; a man of deep devotion, sterling integrity, who, with real prophetic voice had set forth the claims of the missionary enterprise all across our brotherhood.

I will never forget the evening, after Mr. McLean had written his reply, when he went out to the Cincinnati home of F. M. Rains, the senior secretary of the society, and read to two or three friends who had gathered, including me, what he had written. His article was strong, incisive, and contained tremendous implications, but we all felt that it should be published if the *Christian Standard* would print it. Mr. McLean subsequently gave his article to the *Standard* and, under the circumstances, it could do nothing but publish it (*Christian Standard,* September 21, 1907, pp. 1559 ff.). It created a sensation and so many letters of commendation came pouring in to Mr. McLean in the Cincinnati office that extra secretaries had to be secured to answer them.

During this controversy, Mr. McLean and I were out in a campaign of missionary rallies across the brotherhood. During the whole three months which we spent on the field, we did not hear more than half a dozen criticisms on taking the Rockefeller money for the missionary work. Even John W. McGarvey said that he "would take money from the devil and use it in the serv-

ice of the Christ." (Quoted in an article, "Concerning the
Rockefeller Gift," by A. McLean, *Christian Standard,* July 27,
1907, p. 1227.)

The Attack on Archibald McLean

It was following the publication of Mr. McLean's reply in the
Christian Standard that the controversy became more harsh.
The editorials began to accuse him of unfaithfulness, hetero-
doxy, and being influenced by a group of "destructive critics."
Mr. McLean bluntly told what he deemed to be the truth in
his first article, but attempted to do it in a Christian spirit.
The continued personal attacks finally drove him to decide that
he should write another article, which he did.

This time, Mr. McLean rolled up his sleeves and gave it to
the *Standard,* blow for blow. He showed what he considered
the inconsistency of the *Christian Standard* on three points:

First, J. A. Lord, editor of the *Standard,* had been a private
agent for an oil company and endeavored to sell stock in its
undertakings. He solicited this sale from his Christian friends.
He even stated that his company was a subsidiary of the Standard Oil Company in order to make his point more conclusive.

Second, the *Christian Standard* had been continuously receiving Standard Oil "tainted" money. It ran paid Standard Oil
advertisements in the paper. It also published patent medicine
advertising, such as "Piso's Cure for Consumption" (*Christian
Standard,* January 13, 1906, p. 76) and similar advertisements.

Third, the *Standard* editor, Mr. Lord, wrote strong editorials
against taking "tainted" money and demanded that the Foreign
Christian Missionary Society return the entire amount to Mr.
Rockefeller. Yet Russell Errett, owner of the *Christian Standard,*
apparently wrote editorials for one of his papers in which he
took the other side of the issue. (See "Several Things," *Christian Weekly,* September 16, 1905, p. 10, published by the Standard Publishing Company, under the editorship of J. B. Briney,
H. Bowen, and John T. Brown.) In these statements, Mr.
Errett showed the unreasonableness of refusing money from such
a source and advocated the taking of all that could be secured
for a good purpose. He did not sign these articles, but afterwards F. M. Rains complimented Mr. Briney for this writing.

To which Mr. Briney replied: "I did not write that. Russell Errett wrote it." Mr. McLean, in this second article, accused Mr. Errett of doing so and he never denied it.

I personally took the second article, which Mr. McLean wrote, to the *Christian Standard* and asked for its publication. Mr. Lord, the editor, looked at the title, but did not read the article, then handed it back to me, saying, "We can not publish that." Following this episode, Mr. McLean published it as a 16-page pamphlet at his own expense in 1907, and sent it broadcast throughout the brotherhood under the title, *Debarred From the Standard!* This article, or pamphlet, created widespread interest and great numbers of letters were received by Mr. McLean in approval. Many Christian people were sorry for the controversy. Yet on the other hand they felt that the time had come when the apparent attempt at domination of our brotherhood's life and thinking by the *Standard* should be opposed. No one in our fellowship at that time could have opposed the Standard with more respect and confidence than Mr. McLean held everywhere.

While one cannot give space to the entire articles in the *Standard* by A. McLean and the editorial replies, or to the article of Mr. McLean that was refused publication in the *Standard,* yet it is interesting to quote some of the paragraphs in this controversy. A quotation from Mr. McLean's first article (*Christian Standard,* September 21, 1907) follows from page 1561:

Isaac Errett is dead and his spirit is no longer the dominant one in the paper he founded and made illustrious. Why his name should be kept at the masthead, seeing that the paper advocates the very things it was founded to oppose, and opposes the very things it was founded to advocate, is something of a mystery to many. . . .

All the missionary societies have been attacked in turn. The Woman's Board was attacked on the ground that some of its agents were unsound. The American Society was attacked because of some alleged relation to federation. The Board of Church Extension was attacked and its secretary declared to be unworthy. . . . Now the Foreign Society is having its turn. . . . If the men and women who are at the head of the missionary societies would approve the reactionary policy of the *Standard* and would agree to push its interests and pledge themselves not to put any one on any program who is not *persona grata* to the management of the *Standard,* they would be as cordially supported as are some persons whose reputations are somewhat shady, but whose allegiance is undoubted and unlimited. . . .

Thousands have grown unutterably weary of its everlasting nagging and snarling and faultfinding. Many of these were raised on the *Standard* and loved it. Now they have no use for it. They find nothing in it to feed their souls. . . . More than one preacher has discontinued it in order that he may live a Christian life and preach the gospel.

It is interesting, also, to consider passages from Mr. McLean's second article, refused publication in the *Standard*. The following interprets the feeling of Mr. McLean about the *Christian Standard* at that time. The first four paragraphs are taken from the Introductory Note and the others from the refused manuscript, "The Real Issue Studiously Ignored":

I did not wish any controversy, but I could not be silent without betraying my trust. I wrote one article in reply to numerous attacks. . . . I wrote again, but my article was returned. The editor did not read a line of it. . . . he will say many things to the readers of the paper about me, and I can speak no word in my own behalf.

The *Standard* has boasted for years that its columns were open to any man that it attacked. It claims that it believes in the square deal. It complained that some of the men attacked by it made no reply. The brethren will now know how to appraise its vain boast from this time forth.

I call heaven and earth to witness that the *Standard* has been the assailant, and that I have been on the defensive. While the discussion with Brother [Thomas W.] Phillips continued the editor did all he could to help him and to injure me. Nearly everything written in his favor was published; nearly everything written in my favor was excluded. The editor loaded the dice in Brother Phillips' favor. I protested, but in vain. When Brother Phillips closed the discussion I was satisfied to let the brethren decide as to the merits of the question. From the 24th of August to the 21st of September I did not write a line. The *Standard* kept up the fight. . . . There was only one righteous course open to me. It was my bounden duty to speak out in defense of the Society and my own defense. To stay silent longer would have been culpable.

. . . Our organized interests are the real objective. Any institution that refuses to be dominated by that paper must expect its relentless opposition. It can take its choice between submission and destruction. When the brethren know the facts, they will line up in a way that will astonish the men who are waging this wicked warfare upon the Societies and their officials and in their own interests. . . .

In my last article . . . I showed that the *Standard*, while condemning the Society for taking money from Mr. Rockefeller, advertises Standard Oil products month in and month out and year after year, and takes large money for this service. I showed that it promotes the interests of that company every day and every hour. I showed that if the *Standard* believes its own statements about the crimes of the Standard Oil Company, it can not render it aid and comfort . . . I pointed out that there is not a line that the *Standard* has written against the Society that does not apply with far greater force against itself. In the four pages devoted to a reply what is the answer to this count in the indictment? Absolute silence. Not a single word is said. Why? Because no reply could be made in justification of its own action that would amply justify the Society's action. . . .

I gave an account of Brother Lord's experience as an incipient oil king. He was a stockholder in a company that was auxiliary to the Standard Oil Company. He took from that company a dividend of one per cent. a month and prophesied that soon it would be two or three times as much. In urging his friends to subscribe to this stock, the crowning argument was that they were selling their product to the Standard Oil Company, and therefore they were in no danger. Brother Lord took all the Standard Oil money he could get, and felt very bad when the supply ceased. I asked him to explain how it could be right for him to take this money and wrong for the Society to take the same money? . . . What answer is made to this? Nothing at all. Brother Lord is as silent as the grave. Why? Because anything that would justify J. A. Lord would justify the Society. . . .

Instead of meeting the issue like a man or confessing that he could not meet it, the editor throws dust in the air. He wishes to know why these gifts were not published differently. In my last article . . . I said, "The facts are these: The first gift was credited to a friend. That was because it was understood that the donor did not wish his name known. What was done was done in good faith, and with no thought of concealment as if a wrong had been committed. The second gift was acknowledged in the Annual Report like any other gift. See Report for 1906, page 492. . . . The Report was published a few months later, and not after two or three years, as alleged. The third gift was treated precisely as any other gift of the same kind. . . ." . . .

Brother Lord brings in a question that is in no way related to the matter in hand. He intimates that I am a destructive critic. His course in a controversy reminds one of the doctor who could cure fits only. He had to transmute the disease into fits before he could proceed. If Brother Lord can fasten the charge of destructive criticism on a man, the rest is easy. No evidence is needed. No charge could be more baseless or stupid. He could as easily prove me a Mongolian or a Hottentot. I have as little sympathy with any teaching or teacher that would discredit the Lord Jesus Christ or that would undermine the authority of the Holy Book as any man alive. . . . I do not feel called upon before missionary conventions or elsewhere to pronounce upon questions about which I know as little as the editor of the *Standard*. I exalt Jesus the Christ as the Savior and Lord of all; I magnify the Book and urge all to obey its precepts and to exemplify its spirit.

July 13, 1907.   **CHRISTIAN STANDARD**   (1175)   31

Kansas Notes

I am now in a meeting at Ashland, county-seat of Clark County. This church has had no minister for some time, but is in very good condition otherwise. The people are hearing the truth gladly. We hope to locate a preacher with them soon.

The church at Englewood will co-operate with Ashland in the employment of a minister. The band at this place is small, and they have no house of worship, but they are faithful and willing.

Otto Kennedy, minister at Minneola, is doing a great work. He has had four or five additions during the past month, and is reaching out to the schoolhouses around, establishing preaching-points for Sunday afternoons. Bro. Kennedy has just recently commenced preaching, and he is going to be a success.

The church at Greensburg has employed Bro. Kennedy to minister to them for half time. They are to be congratulated. This church was just recently resurrected, but is now in promising condition.

Bro. Marley has organized a small band of disciples at Bucklin. This is a division point on the Rock Island, and a good little town in western Kansas.

After being without a preacher for some months, the church at Kingman has employed a young man just graduated from Drake University. I am unable to tell his name. I recently preached at Kingman, while passing through, and renewed old acquaintance.

The church at Harper is still without a preacher, but wants one.

L. H. Barnum, minister at Medicine Lodge, is making things move in his diocese. Additions are frequent. Bro. Barnum is preaching some at Sharon, on Lord's Day afternoons, and also at the schoolhouses about Medicine Lodge. Preachers that are doing this class of work are to be congratulated, as it is work that pays wondrously well. We ought to be willing to spend and be spent for the Lord Jesus, and it is the true apostolic spirit that does this class of work.

I am due in the Texas Panhandle for the month of July, to work in a camp-meeting at Lipscomb. This is forty miles from a railroad, but a large attendance is always there, and a most enjoyable time, a feast of spiritual and other good things.

I will begin a meeting with a singer at Hazelton, Kan., about the first of August. There was formerly a church here, but they became too strenuous over the organ, and kindred questions, and evaporated.

In September we are due to begin a meeting at Hartford, Kan. P. E. Hawkins is the minister, and is now beginning to prepare for the meeting.

H. C. Clark is the efficient minister at Ingersoll, Okla. He has added nearly fifty to the church there since beginning his ministry with them a little over a year ago. He has had nearly the same number of additions at other points.

I would like to get items of news from Kansas and Oklahoma, that we can keep things interesting for the readers of the Standard in this section. Why not drop me a line, and say what you have been doing, and what you are going to do? I make this request of both preachers and churches.   M. B. INGLE.
Harper, Kan.

Kentucky Kernels

Now, don't that jar you? Those Canadians have done gone and shown how it is done did, and that man Lord has done gone and did it—does *federation* one better. His heart is in the right place, no matter how far his pen may stray, and when he does do something he does something what is something. To scribe visited the editorial sanctum sanctorum recently, and there that man Lord sat in the agonies of composition and the delirums of blue pencil, as meek as your mammy's mockingbird, over this great achievement of hisn. In the World's Fair at Chicago, Canada took the prize for the best educational system in the world, and if we don't watch out she will take the prize for the best Christian union system. Keep your eye on Canada and keep your eye on Lord!

Latonia is expanding. A new addition is going up to the church there, which will be as large as, or larger than, the church proper. The reason—the State Convention is to be held there and they must expand, and thus they have an expanding preacher and an expanding membership. Runyan makes things run.

Glasgow is getting there. A large meeting by Small soon. The minister, Payne, though quite sick, is all alive to the interests of the church, and on his sick-couch plans for her progress.

Columbia, historic Columbia, is still doing

herself proud, with Williams as minister and Ashill as elder.

Edmonton, weak but wiry, bemoaning the loss of Buckingham, but with another minister in view.

Summer Shade, struggling toward the light. At each of these places have I preached during my vacation wanderings, and for awhile I intend to stay in the shade, and correspondents may address me at Summer Shade, Ky.
CLARIS TRUELL.

Missouri Bible-school Work

The Sedalia Convention was one of the largest and best ever held in our history. The reports of the past year were inspiring. The minutes of the convention containing the annual report of the Board are now in the hands of the printer and will be ready for distribution in a few days. Our faces turned to the new year as soon as the benediction was pronounced at Sedalia, and now our office is humming with preparations for the best year of all. Steps are now being taken to secure pledges from all those schools which were not represented at the convention; if a blank pledge-card comes to you, kindly fill it out and mail it back to the office at once. Remember that all pledges are payable quarterly the first of July, October, January and April. Send the payments promptly. If you need the help of the Association, let us know. Help us to help our great cause in this great commonwealth.
J. H. HARDIN, State Supt.
811 Century Bldg., Kansas City, Mo.

Save Your Postage

Letters are coming one way! Word must have gotten out that the church at Lafayette, Ind., is out of a minister. It is a mistake. Poor excuse as he is, the church is disposed to hold to what they have a few more weeks! Brethren who forgot to send postage will please take this as a reply to their inquiries.
Semi-seriously,   A. W. CONNER.
Lafayette, Ind.

Courtesy, Butler School of Religion Library

A. McLean referred to advertisements of the Standard Oil Co., which the "Christian Standard" published. This is such an advertisement, upper right, from that paper for July 13, 1907, p. 1175.

I recall the time when Brother Lord used to come into the mission rooms and argue in favor of admitting the unimmersed into our churches. He claimed that that was the only logical position for us to take and that we had to come to it. I did my best to defend the teaching of the Scriptures and the observance of the ordinances as Christ gave them to the church. I did what I could to convert him from the error of his way. In those days I was to him a "conservative" and a "fogy"; I am now precisely what I was then. . . .

Mr. [Russell] Errett speaks of the wonderful things that he did for the Society, of the "ten years' debauch of missionary enthusiasm." . . .

He gives some figures and seeks to leave the impression that he has done more for missions than his father. His figures are worthless for the purpose for which they are given. The question of space is only a small part of the truth. If he had given an acre instead of a column, that of itself would signify nothing. A sneer and a stab will do more harm than an acre of space can do. It is the spirit and attitude that avail to help. Isaac Errett prayed for missions; he gave time and thought and money; he made great addresses and wrote great articles; he gave the first place to the subject. As the splendors of eternity enveloped him, his chief concern was about our missionary enterprises, and his chief delight was in the prosperity. . . . There was no fight interjected into a missionary campaign to divert attention and to reduce the receipts. The National Conventions were reported fully and fairly. Can that be said now? I leave the readers to answer. . . .

Mr. Errett may flatter himself that he did far more for the Society than his father did. I disagree. One year of his father's advocacy did more for the work of missions than all that he did since he was born. Such, at least, is my conviction.

It is significant in connection with the refusal of the *Standard* to publish the second article by Mr. McLean to note a short article, "Journalistic Honor," by Russell Errett in the *Christian Standard* (November 3, 1923, p. 102), as follows:

There was one feature of our journalism in our earlier days that was unique—unique, that is, in religious journalism—the habit of representing an opponent fairly. It was held to be only decent, in reviewing a writer, to represent him in his own words; to let him be heard in his own defense as fully as he was reviewed.

This honorable custom was inaugurated by the *Harbinger*, and has been followed by every editor among us who has been at all a representative of the honor of the brotherhood. . . .

I am proud to say that the *Standard* has never departed from the honorable course established by its founder. Through all the controversies in our own ranks it has habitually let the opponent speak for himself, even to the extent of blackguarding both publisher and editor.

After Mr. McLean's second article was published in pamphlet form, the Standard Oil and patent medicine advertising were dropped from the *Standard* pages. . In an editorial announcement, "Our New Advertising Policy" (November 23, 1907, pp. 1927 f.) the *Christian Standard* stated: ". . . every effort will be made to free the paper from this time out of every advertisement that can reasonably be objected to." H. C. Hall, advertising manager, had told F. M. Rains, a secretary of the Foreign Christian Missionary Society, that the magazine lost many thousands of dollars through the canceling of those advertisements.

It is of interest that for several years now the *Christian Standard* has published no advertisements from brotherhood agencies or outside commercial concerns. Its advertising space is used exclusively to promote publications and materials of the Standard Publishing Company.

In an editorial of the *Christian Standard* dealing with the Rockefeller money controversy ("A Disclaimer," October 12, 1907, pp. 1633 f.), there was the following sentence: "That the assault on the editor and business manager of the *Standard* was part and parcel of a scheme to float a new publishing-house, at the expense of the Standard Publishing Co., is too plain for denial." That was an unproved statement.

In a *Christian Standard* editorial ("A Standard Oil Coincidence," July 22, 1905, p. 1168), the following statement was made:

Of course, there are boards of trustees shortsighted and, shall we say, base enough, to take the [Rockefeller] money and become a partaker of this man's sins. But we would be humiliated indeed if we thought that any college among the Churches of Christ in the restoration movement, however urgent its needs, would accept a gift from a man who is charged in the public prints with business corruption and perjury . . .

Of course, during the following years, many of our colleges accepted gifts from the General Education Board, endowed by John D. Rockefeller, Sr. While the *Christian Standard* raised no great cry about the source of those funds, the educational institutions were by then under attack by the magazine on many counts.

Following the writing, publication, and widespread distribution of the second article in pamphlet form, the *Christian Standard* ceased this particular attack. However, the periodical soon launched an attack on the organized life of our brotherhood from another angle. Its opposition seemed especially strong against the Foreign Christian Missionary Society. With the coming of a new editor, Samuel S. Lappin, to take the place of J. A. Lord, the periodical was soon in the midst of another controversy.

The End of the Attack on the Rockefeller Gifts

One of the most revealing things about the controversy over the Rockefeller gifts was the way it all ended. The National Convention was held at Norfolk, Virginia, in October, 1907. The *Christian Standard,* with much emphasis, claimed that the Rockefeller gifts should be repudiated by the brethren and demanded that the money be returned.

The Norfolk Convention met. During the early days of the convention the annual meeting of the Foreign Christian Missionary Society was held in the Norfolk Christian Church. Members of the Society from all over the United States were there in large numbers. The building was filled.

As the time approached for the discussion of the Rockefeller gifts, Thomas W. Phillips arose and made a speech against the acceptance of this money and demanded that the funds be returned. Silence fell upon the audience. Several minutes elapsed, but nobody in the large group would second his motion. It became embarrassing to Mr. Phillips. He even appealed for a second to his proposal.

Finally, O. G. Hertzog, who was field secretary for Hiram (Ohio) College, arose and stated that he entirely disagreed with Mr. Phillips, but that to get the motion before the house he would second it. His second was recognized. The motion was called for. There were a very few who gave an almost indistinguishable vote in favor of the motion. When the negative was called for, there was a nearly unanimous roar against the necessity of returning the money.

Russell Errett and J. A. Lord were seated in the back of the room. During the episode, they did not even arise to say one word in favor of the months of publicity they had given in the *Christian Standard* in opposition to the Rockefeller gift money.

An interesting incident occurred during this Norfolk meeting. Prof. Charles Louis Loos, who was then teaching at Transylvania College, Lexington, Kentucky, had expressed himself as against the reception of the Rockefeller money. It was generally understood that the *Christian Standard* had made it possible for Prof. Loos to attend the convention. Preceding the motion of Mr. Phillips, Prof. Loos arose and began to speak. He had formerly served on the Executive Committee of the Foreign Christian Missionary Society and very fond memories came back to him. He began by praising the Society and all that it had done for the extension of Christianity. He uttered no word of criticism, but only praise. Either because of his age— he was 83 years old at that time—or because his better judgment controlled him, Prof. Loos apparently proved to be a great disappointment to the *Christian Standard!*

So the whole controversy in which the *Christian Standard* had strained every resource it could find to carry its point had come to naught—all the debate and argument and all the pages of publicity.

During this meeting in Norfolk, F. M. Rains, senior secretary of the Foreign Christian Missionary Society, stated that in order to end the controversy that was injuring the missionary work, the Society would not again solicit gifts from Mr. Rockefeller. This decision, made in the interests of brotherliness, was hardly necessary, for it was only a short time afterwards that our colleges were appealing for money from the General Education Board, endowed by Mr. Rockefeller. Ten years later the Rockefeller Foundation made generous contributions to the hospitals of the Foreign Christian Missionary Society at Luchowfu (Hofei) and at Nantungchow, China. So the contention was defeated and at an end. The *Christian Standard*, however, turned to other avenues through which it opposed the cooperative work of the Disciples of Christ.

Nanking University and the Pittsburgh Program

The next three years, from late 1907 to 1910, of the *Christian Standard* were fairly quiet, as far as the editorial controversies were concerned. It did, however, make two attacks. The one was on the participation of the Disciples of Christ in the Union Christian University of Nanking, China. The other was on the program of the 1909 Pittsburgh Centennial Convention, celebrating one hundred years of our history.

In Nanking, China, our missionary, F. E. Meigs, had been the leader in getting together the Methodists, Presbyterians, and Disciples of Christ for the support and operation of a union school there. Each religious body had previously maintained a small and struggling boys' school. Mr. Meigs felt that it would be helpful to present a solid front in Christian education to the Chinese with an institution that could be backed by the three boards far more successfully than any one board could conduct a school. He also declared that, since we were standing for Christian unity, a cooperative effort of this kind would be just what Disciples should do.

The Foreign Christian Missionary Society gave its approval to the venture and the Presbyterians and Disciples came together first. The Methodists at the time were stronger and held out until the experiment between the other two had been tried and found successful. After a year or so the Methodists decided to cooperate and the University of Nanking was established in 1910.

The school became afterwards one of the most outstanding Christian universities in all mission fields. A feature of the understanding was that each religious body should have its representatives on the faculty and would have equal authority with the others in the direction of the school. It was a success from the beginning. No one yielded anything of convictions, or purposes, in this cooperative effort to present a united front to the Chinese people in Christian education. It gave Disciples of Christ much recognition and more appreciation of their leadership than anything that ever happened in our work in foreign fields. Each communion had its own church near the campus for the Chinese Christians.

The *Christian Standard* launched an editorial campaign against this undertaking in Nanking. The thesis of the protest was that it objected to the impression given to the Chinese that we are "one" in Christ! It stated, "The missionaries of the

F.C.M.S. in China have adopted the denominational conception of the church and given up the plea for the union of God's people through the restoration of the Christianity of the New Testament" (*Christian Standard,* June 25, 1910, p. 1091). Other later editorials followed the same lead. But the people who were supporting the missionary cause gave practically unanimous approval to this significant step in Christian co-operation.

Great plans were made for the Centennial Convention of Disciples of Christ in Pittsburgh, Pennsylvania, October 11-19, 1909. During the development of the celebration, a representative committee was appointed to secure the speakers for the great gathering. The *Standard* immediately began to announce the sort of program that should be presented and the men who should participate on that program. Those in charge of the Centennial Convention program decided that it should be representative and consequently men should be asked to participate who were members of our churches, with different theological attitudes, so that the convention would represent a cross-section of the entire brotherhood.

Dr. Herbert L. Willett, then an outstanding preacher and a professor in the department of Hebraics of the University of Chicago, was chosen as one of the speakers. The *Standard* had previously attacked him because of his views regarding Christian baptism. Editorials of the *Standard* proclaimed that no one should take part on the Centennial Convention program who did not "speak the same thing." It later stated that it did not disapprove of Dr. Willett's address, as given at the convention, but of his being placed on the program at all.

The Standard Publishing Company issued the report of the 1909 Pittsburgh sessions under the title, *Centennial Convention Report.* A Publisher's Note, signed by Russell Errett, Manager, stated:

The publication of this report was undertaken by the Standard Publishing Co., only on the express understanding that we were privileged to disclaim in this way all responsibility for the appearance of the names of Prof. H. L. Willett and P. J. Rice in its pages; and that the opposition of a great part of the brotherhood to their appearance on the program, as representative men, should here go to record. . . .

This opposition, so far as we had any hand in it, was based entirely on the public record of these gentlemen, for teaching contrary to and subversive of the principles for which the disciples of Christ contend, principles which it was the object of the Centennial to honor. That opposition is in no degree diminished, and we again enter our protest against the recognition of these men as public teachers on this or any other program, representative of the principles of the Restoration.

On the same principle that compelled us to object to the publication of the address of Col. S. H. Church, we object to the recognition, as representatives, of men who are notorious for public utterances that conflict with the plain teaching of the Scriptures.

Samuel Harden Church of Pittsburgh, a grandson of our spiritual forefather, Walter Scott, delivered an address at the Pittsburgh Centennial Convention on, "Progress and Achievements of a Hundred Years." It was published in the *Christian Standard* of January 1 and 8, 1910. Yet it was omitted from the *Centennial Convention Report,* although Mr. Church's small photo, as a member of the Centennial Convention Executive Committee, was published on page 19 of the volume. Because of the omission of his address from the *Report* book, Mr. Church issued his speech in 1910 in an enlarged form as a pamphlet under the title, *Religious Progress in America.* The *Christian Standard* accused him of "infidelity" and as a result of those attacks, Mr. Church left our people and became a Presbyterian. For many years he was president of Carnegie Institute of Technology in Pittsburgh. He died in 1943.

It was the feeling among many who agreed with the Pittsburgh Program Committee that doctrinal divergence should not be made a test of fellowship in the program of the Centennial Convention. Remembering the great differences which existed between persons and groups in the early days of the movement, and that personal loyalty to Christ was a sufficient bond of union without the aid of creedal agreements, the committee felt that the widest liberty should be accorded to participants on the program.

During the year of 1909, R. A. Long of Kansas City, Missouri, wealthy and generous lumberman of the Disciples, purchased the Christian Publishing Company of St. Louis, Missouri, including the weekly periodical, *The Christian-Evangelist,* from J. H. Garrison and other stockholders for $129,000. The property was given to the Disciples and it is managed as a cooperative, brotherhood corporation by a self-perpetuating board of directors like most of our colleges. The publishing house was renamed the Christian Board of Publication. This generous gift was made with the understanding that all income above necessary expenses and improvements for the business should be contributed to one or more of the various missionary, benevolent, educational, or other agencies of our fellowship. The publishing house became a factor in the brotherhood controversies that followed.

The "Hors de Rome" Movement

Since the *Christian Standard* so strongly attacked the organized missionary work of the Disciples through its controversy over the Rockefeller gifts, the question was raised as to whether it was interested in the missionary enterprise. Significantly, then, it started a missionary venture of its own. This effort was called the "Hors de Rome" (out of Catholicism) movement which began in 1909 in Paris, France. It was a venture to establish a church, or churches, of the New Testament faith in the city of Paris, using a division in the Roman Catholic Church and the conversion of some of its priests to Protestantism as the entering wedge. One of our ministers, Alfred E. Seddon, with his family, was settled in Paris. This missionary was a good writer and propagandist. Consequently the pages of the *Christian Standard* began to carry reports of this new venture and many appeals for the financial support of this "French Christian Mission."

Mr. Seddon's attack on Roman Catholicism was given much space by the *Christian Standard*. The arguments were well stated. Being in the heart of a great Roman Catholic metropolis, the correspondent had plenty of material at first hand with which to attack Catholicism. However, the real missionary end of the effort was rather insignificant and not in keeping with the large amount of space given to the "Hors de Rome" movement. There was much skepticism about the usefulness of this program on the part of people who understood the situation in France.

I remember quite distinctly my own experience in visiting this mission in 1912 on my way to our Belgian Congo Mission. On reaching Paris, I telephoned Mr. Seddon. I told him I would like to attend services at the church. With some hesitation he told me, and to my surprise, that he had no church in Paris, but was meeting in one of the suburbs. I found out what tram we should take to get to the church. There was no morning service. So, on Sunday evening, I went out to the mission, accompanied by Mrs. Corey and three friends.

The mission was most disappointing. In the small, rented place, including the five persons in our party, plus the missionary, his wife and one daughter, there were fifteen persons present. A converted Roman Catholic priest spoke in the French language which we could not understand. Obviously, it was difficult for a Protestant work such as that to progress in an environment so solidly Roman Catholic. However, neither the interest shown, nor the appearance of the priest-convert, represented in any significant way the tremendous publicity of the *Christian Standard* with regard to this movement in France. Shortly after World War I broke out in 1914, this work was abandoned.

Chapter 2

MISSIONARY AND THEOLOGICAL "HERESY"

Because of a very general criticism throughout the brotherhood of Disciples of Christ concerning the attitude of the *Christian Standard,* especially its editorial-controversial emphasis, it was thought that a new day had come. That was in 1909, when Samuel S. Lappin, a good writer, became editor of the *Standard* after about a year as associate to J. A. Lord (*Christian Standard,* April 6, 1946, p. 215). Mr. Lappin went to Cincinnati from the pastorate of the Stanford, Illinois, church where he served well. The feeling was quite general among Disciples that there would be a change in the policies of the periodical. However, it was not many months before the old antagonism began to arise again.

The Guy W. Sarvis Attack

An occasion soon arose which afforded Mr. Lappin and the *Standard* another basis for controversy along theological lines. A young man, Guy W. Sarvis, was appointed in 1908 by the Foreign Christian Missionary Society to serve in China. He was graduated from Drake University that same year and was a member of the University Place Church in Des Moines, Iowa, of which Charles S. Medbury was pastor.

This young man was approved heartily as a missionary candidate by both Mr. Medbury and other persons who knew him intimately. He passed the examination of the Executive Committee and the secretarial staff of the Foreign Christian Missionary Society. This included physical tests and a thorough questioning and study of his general motives and attitudes, scholarship ability, Christian beliefs, life, and service, including the candidate's acceptance of the ideals and purposes of the Disciples of Christ.

Since Mr. Sarvis was appointed to teach in the University of Nanking, then in process of organization, it was thought wise by both the candidate and the Society for him to go beyond his undergraduate college work and to take some graduate training in education. The Society approved his enrolling in the University of Chicago where this sort of academic training was available. He was a brilliant young student, a man of consecration, with a great desire to enter foreign missionary service. He was one of the first foreign missions candidates of the Disciples of Christ to go beyond collegiate biblical courses for post-graduate study.

Mr. Sarvis enrolled in the University of Chicago and became a member of the theologically-liberal Hyde Park Church (now the University Church of Disciples of Christ), where Edward Scribner Ames was minister, adjoining the university campus. Mr. Sarvis later became Dr. Ames' pastoral assistant, thus serving and also earning expenses for his graduate study in Chicago. These facts gave occasion for the *Christian Standard* to claim that Mr. Sarvis was unorthodox.

Editorials began to appear in the *Standard* in 1911, as the time neared for Mr. Sarvis to leave for China, attacking the Foreign Christian Missionary Society for sending such a man, with such a background, to the mission field. These suspicions spread broadcast over the brotherhood called forth criticism from certain quarters.

A fellow ministerial student with Mr. Sarvis in Drake University, together with two or three persons in Mr. Medbury's church, informed the *Christian Standard* of their opposition. G. W. Elliott, then of Huron, South Dakota, who had baptized Mr. Sarvis, put him on the grill of personal examination. Then, when Mr. Sarvis returned for a visit to his home town of Highmore, South Dakota, where he was one of the first members when our church was organized, Carl E. Smith took exception to what he claimed Mr. Sarvis believed and attacked the young missionary candidate through the *Standard* (May 20, 1911, p. 806).

Mr. Sarvis was inexperienced, but brilliant. He objected to what he felt was the legalistic attitude of the man who was his former pastor and who had baptized him. In the discussion that followed, Mr. Sarvis argued that a person did not necessarily have to be immersed in order to be saved. He stated that William Jennings Bryan and Robert E. Speer were as good Christians, or better, than he was.

This set off a thunderous assault. It was claimed that Mr. Sarvis was an advocate of "open membership," that he was untrue to the New Testament position of the Disciples. A good deal was also said and some things published by a small opposition group in Mr. Medbury's Des Moines church. This was embarrassing to Mr. Medbury, who was one of our leading preachers, a man of rather conservative views himself, but who believed in Guy W. Sarvis and told the Foreign Christian Missionary Society that it should send him to China.

I shall never forget those days of controversy. I knew Mr. Sarvis and his wife, formerly Maude Taylor, personally and had every confidence in them as devoted and true Christian people. A couple of persons in Mr. Medbury's church demanded that Mr. Sarvis be brought to Des Moines to undergo further examination. F. M. Rains, the senior secretary of the Foreign Christian Missionary Society, had been on a visit to our mission fields. He returned to the United States, via the Portland, Oregon, National Convention of Disciples in July, 1911. President A. McLean was away from the Cincinnati office of the Society, attending conventions. Being alone at the office, I conferred with Prof. S. M. Jefferson of Transylvania and The College of the Bible of Lexington, Kentucky. He was a member of the Society's Executive Committee and one of the noblest and most level-headed men I have ever known. He was a person of keen intellect, conservative attitude, and human sympathy.

Prof. Jefferson said to me, "Let us go out to Des Moines and see what's up." So we went. It was in July, 1911.

When we arrived in Des Moines, Mr. Medbury was out of the city. We met in a corner of the University Place Church sanctuary with a small group of people. Prof. Jefferson was made moderator of the meeting. He served with rare discretion and fairness.

The main issues that came up in the meeting that day, July 15, 1911, were two. In the first place, a Drake ministerial student had been in a debate with Mr. Sarvis. The debating question was whether Shakespeare was inspired. Mr. Sarvis, for the affirmative, contended Shakespeare was inspired, while the other young preacher upheld the negative. As I recall, Mr. Sarvis' side won the debate. The contention of the young minister was that since Mr. Sarvis spoke so strongly for Shakespeare's inspiration, his attitude proved that he believed Shakespeare was inspired like Paul and other New Testament writers. Mr. Sarvis vehemently denied that he had any such intention, but insisted that he believed the New Testament writers were inspired in a far different way than Shakespeare, that it was a difference of degree and that Shakespeare's inspiration was extremely limited as compared to the others.

The other main witness was an elderly lady who was a member of Mr. Medbury's church and who conducted a boarding house. Mr. Sarvis had roomed at her place. She was a highly excitable person and limited in her understanding of anything like scholarship. She had scolded Mr. Sarvis strongly for going to such a "heretical" school as the University of Chicago. He had laughingly replied that he was rather anxious to go, that it would do him a lot of good, that perhaps he would learn some new things there, that he hoped he would, which was, indeed, the purpose of his going. The old lady took this to mean that he had gone "haywire" theologically and the gossip that ensued started things buzzing around this Des Moines church.

There were other things that came up during the meeting in Mr. Medbury's church, but nothing of great importance. Prof. Jefferson, Mr. Rains (who had reached Des Moines from the Portland Convention), and I left Des Moines, accompanied by Mr. Sarvis as far as Chicago, feeling more committed to the fine young candidate than ever before.

The *Christian Standard* had a reporter at the Des Moines conference and subsequently many columns were devoted to the examination, with all kinds of questions raised and strictures made, entirely outside the real atmosphere and the real conclusions of that meeting.

Following the Des Moines examination, Mr. Medbury wrote to A. McLean, president of the Foreign Christian Missionary Society, and said: "Send Sarvis out to China. I am ready to trust him. He will make good."

As previously stated, Mr. Sarvis was a member of the Hyde Park Church of Chicago and assistant to the pastor there. This congregation offered to support Mr. Sarvis as its "living link" on the mission field. These facts were used by the *Christian Standard* to argue that, of course, Mr. Sarvis agreed with the policy of the Hyde Park Church in receiving unimmersed believers, who presented letters, "as members of the congregation" (*The Scroll,* December, 1906, p. 60). In an editorial, "The Hype Park Living Link," the *Standard* attempted to bolster that argument with a statement from Carl E. Smith of Highmore, South Dakota. After a visit of Mr. Sarvis in Highmore, Mr. Smith wrote that "both publicly and in private he [Mr. Sarvis] has expressed himself as believing in the plan of admitting unimmersed Christians as members of the congregation" (*Christian Standard,* May 20, 1911, p. 806). The editorial of the same issue (p. 808) stated:

Mr. Sarvis is openly and avowedly an advocate of the Hyde Park system, by which a Romish invention is recognized as a substitute for the baptism commanded by our Lord and practiced by his apostles . . .

The Foreign Christian Missionary Society, by sending Mr. Sarvis to the field under pay of the Hyde Park Church, becomes party to the Hype Park anomaly. They have no right thus to betray the trust reposed in them.

Mr. Sarvis answered in the *Christian Standard* of June 10, 1911 (pp. 926 f.):

I do not desire, and never have desired, to carry out the Hyde Park plan in the mission field. I have never advocated the Hyde Park system, either in public or in private. I do not recognize, and never have recognized, any "Romish invention" as a valid substitute for baptism. I believe that my position on baptism is in accord with the teaching of the New Testament and with that of Alexander and Thomas Campbell. Mr. Smith's communication is based on the fragmentary conversation of a very small part of one day, on one public address in which I did not discuss any of the matters referred to in his article, and on hearsay gathered from a week's visit among my friends, during nearly all of which time he was absent from the town.

I did discuss the union educational work in Nanking, China, and expressed my approval of it. If I did not approve of it, I should not participate in it.

The *Christian Standard* paid no attention to these assertions by Mr. Sarvis. As a secretary of the Foreign Christian Missionary Society, I replied for the Executive Committee in the *Standard* (June 10, 1911, p. 927) to the magazine's charges, as follows:

It was published in an editorial in the *Christian Standard* of April 29, that the Hyde Park Church selected Guy W. Sarvis as a missionary to China, and the impression was left upon the mind of the readers that he was selected because he was in accord with the views of the Hyde Park Church and Dr. Ames, its minister . . .

This representation of the facts is entirely erroneous and misleading. There is no basis for it either in fact or in truth. The Hyde Park Church did not select Guy W. Sarvis, and had nothing whatever to do with his selection and appointment. The society was in correspondence with Bro. Sarvis for three years. While he was yet a student in Drake University, S. J. Corey visited him with a view to his appointment. The society appointed him without any reference to the Hyde Park Church. . . . Their work will be directed by the society and not by that church.

Nor is it true that Bro. Sarvis approves or desires to carry out the Hyde Park plan on the mission field. When he was before the committee, he was questioned closely as to his faith and his views. His answers were so explicit and so satisfactory that he was unanimously appointed. Since the question has been raised by the *Standard*, he has written that he does not believe in the adoption of the Hype Park plan, either of home or abroad. . . .

It is a matter for profound regret that the *Standard* did not avail itself of the means easily within its reach [here in its very city] for ascertaining the facts as above stated. Instead of publishing harmful statements which have not been proved, and then calling on the society to print a statement correcting them if they are not true, it is only fair to ask that every means be taken to ascertain the truth before publication, to the end that the cause of missions, which is the cause of God, may not suffer injury.

Mr. and Mrs. Sarvis went out to China during 1911, he having received the M.A. degree and she the B.A. degree from the University of Chicago. The Foreign Christian Missionary Society had every confidence in Mr. Sarvis and felt that a responsible mission administration should not yield to his opponents. He served at the University of Nanking with real ability for more than twelve years. He taught sociology and economics and in 1913 was made dean of the College of Arts and Sciences of the University.

I visited the China mission field in 1914. We had no missionary in China who was more constructive in his judgment and more careful in his administration and teaching than Guy W. Sarvis. He neither practiced nor advocated what is called open membership on the mission field. He was looked upon as an outstanding and devoted leader. He had the friendship and confidence of our own staff in China and also that of the Methodists and Presbyterians, with whom we were associated in the operation and maintenance of Nanking University. However, the *Christian Standard* kept up a steady attack on Mr. Sarvis. He never made further reply, but continued faithfully in his work during all of those years.

During the Louisville, Kentucky National Convention of Disciples in October, 1912, Dr. Ames, minister of the Hyde Park Church of Chicago, read the following statement:

> In order to show that there has been no sinister motive in its living link relation with Mr. and Mrs. Guy W. Sarvis, and to promote harmony, and to advance the great missionary work of the Disciples, as its pastor I will urge the Hyde Park Church to relinquish its living link relation with Mr. and Mrs. Sarvis. (*The Christian-Evangelist*, October 24, 1912, p. 1501.)

To which, the *Christian Standard* replied editorially (October 26, 1912, p. 1746), as follows:

> Mr. Ames attempted to clear the sky later on *by withdrawing support from Mr. Sarvis.* Just how it helped we have not been able to see, except that, from now on, the society alone is responsible for Guy Sarvis, and must support him with money from those loyal to the gospel and the movement. Had Mr. Ames asked that the tie *between Sarvis and the society* be severed, and proposed to support him as an independent missionary, that would have been magnanimous. His course is like that of the wasp that stings and flies away, leaving the stinger in.

Contrast the repudiation by the *Christian Standard* of this gracious gesture on the part of Dr. Ames and the Hyde Park

Church with editorial comment by *The Christian-Evangelist* (October 24, 1912, p. 1501), then under the managing editorship of A. C. Smither with J. H. Garrison as the editor-emeritus, as follows:

The magnanimous statement was received with great applause. . . . . It was explained that this does not involve the recall of Brother Sarvis from the mission field, unless his course there should demand it, nor does it prevent the Hyde Park Church from contributing to the foreign mission work. At this happy solution the convention rose and sang "Praise God from whom all blessings flow." It was a triumph of the Spirit of Christ over any personal feeling and prejudice that may have existed. The action of Prof. Ames provoked a great deal of commendation.

Opposition to the International Convention

At the Louisville, Kentucky, National Convention in 1912, there was a strong committee report favoring the organization of a General Convention of Disciples of Christ. Up to this time our so-called National Convention was in fact a series of separate, and only indirectly related, annual meetings of our three missionary organizations, namely, the American Christian Missionary Society, the Christian Woman's Board of Missions, and the Foreign Christian Missionary Society. Other brotherhood interests usually had their meetings and programs also. These assemblies were generally attended by the same group of Disciples.

There had been much discussion as to whether a General Convention, to which all agencies of the brotherhood should report, should be a delegate assembly. That would have meant having representatives elected from our churches who might have some backing and advisory direction given to them to act in a representative way upon matters that might come before the convention. With nearly unanimous approval, the convention reorganization was authorized at Louisville.

The *Christian Standard* strongly opposed the delegate convention and mainly because of this, when the International Convention was later formed, it was not a delegate body. The *Standard* charged in an editorial ("The General Convention and Ecclesiasticism," September 26, 1914, p. 1661) that "a convention made up of delegates representing churches is an ecclesiasticism."

When the General Convention met in Toronto, Ontario, Canada, in 1913, the new constitution was ratified with an overwhelming vote of approval. Every effort was made to placate the *Christian Standard* and to secure its support of the convention. But the paper turned strongly against it.

In 1916, Russell Errett, during the absence of S. S. Lappin, editor of the *Standard*, published a letter on the editorial pages which he had addressed to C. M. Chilton, pastor of St. Joseph, Missouri. After charging that the convention "has made its sole plea on the ground that we are a 'church' or sect" and stating that the periodical "will oppose it as it will any other sect," Mr. Errett then added (September 9, 1916, p. 1686):

(1) It has been perverted from its avowed purpose—i.e., to unify our voluntary association of individuals—into the formation of an ecclesiasticism, with our free congregations as units in an organization which intends to control officially the missionary and other interests of the brotherhood.

(2) It was "adopted" (not by the congregations themselves, but by a few hundred votes in a mass-meeting of four thousand), as a *delegate* Convention, under a constitution by which the delegates were to control, and were to elect the officers. . . . .

(3) While it is wholly irresponsible, and, in the eyes of the law, is a pure nonentity, it has planned to take charge of our largest corporate interests and announces its intention to assume control of all affairs of the brotherhood, or "church," as it prefers to call it. . . . .

(4) Its pretense of regard for the authority of the churches is only a pretense. . . . . It is crooked in all its ways.

In this same statement, Mr. Errett had stated that "the management of the organization has been without rectitude throughout." Later, the same year, in an editorial, "Why Protest" (*Christian Standard*, December 23, 1916, p. 371), the magazine stated:

The "General Convention"—an organization in direct conflict with the fundamentals of the Restoration plea, subsisting on charity because it can not be legitimately financed by the brotherhood, an ecclesiasticism if regulated by its proposed constitution, and a connecting link with denominationalism—is now being thrust into our annual missionary assemblies and into the highway of our progress.

At the 1916 convention in Des Moines, Iowa, Z. T. Sweeney, a member of the Columbus, Indiana, Tabernacle Church and formerly its minister, offered a resolution asking for a committee of five persons to meet with officers of the convention, representatives of the societies, editors and owners of newspapers, to provide changes in the convention constitution and thus bring harmony to the brotherhood. The convention approved the resolution and the committee was appointed. This is another example of the successive attempts made to bring harmony between the *Christian Standard* and progressive Disciples.

The next General Convention was held in Kansas City, Missouri, October 24-31, 1917. The Committee on Revision of the Constitution had been at work during the year. A final meeting was held in St. Louis, Missouri, at which Russell Errett, Z. T. Sweeney, representatives of the societies and other brotherhood organizations were present. The revised constitution, practically drafted by Mr. Errett and Mr. Sweeney, abandoned the delegate convention and thus gave all members of our churches attending the convention the privilege of voting on all matters. The name was changed to the International Convention, since the churches of both the United States and Canada are represented. Every concession was made to the *Christian Standard*, as represented by Mr. Errett, its chief owner. It was thought that a time of peace had come for our brotherhood when the revised constitution was approved in Kansas City with great enthusiasm, Mr. Sweeney presenting it from the platform.

Commenting on the new constitution of the International Convention, the *Christian Standard* (November 10, 1917, p. 174) stated:

> Time will, of course, change the constitution adopted at Kansas City—all human documents that live must change, and accommodate themselves to the situations through which they pass. But it is our conviction that the Kansas City Convention mapped out a program on which we can depend for unity and substantial results for several years to come, and likewise a program that will expand and bear fruit a generation hence.

Sad to say, however, only a little time passed until the reorganized convention was under attack by the *Christian Standard*. An editorial, "The Challenge of the Hierarchy" (October 8, 1921, p. 2750), stated:

> The president of the International Convention at Winona [George A. Miller], in his address—the key-note address—issued the following chal-

lenge to the members of the free churches of Christ, known among themselves as "The Restoration":

"Now, as a result of what I have said, I make my final proposition, which is, *that all agencies—missionary, educational, and philanthropic—asking the aid and support of our general brotherhood, should report to this Convention, have its books audited by it, and its officers nominated and elected in its general assembly.*"

This challenge was uttered immediately after a strong public protest against the apparent tendencies of the Convention towards ecclesiasticism, and against its disregard of its solemn pledge to abstain from all show of ecclesiastical authority.

As time for the 1922 International Convention at Winona Lake, Indiana approached, the *Standard* published an editorial, "We Can Not Participate" (August 19, 1922, p. 3869), in which it said:

The *Standard* will not be represented at the Winona Convention because it believes that the contemplated amendments to the constitution of the International Convention pass beyond the pale of expediency and are utterly foreign to a true Restoration movement. . . . .

We consider this attempt to arrogate to an "international convention" direct authority over agencies an inexcusable patterning after denominational schemes of government which must heavily becloud our true position as an undenominational movement.

Despite the editorial announcement of the *Christian Standard* in 1922, it was some years before the periodical and the Standard Publishing Company practically ceased to have anything to do with the International Convention when it convened.

Attack on Transylvania and The College of the Bible

Perhaps the most significant attack of the *Christian Standard,* aside from that on the United Christian Missionary Society and its predecessor organizations, was its opposition to Transylvania College and The College of the Bible of Lexington, Kentucky. This had begun as far back as 1912, when Dr. A. W. Fortune, minister of the Walnut Hills Christian Church, Cincinnati, went to the faculty of The College of the Bible. John T. Brown, of Louisville, Kentucky, one of our evangelists, then attacked what he called the "heresy" of Dr. Fortune. This attack was published in the *Christian Standard*, beginning with the issue of July 27, 1912 (p. 1206) and continuing for several weeks thereafter.

The Board of Trustees of The College of the Bible, composed of sixteen well-known Disciples, made a statement concerning this attack. The board introduced it by saying that it had made a thorough investigation of Dr. Fortune's preaching at the Walnut Hills Church, of statements that he had made, of his sermons, etc., before calling him to the teaching position. In reply to Mr. Brown, the statement related the board's answer thus (*Christian Standard*, December 7, 1912, p. 2018):

> The Board would call attention to the fact that Mr. Brown presented no record or documentary evidence, but only the recollection of several men as to their impressions received at various times from hearing utterances of Mr. Fortune. The uncertainty and unsatisfactory nature of such evidence is easily apparent.
>
> After full investigation and mature deliberation, we the Trustees, each speaking his independent opinion, find that Mr. Fortune is not only a profound scholar, an excellent teacher, a man of great natural ability and charming personality, but that he is also a devout, consecrated man of deep spirituality and thorough soundness in the fundamentals for which the disciples of Christ stand, and is in every way worthy to fill the position to which he has been called. We find that none of Mr. Brown's charges has been sustained by the evidence.

Later, in 1917, the *Christian Standard* launched its all-out attack on these two institutions. The background for this attack was as follows:

John W. McGarvey had been for a long time the revered teacher and president (1895-1911) of The College of the Bible. He was recognized as a scholar and was looked upon as one of the leaders in the ultra-conservative school of theological thought. As he approached the end of his career, he undoubtedly wished to have somebody leading The College of the Bible who would follow in his footsteps. He apparently chose one of his students, Hall L. Calhoun, to prepare himself for this place. Mr. Calhoun, as President McGarvey felt, needed the academic standing which training in the great universities would give him, if he was to become president of The College of the Bible. He, therefore, went to Yale and Harvard Universities for his graduate work, receiving the Ph.D. degree from the latter institution in 1904.

However, after President McGarvey died on October 6, 1911, at the age of eighty-two, R. H. Crossfield was chosen president

of the two institutions, Transylvania College and The College
of the Bible.   Many persons felt that this was a keen disappointment to Dr. Calhoun.   With the presidency of The College of
the Bible again filled, Dr. Calhoun was made dean of the seminary in 1912, succeeding W. C. Morro.

In the meantime, other important things had happened.
Older men besides President McGarvey had died, men who had
been teachers in The College of the Bible.   These included S.
M. Jefferson, Charles Louis Loos, and I. B. Grubbs.   Thus
nearly a whole new faculty became necessary.   To fill these
positions, A. W. Fortune, William Clayton Bower, G. W. Hemry,
and Elmer E. Snoddy were chosen.   These were all devout and
scholarly men who were sympathetic with many of the developments of historical biblical research and the newer methods of
teaching, especially for graduate students.

W. C. Morro had gone to Butler University from the faculty
of The College of the Bible.   He afterwards went to teach at
Brite College of the Bible of Texas Christian University, Fort
Worth, where he taught until his death in 1943.   In his book,
"Brother McGarvey" (p. 233), Prof. Morro, in interpreting
President McGarvey's teaching, said: "This means that McGarvey's method fitted his day.   It was not adaptable to times of
better educational preparation."   Then, Prof. Morro makes this
additional observation (p. 250):

The viewpoint and the motive in studying the Bible today differ
from those of McGarvey's time. · Hence this age can profit from McGarvey, not by literally doing and teaching as he did, but by meeting the
problems that confront it in the spirit and with the ideals of McGarvey.
In this way only can a person of the past be of value to a later generation.

Prof. Morro was a man of modern training and he had prepared the way somewhat at The College of the Bible for the
coming of these new men.   The transition from the old type of
teaching carried on by President McGarvey, to the newer peda-
gogy being adopted quite generally among educational institutions, both secular and religious, provided some difficulty, of
course.   This, added to the fact that Dean Calhoun, although
educated at Yale and Harvard, still held to the old type of

teaching and an extremely conservative theology, made the transition even more difficult.

Another fact augmented the problem which arose. In those days there were numbers of students in The College of the Bible who had very little preparatory training and some who had only the equivalent of high school education and yet were men of rather mature years. For them to adjust themselves to new methods of teaching and thinking was very difficult. Encouraged by outside journalistic propaganda, some of these students became very critical of the new professors.

The teaching of President McGarvey had been of the question and answer type. His notes were carefully prepared and answers worked out by him. Good scholarship on the part of the student depended largely on how accurately he could stick to President McGarvey's notes and give the answers that he had formulated. Mr. McGarvey's *Class Notes on Sacred History*, covering books of the Bible from Genesis through the Acts of the Apostles, published in four volumes, were used as textbooks in his courses. Most of the outside reading was from authors who supported President McGarvey's point of view. Thus, the student was kept in a limited academic channel.

Colby D. Hall was a professor and dean for many years at Brite College of the Bible, Texas Christian University, Fort Worth. A former student of President McGarvey's, Dean Hall writes: "I studied under him for three years; the only books he ever referred to were the Bible and the *Lands of the Bible*. Never did he suggest that we use the college library."

On the other hand, the method of teaching used by the new members of the faculty of The College of the Bible was entirely different. The lecture method of teaching and cooperative inquiry between student and teacher, with much reading by the student on all sides of a question, was the accepted procedure. There was give and take in the class and much freedom of discussion and stimulation of the students to come to their own conclusions, after thoroughly investigating all sides of every proposition that came up. In those days the question of historical study of the Bible—"Higher Criticism" it was called— and the question of the evolutionary principle were warm themes. Every liberty was given for the discussion of those propositions in and outside of the classes. The professors had accepted many of the conclusions of historical criticism advanced by modern scholars and they also accepted a Christian view of evolutionary principles.

These two points of view afforded some of the more conservative students and Dean Calhoun an occasion for criticism. Another factor also entered into the situation. The new methods of teaching and the new professors were very popular with the majority of the students. Thus, there was a rather clear line of demarcation between groups of students. Some of the more conservative students began to take notes on the remarks of the professors. They had the confidence of Dean Calhoun, who undoubtedly encouraged them.

At this juncture, the *Christian Standard* took a hand. The controversy had waxed rather hot on the campus and the Standard Publishing Company sent the editor of the *Christian Standard*, George P. Rutledge, down to Lexington to take an active part in the controversy! Then the wrangle began in earnest with all the accusations which could be mustered for a delicate situation.

On March 31, 1917, the *Christian Standard* published charges and counter-charges against The College of the Bible. The same issue included a letter (p. 764) by Ben F. Battenfield, one of the older students, about "heresy" at The College of the Bible. This letter was endorsed by nine students in a covering letter. Later, five of these removed their names, saying the endorsing letter was hastily signed and by some without the letter being read. The letter of Mr. Battenfield had quotations from faculty members and students which were declared to be heretical. To this, the faculty, composed of R. H. Crossfield, W. C. Bower, E. E. Snoddy, A. W. Fortune and G. W. Hemry, replied, as follows (*Christian Standard*, March 31, 1917, p. 764):

We desire to state that the letter published by Mr. Ben F. Battenfield under date of March 12, 1917, . . . does not represent our positions.

In many cases statements have been lifted out of their context in such a way as to give a content they do not contain and entirely pervert their meaning, and, ... contradict the fundamental positions held by us. . . . .

In the presence of such an attack upon the integrity of the administrative policy of the College of the Bible and the Christian faith and devotion of the greater part of the Faculty, we take occasion to affirm our fidelity to the fundamental truth of Christianity as revealed in the Bible, and to the historical principles of the Disciples of Christ.

In this same issue of the *Christian Standard* (March 31, 1917, p. 769), there was an editorial asking that a committee outside Transylvania and The College of the Bible and without "representatives of any of our colleges" investigate the charges. Following this, the *Standard* published pages of letters of protest with sensational and accusing headlines, playing up the term "destructive criticism." To Disciples, unfamiliar with scholarly biblical study and lacking a modern conception of scholarship, these startling headlines in the *Standard* became a warning signal of danger. In one issue (April 14, 1917, pp. 830 ff.) the magazine published more than seven pages of letters in favor of a "heresy" investigation and less than one page in opposition. The propaganda was issued for weeks.

In the whole discussion, there seem to have been three points at issue: (1) Academic freedom in teaching. (2) Should any teaching be allowed on historical criticism and should any theory of evolution whatever be given a place in the teaching? (3) Can you trust competent trustees to supervise an educational institution?

The investigation of the "heresy" charges was conducted by the Board of Trustees of The College of the Bible. Although Transylvania and The College of the Bible had the same president in those years, the two institutions had separate governing boards of trustees. The faculty members of The College of the Bible stood their ground without relinquishing their Christian convictions or their intellectual integrity. After meetings of the Board of Trustees and a full opportunity to discover what the criticisms were about, including the attitude of the professors, the criticisms of Dean Calhoun and a certain group of students, the findings were released. Under the chairmanship of Mark Collis, then minister of the Broadway Christian Church in Lexington, the Board of Trustees of The College of the Bible made a statement dated May 9, 1917, clearing the professors of blame (*Christian Standard,* June 2, 1917, p. 1027).

10   (830)   CHRISTIAN STANDARD   April 14, 1917.

IN FAVOR OF THE PROPOSED IMPARTIAL INVESTIGATION
OF THE COLLEGE OF THE BIBLE

Courtesy, Butler School of Religion Library

This is the first of more than seven pages of letters in the "Christian Standard" of April 14, 1917 (p. 830) endorsing a proposed theological investigation at The College of the Bible.

An incident which entered into the investigation is most interesting. Dean Calhoun, holding to the older teaching methods and views, insisted on using Mr. McGarvey's notes in his classes. This seemed to many of the students to be simply a surrender to the conviction and method of another man and they protested. President Crossfield received a petition from these students, requesting that Dean Calhoun change his method of teaching. This, together with the fact that the Board of Trustees finally cleared the professors of all charges, led to Dean Calhoun's resignation on the floor of the investigation (*Christian Standard,* May 12, 1917, p. 948).

After Dean Calhoun had resigned, he began presenting his charges to the brotherhood through the *Christian Standard.* A series of articles began with the issue of May 19, 1917, and concluded in the number of September 15, 1917. The attack of the *Standard,* with conspicuous headlines, was kept up through 1917 and into 1918. In this way there was the sorry spectacle of a religious periodical conducting a greatly publicized attack with much propaganda.

Further developments concerning Dr. Calhoun are quite interesting. He became the T. W. Phillips Professor of Old Testament Language and Literature at Bethany College, Bethany, West Virginia, from 1917 to 1925 (*Gospel Advocate,* October 31, 1935, p. 1046). Then, he was a member of the Executive Committee of McGarvey Bible College which started in Louisville, Kentucky, October 1, 1923 (*Christian Standard,* September 1, 1923). The present Cincinnati (Ohio) Bible Seminary, which began its first session September 23, 1924, was a consolidation of McGarvey Bible College and the Cincinnati Bible Institute that began in 1923 (*Christian Standard,* March 22 and September 6, 1924).

From Bethany, Dr. Calhoun returned to Tennessee. For one year, 1925-1926, he was associate president of the Freed-Hardeman College, a Church of Christ institution at Henderson. He then went to Nashville, Tennessee, where he preached in Churches of Christ and over the radio for their Central Church. He also taught for two years at David Lipscomb College, another Church of Christ institution in Nashville. These facts were related in an obituary published in the *Gospel Advocate*

(October 31, 1935, p. 1046), a weekly of the Churches of Christ, issued in the Tennessee capital city by the McQuiddy Printing Company.

This, no doubt, was really where Dr. Calhoun belonged. The rest of his life, until his death in 1935, was spent in strongly advocating the principles, theology, and program of the group now known nationally as Churches of Christ, which is opposed to the use of instrumental music in worship and to missionary societies. He held a number of evangelistic meetings in West Kentucky among rural churches and succeeded in turning most of them to the non-cooperative Churches of Christ.

A significant incident occurred during The College of the Bible investigation which illustrates how extreme and foolish charges may become in a theological controversy. Prof. Alfred Fairhurst, trustee of The College of the Bible and a professor-emeritus in science at Transylvania College, had criticized the professors for their stand on evolution. He was especially antagonistic to Prof. E. E. Snoddy, who taught in both schools. Prof. Snoddy had been criticized by students for some position that he had taken on an issue in some of his classes and the criticism had been passed on to Prof. Fairhurst.

In the investigation, Prof. Snoddy asked the privilege of making a statement as to his position on evolution. Prof. Fairhurst, who sat with the group of trustees, consented and the permission was granted. Following this, Prof. Snoddy read a brief statement. Prof. Fairhurst immediately took exception to it. Prof. Snoddy then revealed that what he had read, as explaining his own position, had been taken verbatim from a statement of Prof. Fairhurst, as expressing his conviction in a book he himself had written entitled, *Organic Evolution Considered!*

The reaction of a conservative, but peace-loving brother, R. D. Harding, pastor of the church at Dayton, Kentucky, is worth quoting from the *Christian Standard* (April 7, 1917, p. 796), as follows:

In my judgment, the trustees of the College of the Bible are well qualified to settle this matter right. I am firm in the conviction that the *Standard* has done this school more harm than it will ever be able to do this or any other cause good. When a decision has been reached by competent people, and after mature consideration, it is time enough to publish facts, and not try to ruin a man through the columns of your paper, whether innocent or guilty.

In its attack on Transylvania and The College of the Bible, the *Christian Standard* struck at two of our strongest educational institutions, with the oldest history, and the most popular in the training of the Christian ministry. If it had succeeded in its attempt, intellectual and religious liberty would probably have gone by the board in most of our schools. The outcome really turned the tide in our brotherhood for the educational institutions. Today, what the faculty of The College of the Bible stood for so valiantly has become mainly the conviction and the working principle of the faculties in all of our schools holding membership in the Board of Higher Education of Disciples of Christ. Of course, in the schools now endorsed by the *Christian Standard*, very little, if any, of the modern concepts of scholarship and teaching are accepted and the methods and conclusions of extremely conservative schools of forty or fifty years ago are still held by them.

The *Christian Standard* conducted all of this in a sensational way, attacking both Transylvania and The College of the Bible, and charging Professors Fortune, Snoddy, Bower, *et al.*, with "destructive criticism" and disloyalty. The only claim against them, actually, seemed to be that they were persons of modern scholarship. The *Standard* called this "infidelity," against all for which Disciples stand. The periodical forgot, overlooked, or ignored the fact that Alexander Campbell, himself, in his day was attacked in the same way because of his liberal attitude toward the Old Testament and his distinction between the Law and the Christian message. He was one of the first theologians in America to take the position now accepted by historical criticism, that the Bible, like any other book, should be subjected to sincere study of the origin, historical background, and scholarly basis of its claims (*The Christian-Evangelist,* September 8, 1938, p. 957). A quotation from Campbell's *Christian Baptist* (Vol. 6, No. 1, August 4, 1828, p. 461) is enlightening:

Truth has nothing to fear from investigation. It dreads not the light of science, nor shuns the scrutiny of the most prying inquiry. . . . it challenges the fullest, the ablest, and the boldest examination.

And again, from *Debate on the Evidences of Christianity* (p. 266 f.), a debate between Campbell and Robert Owen, note what Mr. Campbell said:

> We will submit the question of authorship to be tried by all the canons, or regulations, or rules, which the literary world, which the most rigid critics, have instituted or appealed to, in settling any literary question of this sort.

During the time of the controversy at The College of the Bible, the *Christian Standard* was yet within the structure of the brotherhood life of Disciples of Christ and its cooperative enterprises. It was an influential publication and this gave it a formidable position in a controversy like this. Of course, such an attack now would mean little since the *Christian Standard* apparently considers itself entirely apart from the organized and cooperative structure of our brotherhood life. Its present influence in the brotherhood of Disciples of Christ is small except with the group that has followed its leadership. The periodical claims that the whole organized and cooperative life of the brotherhood is a departure from the original principles of the Restoration Movement. It so judges everything in any way connected with the International Convention of Disciples of Christ.

The *Christian Standard* carried on its publicity into the Restoration Congress which it called to meet just prior to the 1919 International Convention in Cincinnati. After that, though not entirely abandoning its fight on Transylvania and The College of the Bible, the magazine changed its emphasis once more. It began a prolonged attack against the United Christian Missionary Society. This will be discussed in the next chapter.

The C. W. B. M. and Mexico

In 1919, the *Christian Standard* strongly criticized the Christian Woman's Board of Missions for leaving the Monterrey field in Mexico ("Federation in Mexico As an Example," April 19, 1919, p. 701). In this situation the paper raised a question as to comity understandings with other religious bodies.

Previous to this date, a civil war had been raging in Mexico and all of the Protestant missionaries had to leave the field. It then became clearer than ever to the mission boards working in Mexico that they should have a conference to analyze the situation as to the areas occupied, together with a study of the territory that needed occupation, but which had not been entered by any board.

Consequently, the first conference was held in the mission room of the Foreign Christian Missionary Society in Cincinnati, beginning June 30, 1914. Eleven boards were represented by sixty-five missionaries and delegates, including ten from the Christian Woman's Board of Missions. A similar meeting, convened in Panama in February, 1916, was called the Congress of Christian Work. It resulted in the formation of the Committee on Cooperation in Latin America and our own former missionary, Samuel Guy Inman, was named the executive secretary. This committee then called a conference in Mexico City, February 17-24, 1919, to which eleven boards sent sixty-seven persons. Among the representatives of the Disciples were Mrs. Anna R. Atwater, president of the Christian Woman's Board of Missions; A. McLean, president of the Foreign Christian Missionary Society, and Mr. Inman (*History of the Christian Woman's Board of Missions* by Ida Withers Harrison, pp. 101 f.; also *World Call*, May, 1919, p. 49).

It was discovered, following studies made in these conferences, that the missions boards in Mexico were overlapping in their work. In other sections, no one had entered the area. The field was large and most inadequately covered. The spirit of cooperation was genuine and a new day seemed to be ahead for the Mexican work.

The Christian Woman's Board of Missions had been at work in Monterrey of Northern Mexico. There the Methodists were strong while the Disciples were weak. It seemed to be poor missionary strategy to compete with one another in this field, while large sections of Mexico were entirely unoccupied and needed evangelistic effort. The primitive state of Yucatan had no missionaries in it. The Presbyterians U. S. A. (Northern), working in Central Mexico in a rather new enterprise, volunteered to leave that field and to go to Yucatan for pioneer work. The Presbyterians offered the field which they occupied to the Disciples.

After careful consideration, the Christian Woman's Board of Missions decided to withdraw its staff from Northern Mexico, strengthen the number of missionaries in all of Mexico, and undertake the work in this field which the Presbyterians were willing to turn over. The new work for the women was in the states of Aguascalientes, San Luis Potosi, Zacatecas, and two small districts of Jalisco. This was an abundant Central Mexico field where Disciples would have a free hand and could extend themselves in a stronger evangelistic and educational work.

It was understood that in Monterrey where the Christian Woman's Board of Missions had been working for twenty years, the native churches were to be left free to carry on. Provision was made so that they could still occupy the church properties, although the Christian Institute was sold to the Methodists. The same understanding obtained in the field released to the Disciples by the Presbyterians—their congregations which desired to do so could remain under native leadership as autonomous Presbyterian churches. Other properties there were sold to the Disciples. It was felt by the Christian Woman's Board of Missions that after twenty years of work, largely supported from the United States, these churches in Monterrey which it was leaving could undertake self-support.

A Mexican minister named E. T. Westrup took strong exception to the removal of the Disciple missionaries from Monterrey and the leaving of him and the native churches to their own self-support. He found ready publicity for his complaint in the columns of the *Christian Standard* (May 31, 1919, p. 851). As was stated in the opening paragraph of this section, the *Standard* attacked the Christian Woman's Board of Missions for leaving the Monterrey field where the Methodists were strong and entering the larger field from which the Presbyterians were withdrawing. In its editorial attack, the *Standard* took exception to the statement of the Christian Woman's Board of Missions that it was avoiding "overlapping" and joining hands with others in the "practice of Christian unity." The magazine maintained that this sort of an arrangement was "federation," to which it had been opposed always.

Later an editorial appeal for financial support of the Monterrey Mission, under the leadership of E. T. Westrup, was published by the *Standard* ("To the Rescue of the Mexican Mission," June 14, 1919, pp. 900 f.), as follows:

However, everything must have its beginning, and now that the task to save and make great and powerful the Monterey Mission has been undertaken, we anticipate an immediate response that will be both general and generous. The appeal of our Mexican brethren should be met with a loyal response from individuals, churches and church organizations.

Since that time the Monterrey Mission has been one of the many undertakings endorsed by the *Standard*.

Before concluding this chapter, I wish to mention two other matters briefly for the record.

First, the Association of Colleges of Disciples of Christ was organized in 1911. This became the Board of Education in 1914 and later the Board of Higher Education of Disciples of Christ. In time, it was repudiated by the *Standard*.

Then, a significant step in unity was inaugurated for the Disciples of Christ in 1913 with the launching of the Men and Millions Movement. This was led by Abram E. Cory and Raphael H. Miller. Cooperating with the movement were all of the missionary organizations of the brotherhood and the educational institutions affiliated with the Association of Colleges. More than $6,000,000 was raised. The *Christian Standard* was not helpful in the campaign, stating in its issue of October 18, 1919 (p. 57) that it "gave it only a modified support."

Chapter 3

THE UNITED CHRISTIAN
MISSIONARY SOCIETY

No International Convention was held in 1918 because of the influenza epidemic. St. Louis, Missouri, was to have been the site, but plans for the assembly were canceled. The convention for 1919 was held on October 13-19 in Cincinnati. This was when the proposed constitution for the United Christian Missionary Society was acted upon. As far back as the Norfolk Convention in 1907 a committee had been appointed to work on some sort of coordination among the group of missionary and benevolent organizations which Disciples of Christ were promoting. These were the American Christian Missionary Society, the Christian Woman's Board of Missions, the Foreign Christian Missionary Society, the Board of Church Extension, the National Benevolent Association, and the Board of Ministerial Relief.

The offerings for these various organizations had mainly been raised on certain special days during each year. The many days and appeals caused great confusion. There was overlapping of interests and, many times, competition. Numerous ministers and churches had criticized this tendency and asked for some coordination which would prevent the seeming rivalry and the expense of so many groups. After much work and many proposals, it was decided that the best results could be obtained if these several boards were united in one society with a careful program worked out for the churches that would end competition, bring solidarity and loyalty to all the work, and increase the general missionary enthusiasm.

At first there was hesitancy on the part of the officers of the societies to have the old, established order changed. However, after many conferences, all of these organizations had reached an agreement for a united society and there was great enthusiasm for it. It was thought that if a real, democratic plan could be developed for such an organization, it would bring a great degree of harmony and efficiency in our missionary and benevolent undertakings. Some such plan had been discussed in nearly every convention for years and the tide of approval and expectation was running high. The proposal for a united organization really came out of the pressure of the churches and the pastors for some more seemly and cooperative plan.

However, the *Christian Standard* with its usual attitude of criticism, began to question seriously any such movement as a United Society. Early in 1919 the periodical launched a campaign of opposition to the organization of the proposed new society. It began first by attacking the various agencies for their "officious" attitude in promoting a united board, claiming that the Restoration Movement was not a denomination and, therefore, should not have denominational tendencies.

The brotherhood agencies had previously joined in publishing an annual *Year Book*, now known as the *Year Book of Disciples of Christ*. The 1885 and 1888 volumes were issued by the Standard Publishing Company. The volumes from 1897 through 1920 were published annually by the American Christian Missionary Society. The United Christian Missionary Society was the publisher, 1921-1935. The Year Book Publication Committee issued the volume, 1936-1946 ("The Story of the Year Book," *Discipliana*, April, 1944). Since 1947 the volume has been published every year by the International Convention of Disciples of Christ.

The *Christian Standard* of June 21, 1919 (p. 925) called the *Year Book* an "effrontery" and claimed that it meant that the agencies "have announced to the brotherhood, and to the world, that they constitute the movement to restore New Testament Christianity." This annual *Year Book* has been almost universally used as a reference volume by the ministers and churches.

Under the heading, "Shall There Be a 'United Missionary Society'?" the *Standard* published six editorials, beginning June 7, 1919 (p. 876) and concluding July 12, 1919 (p. 996). In these editorials the magazine set forth what it claimed to be the growing autocracy of certain groups of Disciples. It cited certain "tendencies," such as the Men and Millions Movement,

Year-Book

OF THE

DISCIPLES OF CHRIST

THEIR

Membership, Missions, Ministry, Educational
and Other Institutions.

CINCINNATI
STANDARD PUBLISHING COMPANY
1888

Transylvania and The College of the Bible, the American Christian Missionary Society and the *Year Book*, the Guy W. Sarvis controversy and changes in China, and the Monterrey, Mexico "abandonment." It stated that these were dangerous trends, therefore, beware! (June 28, 1919, p. 948).

Later the paper instituted a still stronger build-up. In the issue of July 5, 1919 (p. 972), the editor stated:

The conflict between the Restoration advocates and Restoration wreckers will be hot, and it will continue for perhaps years. The propagandists are struggling for supremacy in the local church, in the college classroom and especially in our co-operative enterprises.

. . . the *solid* support which the propagandists are giving the merger challenges serious thought upon the part of every one who really values the mission of the Restoration movement.

These "propagandists" apparently were *The Christian-Evangelist, The Christian Century,* and the Campbell Institute, along with the various agency officials and others.

Writers came to the defense of the proposed United Christian Missionary Society on the grounds that it would (1) be more economical, (2) eliminate rivalry, (3) eliminate too many appeals, and (4) further our unity. The *Standard,* however, paid no attention to the logic of these statements. It kept on opposing the proposed united organization.

On July 12, 1919, the *Standard* attempted to make much capital of the fact that *The Christian Century,* liberal weekly published in Chicago, favored the proposed society. The *Standard* stated that all of the "rationalists" and "propagandists" favored the proposed organization, adding that an expensive program was "already hinted at which contemplates a gigantic office building, possibly in New York." Apparently, the only basis the *Standard* had for the latter statement was the fact that several cities had been mentioned as a possible headquarters for the proposed missionary organization. Among these cities were Chicago, Cincinnati, St. Louis, Indianapolis, and New York, although the last-named was given little consideration.

In the issue of July 26, 1919 (p. 1045), the *Standard* devoted the front, cover page to an announcement that stated, "To the Rescue of the Restoration Movement." The text said that a meeting of protest would convene at the Odd Fellows' Assembly Hall in Cincinnati for two days prior to the opening of the International Convention. The announcement carried the names of a considerable number of people. In addition, an adroit sub-heading appeared (p. 1051) with the announcement, as it was continued to the inside pages, as follows: "In no uncertain terms ministers and leaders the brotherhood over declare their allegiance to the New Testament plea and their determination to protect it from methods of compromise and from materialistic philosophy." An editorial in the same issue (p. 1052) was entitled, "To the Rescue of the Restoration Movement." Also, the same page carried another appeal with the heading, "To the Rescue of the Mexican Mission."

The build-up for the protest meeting prior to the convention increased. Edgar DeWitt Jones, then a pastor at Bloomington, Illinois, was president of the International Convention that year. He had issued a proper call (*Christian Standard*, August 2, 1919, p. 1088) for attendance and support of the convention. In the same issue, the *Standard*, referring to his call, stated: "It is a call to battle between the loyal advocates of the Restoration cause and the propagandists who are endeavoring to swing the Restoration movement away from its mission" (p. 1077).

Repeatedly, in each issue up to the meeting of the Cincinnati convention, the *Standard* had headings, "To the Rescue of the Restoration Movement" and underneath printed the names of those protesting.

Before the Cincinnati convention, in harmony with the plans for unification, the various brotherhood organizations had united in publishing a monthly magazine that was named *World Call*. Formerly each board had issued its own small periodical. This caused confusion and much expense. There was a long editorial in the *Standard* on *World Call* and the proposed United Christian Missionary Society (August 16, 1919, p. 1127). This editorial stated:

The question may be justly raised: Can, and will, the United Missionary Society, whose official organ [*World Call*] has already grown so bold as to lend itself to a propagandism which now disturbs the harmony of the brotherhood, be depended upon to stand squarely for Restoration principles?

World Call continues to represent our whole cooperative life, being published by five of the national agencies of the Disciples.

CHRISTIAN STANDARD

SUBSCRIPTION, $2.00 PER ANNUM
PUBLISHED WEEKLY

CINCINNATI, JULY 26, 1919

VOL. LIV.—NO. 43
OFFICES: EIGHTH, NINTH AND CUTTER STS.

TO THE RESCUE OF THE RESTORATION MOVEMENT

THAT there is an impending crisis in the affairs of the Restoration movement, coincident with the spread of modern rationalism, is apparent even to the most thoughtless.

1. Under this influence the Scriptural unity of doctrine is disturbed, among other evils, by the attempted introduction of "open membership," threatening the peace of all our congregations, and the very integrity of the Restoration plea.

2. As a result, our evangelistic work has been well-nigh brought to a standstill.

3. Our wonderful Bible-school progress has been halted.

4. In most of our colleges, classes for the ministry have dwindled alarmingly.

5. In several instances, public journals, professedly loyal, champion the cause as a separate denomination or sect, rather than as the divine cure for sectarianism.

6. Instead of forming a training force sufficient for a great Bible-ministry, our colleges are too largely spending their energies in a feeble rivalry of State institutions, under secular, and not under Scriptural, standards of efficiency.

7. With a foreign element of forty million souls within our borders, we are doing next to nothing to win them to Christ, and, through them, to open the way into their home lands.

All this, and much more, at a time when our country and the whole world are crying aloud for the message committed to us in the providence of God.

This message receives scant attention at our national gatherings, and there is an imperative need for an open congress of earnest spirits who are resolved that it shall be heard, and heard in no doubtful tones, and who will take steps to remedy the evils that now hinder it.

With this purpose in view, we invite all who are resolved to maintain the Restoration plea intact, to meet with us at Cincinnati, O., Oct. 13, 1919, at the Odd Fellows' Assembly Hall, Seventh and Elm Streets, at the hour of 9 A. M., to remain in session for two days.

This call is issued to our ministry generally, and to the manhood and womanhood of the Restoration movement.

The time and place have been so arranged as to enable those who take part in it to attend, without undue expense, the annual Conventions which follow.

Ample hotel accommodations have been engaged in our leading hotels. Terms, etc., will be forwarded on application to Willard Mohorter, Box 5, Sta. N, Cincinnati, O.

Confident, both from the enthusiastic response to a similar call last year, and from the still growing insistence throughout our loyal hosts that positive steps be taken to make the world ring again with the New Testament message, that the meeting here proposed will commend itself to a loyal brotherhood, we submit it to their judgment and appeal for their support.

Faithfully yours,
E. C. Sanderson, Russell Errett, Z. T. Sweeney, O. J. Sharp, P. H. Welshimer, Fred D. Kershner, T. W. Phillips, Jr., W. N. Briney, Marshall

Continued on page 6.

Objectives of the Proposed Congress

Our deliberations will be addressed:

1. To a renewal, on the widest possible scale, of the New Testament evangelism, which is the crowning glory of the Restoration.

2. To the repudiation of the materialistic philosophy which discredits the Scriptures.

3. To the repudiation of methods of compromise which would substitute a variety of human creeds for the simple creed of the New Testament.

4. To take such action as may be found necessary to reassert the New Testament plea with clearness and increased vigor, and to insure its perpetuation unimpaired.

Courtesy, Disciples of Christ Historical Society

The "Restoration Congress" that met in Cincinnati in 1919 was first announced by the "Christian Standard" on the cover (p. 1045) of its issue for July 26, 1919.

The publication has now grown to be one of the most highly-praised and widely-circulated religious periodicals in America.

Another issue of the *Standard* carried an editorial (August 30, 1919, p. 1182) quoting from J. H. Garrison, the editor-emeritus of *The Christian-Evangelist.* Mr. Garrison criticized the *Standard* for calling the Restoration Congress before the International Convention. He wrote: *"Do not do it.* Instead, attend the International Convention, and request time to state your opposition." The *Christian Standard* reply stated that (1) Mr. Garrison "is a member of the Campbell Institute," (2) "he has endorsed *The Christian Century*," (3) "he gave the Transylvania administration a clean bill of health," and (4) he has given comfort "to the propagandists."

In the *Christian Standard* for September 13, 1919, just preceding the Cincinnati convention, there was an appeal for attendance at the Restoration Congress and many personal statements of utmost loyalty to the Restoration principle. There was, again, an attack upon the Christian Woman's Board of Missions for leaving the Monterrey, Mexico mission field ("C.W.B.M. Officials Should Answer a Question," p. 1231). This editorial replied to a statement by Mrs. Anna R. Atwater, president of the Christian Woman's Board of Missions, as follows:

We are not planning to sell any of our churches or chapels to any other people. We have told the congregations where we own chapels that they may continue in possession of those chapels. . . . those we do have are left in the possession of the little congregations that are worshiping in them.

Mrs. Atwater then added that it was expected the school building would be sold "either to some body of people who wish to conduct a school in it, or for some business enterprise." She continued, "We think our larger opportunity for Christ is in central Mexico."

Then the *Christian Standard*, with more publicity for its Restoration Congress, announced the subjects for the meeting. This was in the issue of October 4, 1919 (p. 5), as follows: "Relation of Our Co-operative Agencies to the Inter-Church World Movement," "United Christian Missionary Society," "Attitude of Restoration Movement Toward Present-Day Union Movements," "Materialistic Philosophy," "New Testament Evangelism," etc.

In this issue the magazine published various resolutions from local congregations deploring the tendency toward "denominationalism."

In the issue of October 11, 1919 (p. 34), just before the Cincinnati convention met, besides the continued advertising of its Restoration Congress, the periodical attacked the American Christian Missionary Society for its cooperation with the Home Missions Council, an inter-church agency, and various churches in a program in Montana.

The 1919 Convention in Cincinnati

No newspaper, preceding a big national political convention, would likely have resorted to more appeal for loyalty than did the *Christian Standard* in the weeks and months of increasing build-up preceding the Cincinnati convention when the United Christian Missionary Society was to be formed. In most instances, there were emphatic headlines of protest concerning the proposed organization.

In ignoring J. H. Garrison's appeal in *The Christian-Evangelist* to go on the floor of the Cincinnati convention and state its case of opposition to the trend of things, the *Standard* resorted to the undemocratic principle of building up the biggest tide of opposition possible instead of appealing to reasoning and careful judgment. All the time, actually, the periodical was opposing the study as well as the logic of the brethren who were attempting to unify the missionary and benevolent program of the Disciples of Christ.

With October came the 1919 International Convention in the Queen City of Cincinnati, Ohio, preceded by the two days of the Restoration Congress. The Congress, so consistently promoted by the *Christian Standard*, brought together an attendance of possibly 1,500 persons, some curious perhaps, but many disturbed and aroused by the accusations of the periodical.

Several years had been spent in carefully drafting the constitution of the proposed United Christian Missionary Society so that it would be readily responsive to the will of Disciples of Christ supporting it. The constitution provided that the annual meeting be composed of all persons in attendance who had given either moral or financial support to the program of the organization. The Board of Managers was composed of sixty men and sixty women, so that all of the states and Canada could be adequately represented. The Board of Managers was given power to choose from its own number an Executive Committee of ten men and ten women.

As to the opposition and the part it took in the Cincinnati International Convention, I quote from *The Life and Labors of Archibald McLean* (pp. 273 ff.) by William Robinson Warren, published in 1923, as follows:

For months prior to the Cincinnati convention of 1919 the opposition waged an aggressive campaign throughout the country, to assemble for the two days previous to the convention the largest possible number of men and women who felt, or could be made to suspect, that the faith of our fathers was in danger. . . . This campaign was the culminating effort of years of . . . sowing and thoroughly cultivating the seeds of suspicion.

When one remembers that the Disciples had nine national boards and twenty-seven colleges; that even the wisest and most devoted men and women are liable to err; that people are easily mistaken in regard to facts and especially beliefs and motives; that misunderstandings, rumors and grievances grow and multiply with time and repetition, it is easy to see how natural it was that hundreds of people should respond to the call and come to Cincinnati for a pre-convention congress.

After the active participants in the congress had spent two days in public and private discussion of their suspicions and injuries, . . . they moved into the convention at Music Hall. . . .

They chose for their attack the session of the American Christian Missionary Society, over which President F. W. Burnham was presiding. The board's recommendation that the society join with the Foreign Christian Missionary Society, Christian Woman's Board of Missions, National Benevolent Association and Board of Ministerial Relief to form the United Christian Missionary Society was the signal for the offensive. The air was electric with the impending storm. Leaders of the opposition broke forth with charges of autocratic methods, unscriptural teachings and luxurious extravagance against all the officers of all the boards. The purport of it all was that, both those who had grown gray in the service and those who had been called but recently from responsible pastorates, were . . . to deliver the churches of Christ over to German rationalism, . . .

The . . . indictments were comprehensive enough to include every officer of every board. The critics were shown every courtesy and allowed to express themselves without reserve. This in itself was a clear refutation of one of their gravest charges. When an accusation against the chairman became definite enough for a categorical denial he promptly made it and challenged the accuser to produce his evidence. This immediately faded into a report of a repetition of a five-year-old conversation of entirely different import. Other charges were manifestly twenty years old and concerned former administrations. Some of the most violent were aimed at F. M. Rains, a hero of Christ's service who was known to be on his deathbed at that moment, twenty years before his time because of his abundant labors. With quiet self-control the officers allowed the storm to break its fury upon its own violence. Even the opposition paid high tribute to the forbearance and fairness with which they were heard. Most of those present recognized the plain marks of strength and courage, integrity and unselfishness in all of the official group. The vote was overwhelmingly in favor of organizing the United Christian Missionary Society as proposed, and later for all other recommendations of the boards.

Thus, another attempt to turn the tide against progress among the Disciples of Christ came to naught in the 1919 Cincinnati Convention. However, much harm was done among the churches and their thousands of members, throughout the brotherhood in the United States and Canada, in creating doubt about the cooperative organizations, leaders, and programs of the Disciples. Yet the opposition did not accept defeat, in a convention attended by thousands of their brethren and which gave fair-minded consideration to the questions raised.

The leading editorial in the *Christian Standard*, following the Cincinnati Convention, carried the title, "A Sign-Board Lifted High" (November 1, 1919, p. 117). Among other statements made therein were the following:

As a sample of the objections, that are coming to us by mail, thus early, we shall here quote a sentence from a letter dated October 21, and received a few minutes ago. It reads:

"Of the members of the Board of our United Society, four are from Lexington—all Transylvania partisans."

Also, the fact that the management of the United Society is composed, throughout, of half men and half women (60 men and 60 women) is a cause of widespread dissatisfaction. Those who object to this feature are not opposed to women holding office in missionary societies. However, they know the tendency (chivalry) among men to defer to women, and they express the fear that the C. W. B. M. will practically dictate the policy of the society. This, in the light of the Mexican federation and State Bible-chair experiences, naturally causes brethren, who are not in accord with compromises and destructive teaching, to look with disfavor upon the United Society.

To sum the whole matter up, the signboard points to a division of missionary funds upon a gigantic scale. It is our conviction that the

Cincinnati gathering will go down in history as the black convention of the so-called regular societies.

Robert E. Elmore, who had succeeded A. W. Fortune as minister of the Walnut Hills Christian Church, Cincinnati, during 1912, and for a time had been a popular pastor, had lost some of his popularity during this period. In 1917, George P. Rutledge, upon becoming editor of the *Christian Standard*, had joined the Walnut Hills Church as one of its members. His membership caused some concern among the leaders of this progressive congregation for the overwhelming majority of the Walnut Hills Church members were opposed to the program of the *Standard* which they had observed for many years in their city. Mr. Elmore and Mr. Rutledge were close friends, born and reared in the same county in Virginia.

Mr. Elmore had served as a member of the Executive Committee of the Foreign Christian Missionary Society and was its recorder, October 12, 1917 to July 9, 1920. In his capacity as one of the officers, he had agreed to practically all of the policies of the Foreign Christian Missionary Society and had passed on the appointment of missionaries whom he afterwards attacked.

After some time had elapsed, Mr. Elmore adopted the *Christian Standard* attitude and attacked the newly-formed United Christian Missionary Society from his Walnut Hills pulpit. The result was that he left that pastorate. He was later employed by the Standard Publishing Company and put on its editorial staff. He proceeded to attack the United Christian Missionary Society and its officers. This opposition has continued and increased across the years since.

The China Mission and Church Membership

While Mr. Elmore was still recording secretary of the Foreign Christian Missionary Society, before the United Christian Missionary Society had been formed, a movement was under way in China for the United Church. A need for unity in a vast field like China was evident to the missionaries and even more so to the nationals. The whole matter was in the stage of a preliminary study when the different churches represented in China were considering what could be done to draw the Christian forces together in a united effort. The Disciples of Christ Mission, in its annual meeting in China, had considered the matter and was favorably inclined, but, of course, could take no final action without approval of the Society at home.

The real launching of the united Church of Christ in China did not take place until October, 1927, but previous to that for a number of years, there was a great deal of discussion about its possibility. Our own missionaries, under the Foreign Christian Missionary Society, a year or so before the United Christian Missionary Society was formed, had seemed to feel that the real question in the way of unity on the part of Disciples of Christ would be that of the recognition of the church membership of Chinese from other communions coming into the centers where we were working.

The situation on the mission field, as a rule, is quite different from that here at home, as the different communions usually have their own distinct territory which they have chosen. Because the field is so large and much of it entirely unoccupied, there is hardly any overlapping. As a consequence, there are very few churches of different communions in the same community, except in the larger cities like Nanking, Shanghai, and Peking.

In the preliminary discussions in our convention in China, it appeared that the missionaries would be in favor of the union if it could be worked out and if approval came from home. Frank Garrett, secretary of the China Mission, wrote home to the Foreign Christian Missionary Society. He said that the China Mission favored union, that the union was still a long way off and he also stated that there needed to be a good deal of study of what was involved.

Mr. Elmore, then a member of the Executive Committee of the Foreign Christian Missionary Society, raised objection to the attitude of our China missionaries. After the United Christian Missionary Society was formed in 1919 in Cincinnati and he was no longer with the Foreign Christian Missionary Society or the Walnut Hills Church, but was in cooperation with the *Christian Standard,* he attacked missionaries of the Society in China and accused them of disloyalty to the historic position of the Disciples and of belief in open membership. He wrote articles for the *Standard*, attacking the China Mission and the new United Society.

In the meantime, the new organization of the United Christian Missionary Society had moved its headquarters to St. Louis, Missouri, that being the city which was chosen out of the several that had been under consideration.

There was an interesting point in the procedure of the *Christian Standard* while promoting the Restoration Congress that preceded the St. Louis International Convention of 1920 and its further attack upon the United Christian Missionary Society. Although F. W. Burnham had been chosen as president of the new Society, the *Standard* sent out thousands of blank ballots for preferential voting on a proposed new president for the United Society. Much space was given to this and the paper published the following list and nominating endorsements concerning those suggested for president (*Christian Standard*, July 31, 1920, pp. 1083 f.):

P. H. Welshimer, Canton, Ohio, named by Mark Collis, Lexington, Ky.; F. W. Burnham, who was president, suggested by Ellis B. Barnes, Cleveland, Ohio; S. S. Lappin, former editor of the *Standard*, Bedford, Ind., candidate of Peyton H. Canary, Jr., Columbus, Ohio; W. H. Book, Columbus, Ind., selected by A. M. Hootman, Greencastle, Ind.; F. D. Kershner, who had been on the editorial staff of the *Standard* and was then a professor of the Drake University Bible College, Des Moines, Iowa, endorsed by Walter S. Hopkins, Niagara Falls, N. Y.; and A. McLean, former president of the Foreign Christian Missionary Society, nominated by John W. Ligon, Morganfield, Ky.

On August 7, 1920, the *Standard* published a first-page article by R. E. Elmore entitled, "Does China Mission Endorse Open Membership?" (pp. 1107 ff.). On August 14 of that year, Russell Errett wrote in the *Standard* (pp. 1131 ff.) under the heading, "Missionary Agencies Challenged." He attacked the United Christian Missionary Society for enrolling as a unit in the Inter-Church World Movement under the name of "Disciples of Christ." He affirmed the proposition that the constituent boards of the Society were "guilty of a gross imposition when they assumed ecclesiastical character to commit the independent

August 28, 1920. **CHRISTIAN STANDARD** (1187) 11

ARMENIAN AND SYRIAN RELIEF

IN reading the proof of receipts for Armenian Relief for the issue of the STANDARD dated July 24, a mistake occurred. The Fairview Christian Church, Durmid, Va. (by Geo. C. Dalton), was credited with a contribution of $8, instead of $28. The total given in that issue, however, is correct, as the $28 is included.

A Friend, Saranac, Mich.	$ 2.00
M. L. Miles and Wife, Waco, Tex.	2.00
Mrs. C. T. Numbers, Akron, O.	5.00
Mr. and Mrs. Jay W. Smith, Muskegon, Mich.	3.00
Mr. and Mrs. T. O. Wilson, Miami, Fla.	25.00
First Church Bible School, Yates Center, Kan.	2.00
Mizpah Bible School, Bula, Va.	5.00
Bible School, Dexter, Mo. (by J. I. Moore)	10.00
Shadyside (O.) Church	6.00
Grassy Springs Bible School and Church, Woodford County, Ky. (by A. Fairhurst)	20.60
C. H. Brown and Family, Osawatomie, Kan.	6.00
Mrs. George McGaw, Osawatomie, Kan.	1.00
Mrs. J. C. Burroughs, St. Cloud, Fla.	5.00
Miss Irma Burroughs, St. Cloud, Fla.	5.00
First Church, Cowden, Ill.	40.70
L. H. Thompson, Mount Gay, W. Va.	5.00
Waynetown (Ind.) Bible School	41.00
Mrs. D. C. Johnson, College Springs, Ia.	10.00
Thomas Smith, Oelwein, Ia.	5.00
Elsie Brownlee, Truman, Minn.	4.00
Martha E. Evans, Bucklin, Kan.	1.00
W. S. and Floyd E. Betts, Longmont, Col.	6.00
Mrs. A. T. Felix, Los Angeles, Calif.	5.00
I. M. McKay, Washington C. H., O.	5.00
M. J. Lackman, Mirabile, Mo.	1.00
Frances Franklin and Mrs. Herman Lowell, Princeton, Minn.	3.50
Citrus Center (Fla.) Union Bible School	14.72
J. H. Johnston, Middletown, O.	1.00
Perkins Baptist Bible School, Bula, Va. (by W. T. Davis)	10.00
Mizpah Christian Bible School, Bula, Va. (by W. T. Davis)	5.00
Total	$ 255.81
Previously reported	39,441.01
Grand total	$39,696.82

JUST AS WE EXPECTED

THE *Christian Century*, in its issue of August 19, editorially endorses the proposition to practice open membership in China, and likewise the sympathetic attitude of the Foreign Christian Missionary Society toward Secretary Garrett, the self-confessed open-membership advocate.

No one doubted that the *Century* would refrain from complimenting both the China Mission and the Foreign Society. It is human nature to eulogize those who agree with us, and do the things we want done.

"A MINISTER'S DUTY"

THE boxed article, bearing the above title, by T. W. Phillips, Jr., which appears on page 5, is one of many expressions concerning R. E. Elmore's exposé of conditions in the Foreign Society that are coming to this office.

One of our preachers, in a personal letter, says: "If the Foreign Society declines to recall Frank Garrett and to thoroughly investigate the entire China Mission, it will be conclusive proof to me that men who advocate a departure from Restoration principles constitute the majority in the Executive Committee." And many others write in a similar vein.

A preacher of renown among us, and who has traveled extensively this summer, called at our office just yesterday, and when we asked what the brethren are saying about Mr. Elmore's article in the STANDARD of August 7, he answered: "They are simply amazed."

Also, many are asking: "Why does not the Foreign Society answer Mr. Elmore?" Our only answer is: We don't know.

ANOTHER WORD ABOUT VOTING

IT appears that the rule which governs the straw vote for president of the United Christian Missionary Society is not yet perfectly clear to all the brethren.

One writes: "Send me four hundred ballots for distribution in our congregation." Another writes: "Send me ballots and I'll have our entire church vote for ——." And so it goes.

Just why there should be confusion we do not know. Nevertheless, confusion exists.

Hence the necessity for further explanation:

1. All members of a church of Christ can vote.

2. Each member must do his or her own voting.

3. The voter must either clip the ballot printed in the STANDARD each week and use it or use a card ballot.

4. Card ballots can be sent only to those whose names and addresses we have in the STANDARD office.

5. It is not necessary to be a subscriber to the STANDARD or to any other paper to cast a preferential ballot.

PREFERENTIAL BALLOT

I indicate below by cross (X) my choice for President of the United Christian Missionary Society

☐ A. McLEAN, of Cincinnati, O.
☐ P. H. WELSHIMER, of Canton, O.
☐ W. H. BOOK, of Columbus, Ind.
☐ F. W. BURNHAM, of St. Louis, Mo.
☐ F. D. KERSHNER, of Des Moines, Ia.
☐ S. S. LAPPIN, of Bedford, Ind.

(Write on above line the name of any other preferred)

Name of voter ....

Address ....

Vote for only one candidate and sign your name and address, if you wish your ballot counted. If, by chance, a second ballot reaches you, do not vote a second time, but pass it on to some other interested person.

Week Ending August 21 Shows No Change in Relative Standing in Preferential Ballot

Courtesy, Library of The United Christian Missionary Society

The preferential ballot and cartoon were published by the "Christian Standard" (August 28, 1920, p. 1187) for voting on a proposed new president of the United Society.

churches of Christ to membership, as a body, in an association of denominations (sects) only." The paper, also, in the same issue, printed an approval of affiliation with the Inter-Church World Movement by E. L. Powell, Louisville, Kentucky. This was followed by a debate between other persons in succeeding issues. A second installment of the Errett vs. Powell debate appeared in the *Standard* of September 18, 1920 (pp. 1251 ff.).

The Inter-Church World Movement was a united organization of most all of the Protestant churches in America for a great missionary and educational campaign. It had headquarters in New York City and outlined an extensive program. A. E. Cory, who formerly had been a leader in our own Men and Millions Movement, was the main leader from the Disciples of Christ in the effort. A quotation from *Survey of Service* (pp. 15 f.), W. R. Warren, editor, gives additional information on the Inter-Church World Movement:

The same Cincinnati convention of 1919 that authorized the formation of the new [United Christian Missionary] society directed the same old boards and the Board of Education to participate in the Inter-Church World Movement, in full confidence that the success of wartime Red Cross, Liberty Loan and United War Work campaigns would be repeated. Instead of receiving several million dollars of increased funds, the Inter-Church askings of its constituent boards, the United Society had to begin its life in 1920-21 by taking the lead, in cooperation with the Board of Education, colleges and state societies, in raising over six hundred thousand dollars, underwritings of the Disciples of Christ organizations for the defunct movement. Even in this effort there was a fine example of brotherhood solidarity. Some churches that had opposed entering the movement heroically paid their quotas on what they considered a debt of honor.

As the quotation indicates, and as many persons will recall, the Inter-Church World Movement finally failed financially and the Disciples of Christ, being a party to the movement, undertook to pay their share of the debt which was involved and did so with credit.

A first-page "Open Letter" from P. H. Welshimer, Canton, Ohio, minister, was published in the *Christian Standard* for September 11, 1920 (p. 1225). Mr. Welshimer quoted from an editorial in *The Christian Century* of Chicago for August 26, 1920, as follows:

The mission churches have already exercised their congregational prerogatives and taken action.

Most, if not all, of the mission churches of Disciples in China have been for some time receiving unimmersed Christians into their membership. . . . The membership reports sent to missionary headquarters in America have made no distinction between the immersed and unimmersed members.

This editorial of *The Christian Century* later revealed a curious situation which had arisen between its editor, Charles Clayton Morrison, and one of the missionaries in China, George Baird, at the station of Luchowfu (now Hofei). The missionary had personally advocated the reception of Christian people who had not been immersed into one of the native churches, but he had been resisted unanimously by the China Mission, composed of the other missionaries. It seems, however, that on his own responsibility he had placed the names of certain people on the card index or church roll.

These were Chinese Christian people who had come from some distance, usually hundreds of miles, where other mission boards were working. They had become identified as teachers in the Chinese schools and in other rather professional work in the city where this mission station was located. Upon arriving in the city, they had instantly asked where the "people of God" met and had joined with their Christian brethren in our church, the only one in that whole section of China. They had entered its work with great earnestness. A number of these Christians were talented and were put to teaching Sunday school classes and other activities in the church, even sometimes helping in the communion service and in other ways aiding the isolated group of Chinese Christians in their work.

It seems that Mr. Baird had carried on a correspondence with the editor of *The Christian Century* in regard to the situation, unknown to the China Mission, or to the Missionary Society at home. Because of this, Mr. Morrison, who himself was an advocate of what was called open membership, agreed with the editor of the *Christian Standard* in his statements, although from a different point of view. Each journal had been very antagonistic to the other.

The sequel to this situation was, likewise, strange. When the little group of Presbyterians, Methodists, and Episcopalians, who were worshipping in our church at Luchowfu discovered that an issue had been made, with regard to their church membership, they held an indignation meeting of their own and declared that they still held membership with their home churches miles away and had never intended to have membership in the local church or to belong to the religious group called the Disciples of Christ! They were very much offended at what they felt was the advantage which had been taken of them. Because of this, the question would naturally arise whether a person could become a member of a local church and not know it, or not desire it!

This incident, which was unfortunate and led to misunderstanding, only illustrates the fact that on the mission field, especially in the younger churches where sufficient attention has not been given to careful organization, the main emphasis has been on grouping together the people who are followers of Christ as opposed to the great non-Christian population surrounding them. However, no explanations of this kind seemed to satisfy the *Christian Standard*, which adhered to its literal point, trying, if possible, to win the issue.

It is interesting to note that the "right hand of fellowship" cannot be exercised in the Chinese churches. The Chinese people do not shake hands with each other. They bow to each other and shake hands with themselves, pressing their hands together in front. When other Christians come to worship, they are asked to stand. This they do as they bow and are recognized as God's people. This is about all there is to the matter.

The church in China practiced immersion and immersion only and sometimes one of these people would wish to be immersed and that would follow. In most instances, however, they expected to return to their home church and only regarded themselves as guests among Christian people. R. A. Doan, layman secretary for the Foreign Christian Missionary Society and afterwards with the United Christian Missionary Society, had visited China. He said that Mr. Baird, the missionary involved at Luchowfu, "has always believed that the recognition of members of other churches as Christian and the use of them in the work of the local congregation is a recognition of their church membership" (*Christian Standard*, November 13, 1920, p. 1497; *World Call*, November, 1920, p. 35).

Later, in 1922, the whole staff of our eight missionaries who were stationed at Luchowfu sent a signed statement to the

United Christian Missionary Society in St. Louis, as follows (*World Call*, July, 1922, pp. 36 f.) :

We, members of the Luchowfu Station, in compliance with the request of the Advisory Committee for a statement regarding our practice in receiving members into the church, wish to make the following statement:

We feel that it would be useless to avow that we do or do not practice open membership for the simple reason that no definition we could make would satisfy all whom it concerns. Terms are too elastic and interpretations too many. But we are willing to make known very definitely what has been our practice and each member of the Brotherhood may decide for himself whether or not we have practiced open membership.

To the best of our knowledge there are no recent innovations in the practices of the Luchowfu Church. Our present practices are those which have been followed since the beginning of our work, without any effort at concealment. It has not been our custom to formally receive any members into the local congregation, either immersed or unimmersed. Christians coming to us find a church home where they may worship, partake of communion and work in whatever capacity they are best fitted. In that way unimmersed Christians have been used as teachers and members of church committees.

But unimmersed Christians coming to us from various denominations have not given up their identity with their denominations. They do not consider themselves members of the brotherhood known as the Disciples of Christ, and upon leaving our local congregation do not seek to proclaim themselves members of our brotherhood, but return to the denominations of which they have considered themselves members even while working with us. They recognize us an an immersionist body; we are known as such both within and without the Mission.

Furthermore, we reaffirm our determination, as long as we remain members of this Mission, in these and in all other matters, to adhere to the policies formulated for our guidance by the authorized representatives of the Disciples of Christ in America.

Signed:

Lillian B. Collins, Blanche A. Parker, Frank Vierling, Laura Lynne Major, Lyrel G. Teagarden, Mabel A. Vierling, Albin C. Bro, Margueritte Harmon Bro.

The following statement concerning church membership at our Nantungchow, China, mission station is so fair and explicit that it answers in itself the accusations concerning open membership. It only needs to be said that the church at Nantungchow comprised the only Christian group of any communion for many miles around in a population of several million.

The statement was written by Mrs. Ruby S. Hagman, wife of Dr. G. L. Hagman, the medical missionary, both now retired. He was away when she wrote the statement. These devoted missionaries were located at this station for a long period of years, beginning in 1915. What she wrote was published in a *Statement of the Executive Committee of the United Christian Missionary Society* . . . . (first in 1922, then reprinted, 1924) and accepted by the Board of Managers and by the Society in the 1922 International Convention at Winona Lake, Indiana. The statement, published also in *World Call*, July, 1922 (pp. 37 f.), follows in full:

Nantungchow, China,
February 22, 1922.

To Whom It May Concern:

Statement concerning unimmersed believers in Nantungchow.

As the oldest resident member of the station, I would like to give a bit of history concerning the Nantungchow church.

When the undersigned arrived here, in 1915, the church had just gone through deep waters and was much reduced in numbers and quite disorganized. The missionaries here, with the remaining Christians, met for regular Bible study, worship and communion. A constitution of a simple nature was adopted and written in the secretary's book. The members of the church all signed it. All were immersed believers.

Before many months had passed there were changes in both Chinese and foreign pastors and with the changes passed the custom of having members sign this constitution. In fact, it was disregarded in most respects and the fellowship was most informal. With the coming of teachers, doctors, nurses, etc., from other stations, letters were sometimes brought but often not. When letters were brought they were presented to the church. Often these letters came long after the individual had established himself with us. Sometimes none came. New converts were admitted to the church by immersion and they all received the same warm welcome. All members have been encouraged to take part in the work, teaching a Bible class, leading the weekly prayer meeting, etc. Those able have taken their turn in preaching.

Three years ago Mr. Alexander Lee, a teacher and member of our church, came to our city to reside. He had long been in the employ of the Mission and previously educated in our schools both in China and America. Upon his arrival in Nantungchow he immediately took an active part in all the church work. I believe he brought no church letter with him, and I recall no formal recognition of his coming to this church. He simply went to work just as he had been doing in the Nanking church. A few months later his wife and children arrived to make this their home. At that time the undersigned was in America and the other missionaries away on summer vacation. Mrs. Alexander

Lee came to China from Honolulu, where she had married Mr. Lee. She was a member of the Episcopal Church there, and brought some such statement with her when she went to Nanking as a bride. When Mrs. Lee came to Nantungchow she was received as the wife of Mr. Lee, who had already made his influence felt in the local church. She entered into the church life just as the other believing women here entered into it. She has been on the list of contributors and has been very faithful in this respect. The Chinese pastor of the church keeps a roll of the Christians. On this roll he has Mrs. Lee enrolled in a manner different from her husband. She is what he called an associate member. Mrs. Lee states that she does not consider it necessary to observe the ordinance of baptism more than once.

Just two years ago Mr. Y. C. Lee came to the Nantungchow church as the Chinese pastor. He too is a product of one of our Mission Schools and is a member of our church. For the fourteen years previous to his coming here he had been teaching in a Southern Presbyterian Boys' School in Chinkiang. While in Chinkiang he married a young woman who had been educated in the Methodist Girls' School there. She, I believe, was an orphan who had first been in the care of a Baptist, but later educated in the Methodist school. She was sprinkled and became a member of the Methodist church. When she married Mr. Lee she went to work with him and the Presbyterian missionaries with whom he was associated. Shortly after Mr. Lee came to Nantungchow his wife and children followed him. The undersigned was still in America, but has the word of one here at that time that Mrs. Y. C. Lee had no official recognition as a new member entering the church. She simply came and went to work as she thought a pastor's wife ought to, and everybody was happy to have her do so. Upon recent investigation we find that her husband has placed her upon the church roll as an associate member, along with Mrs. Alex Lee.

Soon after Mr. Y. C. Lee came to Nantungchow, a friend of his who was a Presbyterian in Chinkiang came here to work for the Standard Oil Company. This young man immediately associated himself with the Nantungchow church for fellowship in worship, communion and giving. He too is enrolled in the same manner as the two Mrs. Lees.

There is another unimmersed believer living in Nantungchow, an old lady, the mother of a former pastor. She conducts herself as a Christian and worships with us in the same manner as do the above mentioned persons.

In the eyes of the heathen world these four individuals are counted as Christians and well they may be, if life is any testimony. To do otherwise would be a denial of Jesus Christ.

Respectfully submitted,

(Signed)   Ruby S. Hagman

The membership situation, as above described, came under the attack of John T. Brown, the *Christian Standard*, and *The*

Touchstone. These, and similar statements from other stations in China were published by the United Society and sent to all of our churches, as well as to the news publications of the brotherhood. The *Standard*, however, maintained its opposition to the "unfaithfulness" of the China Mission.

It has always been the feeling of officials of the United Society that the missionaries who give their lives to the work could be trusted to work out problems which were peculiar to the different fields of effort where conditions are so different from those in America. The missionaries make mistakes and they are the first to acknowledge them. Indeed, we in the homeland are hardly expected to monopolize the matter of mistakes in Christian work. We will have to acknowledge that we make plenty of them!

The United Christian Missionary Society began to function in St. Louis, Missouri, where its first headquarters were established, on October 1, 1920. The first International Convention of Disciples of Christ after the Society was formed was held in St. Louis on October 18-25, 1920.

The *Christian Standard* had again preceded the convention with much publicity of another Restoration Congress. This Congress met for four days preceding the convention. Sessions were at the Odeon Theater with several hundred persons attending. P. H. Welshimer, minister of Canton, Ohio, was the chairman.

A. McLean, then vice-president of the new United Society, asked for the floor in a session of the Congress. He was granted it and spoke concerning the United Society and its purposes, as well as answering some statements that had been made.

At this meeting, Robert E. Elmore made many accusations concerning the United Society, its officials, the missionaries in China, and open membership. After Mr. Elmore had spoken, Bert Wilson, then a secretary of the United Society, asked permission to speak. Chairman Welshimer recognized him. So Mr. Wilson went to the platform, took Mr. Elmore by the arm after the latter had taken a seat at the back of the rostrum following his remarks and led him to the front. There Mr. Wilson interrogated Mr. Elmore for several minutes. Mr. Wilson took exception to many things that Mr. Elmore had said.

Bert Wilson later answered Mr. Elmore's repeated attacks on
the attitude of the China Mission towards Christian union in
China, including the charge that our China Mission was committed to open membership and practicing it. Mr. Wilson's reply to Mr. Elmore, published in the *Christian Standard* of February 25, 1922 (p. 3251 f.), summarized the following points
thus:

Twenty-seven missionaries in one meeting said that open membership
had not been practiced in China.

Nearly a dozen missionaries home on furlough last year said the same
thing.

Six missionaries home on furlough now say the same thing.

Walter Scott Priest, who visited the field, says the same thing.

Mr. Priest was then minister of the Central Christian Church
of Wichita, Kansas. Earlier in this same article, Mr. Wilson had
explained:

When Walter Scott Priest was in China last year, there was a conference of missionaries during his stay in Nanking. There were twenty-
seven missionaries present. After Mr. Priest's address to the missionaries, he said: "Has any one of you, or has any mission in China, ever
advocated, does now advocate, the reception of the unimmersed into the
fellowship of the churches of Christ in China?" Mr. Priest writes:
"Then I put it to a vote, and there was an emphatic 'No' from every
one present."

L. N. D. Wells, then pastor in Akron, Ohio, and later for
many years minister of the East Dallas (Texas) Christian
Church, was a member of the new Board of Managers of the
United Society. During a discussion in one of the St. Louis sessions, Mr. Wells was asked a question regarding open membership on the mission field.

"If I were in China," Mr. Wells replied, "the facts as they
presented themselves to me from China would help me to make
my decision."

"Does geographical location make a difference?" some person
inquired from the audience.

Mr. Wells then answered as follows:

The environment makes every difference. You were discussing the
question of when a person comes from another place to a place where

CHRISTIAN STANDARD

SUBSCRIPTION, $2.00 PER ANNUM
PUBLISHED WEEKLY   CINCINNATI, FEBRUARY 25, 1922   OFFICES: E?   ʻER STS.

Who Is Responsible for the China Controversy?

President Burnham's statement in the "World Call"

More that must be told to make that statement clear

Is the Sweeney resolution to be considered a part of the old "hide and seek" policy?

Letters from members of the Board of Managers

Bert Wilson Answers R. E. Elmore

U. C. M. S. Secretary presents long-awaited reply to Louisville Congress address on "The China Mission and the U. C. M. S."

Open Letter to Managers of U. C. M. S.

Wherein are presented some statements of public record which require more detailed explanation than a blanket denial that the issue, on which they are based, exists

The Strange Obsessions of Peter Ainslie

The President of the Association for the Promotion of Christian Unity explains the personnel of the Sunday evening program at Winona Lake Convention

Atheism in Our Colleges

Chas. W. Eliot, President Emeritus of Harvard, and Arthur T. Hadley, Ex-President of Yale, answer the late Professor Fairhurst's questionnaire on evolution

A Heathen from Africa Finds the Light and Walks Therein

W. H. Book tells the story of Thomas Kalane

The Restoration Congress at Poplar Bluff, Mo.

Courtesy, Disciples of Christ Historical Society

This cover (p. 3245) from the "Christian Standard" of February 25, 1922, illustrates the size and kind of headlines used to publicize attacks on the United Society while the periodical promoted its own causes.

there is only a Disciple church. You let him pass the emblems, teach a class, and fully fellowship with him, but you say, "I will not put your name on my church roll." I can't find anything between Genesis and Revelation that says anything about a church membership roll except, "The Lord added to the church daily them that were being saved." Little attention is paid to a church roll on the mission field. God's people fellowship each other whenever they come together. I do not practice open membership here. It is not necessary. There are churches of all names all about us to which people can go. If I were in China, I think it would be a different matter. If the denominational churches were not close, I think I would receive the pious unimmersed.

Mr. Wells recently confirmed this statement to me as being what he said in St. Louis, other statements to the contrary notwithstanding. The *Christian Standard* labeled Mr. Wells' statement thus: "L.N.D. Wells' Peculiar Reply" in a stenographic report of the St. Louis Congress and Convention business sessions (November 6, 1920, p. 1468).

In a business session, during the annual meeting of the United Society at the St. Louis Convention, a resolution was presented. This was afterwards called the "Medbury Resolution," which would, it was hoped, bring about a greater degree of peace and understanding in connection with criticisms of the missionary work. This resolution grew out of a previous one offered by Mark Collis of Lexington, Kentucky, in which he asked for the recall of Frank Garrett of China. A committee of five persons, of which Charles S. Medbury, Des Moines, Iowa, minister, was the chairman, drew up the resolution that was approved.

This Medbury Resolution dealt with a statement of policy which had been passed by the Board of Managers of the Foreign Christian Missionary Society before the United Society was formed. The prior policy statement was as follows:

That the Executive Committee is committed to the program of the organization and maintenance of work on the mission field in consonance with the teaching and practice of the disciples of Christ in the United States.

These resolutions can have but one meaning, and that is that the Executive Committee does not approve of any control of the local churches by a district association, or of the advocacy or practice of open membership among the missionaries or mission stations supported by the Foreign Society.

The Medbury Resolution, after quoting the above, went on to state (*Christian Standard*, October 30, 1920, p. 1433):

> *Resolved,* That this statement of the Foreign Christian Missionary Society voicing, as we believe it does, the heart of our brotherhood as to points at issue, be submitted by the United Society to men and women engaged in service under their direction, whose teaching or practices have been called in question, to the end that their open avowal of loyal support of such an expression of the thought and life of the brotherhood may restore in the hearts of all, complete confidence in them, or, if in the liberty of conscience such avowal is impossible, may indicate the wisdom of a prompt cessation of service as representatives of the disciples of Christ.

This Medbury Resolution was sent to all the fields of work abroad by the United Society and there was no dissent from it. The missionaries were all willing to follow explicitly the accepted position of the Society.

The 1921 International Convention was held at Winona Lake, Indiana, and was rather uneventful as far as controversy was concerned. It was a well-attended and enthusiastic gathering and people went away hoping that perhaps opposition and controversy had played themselves out. The Board of Managers of the United Society had been elected with the thought that a cross-section of the brotherhood should be in its representation. An evangelist, John T. Brown of Louisville, Kentucky, and Z. T. Sweeney of Columbus, Indiana, where he formerly was the pastor, were chosen as members of this group. They were known to be friendly to many of the positions of the *Christian Standard*.

In one of the meetings of the Board of Managers in St. Louis, which was headquarters for the United Society, John T. Brown said he would like to visit the mission field and study the work of the missionaries, but that he could not bear the expense himself. He stated also that he had been asked to hold some evangelistic meetings in Australia. E. M. Bowman, New York City, a liberal-minded as well as generous lay member of the Executive Committee, immediately suggested that he would pay Mr. Brown's expenses. Mr. Brown had been sympathetic to the policies of the *Christian Standard* and there was considerable feeling in the group that it would be unwise for him to go to the mission field. However, Mr. Bowman's offer had been made

in good faith so Mr. Brown went on his way around the world
with Mr. Bowman paying the cost. Mr. Brown's journey was
so timed that he could make his report at the 1922 International
Convention at Winona Lake, Indiana.

Nearly four pages of the *Christian Standard* for October 1,
1921 (pp. 2719 ff.) were filled with an attack by R. E. Elmore
on the China situation. The paper announced a "Regional"
Restoration Congress at the Broadway Christian Church, Louisville, Kentucky, on December 6-8, 1921. Mr. Elmore addressed
the Congress on the China Mission and the United Society,
claiming that there was evidence of open membership in China
and attacking any union movement in that field. This message was published in the *Standard*, December 31, 1921 (pp.
3055 ff.). Frank Garrett, missionary to China, and F. W. Burnham, president of the United Society, were at that Congress and
stated that there was no intended open membership in China,
but always the recognition of Christian people of other religious
bodies as belonging to the group of Christians which worship
God and turn away from the Oriental religions. This, however,
had no effect upon the attitude of the *Standard* or Mr. Elmore.

John T. Brown's Report on Mission Fields

At the Winona Lake, Indiana, Convention in 1922, John T.
Brown had returned from his tour around the world. He made
a lengthy report to the United Christian Missionary Society's
Board of Managers and also a brief report to the convention.
He stated that he had visited India, the Philippine Islands, and
China. His interests, however, seemed to lie in seeing if he could
find any cases of open membership, rather than the great aims
and problems of the mission fields.

Mr. Brown reported that India was all right.

In the Philippine Islands, he stated that the only question was
E. K. Higdon and the Taft Avenue Church opposite the University of the Philippines in Manila. This congregation was
conducted in connection with a student dormitory maintained
by our Mission. The membership and attendance were, therefore, largely composed of students who were there temporarily.

Mr. Higdon had said that when the church was organized, it
was agreed by the Mission station that there might be two mem-

bership lists. One was to be for penitent believers who had been immersed. The other for those Protestants, whether immersed or sprinkled, who desired to work with and have a home in the congregation. Mr. Brown quoted Mr. Higdon as saying that he had no doubt gone beyond his authority in that he had received unimmersed persons and sometimes had put them in as deacons of the church. But Mr. Higdon emphasized that he had no intention of causing difficulties for the Executive Committee of the United Society or the churches at home which had sent him out as a missionary.

Following Mr. Brown's visit to the Philippines, Mr. Higdon wrote a letter to the United Society, stating that he would abide by the policy of the Society with regard to church membership. He added, also, that before Mr. Brown left Manila he read his proposed report to him. Mr. Higdon stated to Mr. Brown that he had misinterpreted the practice of the Taft Avenue Church when he described it as open membership.

In China, at the rather new station of Nantungchow, Mr. Brown found that the wife of the pastor, and one other person, had their names on the church roll as members, although they were not immersed. They were very earnest Christians. When the question was raised, the statement was made that these names had been placed on the guest roll, rather than on the regular membership roll. At Wuhu, China, a Bible woman was a Presbyterian, but the church had unanimously agreed to employ her since good workers were scarce. She, however, in working with people, had led them to follow the rule of the church and be immersed. Luchowfu (now Hofei), Mr. Brown stated, had twenty-three members who were never immersed and who were considered members until the controversy arose. The fact was that after the controversy arose, these people, all from other cities, got together and stated that they never intended to leave their home churches where their membership remained. They had simply joined with the people of God in Luchowfu for a church home and an opportunity to serve.

Mr. Brown stated that the China Mission had signed a statement that it would abide by the policy of the United Christian Missionary Society.

Then he said, "I think that most of the missionaries on the foreign field will agree, or have agreed, to work in harmony with the policy of the society" (*Christian Standard*, September 9, 1922, p. 3949). He praised the missionaries for their devotion and said he believed they could be trusted to do what was right.

At the 1922 Winona Lake International Convention, the statement of the United Christian Missionary Society concerning church membership was approved. This statement by the Society's Board of Managers was as follows:

As a purely administrative policy, the Board of Managers of the United Christian Missionary Society announces the following:

In harmony with the teachings of the New Testament as understood by the Board of Managers, the United Christian Missionary Society is conducting its work everywhere on the principle of receiving into the membership of the churches at home or abroad, by any of its missionaries, only those who are immersed, penitent believers in Christ.

Furthermore, it is believed by this Board of Managers that all of the missionaries and ministers appointed and supported by this Board, are in sincere accord with this policy, and certainly it will not appoint and indeed it will not continue in its service any one known by it to be not in such accord. It disclaims any right and disowns any desire to do otherwise.

There was a long debate in the convention over whether such a statement was "creedal." It finally was approved by a large majority. Z. T. Sweeney was on the committee which drafted the statement.

The *Christian Standard* published the statement in its issue of September 9, 1922 (p. 3949). Also, it was issued in 1922, and reprinted in 1924, as a part of the *Statement of the Executive Committee of the United Christian Missionary Society, Together With the Latest Report of the China Mission and All the Missionaries in China.* The statement was subsequently printed in the *Foreign Missionary Manual of The United Christian Missionary Society (Disciples of Christ)* for the guidance of all missionaries. Careful observance of the position of the Society followed.

Following the 1922 convention, the Foreign Department of the United Society recommended to the Executive Committee of the Society that the department be authorized to answer Mr. Higdon's letter, in which he stated his position, and asked for

the Society's position with regard to it. The recommendation
of the Executive Committee was as follows (*Second Annual Report
of the United Christian Missionary Society, July 1, 1921-
June 30, 1922,* p. 251):

We interpret the statement with regard to "being in sincere accord"
with the policy pronounced to mean that the missionary should be willing to earnestly carry on the work in the manner suggested. We feel
that this was not meant in any sense to infringe upon private opinion
or individual liberty of conviction "so long as none judges his brother,
or insists on forcing his own opinions upon others or on making them
an occasion of strife."

This statement, likewise, was approved by Z. T. Sweeney. Mr.
Higdon was written to this effect and in answering he gave his
full approval.

To the surprise and chagrin of most Disciples concerned,
John T. Brown went to the *Christian Standard* following the
1922 Winona Lake Convention and arranged for the complete
publication of his report on his visit to the mission fields. This
report took eighteen pages in the periodical for the issue of October 28, 1922 (pp. 109 ff.). It included all of his personal in-
terviews, his questions asked and the answers, and many things
of a strictly personal nature. In connection with publication of
the report, the *Standard* issued a long editorial, "Index to the
Brown Report," attacking the United Society and its missionaries on the fields (October 28, 1922, p. 127 f.).

On December 9, 1922, the *Standard* began publication, near
the back of each issue, of a controversial page labeled, "The
United Society Has Broken Faith." It was edited by Robert E.
Elmore, then of Carlisle, Kentucky. The page contained a rehash of data from John T. Brown's report and attacked what
was termed open membership on the mission fields. The facing
page, announced for the Society's use, was to be designated, "The
United Society Merits Support."

The page reserved for the United Society was partially blank
the first time that the feature appeared, December 9 (p. 295).
The page reserved for the Society in the issues of December 16
(p. 319) and December 23 (p. 351) were mainly blank. A
small, boxed, note stated, in capital letters: "THIS PAGE IS
RESERVED FOR USE OF U.C.M.S. FOR FRANK DE-

FENSE OF ITS POSITION, WHENEVER IT DESIRES DI-
RECTLY, OR THROUGH WRITERS OF ITS NAMING,
TO REACH THE 'STANDARD' READERS."

By the issue of December 30, 1922 (p. 374), the *Standard* had
a boldfaced, boxed sentence at the bottom of the page used to
attack the United Society. That sentence read: "Equal space
is offered to the U.C.M.S. whenever desired for defense of its
position." The space was never used by the Society or any of
its friends. The feature was discontinued with the issue of
March 31, 1923.

Robert E. Elmore edited "The United Society Has Broken
Faith" pages, as stated. He became a member of the editorial
staff of the Standard Publishing Company to advance its "Christian Unity Fellowship" (*Christian Standard*, September 8, 1923,
p. 1411; June 13, 1925, p. 904). He wrote a primer, *Christian
Unity*, of thirteen lessons. When one of these was published in
the *Standard* (March 22, 1924, p. 627 f.), Mr. Elmore's by-line
had "Christian unity specialist" underneath it. A regular page
called "Christian Unity Fellowship" appeared in the *Standard*
for a number of months about this time.

The visit of John T. Brown to the mission fields and his taking the detailed report to the *Christian Standard*, so contrary to
his presentation to the Board of Managers of the United Society
and to the 1922 Winona Lake Convention, was one of the sad-
dest episodes ever suffered by our people. The material was
publicized by the writer and by the *Standard*. Suspicion and
distrust were created, especially among readers who were entirely ignorant of conditions on the mission fields. The answer
of the 120 members of the United Society's Executive Committee and Board of Managers, a representative group from forty-
one states and several Canadian provinces, will give some idea
of the reaction.

Let it be recalled that on Mr. Brown's return from the Orient,
he met with the United Society's Board of Managers, of which
he was a member. While the facts of his journey were thus
fresh in his mind, he indicated that some situations on the fields
did not meet with his approval. He had called these to the attention of the missionaries and said that he was satisfied correc-
tions were being made. On August 29, 1922, addressing the

22 (318) **CHRISTIAN STANDARD** December 16, 1922

THE UNITED SOCIETY HAS BROKEN FAITH

A PAGE EDITED IN BEHALF OF OPEN DISCUSSION AND FRANK CRITICISM OF UNITED SOCIETY MANAGEMENT AND POLICY

R. E. ELMORE, CARLISLE, KY., EDITOR

WHY WE CAN NOT SUPPORT THE U. C. M. S.

In a letter from a friend, reference is made to a preacher who was asked as to his attitude to the United Society, and who replied: "I am going to support them this year, and if they carry out *what was done at the Winona Convention*, I will continue to support them, but if they do not I will not support them."

Since through a high-power hoax the impression was sent abroad that the 1922 Convention did something to restore confidence in the United Society, it is well to consider just what was done at the Winona Convention.

The only thing the United Society administrators have ever done, looking toward a housecleaning, was done in January, 1922, when a minority of the Board of Managers adopted the Sweeney resolution, which, if enforced, would bring back from the field every missionary who favors open membership.

Now, what did the Winona Convention do? Good psychology required that the Convention ratify the Sweeney resolution. With customary docility the Convention obeyed orders and ratified, *not the Sweeney resolution*, but *the Sweeney resolution with a rider*, designated as "the interpretation as given in the Higdon case."

The wayfaring man, yea, a fool, could understand the Sweeney resolution without interpretation. In the simplest terms it declares that the U. C. M. S. will not keep in its employ any missionary who is not *in sincere accord* with the principle of receiving into the membership of the church only those who are immersed, penitent believers in Christ.

But since the real rulers of the U. C. M. S. did not relish the Sweeney resolution, it became necessary for them to "interpret" it in order to keep in the field the missionaries who have been advocating and practicing open membership.

This is "the Higdon case"—Mr. Higdon, a United Society missionary in Manila, said to John Brown: "I have received into the church unimmersed persons and have put them in as deacons of the church. At the present time we have three deacons who have not been immersed."

This is "the interpretation as given in the Higdon case"—and *this* is what the Winona Convention ratified:

> Can a missionary continue as a worker of the United Society who personally holds it advisable to receive unimmersed Christians into church membership on the mission field, but refrains from doing so and endeavors to logically carry out the policy pursued in the past [sic] and recently stated by the society through its Board of Managers?
>
> We interpret the statement with regard to "being in sincere accord" with the policy pronounced to mean that the missionary should be willing to earnestly [sic] carry on the work in the manner suggested. We feel that this was not meant in any sense to infringe upon private opinion or individual liberty of conviction.

The author of the Sweeney resolution, who also seconded this interpretation, says: "The United Society has cleaned house and then some." An eminent leader says he is "satisfied with things as they are—plus." Another prince in Israel says: "We believe the sentiment of our brotherhood was expressed in the great Convention at Winona." It is not pleasant to disagree with these beloved brethren, but we believe that the house is now more polluted than ever, that "things as they are" are worse than they ever have been, and that the sentiment of our brotherhood was not expressed at Winona. The Convention, in action great or "epoch-making," did not "give Morrisonism a black eye." It gave the Sweeney resolution a black eye.

This "Higdon interpretation," originated by the Foreign Department of the United Society, ratified by the Executive Committee, endorsed by the Board of Managers, and approved by the Convention, kills the recall clause of the Sweeney resolution and grants official immunity to the army of missionaries, who have advocated and practiced open membership, retaining them in the field. Poor Baird, it appears, resigned too soon, before he was apprised of this latest "interpretation."

THE MORAL ISSUE.—The official interpretation of the Sweeney resolution in the Higdon case, which the Convention ratified, is the open and unblushing announcement of a doctrine so pernicious as to be inconceivable in a Christian council. Were it not for the fact that our Conventions habitually approve, without careful consideration, the recommendations brought down from "headquarters," the ease with which this vicious principle was promulgated at Winona Lake would be utterly astounding.

Here we find a group of foreign missionary secretaries coolly informing their employees that "being in sincere accord" with a given principle or rule of conduct does not involve their private opinion or personal conviction. Here are the officials of a missionary organization called "Christian" inducing a mass-meeting of their constituents to endorse this monstrous immorality. Here are the administrators of the U. C. M. S. teaching their agents to stifle self-respect, violate honor, murder conscience and live a life of fraud and falsehood among a pagan people.

Astonished and bewildered, many are wondering how some of our true and loyal brethren have become enmeshed in this sophistry to the extent of lending their aid to the most shocking intellectual dishonesty and moral anarchy.

This casuistry—inconceivable in men and women who rank themselves as leaders in the holy work of spreading over the world the righteous teaching of Him who is the Way, the Truth and the Life—this unthinkable immorality involves missionary and missionary officials alike, in the face of which the question of open membership fades into insignificance.

The Medbury resolution was not carried out. The Sweeney resolution was not carried out. The good Lord pity us if the brethren permit the U. C. M. S. to carry out the Sweeney resolution with the Higdon rider.

FRANK GARRETT

Early in 1920, R. E. Elmore offered a resolution to the Executive Committee of the Foreign Society for the recall of Mr. Garrett. It was ignored.

At the St. Louis Convention, the same year, Mark Collis introduced a similar resolution. It met the same fate.

These resolutions were based on the facts that Mr. Garrett, as secretary of the China Mission, had participated, and probably led, in the memorable action of the mission in endorsing open membership, and S. J. Corey's statement that Mr. Garrett "was *decidedly* for the movement."

These facts have been treated expertly by Mr. Garrett and his employers, but these facts stand.

In apologizing for jumping into an affair described by A. McLean as "a departure from what is believed by our people," Mr. Garrett said: "We had been told [through the Chicago subway, no doubt] that many of our leading men in the brotherhood at home approved of this practice [open membership] and that an increasing number of churches were introducing it."

The *World Call*, commenting brilliantly on Mr. Garrett's letter containing the above "correction," as Mr. Wilson puts it, assured us that Mr. Garrett's statements "make all clear and plain, and confirm the statement of the officers of the society to the effect that open membership has been neither practiced nor advocated by the China Mission."

Some brethren failed to see it that way, so Mr. Garrett appeared at Winona Lake to speak peace to the troubled waters. Mr. Garrett is one of the missionaries described as not having "anything to keep from the brotherhood." He had said to the Executive Committee: "You may not be prepared to have this question come before the brotherhood in any way as having the approval of the China Mission." But the brotherhood had found it out.

In China, in 1919, Mr. Garrett and his associates stood for open membership. In 1921, in America, what did Mr. Garrett stand for?

He stood for evasion. His misrepresentations were so raw that J. E. Brown, for fourteen years missionary at Luchowfu, listening to Mr. Garrett at Winona Lake, desired to take the floor and state the facts. Mr. S. J. Corey, of the U. C. M. S., described by John Brown as not having "anything to keep from the brotherhood," prudentially restrained him.

However, amidst his sinuous explanations and artful irrelevancies, Mr. Garrett, under the veneer, was still the champion of open membership. The *Christian-Evangelist* reported: "Being pressed on the point whether he would practice open membership if the Convention so authorized, he answered that he would."

Later, in his apostleship among the churches in America, Mr. Idleman introduced Mr. Garrett as "the emancipator of our brotherhood, emancipating us from old ways to new ways."

The liberal Presbyterian organ, the *Continent*, referring to Mr. Garrett's embassy to America, exults: "The Rev. Frank Garrett did come home—but not to resign.".

Mr. Bert Wilson says, "Mr. Garrett corrected himself," referring to his incriminating letter of Aug. 11, 1919, and to his later letters to the Executive Committee. Mr. Wilson can only mean that we had wronged Mr. Garrett in our charges.

Now it becomes necessary for Mr. Garrett and his defenders to "correct" his letter to Mr. Baird in 1919. When Mr. Baird was put on the China convention program, he wrote to Mr. Garrett and suggested that some one else should deliver the address because F. M. Rains had asked him to resign in 1911, when he had made a similar speech advocating open membership. *Here was Mr. Garrett's chance.* In Mr. Garrett's reply to Mr. Baird urging him to remain on the program and deliver his ardent open-membership speech, we find the following things which merit "interpretation" from St. Louis: "This is a time when we must probe this question to the bottom. We can no longer take a traditional view. The crisis is upon us. . . . . Your outline is good. . . . *Do not let your former experience* [with F. M. Rains] *trouble you now.*"

Thus Mr. Garrett put his O. K. upon Mr. Baird's address and pushed him before the Convention with a speech which resulted in the unanimous endorsement of open membership by the China Mission.

Now Mr. Garrett crawls from under and leaves Geo. Baird to be gibbeted. With pious benedictions and official unction, Mr. Garrett goes back to China, while Mr. Baird "resigns." This is an elegant brand of administrative hypocrisy.

In the added light from John Brown's report, we now find that Mr. Garrett not only advocated, but practiced, open membership. He received Mrs. Alexander Lee's Episcopal certificate of membership in Nanking. Later he moved to Nantungchow, as did also the Lees. Mrs. Lee says that when she came to Nantungchow, her "name was put on the list of the church." Y. C. Lee, the Chinese pastor, says: "We have counted these people members—sprinkled people—until Mr. Garrett came to me sometime ago and said, '*On account of the trouble in America*, we would have to put them on the social list.'" Yes; he practiced open membership until trouble arose in America, and then resorted to the subterfuge of the "guest roll," a fiction for American use purely, as it did not change the status of the unimmersed members in China. In fact, the juggling consisted merely in writing "guest" after their names on the regular church roster. Neither Mr. Garrett, nor any other missionary, had ever mentioned immersion to these Lee women.

If anything further is needed in Mr. Garrett's self-revelation of unthinkable duplicity, we submit the following fragment from John Brown's report: "Bro. Garrett wrote Bro. Baird, *while we were in China*, that he was told of one wealthy man in Chicago who would put up this year all the money that the society *lost* because *of the practice of open membership.*"

The demand for Mr. Garrett's recall was originally based upon his favorable attitude to open membership and his shrewd apostleship in spreading this heresy throughout the China Mission.

Now the demand for Mr. Garrett's recall is reinforced by proof that he shared responsibility in the practice of open membership.

To all this is added indisputable evidence that Mr. Garrett, for many years, has deliberately deceived the brotherhood which supports him. In public addresses in America last year, he knowingly misrepresented the facts. It was under his smooth, Chicagoesque tutelage that the China Mission, far-away outpost of New Testament Christianity, surrendered its high charge and became the willing tool of the effervescent cult of modernism.

And now the United Christian Missionary Society has sent him back to complete the job, while it turns to a long-deluded constituency for support.

If the churches knew the facts, the curtain would be rung down on this travesty.

Knighthood is in flower when missionary secretaries use aged preachers and dependent widows and orphans as their breastworks.

In a letter addressed to the *Christian-Evangelist* from Tokyo, Japan, dated Dec. 26, 1920, P. A. Davey said: "My impression is that, during my twenty-one years in Japan, of the exceedingly few who have openly advocated open membership, *all came here with that point of view.*" Who sent these open-membership advocates to Japan?

Why does the U. C. M. S. continue to defend the missionaries in China? Why deny the fact that they have been practicing open membership? It seems to me, if they want us to trust them, the thing for them to do is to "fess up" and then call home all who are not in sympathy with what we believe.—W. H. Book, Columbus, Ind.

Courtesy, Butler School of Religion Library

This page from the "Christian Standard" of December 16, 1922, p. 318, illustrates a feature that the periodical ran for about four months. Robert E. Elmore was editor of the page.

December 16, 1922   **CHRISTIAN STANDARD**   (319) 23

> THIS PAGE IS RESERVED
> FOR USE OF U. C. M. S.
> FOR FRANK DEFENSE OF ITS
> POSITION, WHENEVER IT
> DESIRES DIRECTLY, OR
> THROUGH WRITERS OF ITS
> NAMING, TO REACH THE
> "STANDARD" READERS.

Courtesy, Butler School of Religion Library

A facsimile of a page reserved for defense of The United Christian Missionary Society
by the "Christian Standard" in the issue of December 16, 1922, p. 319.

Winona Lake International Convention, he said that the missionaries "all seemed to want to do the right thing, and closed by urging those present to stand by the missionaries and the work" (*Facts About the Visit of John T. Brown to Some of the Mission Fields and Answers to His Statements in the Christian Standard*, p. 5).

The following quotations are from the thirty-two-page pamphlet, sent out by the United Society to the churches of the brotherhood in the early part of 1924. This followed the publication of Mr. Brown's detailed report in the *Christian Standard* and a series of subsequent articles written by him for that periodical and published beginning November 17, 1923 and concluding February 2, 1924. The title of the pamphlet is, *Facts About the Visit of John T. Brown to Some of the Mission Fields and Answers to His Statements in the Christian Standard*. The quotations from the pamphlet follow:

In his report Mr. Brown has mistaken the Christian courtesy and hospitality of the missionaries for acquiescence with his own method and activity. Some missionaries regarded him with humorous pity and his whole performance as a ridiculous travesty of Christian ethics and mission principles. The younger missionaries received him with good-natured tolerance. Others viewed him with a sting of tragedy as he walked full-shod into their holy-of-holies, wounded their hearts and hurt those whom they loved. Still others bordered on that fervent mood wherein Christian charity and forbearance have a hot time gaining the victory over impatience and disgust. In one attitude they were unanimous, viz., in regarding his mission on the whole as an unenlightened interruption of their work. . . . [p. 11].

He bore them no loving greetings or expressions of fraternal solicitude from the Brotherhood at home, but chiefly the message that they were under suspicion and would be called upon to clear themselves. He played the role of a critical ecclesiastic, not of a sympathetic Christian brother. Testimony is unanimous that his visit brought no helpful inspiration or constructive counsel. Not a single missionary speaks of having any spiritual help from the visit. . . . [p. 11].

The reaction of our Chinese Churches and their leaders to Mr. Brown's approach and impact is another story which cannot yet be fully told. . . . [p. 12].

The impression on the Chinese was unfavorable and unfortunate in the following respects [p. 13]:

1. Mr. Brown's aggressive and unceremonious procedure led him into glaring breaches of Chinese etiquette and custom. Had he deliberately planned to shock and contravene the most delicate sensibilities,

and to violate the commonest proprieties of the Chinese people, he could scarcely have succeeded better than he did. Take as an example, his dealing with the Chinese ladies, Mrs. Y. C. Lee and Mrs. Alexander Lee [of Nantungchow]. His brusque questions about their baptism and his summary disposal of their Christian standing, causing them to lose face among their friends and fellow Christians were serious enough. And let it not be imagined that these cultured ladies, exquisitely sensitive, do not know that in Mr. Brown's report, in a Christian paper, their names have been blazoned in big black type as "the Lee Women"— and that they have been held up all over America as examples of ecclesiastical delinquency, and made the subject of controversy. Mr. Brown will never know the aftermath of that event alone. The whole Chinese Church remembers it with shame. [These Chinese ladies were respectively the wives of one of our Chinese pastors and one of the Chinese professors in Nanking University] [p. 13].

2. Our Chinese leaders do not feel that Mr. Brown had any heartfelt solicitude for the welfare of the Chinese churches. If irregularities existed, he made no effort to correct them. He looked for delinquencies, they say, and found nothing to praise. Some got the impression that he had come to disrupt and destroy the Churches. One of our ablest and most consecrated pastors, a man of tender heart and habitually gentle speech said: "Mr. Brown did not come as a brother to us Chinese. He approached us from the side of the Devil, and not from the side of God." Following one of his meetings with the Chinese church, the members referred to him as the "criminal judge from America," and his meeting with them as "a short session of the criminal court" [p. 13].

3. Mr. Brown's crusade on church rolls and the details of organization gave the Chinese some unwelcome notions about the United Society and our Brotherhood in whose name he pushed his propaganda. They received the impression that this great missionary organization and communion of their brethren in America, had ceased to be actuated by a desire to spread the Gospel in China; that they were putting the emphasis now on the technical minutiae of Church organization with the objective of reproducing in China a complete reflex of the Americanized church. . . . [pp. 13 f.].

4. Through his reports, alarms and investigations on "open membership"—a phrase most of them had never heard before, and which is almost untranslatable into Chinese—the impression was given that the Disciples of Christ stood in pharisaic aloofness from other Communions— and were demanding of the Mission Churches an attitude of exclusion toward other evangelical churches. . . . they could not follow his argument, except in the point that a Methodist or Presbyterian must not be recognized as a Christian in a Church of Christ. . . . [p. 14].

The above quotations tell something of the background and the propaganda, also the attitude of the missionaries and the

Board of Managers of the United Society. The pamphlet closes as follows:

> The officers of the Society, acting under the direction of the Executive Committee, have refrained from newspaper controversy on matters related herein. They have courteously answered letters of inquiry and have set forth the facts as required. They are men and women charged with serious responsibilities of administration, education and promotion and ought not to be burdened with unnecessary and controversial correspondence. The Executive Committee therefore, has caused this official statement to be issued in order that the entire Brotherhood of Disciples of Christ may know the truth of these matters and that thereby churches and disciples who have been disturbed may have rest. . . . [p. 28].

The *Christian Standard* reprinted the pamphlet, *Facts About the Visit of John T. Brown* . . . in the issue of March 22, 1924 (pp. 638 ff.) with this parenthetical sub-heading, "This document has not been sent to the 'Christian Standard' nor has its publication been requested by the Society." A boxed, bold-faced statement, entitled, "The 'Standard's' Comment" (p. 641) stated:

> Without hesitation, we say that the Executive Committee's report was written by some one or ones who has or have only the corporation lawyer's interest in the truth. . . . Practically every section of the document is either an attempt to discredit Mr. Brown, to hide behind a technicality or to cover up.
>
> . . . a document that is dishonest in spirit and statement.

This was followed shortly afterwards (*Christian Standard*, May 31, 1924, pp. 873 ff.) by John T. Brown's, "The U.C.M.S. Self-Impeached," which was a prolonged attempt to answer the Society's leaflet, *Facts About the Visit of John T. Brown* . . . . Mr. Brown maintained his opposition to the Society and its policies until his death on November 21, 1926, just after the controversial Memphis International Convention.

The 1923 International Convention of Disciples of Christ was held at Colorado Springs, Colorado on September 3-9. The report in the *Christian Standard* by Edwin R. Errett, later an editor of the magazine, bore the sub-title, "The Atmosphere Was Too Light for Heavy Work." The report of John T. Brown was still an issue. Mr. Errett's convention report stated (*Christian Standard*, September 22, 1923, p. 1465):

When the Board of Managers was organized, W. A. Shullenberger, of Des Moines, was elected chairman, and Mr. [John T.] Brown was dropped from the Executive Committee. It was evident that in placing P. H. Welshimer on the Board of Managers and upon the Executive Committee the leaders of the society hoped to placate those who have been demanding reform. It is not at all clear that either the Board or the Executive Committee has been strengthened.

In addition to such comment, the *Standard* published the Colorado Springs Convention address of Raphael H. Miller, a prominent pastor, then of Kansas City, Missouri. Mr. Miller said, "In the United Christian Missionary Society we have a democratically formed organization through which the will of the brotherhood in missions and benevolence may be known and done" (*Christian Standard*, September 22, 1923, p. 1462).

Mr. Errett replied to that pertinent observation the next week (*Christian Standard*, September 29, 1923, p. 1502) in an article entitled, "Organization Can Not Be the Test of Our Unity." He stated it as his conviction that "this speech is an effort to answer John T. Brown without going to the trouble of taking up Mr. Brown's charges in detail."

The 1924 International Convention met in Cleveland, Ohio, on October 14-19. It was a good convention with little to distract and a fine feeling prevailed. The *Christian Standard* did not participate in it. Z. T. Sweeney offered what was called a "peace resolution." A substitute resolution, approved by the Cleveland Convention, said: "In view of the fact that some misunderstanding exists between the management of our organized agencies and certain brethren and churches, and in order to achieve the fullest co-operation of the whole brotherhood . . ." (*Christian Standard*, November 1, 1924, p. 111). This led to the selection of a committee charged with the task of drafting a statement for the next convention in 1925 in Oklahoma City in an effort to bring unity to the brotherhood.

At the Cleveland Convention, the missionary women had the Golden Jubilee celebration of fifty years of organized women's missionary work among the Disciples. A part of the jubilee was the raising of $500,000 to erect the fifty most-needed buildings for the work at home and abroad. The attainment of the goal was announced at the convention.

Also, at the Cleveland Convention, the report of the "Survey of Service" for all of the brotherhood work at home and abroad was made. The report was subsequently published in a volume of 723 pages in 1928 under the title, *Survey of Service.*

During these months the *Christian Standard* continued to protest the alleged unfaithfulness of the United Society.

"The Touchstone"

In September, 1925, the Standard Publishing Company began the publication of a new monthly periodical devoted almost entirely to controversy. The first issue was called *The Spotlight,* but with the second issue of October, 1925, the name became *The Touchstone.* Robert E. Elmore was the editor. The purpose of the new magazine was "to turn the full light of publicity upon departures from the faith and polity of the New Testament Church." The first issue, reprinting a front-page editorial announcement from the *Christian Standard* of August 8, 1925, proclaimed: "Increasing Unfaithfulness of 'Leaders' Demands More Complete Exposure." Several of the issues of *The Touchstone* also appeared as eight-page supplements to the *Christian Standard* with the folio changed. The periodical ceased publication with the issue of January, 1927 (*Periodicals of the Disciples of Christ and Related Religious Groups,* compiled by Claude E. Spencer, p. 131).

Mr. Elmore stated in the pages of *The Touchstone,* and has repeatedly asserted elsewhere since, that he had no use for the United Christian Missionary Society. This same attitude has largely been that of the *Christian Standard* since and is especially true of the *Restoration Herald,* now edited by Mr. Elmore.

Of course, the United Society is nothing without its supporting constituency. Its officers, its committees, and its supporting friends throughout the United States, Canada, and other countries of the world constitute the organization. Mr. Elmore's publications, with their accusations, certainly have given testimony to his personal opposition. The principle themes of his writings in *The Touchstone* were the situations on the mission fields in the Philippines and in China.

A NEW ADJUNCT TO "STANDARD" JOURNALISM

THE SPOTLIGHT

A MONTHLY OF EIGHT PAGES

For the exposure of departures from Scriptural doctrine and of abuses in the administration of trusts,

Expecting to vindicate its right to existence by its usefulness, THE SPOTLIGHT will aim to expose and counteract the evils which

Disturb the Peace of the Brotherhood

1. **By dishonoring the Scriptures**
2. **By fostering denominationalism**
3. **By cultivating ecclesiasticism**
4. **By vitiating the ordinances**
5. **By substituting a sectarian combine for New Testament unity**
6. **By attempting to identify the brotherhood with a corporation**
7. **By warring on the independent agencies**
8. **By warring on the independent press**
   By any and all departures from the New Testament as the supreme rule of the church

THE FIRST NUMBER WILL APPEAR THE TENTH OF SEPTEMBER

This number will vindicate John T. Brown's arraignment of the Philippine Mission by the exposure of the facts with regard to open membership

Terms	**Order Blank**
Single subscription, postpaid, per year . . 25 cents 12 copies to one address, per quarter . . . 45 cents 100 copies to one address, per quarter . . . $3.25 *Specimen Copies Free* FIRST ISSUE READY SEPTEMBER 10	The Standard Publishing Company Box 5, Sta. N, Cincinnati, O. Enclosed find............, in payment of........... copies of THE SPOTLIGHT for........................... Address to Mr... P. O......................County...........State.........

ADDRESS

THE STANDARD PUBLISHING COMPANY

EIGHTH, NINTH AND CUTTER STS. - - - - - - - **CINCINNATI, O.**

Courtesy, Library of The United Christian Missionary Society

This page advertisement appeared on the back cover (p. 1096) of the "Christian Standard" of August 8, 1925. It announced publication of a new periodical that became "The Touchstone."

THE TOUCHSTONE

PROVE ALL THINGS · TRUTH · **HOLD FAST THE GOOD**

SUBSCRIPTION,
25 CENTS PER YEAR

CINCINNATI, O., APRIL, 1926

VOL. I. No. 8
PUBLISHED MONTHLY

Entered as second-class matter, Oct. 6, 1925, at the Postoffice at Cincinnati, O., under the Act of March 3, 1879. Printed in U. S. A.

LESLIE WOLFE SACRIFICED

S. J. Corey's Hand-picked Commission Obeys Its Master's Voice and Ratifies Recall of Loyal Philippine Missionary

ANOTHER loyal missionary has been sacrificed to the U. C. M. S. Molock.

Another chapter of disloyalty, dishonesty and defiance has been written by U. C. M. S. officials.

The peace resolution passed by the Oklahoma City convention demands the discharge of all missionaries of the Higdon type, and demands the retention of all missionaries of the caliber of Leslie Wolfe.

The U. C. M. S. officials arbitrarily reverse the will of the convention by discharging Leslie Wolfe and retaining Higdon and his kind.

Sept. 12, 1925, S. J. Corey officially recalled Leslie Wolfe. Because of a storm of resentment from the native Christians which jarred the St. Louis office, Corey cabled a stay of execution until his commission could visit Manila and O. K. their master's decree.

March 12, Mr. Corey's vacationist obediently cabled him as follows:

"Executive Committee action sustained. Wolfe must be recalled immediately. This is imperative."

April 1 the secretaries officially announced in the *Christian Evangelist*: "Mr. and Mrs. Wolfe will retire from the service of the Society."

The Wolfe case is but another symptom of the disease, only another example proving the doctrinal and moral decay of the U. C. M. S.

How long will a great people put up with this abomination of desolation?

DISLOYALTY

Month by month, piling up mountain high, the evidence accumulates, proving the gross unfaithfulness and incompetency of U. C. M. S. officials.

According to the testimony of the Ohio Secretary of State they have been operating illegally from the beginning.

They have misused special funds and trust funds.

They have blacklisted and boycotted good ministers of Christ because they would not submit to the U. C. M. S. yoke.

They have broken the peace and unity of local churches by their policy of rule or ruin.

They have hamstrung State mission work in pursuit of their own selfish ends.

They have made war on free agencies which are engaged in missionary and benevolent work independent of their domination.

They have misrepresented and compromised the churches of Christ in sectarian alliances.

They have exerted their full influence to nullify our plea and denominationalize the Restoration movement.

They have built up and are ruthlessly operating a centralized ecclesiastical machine.

They have denominationalized the foreign mission work under their control, introducing open membership and other sectarian inventions.

They have filled mission stations with so-called modernists, squeezing out missionaries who are loyal to New Testament teaching.

They are in intimate bonds of harmony with Morrisonism and Ainslieism, the radical cult which is destroying the purity and unity of the brotherhood.

DISHONESTY

The disloyalty of U. C. M. S. officials is equaled only by their dishonesty. They are prize men in the art of pious deception. Their methods are secret diplomacy, suppression of facts, honey-tongued "explanations" and expert "interpretations."

Why did not S. J. Corey honestly give the facts in the Wolfe case to the people? Why did he not state that Leslie Wolfe is not in sympathy with the secretaries' policy of modernism, federation and open membership, and that because he could not co-operate in

this policy they judged it wise to call him home?

Instead of squarely stating this fact like men, the officials hide behind a tangled skein of deceptive, untruthful phrases such as "incompatibility," "uncompromising attitude," "display of temper" and "unethical propaganda."

The sad part of it is that so many good people have no inclination to take the time to sift these things to the bottom, and softly accept what gentlemen of guile pour into them.

DEFIANCE

U. C. M. S. officials will brook no interference from the brotherhood.

Ordered by the St. Louis convention in 1920 to call home open-membership missionaries and clean house, they defied the will of the people and repudiated the convention resolution.

Ordered by their own board of managers through the Sweeney resolution in 1922 to call home open-membership missionaries and clean house, they "interpreted" the resolution to mean precisely the opposite from what it said, and worked more vigorously to fill the mission stations with open-membership hirelings.

Ordered by the Oklahoma City convention to call home open-membership missionaries and clean house, they "interpreted" the peace resolution and proceeded to recall loyal missionaries and decorate the Higdons and Pauls.

COREY TO STIPP

"We were disappointed in the resolutions which were passed [peace resolution] but we are trusting that the work will go on without interruption and just as before on all the fields."—Letter dated Oct. 27, 1925.

"I COVET SUCH MEN"

Upon learning of the "nefarious petition" (as he correctly dubbed it) which the Higdon group had signed for the recall of Leslie Wolfe, a distinguished leader of a denominational board (immersionist) wrote Mr. Wolfe as follows:

"Praise the Lord for such stalwart defenders of the faith as you are. I am standing shoulder to shoulder with you. . . . I covet such men as you for the cause. If this scheme really succeeds, and your Board can be so blind as to accede to such a request, how about considering a possible call here? . . . Thank God with what courage that He has called you to suffer for His name's sake. Thank God for the loyal Filipinos who are defending you in your position."

COREY TO STIPP

"The whole situation is a sad one. But we must always remember that not many years back most of us looked at this thing very much as these brethren do now. . . . We have opposed such a resolution from the very beginning [the peace resolution], and now it remains to be seen what can be done."—Letter dated Nov. 30, 1925.

Courtesy, Library of The United Christian Missionary Society

A cover page of "The Touchstone" (April, 1926) showing the attack that was made on the foreign missions program of the United Society through Stephen J. Corey, a vice-president.

SUPPLEMENT TO THE AUG. 14, 1926

CHRISTIAN STANDARD

A CALL TO ACTION

To All Who Accept Christ Alone as Their Creed, Rejecting All Authority that Is in Conflict with His Word, Greeting

BRETHREN AND SISTERS:—We address you in an emergency that threatens disaster to the cause we love—the restoration of New Testament doctrine and ideals.

Three times have well-known champions of our cause secured adoption by the convention of resolutions that, if carried out, would have severed all connection of the Society with those of its employees who are committed to open membership and prevented the employment of any such in the future. Three times that vote has been defied by a group of men who favor this divisive and unscriptural thing, and are able, in some hidden manner, to control the policies of the Society.

The resolution of the Peace Conference Committee, adopted at Oklahoma City in October, 1925, was the latest to be thus set aside. That story is as follows:

The Cleveland Convention, at the instance of the late Z. T. Sweeney, and others, provided for a "Peace Conference Committee" which would hear what occasions for discord there might be over missionary policies, and report them, suggesting a remedy. The following well-known and highly respected disciples were named on that committee: Claude E. Hill, Mrs. C. F. Latshaw, Thomas C. Howe, M. M. Amunson and Will F. Shaw. A commission of five brethren met this Peace Conference Committee and, represented that the cause of disturbance and discord is the persistent and underhand working of a factionist minority who favor the reception of unimmersed persons into churches of Christ. It was urged that all missionaries in the employ of missionary societies, who are identified with this contention, ought to be released from service and no more such employed.

The Peace Conference Committee heard with consideration, and, in its report to the convention, urged the course that had been suggested. In spite of the combined opposition of those known to favor

open membership and those connected officially with the United Christian Missionary Society, the committee's report was adopted by an overwhelming majority. It was left to the officials, who had opposed its passage, to carry out the expressed wish of the convention.

At a meeting of the Board of Managers of the Society held in St. Louis on December 4 and 5, thereafter, an "interpretation" was adopted that rendered the resolution null and void.

The resolution asked that those "committed to the belief in or practice of the reception of unimmersed persons into churches of Christ" be recalled. The interpretation adopted was to the effect that "committed to belief in" should mean only "such open agitation as would prove divisive."

Almost simultaneously, while the Board of Managers was being induced to adopt this interpretation, a group of representative open-membership advocates met in conference at Columbus, O., and laid plans to rally a "committee of one thousand" of their allies and go to the convention at Memphis in November, 1926, to attempt to destroy the Peace Committee Resolution.

It seems clear from this and other evidences that the entire open-membership constituency, in-

cluding the management of the United Christian Missionary Society and the troublesome minority already mentioned, are aroused and massed for such action as would not only seize and divert the funds and properties controlled by the Society, but would also, in the eyes of the world, place the brand of open membership upon the churches of the Restoration Movement.

The success of this effort means the surrender of the older agencies, now operating under the United Christian Missionary Society, with all their funds and prestige, into the hands of the deadliest enemies of the faith. For in the group mentioned are those who reject the Scriptures as a rule of faith and practice, scoff at the virgin birth and the resurrection of the Lord, as taught in the Scriptures, rank Jesus with the leading teachers of the heathen world. This is not only a raid on resources that are the common property of us all, but it is an assault on the citadel of the Restoration cause, the Bible as the guide in faith and practice.

This is the emergency concerning which we address you.

What shall be done about it? Unquestionably we are at a crisis. Quick action is required.

We call upon all who are deter-

mined to uphold the plea for unconditional surrender to the will of God as revealed in His word to join together and assist in making these facts known to every soul in our brotherhood that every loyal disciple may be aroused to a full sense of the danger to a sacred cause dear to us all.

This call will be offered for publication in every paper accessible to the brotherhood and distributed wherever our people are to be found, to the full extent of our ability and facilities. We invite every loyal advocate of the Restoration cause to join with us in an endeavor to secure for its contents the widest possible publicity.

Our committee proposes no "attack" on any person, office or organization. It will neither lead in nor suggest any "political" gesture of any sort. Our task is a far larger and more important one. The challenge we are accepting is the championship and defense of the Restoration movement.

Our aim is merely to turn on the light. This done, we are willing to abide the results. *We most earnestly urge upon all to be in attendance at Memphis, November 9-17 inclusive, to aid in the protection of the interests now in jeopardy, and in the rededication of them all, and of ourselves, to the service of Christ and His gospel.*

If you think it advisable that action be taken to this end, and that all act together at this time as here proposed, please send us a message that you will help, and you will be kept informed as the movement progresses.

Prompt action is required.

(Signed) W. R. WALKER,
    P. H. WELSHIMER,
    MARK COLLIS,
    WM. E. SWEENEY,
    S. S. LAPPIN, Sec.

"Committee on Future Action," Appointed from a Larger Group Met for Conference at Indianapolis, June 14 and 15. Dated LOUISVILLE, Ky., July 1, 1926.

THE PEACE RESOLUTION

(Adopted at Oklahoma City, Oct. 1925)

1. That no person be employed by the United Christian Missionary Society as its representative who has committed himself or herself to belief in, or practice of, the reception of unimmersed persons into the membership of churches of Christ.

2. That if any person is now in the employment of the United Christian Missionary Society as representative who has committed himself or herself to belief in, or practice of, the reception of unimmersed persons into the membership of churches of Christ, the relationship of that person to the United Christian Missionary Society be severed as employee. And that this be done as soon as possible, with full consideration given to the interests of the person involved, without jeopardy to the work of the Society.

For the service of the brethren of the "Committee on Future Action," whose "Call to Action" is printed above, and for the host whose position they represent, the CHRISTIAN STANDARD offers the use of a supplement, similar to this, which they may use partly or in whole, for the purpose of publicity for their cause of spreading abroad the truth, as often as they desire it, from now until the Convention in Memphis, Tenn., November 9-17.

Courtesy, Library of The United Christian Missionary Society

Pages of "The Touchstone" also appeared as a supplement to the "Christian Standard." This cover page from the issue of August 14, 1926, shows how such propaganda supplements began.

I happened to be the foreign secretary of the United Society during the publication of *The Touchstone*. I carried on the correspondence for the Society with the Philippines and for part of the time with China. So, Mr. Elmore attacked me personally. He accused me of being "the master-hand" and gave me full credit for "the betrayal of our people."

A keen observer of brotherhood affairs in those years was William B. Clemmer, then the circulation manager of *The Christian-Evangelist*. He attended a large number of the state conventions every year and was in a position to get the viewpoint of both ministers and lay people generally. His regular column, "The Circulation Man Says:—" in *The Christian-Evangelist* of May 13, 1926 (p. 608) stated:

Journalistic Religious Bushwacking—
Shall History Repeat Itself?

Disciples of Christ are being treated to the debacle of religious bushwacking—a sorry time for strife among brethren. A triune journalism—three papers from the same press, motivated by the same minds, though one be made the scapegoat, the three agree in one—assails the integrity of the brotherhood, in a program to frustrate unity of action in building the Church of Christ. Feature news loudly heralded must be read with a color screen; rhetorical flourish is made to do duty for sound reason; . . . earnest Christian workers are led into confusion and controversy; the church lags, in spots, through uncertainty and leadership with half-heart halts in making disciples; while divisive reactions ofttimes follow in the local church. The main issue is fogged and full play is given the psychology of prejudice in creating support for divisive movements. . . .

Individual initiative, "Christian liberty" and so-called "Free Agencies" may not be stifled, certainly. But we may rightly ask, "With what body do they come?" Stop and think! Do not the "Associated Free Agencies" proclaim in fact a definite organized program to parallel existing brotherhood agencies . . . with appeal in the local church to its distress? And is not this that sort of schism decried in the New Testament . . . ? It will not do to urge the specious argument that these are not the "Church." The Church is the sum of all its expressions. In these the Church expresses itself in obedience to the last command of Jesus. Shall we then go on to futility and shall history repeat itself in making for permanent divisions?

The Verdict of the Disciples—
"That We May Centralize upon the One Thing!"

Every movement will ultimately go to its own place. The great body of Disciples of Christ are united in faith and action. The presi-

30105

dent of one of our coming State conventions recently wrote as follows, "I am writing to you and to other publishers requesting . . . that no controversial literature be distributed during the convention. This in order that we may centralize upon the one thing before us." The desire for peace, unity and progress is dominant in the hearts of our leaders— ministers and laymen. In every State Convention this year this is the verdict of Disciples of Christ. Will we go forward together with the "grace of consideration"; in the strength of Christian "Inclusiveness" united in heart and soul though differing in personality and preference; free in the one spirit of Christ, free from the bondage of . . . suspicion; free in the voluntary subjection of every power that Christ may be made perfect in redemptive experience in all life and in all the world, through a harmonious working together of the body of Christ in Love! Thus we fulfill the meaning of the history and mission of the Disciples of Christ! And thus only! This is the verdict of Disciples of Christ—that we may "centralize upon one thing"—building the Church of Christ in all the world!

The June, 1926, issue of *The Touchstone* (p. 5) answered Mr. Clemmer in an item entitled, "Mr. Clemmer—Proxy." The reply stated, in conclusion, that "By reasons of his 'unusual qualifications' Mr. Clemmer is an exceptional asset to the *Christian-Evangelist.*"

Chapter 4

THE OKLAHOMA CITY AND
MEMPHIS CONVENTIONS

The Oklahoma City International Convention, October 6-11, 1925, was an exciting one because the Peace Commission, authorized at the Cleveland Convention the year before, made its report. The Oklahoma City sessions were well attended. The constant propaganda of the *Christian Standard* preceding the convention had attracted many people to the sessions who were disturbed and fearful for the unity of the brotherhood. In one of the early business sessions, the Peace Commission resolution was presented. There was one clause in it which created much controversy. The section which contained the clause follows (*Christian Standard,* October 24, 1925, p. 2235; *World Call,* November, 1925, p. 54):

1. That no person be employed by the United Christian Missionary Society as its representative who has committed himself or herself to belief in, or practice of, the reception of unimmersed persons into the membership of Churches of Christ.

2. That if any person is now in the employment of the United Christian Missionary Society as representative who has committed himself or herself to belief in, or practice of, the reception of unimmersed persons into the membership of Churches of Christ the relationship of that person to the United Christian Missionary Society be severed as employee.

The controversial clause called for the discharge of all employees of the United Christian Missionary Society who were "committed . . . to belief in" open membership. Here was something which apparently had to do with a person's inner convictions and the carrying out of which would necessitate certain intellectual policing, which was a new thing for Disciples of Christ. There was much discussion and a great deal of debate. Claude E. Hill, minister of the First Christian Church, Tulsa, Oklahoma, was chairman of the Peace Commission.

Those who argued for adoption of the resolution were: J. B. Briney, Kansas City, Mo.; Mr. Hill; R. A. Long, Kansas City, Mo.; Charles S. Medbury, Des Moines, Iowa; George A. Miller, Omaha, Neb.; Sam I. Smith, Jacksonville, Fla.; Z. T. Sweeney, Columbus, Ind., and P. H. Welshimer, Canton, Ohio.

Persons opposed to the controversial clause who consequently argued against adoption of the resolution were: F. W. Burnham, St. Louis, Mo.; C. M. Chilton, St. Joseph, Mo.; Mrs. W. H. Hart, Benton, Ill.; Edgar DeWitt Jones, Detroit, Mich.; Edwin Marx, Nanking, China; H. O. Pritchard, Indianapolis, Ind., and A. D. Rogers, Memphis, Tex.

The debate was even continued into the next day. A. E. Cory, then pastor at Kinston, North Carolina, went before the convention's Committee on Recommendations and contended that adoption of the resolution would be approval of a creed. The Committee on Recommendations, after long discussion, recommended to the convention that the questionable clause in the report of the Peace Commission be stricken out.

According to the rules of the convention, the motion that was made for the adoption of the report could be approved, rejected, or referred back to the Committee on Recommendations for further consideration.

In the discussion over the resolution on the convention floor, Edgar DeWitt Jones said that if such a resolution were approved it would be an entering wedge for a creedal statement, that is, "writing . . . an enactment concerning belief by an International Convention." C. M. Chilton stated, "It proposes to interfere with the freedom of men's thought," and subsequently added, "it is a dangerous road." F. W. Burnham, president of the United Christian Missionary Society, in a speech opposing the resolution said that he would sign the New Testament, but nothing else (*Christian Standard,* October 31, 1925, pp. 2269 ff.).

Several persons were on the platform awaiting an opportunity to speak, and especially those of the secretarial staff of the Society who had to deal with the problem and who had not been heard. A. E. Cory and I were two of those persons. Suddenly, before further recognition could be granted to any person, R. A. Long, the eighth affirmative speaker, concluded his remarks by moving the original motion or the previous question. He was one of our leading businessmen who had been most generous in his support of the brotherhood's missionary and educational work, having personally given a million dollars to the Men and Millions Movement. He concluded his speech thus (*Christian Standard,* October 31, 1925, p. 2273):

Mr. Chairman [Jacob H. Goldner], we have a lot of other things to do. I don't believe that a further discussion of this question is going to be helpful. I think we should now resort to the original subject, and I move you that we now pass upon the original motion.

Mr. Long's motion meant that the resolution had to be voted upon. Following parliamentary discussion of the motion, the negative report of the Committee on Recommendations was defeated and the original motion in favor of the resolution was carried.

To those of us who had to carry out the processes of such a resolution, and to a host of others, that seemed to be a dark time for the Disciples of Christ. A resolution had been passed in a convention demanding that the minds and personal convictions of those who served the missionary cause were to be investigated and probed. This was entirely contrary to the decision in the case of E. K. Higdon, after the 1922 Winona Lake Convention, which was agreed to by Z. T. Sweeney. The resolution undoubtedly meant, if taken literally, that we had constituted a committee to try the faithful workers for heresy. It was an abhorrent, an impossible situation for many of us who belonged to the Disciples of Christ.

I went to my room at the hotel that night and wrote out my resignation as a secretary of the United Christian Missionary Society. Since I was foreign secretary, it would have been my duty to go to the mission fields and examine those persons who had been working there for years as to their inner convictions. It was not a matter of what they were doing because they were all willing to carry out the policies of the United Society in connection with the membership of the churches. It was a matter of prying into the sacred privacy of people's thoughts and beliefs. I was prevailed upon by members of the Board of Managers to withhold my resignation until the Board had interpreted the resolution.

A meeting of the Board of Managers was held in St. Louis, Missouri, on December 2 and 3, 1925. A long session was spent in discussion of the issues facing the Disciples. The action of the Oklahoma City Convention was held to have been advisory, but an interpretation had to be made as to the course which the Society would take. The question about the practice of open membership had been cleared at the 1922 Winona Lake Convention and there was then no such practice under the United Society anywhere. Also, the matter would be further clarified by a commission going to the Oriental mission fields.

In the resolution passed by the Oklahoma City Convention, the statement that any person "committed . . . to belief in, or practice of, the reception of unimmersed persons into the membership of Churches of Christ" should be recalled was the point of great discussion by the Board of Managers. The serious point at issue was "committed . . . to belief in."

The Board of Managers finally interpreted "committed . . . to belief in" at its St. Louis meeting "as not intended to invade the right of private judgment, but only to apply to such an open agitation as would prove divisive" (*World Call*, January, 1926, p. 38). This interpretation, which was in the spirit of the liberty which the Disciples of Christ had always proclaimed when it came to intellectual freedom, afforded a way in which the resolution could be carried out. The missionaries and all other persons involved proved willing to follow this interpretation faithfully.

However, the *Christian Standard* and *The Touchstone* were in no way satisfied with this conclusion on the part of the Board of Managers and the officers of the United Society.

The Commission to the Orient

Following the Oklahoma City Convention, the United Society sent a commission to the Oriental mission fields to make a study of the situation. Members were carefully selected by the Executive Committee of the Society. The commission was composed of Cleveland Kleihauer, Seattle, Wash., chairman; John R. Golden, Decatur, Ill., and Robert N. Simpson, Birmingham, Ala. A few friends paid the expenses.

Leslie Wolfe, unable to engage in teamwork with his fellow missionaries in the Philippines on hardly any matter, was a source of controversy and dissatisfaction on the field for years. At the request of nearly the entire missionary staff in the Philippine Islands, the Executive Committee of the United Society voted to recall Mr. and Mrs. Wolfe (*United Christian Missionary Society Minutes, Volume 9, September 8, 1925,* pp. 462, 509).

Even as far back as 1914, when Prof. W. C. Bower, R. A. Doan, and I visited the Philippines, a committee of American members of Christian churches in Manila had requested that Mr. Wolfe, then on furlough, not be permitted to return to the Philippines. The Foreign Christian Missionary Society, under whose auspices Mr. Wolfe served before the organization of the United Society, however, took a generous attitude. After counseling with Mr. Wolfe, the Society sent him back to the Philippines. While on his second furlough in 1920, Mr. Wolfe was sent to Jamaica where he helped to solve some missionary problems. After returning to the Philippines in 1922, Mr. Wolfe was our Mission's representative, beginning in January, 1923, on the Board of Trustees of the Union Theological Seminary, Manila (*Minute Book and Records,* Advisory Committee, Philippine Christian Institute, February, 1920, to August, 1927, p. 41).

Mr. Wolfe's recall, however, after being asked to return home, awaited the visit of the Commission to the Orient to study the situation. After a thorough investigation on the field, the commission cabled the United Society thus on March 12, 1926: "Executive Committee action sustained. Wolfe must be recalled immediately. This is imperative" (*The Christian-Evangelist,* April 1, 1926, p. 408).

However, instead of returning home, Mr. and Mrs. Wolfe became "independent" missionaries. He appealed to the *Christian Standard* for support. In endorsing the Wolfes and their missionary labors, the magazine made additional attacks upon the United Society and the conduct of its work in the Philippine Islands. *The Touchstone,* published by the Standard Publishing Company, set the pace.

In one brief editorial of *The Touchstone* ("The Master Hand," October, 1925, p. 4), my own name was mentioned twenty times. A boldfaced sub-heading across the front page of the April, 1926 issue of this periodical declared: "S. J. Corey's Hand-picked Commission Obeys Its Master's Voice and Ratifies Recall of Loyal Philippine Missionary." This headline failed to recognize the fact that the members of the commission were chosen by the Executive Committee of the United Society after careful consideration.

I never answered *The Touchstone* and do not intend to do so now. Again and again, friends wrote to me and inquired why I did not take some legal action in regard to the charges that were made. To this I paid no attention. I had to live with myself, keep my own conscience clear, and try my best to face life and my tasks with a Christian spirit and attitude.

I wrote an article for *World Call* (March, 1926, pp. 31 ff.) entitled, "Baptism on the Mission Fields." It did not deal with the controversy, but with the situation which the missionaries had to face. It is too long to reproduce here. The article discussed the situation missionaries face in pagan or semi-pagan lands so as to keep people from any "magic" conception of baptism when magic saturates the ideas of the population. Also, it related how spiritual ideals must be emphasized constantly, else we may have a paganized church instead of one of penitent believers.

The statement of Isaac Errett from his widely-known leaflet, *Our Position,* was quoted, as follows (pp. 14 f.):

> With us, regeneration must be so far accomplished before baptism that the subject is changed in heart, and in faith and penitence must have yielded up his heart to Christ—otherwise baptism is nothing but an empty form.

In Central China, at Luchowfu (now Hofei), it would be unwise for a man to baptize a woman, because of the Chinese feeling about a man touching a woman not his wife. Therefore, at that station, about 1926, a group of women and girls was immersed by one of the missionary women. In the Belgian

Congo, it is rarely advisable to baptize a person in the native villages at the time of the confession of faith in Christ. That is because one might make the confession while remaining a polygamist or remaining guilty of some other pagan practice. Hence, care must be taken that a new convert is really a penitent, understanding believer before baptism. Because of this, the "inquirers," as they are called, are instructed for some time before confession and baptism.

During 1926 the *Christian Standard* and *The Touchstone* began to build up an enthusiasm for a Restoration Congress preceding the Memphis International Convention. The Christian Restoration Association had been formed in Cincinnati through *Christian Standard* support in September, 1925. Appeals were issued for the financial support of Leslie Wolfe in the Philippines. This Christian Restoration Association lost no time in communicating with Mr. Wolfe after his dismissal by the United Christian Missionary Society.

In the Philippine Islands Mr. Wolfe turned quite a number of the native congregations, who, of course, had no real understanding of the situation, to his side of the controversy. Reports from the *Christian Standard* and *The Touchstone* went to the field and the distribution of these among the confused natives caused alarm and distrust. Mr. Wolfe was head of the evangelistic work in the Tagalog District around Manila. The churches of this district were especially susceptible to his call for loyalty. The larger work of the Disciples of Christ in the northern part of the Island of Luzon, where Mr. Wolfe had no contact, was not disturbed by the controversy.

An incident occurred in the autumn of 1927, when I was on a secretarial visit to our Mission in the Philippines. It will indicate the methods that were used to alienate people from the Mission of the United Christian Missionary Society.

On one Sunday I went with one of the missionaries to a town south of Manila where we had a fairly strong church. Mr. Wolfe had divided the congregation, but a considerable group had pulled off from his controversial aggregation and was quietly meeting in a residence, planning to purchase a lot in another part of the town and continue with their work in a peaceful way. At their request, we met with them that day for conference and planning. These people were thoroughly disgusted with what had happened and wanted to continue their work unhampered.

Mr. Wolfe was there with his supporting constituency on that Sunday, meeting in the church building less than a block away from the place where we were assembled. They had hired the town's brass band for the day and in the midst of our service a parade was staged to pass our building with all the noise and excitement that could be drummed up. A good many children, along with others, took part in the parade. They displayed a banner which in large letters denounced the United Christian Missionary Society as untrue to the faith. They marched back and forth before our meeting place for a long time. Copies of *The Touchstone* were freely distributed among the people!

It was a pathetic spectacle in a new mission field, where people were ignorant about what was going on in the United States. Every possible harmony and understanding should have been sustained in order for the mission work to proceed. The outcome was an uncalled-for division and weakening of the cause.

During this time the *Christian Standard* and *The Touchstone* strongly attacked the program of comity in the Philippine Islands. In one case, an agreement was reached with the Presbyterian Mission so that each Mission would be responsible for a certain large field near Manila and thus able to do more effective work without controversy between the two groups. This was regarded by the *Standard* as a "sell-out to the denominations."

There was a contradiction in all of this controversy. It happened that Mr. Wolfe had been on the committee that arranged the agreement with the Presbyterians some years before. He wrote a letter to R. A. Doan, a secretary of the Foreign Christian Missionary Society, advising of the comity understanding. The letter, bearing Mr. Wolfe's signature, and the accompanying comity agreement which he endorsed are reproduced in facsimile on succeeding pages.

The "History of Philippine Mission Churches of Christ" by Robert and Eleanor Wolfe Hanson, son-in-law and daughter of Mr. Wolfe, appeared in the four issues of the *Christian Standard*

CHRISTIAN MISSION
1854 AZCARRAGA, MANILA, P. I.

LESLIE WOLFE, Missionary   July 13, 1918.

Mr. R. A. Doan
Box 884, Cincinnati, Ohio.

Dear Brother Doan:-

Herewith is inclosed an agreement made between a committee of
the Christian Mission and a committee of the Presbyterian Mission relative to the evangelization of Laguna province, Philippine Islands.
Never before in the history of our Philippine work has the
Christian Mission ever entered a written agreement as to territory
with another mission. There was opposition on the part of some of the
Filipino workers to our entering any kind of an agreement. In fact
this agreement has not the formal indorsement of any of the native
workers. Some of us approached this matter with fear and trembling,
and in order to make possible a discontinuance of what may prove to be
an undesirable arrangement, it is provided in this agreement that it
shall be in force for three years from date. It is understood that this
agreement is only binding upon the missionaries and paid workers of the
Christian Mission, though we will urge the volunteer workers to cooperate
with us in carrying out the program.
We have entered this agreement with the hope that it would greatly
advantage our work, as it would afford us an opportunity to intensify our
efforts, establishing our work in contiguous towns. At present we have
about twenty-five churches scattered over nine Tagalog provinces. With
our limited resources it has been impossible for us to care for and develop properly these widely separated congregations. Most of them are
weak and more than half of them have not the service of a trained minister.
The district mentioned in this agreement is approximately twelve
miles square, the northern limits being the lake of Laguna de Bay and
the southern limits the wellknown mountains of Banahaw and Cristobal.
It is in the coconut district and for that reason the people are more
prosperous than the average. The population of these nine municipalities
with their 186 barrios, which constitutes the whole district, was 63,255
according to the census report. We have churches or groups of brethren in
San Pablo, Pizal a barrio of Magcarlan, Lilio, Majayjay, Pila, Bay and
Los Baños. Besides developing the work in these towns, our immediate duty
is to establish churches in Magdalena, Magcarlan and Calawan. At present
there are three preachers supported in this district laboring in four of
these municipalities. The least that will suffice will be three additional
men for this district - six in all. The four evangelists employed outside
of this district cannot well be spared from their work to be sent to this
district, so that it is hoped that in next year's appropriation provision
can be made for the employment of at least three more men. We have
assumed the responsibility for the evangelization of this district, and
it will be a cause of much shame on our part if after three years we
have not accomplished something definite in all the towns of this district.
A word of advice or encouragement from you will be appreciated.

Faithfully yours,

[signature: Leslie Wolfe]

Courtesy, The United Christian Missionary Society

This is the facsimile of a letter written by Leslie Wolfe, and bearing his signature,
to send the accompanying comity agreement reached with the Presbyterians in the
Philippine Islands.

Agreement Between the Representatives of the Presbyterian and
Christian Missions Regarding Division of Territory
in Laguna Province.

For the more complete evangelization of Laguna Province and with
a view to greater harmony in the prosecution of this work of the Lord,
the following agreement has been reached as the basis of operation by
the two Missions concerned:-

1. The following towns are recognized as the exclusive field of the
Christian Mission, it being understood that the towns are intended to
include their respective barrios:- Nagcarlan, Majayjay, Lilio, Magdalena,
and Calawar; in addition, it is recognized mutually by the Missions which
are parties to this agreement that in the towns of San Pablo, Pila, Bay
and Los Banos, both Missions have the right to labor. The rest of the Province, not mentioned in the above groups, is recognized as the exclusive
field of the Presbyterian Mission.

2. Each Mission engages to restrict the activities of its salaried
workers to the towns indicated as its own assigned territory and will urge
them to help secure the cooperation of volunteer workers to develop in a
religious way only the towns assigned to it, as indicated in the preceding
paragraph.

3. Regarding members of the churches of either Mission residing in
the territory of the other Mission, they are left free to fellowship as they
choose, as it is realized that any effort to force them may result badly
for the common cause in betraying the common principle of liberty, and that
the Spirit of the Lord will guide in the final adjustment of any such problems arising.

4. This agreement is entered into with the understanding that it shall
be in force for three years from date, and that then such further agreement
may be made as the experience of the three years intervening may indicate
as wise.

```
                              (  SIGNED:
                              (
                              (   W. H. HANNA
     Representatives of       (
   the Christian Mission      (   LESLIE WOLFE
                              (
                              (   KARL BORDERS
                              (
                              (  ─────────────────
                              (
                              (  SIGNED:
                              (
                              (   JAMES B. RODGERS
                              (
     Representatives of        (   CHARLES P. HAMILTON
   the Presbyterian Mission   (
                              (   J. L. HOOPER
                              (
                              )
```

Manila, P. I., June 13, 1918.

Courtesy, The United Christian Missionary Society

Comity understandings with the Presbyterians in the Philippine Islands were set forth
in this agreement, which Leslie Wolfe endorsed, as shown. The word "barrios" in
the first section means the neighboring areas, adjacent to the towns.

of November, 1949. The articles were later reprinted as a sixteen-page leaflet under the same title. The Hansons claimed that Mr. Wolfe did not support comity in the Philippines and challenged the United Christian Missionary Society to produce any evidence that he did (*Christian Standard*, November 5, 1949, p. 717; *History of Philippine Mission Churches of Christ*, p. 4). The charge, in one way or another, is continuously reiterated in the columns of the *Standard*.

Two editorials of the *Christian Standard* called attention to and endorsed the Hanson claims. These editorials were, " 'He, Being Dead, Yet Speaketh' " (November 12, 1949, p. 730) and "Philippine Mission History Available" (June 17, 1950, p. 378).

Shortly after the publication of the Hanson challenge to the United Society, Spencer P. Austin, an executive secretary of the Society, sent a photostatic copy of the original Wolfe letter and the comity agreement with the Presbyterians to the editor of the *Christian Standard*. No acknowledgment or reply was ever received. The challenge of the documentary proof remains unanswered by either the *Christian Standard* or the Hansons.

It is the custom on mission fields where the Disciples of Christ function through the United Christian Missionary Society to have friendly understandings with other Protestant groups. This tends to prevent controversies or waste of funds in fields where the areas of population are ten times what any of us could occupy effectively. It does not take an open-minded missionary long to realize the wisdom of such an understanding soon after he reaches the field.

I shall try now to explain the practice of comity in the Philippine Islands. On the mission field where the unoccupied territory is large, the workers few, and any contention between different church groups stultifies the witness of Evangelical Christianity before the unreached native population, it is found expedient to take some measures in Christian cooperation which would not be considered under normal conditions here at home. This is especially true in the Philippines, where Roman Catholicism is dominant and aggressive in its opposition. In such a situation, contests for territory by Protestant groups and other differences among them greatly hinder the cause. Open-minded missionaries and native Christians see this and try to avoid contention as well as endeavoring to cooperate with others in every possible way.

We were late in entering the Philippine Islands, reaching that field in 1901, two years after American occupation. The Methodists, Presbyterians, and United Brethren had preceded our missionaries and quite naturally districted the Islands somewhat, designating territory each would attempt to occupy. Denominational pride was rather high in those years and cooperation somewhat negligible, so that our entering the field was fraught with some difficulties. There was plenty of territory for each Mission, however, and as time went on the missionaries of the Disciples of Christ found unoccupied and very needy fields. There was, however, some overlapping and occasional misunderstanding and competition. Later the spirit of cooperation grew and there was counsel together as to how the area could be better occupied by the missionary groups.

It was out of this development that the plan with the Presbyterians was worked out by the missionaries, with Mr. Wolfe's hearty cooperation. The larger comity plan, however, was with the Methodists. They and the Disciples were overlapping in missionary effort in three of the provinces of Luzon. There was an apparent duplication of effort and waste of both personnel and money with unsatisfactory results. Taken as a whole, the progress made has fully justified the wisdom of this agreement between the churches for the early period, although there have been a few sore spots.

One difficult place, the most serious, has been at Aparri in the extreme north of Luzon. Much capital has been made of this by our independent group. It is probable that more care should have been taken in connection with the native congregation there, where the church building, largely built with Mission funds, was sold to the Methodists according to the comity agreement.

In the exchange of territory, following the comity agreement, the congregations were left free to follow their own course and conviction. The Aparri congregation of Disciples of Christ did not agree to the transfer of the property. Faustino Peneyra, the minister there, had a private printing press on the church property and some residences were rented, both being entirely against the rules of the Mission. This financial interest, added to the fact that Mr. Peneyra became a follower of Mr. Wolfe in his independent work, increased the difficulty. The United Society afterwards gave our native Aparri congregation $1,000 to reimburse it for its share in the building. In addition, the Methodists also gave this congregation part of the building lot which the Methodists had purchased from our Mission.

Aparri was a distant field, difficult to supervise and in a province where the Methodists were strong. In the comity agreement, the Methodists consented to the withdrawal of their workers from two or three towns north of Vigan and several places south of that provincial capital as well as from the sub-province of Abra where, in Bangued, the capital, we both had churches.

The Disciples were to shepherd their churches in these regions as far as staff visitation was concerned. But each congregation was left free to follow the course it desired. The Methodists really turned over to our supervision much more than we turned over to them. In Bangued the Methodists even transferred their building to us without expense as our building was incomplete. There, Paul Bringas, our Filipino minister, became the spiritual leader of all with the two congregations meeting under his leadership in the same building. Eventually all but one of the Methodists were immersed and united with the congregation of Disciples. I visited this work in 1927.

Dr. C. L. Pickett, a retired missionary to the Philippine Islands, now residing in Seattle, Washington, writes:

> During the last three years I was in the Islands, residing in Manila, I had almost as many calls to help in Methodist conferences and supply pulpits for them as I had from our own congregations. I answered what I could of them without slighting our own work, and felt it was well worth while.

One other missionary in the Philippine Islands besides Mr. Wolfe took the side of the *Christian Standard*. He was A. G. Saunders, an Australian, who resigned and returned to his own country.

The Commission to the Orient, which had left St. Louis, Missouri, on January 16, 1926, and sailed from Seattle, Washington, on January 22nd, returned after completing its task and reported to the Executive Committee of the United Society on June 29, 1926. The commission had arrived in the Philippines on February 15, 1926, and departed from the Islands on March 14, 1926.

In its report, the commission reviewed the reasons for Mr. Wolfe's recall. They were briefly, as follows: the alienation of native workers from other missionaries, the inefficiency of his work, and incompatibility (*Report of The Commission to the Orient, Together With the Executive Committee's Charge to the Commission,* published July 15, 1926).

As has been stated previously, it was a well understood fact that Mr. Wolfe had not been able to get along amicably with fellow missionaries for more than ten years before the commission made its report. With the hope that he might come to some reasonable understanding with his fellow missionaries, the United Society, and previously the Foreign Christian Missionary Society, had kept him on the field. The tension had become so great, however, that the commission dealt with this phase of the problem in its report, stating (p. 9):

> With great reluctance to pass an unfavorable judgment upon one who had been on the field for such a long term of service, but with the conviction that the progress of the work demanded such action, we confirmed the action of the executive committee.

The foreign missions report to the Executive Committee meeting of the United Society, held May 11, 1926, explains a little-known action of the Society in concluding its relations with Mr. Wolfe. This report stated (*United Christian Missionary Society Minutes, Volume 10,* p. 379):

> It was reported at the last meeting of the executive committee that the Commission to the Orient had sustained the action of the executive committee with regard to the recall of Mr. and Mrs. Leslie Wolfe. A letter has been received from Mr. Wolfe, sending his resignation, and asking that his daughter, Eleanor, who is eighteen years of age, be brought home by the Society. Mr. Wolfe states that he will stay on in Manila in independent work.

This same volume of the official minutes shows (p. 380) that the Executive Committee voted "That Mr. Leslie Wolfe's request that his daughter, Eleanor, be brought home from the

Philippines by the Society be granted" and authorized (p. 344) "expenses home from Philippine Islands for Miss Eleanor Wolfe."

The report of the Commission to the Orient, when it was released, was soon used by the *Christian Standard* and *The Touchstone* for promotional propaganda for the 1926 Memphis International Convention and the Restoration Congress which met for two days before the convention. The *Standard* even published an eight-page supplement (the same pages that made up the October, 1926, issue of *The Touchstone*) which labeled the commission's report as "whitewash" (*Christian Standard*, October 9, 1926, Supplement, p. 4; *The Touchstone*, October, 1926, p. 4).

The 1926 Memphis International Convention

The October, 1926, issue of *The Touchstone,* preceding the Memphis, Tennessee, International Convention, included a front-page announcement that Leslie Wolfe would attend the Memphis Congress and Convention, bringing with him Felina S. Orlina and Juan L. Baronia, president of the Manila Bible Institute which Mr. Wolfe had established. The periodical gave several pages to an editorial attack upon the United Society for comity, open membership, and what was called "corrupt ecclesiasticism." There was also a rehash, on several pages, of the Philippine situation, along with an appeal to save the brotherhood by attendance at the Memphis sessions.

The attack of the *Christian Standard* on the Memphis International Convention, which met November 11-17, 1926, was a super effort by the magazine.

The downtown Pantages Theater was the scene of the Restoration Congress in Memphis. Robert E. Elmore was one of the chief speakers. Addresses were given on loyalty, restoration, and integrity. Mr. Elmore, Mr. Wolfe, and the two Filipinos were given every opportunity to attack the United Society and its policies. This opposition group distributed an issue of *The Touchstone* to each person attending the opening session of the International Convention in Memphis.

It was generally understood at Memphis that the *Christian Standard* had requested the attendance of Mr. Wolfe and his

THE TOUCHSTONE

PROVE ALL THINGS   TRUTH   HOLD FAST THE GOOD

SUBSCRIPTION,   25 CENTS PER YEAR   CINCINNATI, O., OCTOBER, 1926   VOL II—No. 3   PUBLISHED MONTHLY

Entered as second-class matter, Oct. 6, 1925, at the Post-office at Cincinnati, O., under the Act of March 3, 1879. Printed in U. S. A.

MEMPHIS AND WHAT? By S. S. LAPPIN

A Forecast from the Secretary of the "Committee on Future Action," Who Was also Active in Securing Passage of the Peace Resolution

FROM far and near faithful men and women are asking: "What is likely to be done at Memphis?"

The question is oftenest addressed to the "Committee on Future Action," constituted in a conference held at Indianapolis last June. As secretary of that committee, I may venture this word of reply.

In the hope of getting the propagandists of modernism in the open, where its advocates would stand up and fight like men ought to fight, giving blow for blow, the following challenge was published the following:

Canton, O., Sept. 1, 1926.
To the Columbus Continuation Committee:

We, the committee recently appointed at Indianapolis to arrange a program for a Congress to be held in Memphis, Tenn., the day preceding the opening of the Convention, challenge the Columbus Continuation Committee to debate the following question at Memphis, Tenn., on Nov. 10, 1926:

"Resolved, That belief in or practice of the reception of unimmersed persons into the membership of churches of Christ is a disqualification for any representative public ministry among churches of Christ."

Our committee will select two persons to debate this question on the affirmative with two whom your committee may select for the negative.

(Signed)   Will R. Sweeney,
Mark Collis,
W. R. Walker,
P. H. Welshimer,
S. S. Lappin.

A month has gone by and there is no voice of acceptance. The challenge still stands and it is open to all comers.

But, from the first, we foresaw that any sort of open championship of that shameful cause is hardly to be expected; its backers are skilled at intrigue and secret wire-working, but they have never been distinguished for frankness, courage or square dealing.

And so other provision was made. The following propositions will be presented at Memphis by the men whose names are attached, and a thorough discussion of all the issues involved will follow, the debate open to all. •

THE PROPOSITIONS

I.

"Open membership," the current expression of Modernism among churches of Christ, is contrary to the Scriptures, inimical to New Testament Christianity and subversive of the plea for the unity of God's people by restoration of New Testament teaching and practice.—*P. H. Welshimer.*

II.

The United Christian Missionary Society, as an institution, judged by its record, is inimical to the brotherhood of churches of Christ; therefore, it should be dissolved, the old societies of which it is now constituted being left free to operate under their original charters, and on a common plane with other voluntary associations, and appealing for support on the sole ground of merit.—*E. E. Elmore.*

III.

Any missionary society, or other co-operative agency countenancing or temporizing with open membership, the current expression of Modernism among churches of Christ, has sacrificed its right to the support of all who stand committed to the restoration of New Testament teaching and practice.—*S. S. Lappin.*

The time and place for these discussions will be made public later on, so that all may know the details. The fullest attendance of loyal brethren and sisters is urged. Once and for all this dissention-propagandist should be cleared out of our counsels. If the interests at stake and imperiled by the present associations and attitude of the older agencies now operating under the "United Christian Missionary Society" are to be saved to the cause for which they were brought into being, now is the time to do it. If those leading are determined to renounce the principles of the plea we make, and ignore the authority of the Lord, the brethren have a right to know it.

So much for that.

As a member of the committee that articulated the "Peace Conference Committee" in securing the passage of the now historic resolution at Oklahoma City, I have been asked again and again, recently, what I think will be the effect of the report of the "Commission to the Orient" that has recently been made public.

In reply, let me quote my own language, published at the time the resolution was passed:

"I have been fooled once by the paralyzing of the Medbury resolution, and I will not be fooled again. When the Executive Committee calls unscriptural teachers from China and the Philippines, I will give consideration to their claims."

I did not believe it would be done. I did not believe those in the lead *could* recall those favoring open membership, as shown by John Brown's report. I do not now believe it. I do not believe they *dare* to do it.

The adoption of that interpretation of the Board of Managers (?) served notice that nothing would be done. It killed the resolution. It was framed to do just that. The commission need not have gone, so far as settling this—

Continued on page 2.

ALL HAIL! AND GOD BLESS YOU!

Leslie Wolfe

WE are happy to announce that Leslie Wolfe will be in America at the time of the International Convention, and will be at Memphis to meet his friends.

Mrs. Wolfe remains at her post in Manila with her loyal Filipino colaborers, while her honored husband is spending a few weeks visiting the churches in the homeland.

Mr. Wolfe is accompanied by Dr. Felino S. Orlina, pastor of the Gastambide Church, Manila, our greatest church in the Orient, and by Pres. Juan L. Baronia, of the Manila Bible Institute.

Nothing could so inspire our loyal brethren as the privilege of hearing these great heroes of the faith tell of their trials and triumphs in maintaining the Lord's cause in those far-away, sunny isles of the Pacific.

Multitudes of the faithful will be in Memphis to welcome these men of God, and to give them heart and hope for the great work to which the Lord has called them.

Courtesy, Library of The United Christian Missionary Society

The October, 1926, issue of "The Touchstone" heralded the appearance of Leslie Wolfe, dismissed missionary of the United Society, at the Memphis International Convention of Disciples of Christ.

OUT WITH THIS DIVISIVE THING

THE meeting of brethren at Memphis in November ought to become historically significant. It ought to mark the final overthrow of the coterie of dissensionists that has been disturbing our convention life and sowing seeds of discord among brethren and churches for nearly thirty years. That our readers may the more clearly see what is involved in the issue, we here recount some past steps in the sorry unfoldment.

Bethany Park, 1894.—Arthur Hall, an understudy of Garvin at Butler College, was given an hour in which to visualize the subtle, but elusive, something then known as "higher criticism." Henry B. Pritchard, chosen to respond, answered dramatically with

"Twinkle, twinkle, little star,
How I wonder what you are;
Up above the world so high,
Like a diamond in the sky."

That was the beginning. Where are Garvin and Hall now? Who can tell? And Butler, after years of fruitless wandering in the wilderness of speculation, is under new and sane leadership and on a solid foundation. What might not Butler have done in these years, had she been turning out Carey E. Morgans instead of Edward Scribner Ameses!

Hoopeston, Ill., about 1896; District Convention.—Errett Gates, of Chicago, proclaimed several (to him) new things, among them this, that *the church was set up on Pentecost, A. D. 30!* And among his revelations was the then new theory (or denial) of inspiration. He was trounced to a finish by George W. Thomas, in heaven these years.

Albion, Ill., about 1901 or 1902.—Assault on the Scriptures by one afterward a missionary in another country. The veteran John A. Williams, of Salem, Ill., attended to his case.

Chicago, Ill., about 1904.—Campbell Club (afterward Campbell Institute) formed. It goes out as a rumor that the aim is to place a certain type of man, belonging to a certain "school of thought," in all prominent pulpits, college presidencies and Bible chairs of the brotherhood. That work is as sedulously and insidiously begun. Hiram got hers in Rowlinson; Eureka got hers in Boyer, who fathered Higdon and Fonger, of the Philippines, when H. O. Pritchard was president; Butler had hers in the Jenkins that Lexington narrowly escaped, thanks to McGarvey; Drake had hers in Norton; Transylvania had hers in Fortune. The churches had theirs likewise—Kansas City Central; Springfield (Ill.) First; Fulton, Mo.; North Tonawanda, N. Y.; Oakland, Calif.; Monroe Street, Chicago, and several college churches. And all these are now like the innocent citizen who had bought oil stock and lost his money; solicited to buy again, he simply said: "No, thanks; I have had mine."

Pacific Coast, 1906; Hiram Van Kirk.—The Van Kirk defection was a matter of brotherhood news. Not understood by rank and file any more than many in the rank and file now understand what the "interpretation" of the Peace Conference Resolution means. The Lokens, De Jarnetts and Perkimers followed in that blazing comet's train. Coast churches had theirs, but are convalescing happily.

Illinois State Convention, 1906.—Committee on nominations offer name of H. L. Willett for president. One man present (John S. Zeran) made protest. The brethren blinked, looked at him and wondered what he was at, anyway. He knew.

Centennial Convention, Pittsburgh, 1909.—Old regulars and heroes of the faith ignored for program service and many irregulars exploited, including H. L. Willett, then recognized leader of liberals, and Samuel Harden Church. The *Standard* made thunderous protest which began to be loudly seconded by many brethren who were awakening. The *Standard* then (and since) *hailed by organization agents as a disturber of the peace.* Samuel Harden Church makes outstanding radical address, flinging loyalty and faith to the winds; and is openly embraced by Edward Scribner Ames in the corridor afterward. Radicals beginning to get hands on associated agencies. "Brotherhood Publishing House" launched, ostensibly as a boon to the cause, but actually to defeat and overthrow the *Standard*. Beginning of *Standard's* greatest prosperity—brotherhood awakening.

1910, Guy Sarvis.—Guy Sarvis, assistant of Ames at Hyde Park, in Chicago, chosen for service in China, supported by Hyde Park Church because of certain liberal ideals held in common. *Standard* lifts its voice and hundreds join in protest.

1911.—Sarvis sent with ten good men, testifying that they knew him to favor open membership, but with Medbury and one other telling McLean "we can not allow the *Standard* to win."

1912.—Fiasco at Lombville: Ames cuts Hyde Park loose from Sarvis; Doan assumes his support. The society has $1,200 extra money, but *Sarvis stays in China*. These are high spots only. Time would fail if we recounted every item of the long imbroglio. There was the "Disciples Publication Society," the "Delegate Convention" and the "Association for the Promotion of Christian Unity"—all put forward and espoused by the liberal propagandists.

And all the while a progressive exodus of men from ranks in which they found themselves ill at ease: Hiram Van Kirk, C. C. Rowlinson, Harry Burns, Errett Gates, Loken, Guy, Boyer, Armstrong, Reidenbach and others; peace to them all, and to others who may yet go. The marauders, hard hit and closely pursued, have taken refuge in the co-operative agencies built up by the contributions of loyal disciples, much as a coward holds a woman or child between himself and danger. The rat is in the bag and the bag tied up at last. But who hits at him now will certainly be branded as disloyal, for *it is the missionary bag he is in.*

And the resolutions—three of them, all clear, all sincere, *all designed to eliminate the trouble,* and all voted honestly by an unsuspecting people, and all then, forthwith, *interpreted out of existence, to save the day for modernism.* Who are these interpreters—who had the tools or agents of *this divisive thing?*

And, finally, the recent rally of liberal forces at Columbus, O., and the ambitious moves to take a committee of a thousand to Memphis to annul the resolution passed at Oklahoma City. The germ is iso-

lated at last. It is the Jenkins-Ames-Ainslie group, plus the Corey Burnham-Garrett group.

Let Memphis see the largest assembly of loyal brethren and sisters ever assembled at one of our conventions. And then, once for all, *out with this divisive thing,* and on with the Restoration to its God-ordained goal.

We believe that all the movement to restore the lost unity of God's people on a New Testament basis will go on in any event, though hindered it may be, as it has been already. But we believe that the only way to save the interests vested in the older agencies now operating under the United Christian Missionary Society is to make an end forever of the modernist, open-membership propaganda and fumigate the premises. We are pledged to any rational movement that may be necessary to accomplish this purpose.

*

MEMPHIS AND WHAT?

Continued from page 1.

issue was concerned. Even if the men on the commission had not been—as Stephen J. Corey said they would be—"the right type of men," the very order under which they were sent—the interpretation—made it certain that nobody would be recalled. Had not the management confessed chagrin that such a resolution had been voted, and said lamentingly: "And now it remains to be seen what can be done"?

Would any thoughtful person expect such a commission, sent out by such a board, working under such an interpretation, to carry out the wish of the Oklahoma Convention, as enthusiastically voted? I did not, certainly; nor do I now expect anything from either the men now leading the United Christian Missionary Society, or from the Society itself as constituted.

And yet, in the face of all this, there are those who would ask that the churches tie themselves up to a general convention by the delegate system and pledge themselves to support whatever agencies the convention might endorse and approve! Against all this every loyal disciple of the Lord, and every church that values its freedom, must stand as adamant.

At the last moment comes word that Leslie Wolfe and two able brethren from among the Filipino churches will be at Memphis. (See announcement elsewhere in this paper.) Place will be made, of course, for these outstanding men to be heard. After all the talk that has been bandied about as to what has happened and is happening in the Philippines, it will be refreshing to have present these three stalwart and reliable men to tell us the facts. And it is to be hoped that the management of the Society, responsible for the upheaval there, may be present. They will be shown every courtesy. The brethren have a right to know the truth, and they shall know it.

THE FAILURE OF THE U. C. M. S.

The official U. C. M. S. reports disclose the following astounding facts:

1. For the last three years, 1922-23 to 1924-25 (the 1926 report has not been issued), the Society has expended *in the Orient* the sum of $2,352,000.00.

2. The fruits of this enormous outlay may be seen in the following facts, revealed by comparing the 1922-23 Year Book with the 1924-25 Year Book:

Loss in mission stations	1
Loss in outstations	44
Loss in native worker	135
Loss in organized churches	18
Loss in regular meeting places	22
Loss in Sunday schools	88
Loss in Bible colleges	1

QUERY: If the expenditure of nearly two and a half million dollars in the Orient in three years, with a missionary force of results in such astounding loss, how much more money and how many more missionaries must be supplied in order for the U. C. M. S. to wipe out the whole Oriental mission work?

Courtesy, Library of The United Christian Missionary Society

The second page of "The Touchstone" for October, 1926, had this historical statement on "divisive" issues. It was typical of material that the periodical publicized. Note the following page.

2 (Supplement) **CHRISTIAN STANDARD** October 9, 1926.

OUT WITH THIS DIVISIVE THING

THE meeting of brethren at Memphis in November ought to become historically significant. It ought to mark the final overthrow of the coterie of dissensionists that has been disturbing our convention life and sowing seeds of discord among brethren and churches for nearly thirty years. That our readers may the more clearly see what is involved in the issue, we here recount some past steps in the sorry unfoldment.

Bethany Park, 1894. — Arthur Hall, an understudy of Garvin at Butler College, was given an hour in which to visualize the subtle, but elusive, something then known as "higher criticism." Henry R. Pritchard, chosen to respond, answered dramatically with

"Twinkle, twinkle, little star,
How I wonder what you are;
Up above the world so high,
Like a diamond in the sky."

That was the beginning. Where are Garvin and Hall now? Who can tell? And Butler, after years of fruitless wandering in the wilderness of speculation, is under new and sane leadership and on a solid foundation. What might not Butler have done in these years, had she been turning out Carry E. Morgans instead of Edward Scribner Ameses?

Hoopeston, Ill., about 1896; District Convention. — Errett Gates, of Chicago, proclaimed several (to him) new things, among them this, that *the church was set up on Pentecost, A. D. 30!* And among his revelations was the then new theory (or denial) of inspiration. He was trounced to a finish by George W. Thomas, in heaven these years.

Albion, Ill., about 1901 or 1902. — Assault on the Scriptures by one afterward a missionary in another country. The veteran John A. Williams, of Salem, Ill., attended to his case.

Chicago, Ill., about 1904. — Campbell Club (afterward Campbell Institute) formed. It goes out as a rumor that the aim is to place a certain type of man, belonging to a certain "school of thought," in all prominent pulpits, college presidencies and Bible chairs of the brotherhood. That work is assiduously and insiduously begun. Hiram got hers in Rowlinson; Eureka got hers in Boyer, who fathered Higdon and Fonger, of the Philippines, when H. O. Pritchard was president; Butler had hers in the Jenkins that Lexington narrowly escaped, thanks to McGarvey; Drake had hers in Norton; Transylvania had hers in Fortune. The churches had theirs likewise: Kansas City Central; Springfield (Ill.) First; Fulton, Mo.; North Tonawanda, N. Y.; Oakland, Calif.; Monroe Street, Chicago, and several college churches. And all these are now like the innocent citizen who had bought oil stock and lost his money; solicited to buy again, he simply said: "No, thanks; I have had mine."

Pacific Coast, 1906; Hiram Van Kirk. — The Van Kirk defection was a matter of brotherhood news. Not understood by rank and file any more than many in the rank and file now understand what the "interpretation" of the Peace Conference Resolution means. The Lokens, De Jarnetts and Perkinses followed in that blazing comet's train. Coast churches had theirs, but are convalescing happily.

Illinois State Convention, 1906. — Committee on nominations offer name of H. L. Willett for president. One man present (John S. Zeran) made protest. The brethren blinked, looked at him and wondered what he was at, anyway. He knew.

Centennial Convention, Pittsburgh, 1909. — Old regulars and heroes of the faith ignored for program service and many irregulars exploited, including H. L. Willett, then recognized leader of liberals, and Samuel Harden Church. The *Standard* made thunderous protest which began to be loudly seconded by many brethren who were awakening. The *Standard* then (and since) *hailed by organization agents as a disturber of the peace.* Samuel Harden Church makes outstanding radical address, flinging loyalty and faith to the winds, and is openly embraced by Edward Scribner Ames in the corridor afterward. Radicals beginning to get hands on associated agencies. "Brotherhood Publishing House" launched, ostensibly as a boon to the cause, but actually to defeat and overthrow the *Standard*. Beginning of *Standard's* greatest prosperity — brotherhood awakening.

1910, Guy Sarvis. — Guy Sarvis, assistant of Ames at Hyde Park, in Chicago, chosen for service in China, supported by Hyde Park Church because of certain liberal ideals held in common. *Standard* lifts its voice and hundreds join in protest.

1911. — Sarvis sent with ten good men, testifying that they knew him to favor open membership, but with Medbury and one other telling McLean "we can not allow the *Standard* to win."

1912. — Fiasco at Louisville; Ames cuts Hyde Park loose from Sarvis; Doan assumes his support. The society has $1,200 extra money, but *Sarvis stays in China.*

These are high spots only. Time would fail if we recounted every item of the long imbroglio. There was the "Disciples Publication Society," the "Delegate Convention" and the "Association for the Promotion of Christian Unity" — all put forward and espoused by the liberal propagandists.

And all the while a progressive exodus of men from ranks in which they found themselves ill at ease: Hiram Van Kirk, C. C. Rowlinson, Harry Burns, Errett Gates, Loken, Guy, Boyer, Armstrong, Reidenbach and others; peace to them all, and to others who may yet go. The marauders, hard hit and closely pursued, have taken refuge in the co-operative agencies built up by the contributions of loyal disciples, much as a coward holds a woman or child between himself and danger. The rat is in the bag and the bag tied up at last. But who hits at him now will certainly be branded as disloyal, *for it is the missionary bag he is in.*

And the resolutions — three of them, all clear, all sincere, *all designed to eliminate the trouble,* and all voted honestly by an unsuspecting people, and all then, forthwith, *interpreted out of existence, to save the day for modernism.* Who are these interpreters — who but the tools or agents of *this divisive thing?*

And, finally, the recent rally of liberal forces at Columbus, O., and the ambitious move to take a committee of a thousand to Memphis to annul the resolution passed at Oklahoma City. The germ is iso-

---

THE FAILURE OF THE U. C. M. S.

The official U. C. M. S. reports disclose the following astounding facts:

1. For the last three years, 1922-23 to 1924-25 (the 1926 report has not been issued), the Society has expended *in the Orient* the sum of $2,352,000.00.

2. The fruits of this enormous outlay may be seen in the following facts, revealed by comparing the 1922-23 Year Book with the 1924-25 Year Book:

Loss in mission stations	1
Loss in outstations	44
Loss in native workers	135
Loss in organized churches	18
Loss in regular meeting-places	22
Loss in Sunday schools	88
Loss in Bible colleges	3

QUERY: If the expenditure of nearly two and a half million dollars in the Orient in three years, with a missionary force of 228, results in such astounding loss, how much more money and how many more missionaries must be supplied in order for the U. C. M. S. to wipe out the whole Oriental mission work?

---

lated at last. It is the Jenkins-Ames-Ainslie group, plus the Corey Burnham-Garrett group.

Let Memphis see the largest assembly of loyal brethren and sisters ever assembled at one of our conventions. And then, once for all, *out with this divisive thing,* and on with the Restoration to its God-ordained goal.

We believe that the movement to restore the lost unity of God's people on a New Testament basis will go on in any event, though hindered it may be, as it has been already. But we believe that the only way to save the interests vested in the older agencies now operating under the United Christian Missionary Society is to make an end forever of the modernist, open-membership propaganda and fumigate the premises. We are pledged to any rational movement that may be necessary to accomplish this purpose.

* * *

MEMPHIS AND WHAT?

Continued from page 1.

issue was concerned. Even if the men on the commission had not been — as Stephen J. Corey said they would be — "the right type of men," the very order under which they were sent — the interpretation — made it certain that nobody would be recalled. Had not the management confessed chagrin that such a resolution had been voted, and said lamentingly: "And now it remains to be seen what can be done"?

Would any thoughtful person expect such a commission, sent out by such a board, working under such an interpretation, to carry out the wish of the Oklahoma Convention, as enthusiastically voted? I did not, certainly; nor do I now expect anything from either the men now leading the United Christian Missionary Society, or from the Society itself as constituted.

And yet, in the face of all this, there are those who would ask that the churches tie themselves up to a general convention by the delegate system and pledge themselves to support whatever agencies the convention might endorse and approve! Against all this every loyal disciple of the Lord, and every church that values its freedom, must stand as adamant.

At the last moment comes word that Leslie Wolfe and two able brethren from among the Filipino churches will be at Memphis. (See announcement elsewhere in this paper.) Place will be made, of course, for these outstanding men to be heard. After all the talk that has been bandied about as to what has happened and is happening in the Philippines, it will be refreshing to have present these three stalwart and reliable men to tell us the facts. And it is to be hoped that the management of the Society, responsible for the upheaval there, may be present. They will be shown every courtesy. The brethren have a right to know the truth, and they shall know it.

Courtesy, Library of The United Christian Missionary Society

This page appeared as page two of "The Touchstone" for October, 1926, and, also, as page two (supplement) in the "Christian Standard," October 9, 1926. Content of the pages was the same.

two Filipino colleagues for the Memphis sessions and that the Standard Publishing Company was paying their expenses. It had been stated that these three men would spend some time in the United States and that invitations from the churches for speaking engagements would be welcomed. However, as matters turned out, they returned to the Philippines before the end of the year. Mr. Baronia died on July 17, 1953.

Many Filipino Christians were concerned that their two brethren were coming to the United States. They substantiated character attacks on the two men with accredited documentary evidence, sent in advance of the Memphis sessions to officials of the United Christian Missionary Society.

Officials of the United Society felt that the *Christian Standard* should know about the matter. So President F. W. Burnham asked that a group of *Standard* representatives should confer with us during the convention. Those who met included Edwin R. Errett, then editor-in-chief of Sunday school materials for the Standard Publishing Company and later an editor of the *Christian Standard*, and S. S. Lappin, a former editor of the *Standard*. A copy of the documentary evidence received from the Philippines was presented to the *Standard* group.

They asked for time to consider the evidence. So another meeting was called. It was left entirely up to the *Standard* group what should be done about the matter. This group subsequently took the position that the "two men involved quite completely cleared themselves" (*Christian Standard*, November 27, 1926, p. 632). So the men appeared on the program of the Congress in Memphis. The United Society group decided not to reveal the matter to the convention. There are copies of these documents before me as I write these lines.

The Memphis Convention had provided time for a report from members of the Commission to the Orient on the situation as they found it in the Philippines and in China. They spoke of certain irregularities which they had discovered, things which might easily occur on the mission fields, and of certain misinterpretations of these irregularities. They stated that mistakes had been corrected, that the missionaries were loyal to the United Society and were a devoted group of people who were carrying on under difficult circumstances which called for the support and confidence of the constituency at home. The report was well received by the convention and endorsed by its vote of approval on Saturday, November 13, 1926.

The delegation from the Philippines stirred up much excitement in the Restoration Congress. Therefore, those in charge of the International Convention program thought that it would be well to eliminate a couple of hours of the regular program. This was in order to provide time for Mr. Wolfe and the Filipinos to come before the convention and make statements. It was not easy to cancel part of the regular convention program. However, because the proposition seemed fair, the changes were arranged by President A. D. Harmon and Graham Frank, the general secretary of the convention. Mr. Baronia, Mr. Orlina, and Mr. Wolfe all spoke. The Filipinos, of course, were handicapped because they were strangers and the English language was a bit difficult for them. However, they were given every liberty to express themselves freely. There was nothing of particular importance in what they said.

In his statements to the convention, Mr. Wolfe read part of a resolution that had been approved by our Philippine Christian Mission Convention at Baguio, March 28-April 4, 1925. He claimed that the resolution endorsed open membership. However, his reading was rather halting and he did not seem to complete the statement.

H. H. Peters, secretary of the Illinois Christian Missionary Society, who was familiar with the situation, arose after Mr. Wolfe sat down. Mr. Peters said he felt that Mr. Wolfe had stopped before completing the reading of the resolution. Mr. Peters then urged Mr. Wolfe to read the whole substance of the resolution. Others, too, in the audience asked for it. Under such pressure, Mr. Wolfe then, haltingly and in an embarrassed manner, read the entire resolution. As later published in the *Christian Standard* (December 4, 1926, p. 670), the resolution stated:

> WHEREAS, Members of the churches of other communions are often located in communities where we have the only church; and
>
> WHEREAS, We wish to give them the fullest possible recognition in our churches; be it

Resolved, That it is the sense of the Christian Mission that evangelical Christians who have not conformed to our requirements for regularly entering the church should be listed as affiliated members while still retaining their membership in their churches, it being made clear that they are not regular members of the local church.

When the resolution was read in its entirety no such interpretation could be put upon it as was contained in the first two paragraphs which Mr. Wolfe had read. This, of course, put him in a most embarrassing position before the convention.

As an independent missionary, Mr. Wolfe apparently maintained his opposition to the United Society and its policies until his death in the Philippine Islands on March 26, 1945. However, when he resigned from the Society, he wrote on March 23, 1926, that he had "no intention of injuring any part" of the "work that has been built up here."

Robert E. Elmore was asked by the regular Committee on Recommendations of the Memphis Convention to appear before it and make his claims and statements. He refused to do so.

Approval of the report of the Commission to the Orient was recommended to the Memphis Convention by the Committee on Recommendations. Copies of the document were provided to all persons who registered for the Memphis Convention. Several persons spoke during the open discussion. Mark Collis, the minister of the Broadway Christian Church of Lexington, Kentucky, a supporter of the *Christian Standard* in the controversy, was one of these. In fact, he spoke briefly, or asked questions, several times.

Another speaker was W. F. Rothenburger, pastor of the First Christian Church, Springfield, Illinois. After he had concluded his remarks, he was requested by H. H. Peters, the Illinois secretary, to identify an independent missionary who had some identification with the Tokyo Union Church. Mr. Rothenburger then mentioned the name of W. D. Cunningham whom he had met at the Tokyo Union Church.

Mr. Rothenburger had visited some of our mission fields shortly before this time. At Memphis, he had in his hand a leaflet of the Tokyo Union Church that listed Mr. Cunningham as a "counselor" of that congregation, elected for three years, and showing that Mrs. Cunningham was chairman of the women's work in the Tokyo Union Church. The counselor corresponded to a deacon or an elder in one of our churches. The only other offices in the Tokyo Union Church at that time were a clerk, treasurer, and Sunday school superintendent.

About this time in the discussion, Beverly E. Jouett, a layman of Winchester, Kentucky, asked if Mark Collis and his Broadway Church of Lexington did not support Mr. Cunningham. Mr. Collis, when pressed, replied, "Why, certainly" (*Christian Standard*, December 4, 1926, p. 666).

After the Memphis Convention, I wrote to William Axling, Baptist missionary friend of mine in Tokyo, who knew Mr. Cunningham. I inquired about Mr. Cunningham's relationship with the Tokyo Union Church. Mr. Axling replied that Mr. Cunningham was a member of the Union Church in exactly the same way that they were all affiliated with it. He added that Mr. Cunningham was on the committee which received members, as a counselor.

Mr. Cunningham explained his relationship to the Tokyo Union Church in a statement published in the *Christian Standard* (March 12, 1927, p. 247). Excerpts follow:

1. In 1901 W. D. Cunningham and a few others (mostly young missionaries who did not understand the Japanese language) met in Tokyo on Sunday afternoons for services in English. This was kept up for seventeen years without any church organization or any membership-list. They "took turns" preaching.

2. In 1918 while the Cunninghams were in America on furlough, an organization was effected. . . .

6. Quite a number of missionaries, business men and embassy officials attend the meetings without becoming members. From these are chosen occasionally men and women whose advice is sought. Two of the first advisers chosen were not members of the organization.

7. In 1924 W. D. Cunningham, as one of the oldest missionaries in the city, was invited to counsel with them in evangelistic matters. Knowing that membership was not required, he consented. He was called a counselor, but was never considered a member.

8. W. D. Cunningham has never been a member of any church in Japan except the First Church of the Yotsuya Mission, of which he is an elder.

Mr. Cunningham had gone to Tokyo many years before as an independent missionary. The Foreign Christian Missionary Society had refused his services for missionary labors because he had suffered a slight stroke of paralysis before his appointment was completed. He had done what other missionaries do in his yearning for fellowship with American Christians and in his desire to promote the general cause of Christianity. He had, thus, for years enjoyed the happy fellowship of Christian people in the Tokyo Union Church.

There were such union congregations of Christians in cities like Tokyo, Manila, Nanking, Shanghai, and in other great mission centers around the world. Such churches afforded opportunity for Christian people of different religious beliefs and practices to meet together for common worship. They could thus use the English tongue, place their children in an English-speaking Sunday school, and all could have a happy fellowship together as Christian workers of the same race.

This Memphis incident illustrated the unusual conditions on the mission fields to which all missionaries naturally adjust themselves.

In connection with Mark Collis and his position at Memphis, it will be recalled that he opposed Transylvania College and The College of the Bible in the earlier controversy ("Chairman of Board of Trustees Explains," *Christian Standard,* June 23, 1917, p. 1116). Also, he had influenced the Broadway Church to withdraw all support from the United Society. However, the Woman's Missionary Society of the church, a large group and one of the most generous in our entire brotherhood, had remained loyal to the United Society. Mr. Collis refused to allow these women to meet in the Broadway Church and presented them with letters of dismissal. The Woman's Society was compelled to find another place of meeting. The Phoenix Hotel of Lexington gladly provided the women with a meeting place without charge. The women met at the hotel for two years, keeping up their generous contributions to the United Society. They then united with the Central and Woodland Christian Churches of Lexington. Broadway Church became entirely identified with the "independent" movement of our brotherhood in its missionary and educational work, except that children of its succeeding pastors have enrolled as students at Transylvania College across the street in Lexington.

The *Christian Standard* reported the Memphis Convention as "A Convention of Bad Faith." In concluding this report, the writer, Edwin R. Errett, later an editor of the periodical, said (November 27, 1926, p. 636) :

Many devout disciples of the simple Nazarene went away declaring it the last International Convention they would attend . . .

In short, if we had to believe that this gathering at Memphis represents the disciples of Christ in the Restoration movement, then we must conclude that we don't belong.

An editorial, "The Memphis Convention," in the same issue (p. 638) declared:

Loyal brethren returning from Memphis are at last agreed that the U.C.M.S. and the International Convention, as at present manipulated, are hostile to the very purpose of the Restoration movement.

They are agreed that the *personnel* directing these organizations has so given them its devotion as to be utterly unreliable and beyond sense or reason on any question affecting organizational ambitions. Hence further conference with them is folly.

They are agreed, not only that leaders of the organizationists broke faith and resorted to political trickery at Memphis, but that their followers in practice actually placed the machine, right or wrong, above the principles to which the people have been committed.

They are agreed that it is folly longer to hope for improvement, fair play or common-sense action from this group, at least at present. The question can not be discussed on its merits with them.

All in all, the Memphis Convention must have been a great disappointment to the *Standard* group. Those people had protested the recall of Mr. Wolfe, comity in the Philippines, and the necessity of missionaries cooperating with unimmersed Christians. The publicity had been used vainly in an attempt to defeat the officers of the United Christian Missionary Society when the time of election arrived.

A great many of the people who attended the Restoration Congress were in the International Convention sessions. They consequently were disillusioned concerning claims and charges made in the Congress. Their eyes were opened to the fairness of both the International Convention and the United Society in allowing opposite views to be expressed. A great change occurred, no doubt, in their attitude concerning the whole brotherhood situation. When a vote was taken at Memphis, the United Society's board and officers were sustained almost unanimously.

Again, the contentions of the *Christian Standard* had come to naught in an open, democratic convention of Disciples of Christ from all parts of the United States and Canada. However, the magazine's publicity had created suspicion of our cooperative work in many churches not in touch with the International Convention and dependent on the *Standard* for their information.

This concerted opposition to the International Convention and the United Christian Missionary Society came to an end with the Memphis Convention. At least, insofar as the International Convention was concerned as the means to an objective. From this time on the attacks were directed more at local churches.

Chapter 5

BUILDING UP SEPARATISM

Through the rest of the year 1926 and in the early part of 1927, the main propaganda effort of the *Christian Standard* was for the Christian Restoration Association and its sponsorship of independent missionaries.

Much space was given, week after week and month after month, by the paper to the Thomas Evangelistic Mission to white South Africans. This Mission began with the appeal of O. E. Payne, an American working with the colored natives of South Africa at Kimberley. Shortly before his death in May, 1925, Payne wrote to the *Christian Standard*. He said that no progress could be made in the Kimberley work unless a comparable work could be developed in South Africa among the white people.

The Thomas Mission was first announced on the cover (p. 833) of the *Christian Standard*, May 30, 1925. The effort began some months later under the direction of Jesse R. Kellems, an evangelist of the Disciples. This independent undertaking was first financed by a gift of $20,000 from Mike H. Thomas of Dallas, Texas. Later, Mrs. Thomas W. Phillips, Sr., of New Castle, Pennsylvania, contributed "at the rate of $12,000 a year toward the salaries of the team" (*Christian Standard*, August 3, 1929, p. 727). The team, at first, consisted of Mr. Kellems, his wife, Vera, and Mr. and Mrs. Charles H. Richards, singers.

This evangelistic work in South Africa had a promising start. Two churches, both "anti-organ," at Cape Town and Johannesburg, were the nucleus of the Thomas Mission. They were very conservative and small in numbers. Mr. Kellems led them to accept and use instrumental music. Both churches were strengthened by the Thomas Mission. In all, Mr. Kellems re-

10   (374)   **CHRISTIAN STANDARD**   September 11, 1926

THE THOMAS EVANGELISTIC MISSION
TO SOUTH AFRICA

FORWARDING ADDRESS
THE STANDARD PUBLISHING COMPANY
BOX 5, STA. N, CINCINNATI, O.

DURBAN
THE COMING METROPOLIS OF THE UNION OF SOUTH AFRICA

The Thomas Evangelistic Mission to South Africa will soon begin a gospel campaign in Durban, a seaport city of swiftly growing importance, with a large English-speaking, European population.

Already Harold E. Knott, the advance man, has engaged a hall for the campaign, found a half-dozen scattered Christians only, and enlisted their support.

On September 17, Hugh McCallum, young minister at Newberg, Ore., with his wife and babies, will sail for the field to be the minister of the church of Christ that faith has already projected as a living, growing demonstration of New Testament Christianity in Durban. The passage money—over a thousand dollars—has already been underwritten by the church at Johannesburg and the faithful, but unorganized, few in Durban.

The nearly six hundred Christians only in Johannesburg—all but eighteen new in the faith—are not only shouldering every responsibility of caring for the financing of their own new work, but of co-operating with new congregations, as they are organized in other cities, to the end that South Africa may be an independent, self-supporting brotherhood from the start.

All that the American brethren are called on to provide is the initial proclamation of the gospel. Those hearing and obeying will consecrate their pocketbooks as well as their hearts to carrying forward the work.

THE INITIAL IMPULSE MUST BE GIVEN

When there is a congregation of Christians only in Durban, they will provide for their own needs. Before that congregation comes into being, however, the gospel must be preached with convicting power.

The evangelists are on hand, with their salaries provided through the vision of Mike Thomas, of Ft. Worth.

They know the gospel and proclaim it with convicting power, as the results at Johannesburg show.

But—

A central and adequate meeting-place is a necessity, and the meeting must be intensively advertised if the city is to be stirred.

Who will provide the money for the hall-rent and the publicity, that Durban's white population may hear the gospel?

This expense at Johannesburg averaged $400 per week. The expense at Durban will be about the same—the hall alone will probably cost £10, or nearly $50, per night. No small item, to be

[CABLEGRAM]

Johannesburg, South Africa, Sept. 2.—Five hundred and forty-five additions. Continue until Farrows arrive to begin ministry September '3. South Africa wants only men loyal to Book. Its young folks will attend only such schools in America as are of unquestioned loyalty to New Testament Christianity.—Jesse R. Kellems.

sure, but where in foreign fields has so small a total investment brought such spontaneous and abundant dividends! The investment here is a matter of weeks, not years, and the dividends are an indigenous brotherhood, independent, self-supporting, evangelistic, missionary.

The following will have a part in entering all the South African cities. They have made pledges payable monthly for the year of the campaign:

C. H. Dobbs, Mississippi	$ 5
C. L. Baird, Texas	5
Mr. and Mrs. C. H. North, Ohio	5
G. W. Hootman, Minnesota	5
Mrs. Frances A. Shambaugh, Iowa	1
D. E. Sassaman and wife, Kansas	1
Clara J. Banie, Missouri	1
S. S. Lappin, Ohio	10
Mr. and Mrs. W. S. Garvin, Missouri	1
Edward Scharnikow, Montana	10
Women's Bible Class, Chestnut Grove, O.	2
R. E. Jones, Ohio	2
Mrs. Carrie S. Sewell, Kentucky	2
Mrs. Mary McFarland, Oregon	1
Mr. and Mrs. R. A. Mayfield, Mrs. Fannie Burnett, Mrs. Jess Detterstrom and Mrs. Ida M. Balch, Oklahoma	5
The Standard Publishing Company, Ohio	100

A total, per month, of............$152

This is the equivalent of thirty pledges of $5 per month for the purpose of taking South Africa for Christ.

Needed at once—not only generous offerings, but pledges of monthly support from hundreds of brethren, that the work may go forward confidently, and that the workers in Africa may be freed from all anxiety as to support.

Do we want South Africa taken for Christ?

If we do, say it with offerings. Send to-day your gift or your pledge for "The Thomas Evangelistic Mission" to the voluntary forwarding agent, The Standard Publishing Company, Box 5, Sta. N, Cincinnati, O.

Funds are needed NOW to guarantee the Durban meeting.

Make and mail is your pledge to-day.

I, individually
I, in behalf of

pledge the sum of $........ per month for twelve months to keep the Thomas missionaries busy proclaiming the gospel in South Africa. I shall forward this amount each month through The Standard Publishing Company, Box 5, Sta. N, Cincinnati, O.

Signed...............

Address............... Date...........

Courtesy, Library of The United Christian Missionary Society

Appeals for funds for the Thomas Mission to South Africa often appeared in the "Christian Standard" during 1925-1930. This page advertisement was in the issue of September 11, 1926, p. 374.

ceived about 1,200 converts during the first year of the Mission and about 300 more, later, a total of about 1,500 persons.

Under the Kellems leadership, the churches at Benoni and Boksburg were established. American ministers went to serve as located pastors in South Africa. The number included Eugene O. Farrow, Carroll C. Roberts, Hugh N. McCallum, and Len B. Fishback. Mr. Roberts edited the *South African Christian*, monthly journal, at Cape Town, in 1927-29. Basil F. Holt, native of South Africa, became a Disciple in 1927 during the Benoni meeting. A young Baptist minister, he soon became pastor at Johannesburg. He writes: "Unfortunately the work during this phase was operated as an 'independent' mission and suffered for lack of a proper organization at the home base (U.S. A.)" (*Discipliana*, October, 1948, p. 31).

The 1928 International Convention of Disciples of Christ, which met at Columbus, Ohio, April 17-22, heard an address on evangelism by Mr. Kellems. He was a dynamic speaker. Perhaps because of this, the convention voted approval of the Thomas Mission "with the suggestion that the matter of its budget be submitted to the Committee on Budgets and Promotional Relationships for its advice" (*Christian Standard,* May 12, 1928, p. 459).

In spite of that convention approval, however, the Thomas Mission never received much support from our cooperative congregations. Members of the High Street Church, Akron, Ohio, contributed generously. The Central Church, Pittsburgh, assumed support, at $5,000, for the planting of a congregation in South Africa, while First Church, Canton, Ohio, gave liberally. These were the main, large churches that supported the Thomas Mission. The Standard Publishing Company, principal publicity medium for the Mission, "cared for all bookkeeping and forwarding of funds" (*Christian Standard,* August 3, 1929, p. 727).

The treasurer of the American funds was W. R. Errett, then president of the Standard Publishing Company. He was the father of Edwin R. Errett, who became editor of the *Christian Standard* in 1929, a nephew of Isaac Errett and a cousin of Russell Errett (*Christian Standard,* December 2, 1939, p. 1152). In May, 1928, a committee to handle Thomas Mission funds was announced with W. R. Errett as treasurer (*Christian Standard,* May 19, 1928, p. 472). By the summer of 1929, when financial difficulties for the Mission continued, another advisory committee was named. P. H. Welshimer, Canton, Ohio, minister, was the new chairman. Willard L. Mohorter, also an official of the Standard Publishing Company (editor of the *Christian Standard* during most of the existence of the Thomas Mission), was chosen secretary. Again, W. R. Errett was treasurer (*Christian Standard,* August 3, 1929, p. 727).

After the resignation of Mr. Kellems from the Thomas Mission (*Christian Standard,* December 22, 1928, p. 1289), Mr. Holt became the general evangelist early in 1929. Mr. Richards was the singer, his wife and children then being in the United States. Lawrence Bash, a young American, was pianist. Mr. Holt led in founding the churches at Brakpan and Germiston.

By the end of 1929, financial support for the Thomas Mission had decreased, in spite of the continued high-pressure campaigning by the *Christian Standard.* Mr. Holt came to the United States in May, 1930, paying his own travel expenses. He sought more funds for the Thomas Mission and became acquainted with his American brethren. He soon had many unhappy experiences. His salary was stopped that summer since he was no longer actually preaching in South Africa. So Mr. Holt was stranded in the United States by August, 1930, with his wife and two babies in South Africa.

Mr. Holt conducted evangelistic meetings in various places of the United States for about one year. In 1931 he went to the pastorate at Angola, Indiana. In January, 1937, he joined the faculty of Johnson Bible College, Kimberlin Heights, Tennessee. In the fall of 1940, he began a ministry with the Maywood Church near Chicago.

Thus, the Thomas Mission had little continuance of effort. The American pastors returned to the United States, one by one, for lack of support. Much that was originally gained was lost. The infant congregations, left to develop their own resources and leadership, struggled on with lay preaching.

Since 1946, at the request of the South African churches, the United Christian Missionary Society has continued this work by sending and supporting Mr. Holt in South Africa as its representative (*World Call,* January, 1946, p. 19). During these years, 1940-46, in Chicago, Mr. Holt's viewpoint had changed. He had learned that the American brotherhood did not center in Cincinnati around the Standard Publishing Company. Consequently, he became sympathetic with and a supporter of our cooperative work.

When Mr. Holt arrived back in South Africa in 1946, the remains of the widely-publicized Thomas Mission consisted of six churches at Cape Town, Benoni, Boksburg, Brakpan, Germiston, and Johannesburg with 266 resident members (*1946 Year Book, Disciples of Christ,* p. 657). The congregation at Durban had died completely. Three of the churches—Cape Town, Benoni, and Boksburg—had buildings of their own (*Discipliana,* October, 1948, p. 31). The latest report shows a resident membership of 374 for the six congregations (*1952 Year Book, Disciples of Christ,* p. 754).

Early in 1927 the *Christian Standard* began to play upon the word "modernist." Formerly it had been destructive criticism, German rationalism, open membership, betrayal of the faith, and other terms and labels which the paper tagged to those whom it opposed. Disciples who, according to the interpretation of the *Standard,* had left the beaten theological path, were called "modernists."

Edwin R. Errett wrote about J. Russell Morse in the *Christian Standard* of March 12, 1927 (pp. 243 f.). Mr. Errett became editor of the periodical in 1929. Mr. Morse had resigned from the Batang Mission conducted by the United Society on the Tibetan border. He became an independent missionary. Mr. Errett claimed that one reason for the resignation was failure of the Society to open a new station. It was true that the Society did not open a new station as planned and for which several new missionaries were sent to Batang following the death by bandits of Dr. A. L. Shelton. However, additional facts present a different picture from that given by Mr. Errett.

The United Society had sent out this new group of missionaries with high hopes of opening a new station. Batang was a small town in a limited area of population. It could be used wisely only by a small number of missionaries. However, because of difficulties between China and Tibet, and the great dangers due to the disturbed conditions along the border, the Chinese Consul at Tachienlu (nearest outpost in China), the American Consul in West China, and the State Department in Washington had denied the Society, for the time being, permission to open any new station.

Mr. and Mrs. Morse, feeling that there was not adequate opportunity for them with the Batang Mission, resigned early in 1926. When the support of the United Society for the Morses ceased, they were granted the amount of their furlough travel home to the United States. This was because they had completed, lacking a year or so, their first term of service as Batang missionaries. They began independent missionary labors in West China, not far from the Tibetan border.

In 1927, during the forced evacuation of Americans and other foreigners from China, the Morses started home on furlough through Burma. That was considered the safest way because of the warfare in China. Two items from the information reports furnished the United Society's Executive Committee tell of assistance rendered the Morses when they became stranded in Upper Burma:

On July 20, a night letter was received from Mr. Frank B. Kellogg, secretary of state, to the effect that the American Consul at Rangoon had advised that Russell Morse and family were destitute in Upper Burma and requested funds for their relief and transportation. The treasurer, on recommendation of the foreign department, sent $800 to Mr. Kellogg who forwarded it by cable to the American Consul at Rangoon . . . A cable was received from Mr. [Edwin] Marx [secretary of the United Society's China Mission], stating that he had received a wire from Mr. Morse from Rangoon asking for transportation home. Mr. Marx has been authorized to furnish the money needed. It was our understanding with Mr. Morse when he left Batang to take up independent work in Southwest China that if he left the field for the homeland by May, we would meet his expenses to America. It seems quite possible that Mr. Morse left the field late in May, hence the advance we are making him now will be according to our understanding with him (*United Christian Missionary Society Minutes, Volume 12, September 13, 1927*, p. 379).

J. Russell Morse has written from England that he will arrive in New York City on the SS "Minnekahda" Monday, November 7. We are asking Mr. and Mrs. Morse to visit the office en route to his home. The committee will remember that Mr. Morse has been a missionary at Batang, but less than a year ago resigned to undertake independent work in Yunnan Province with the understanding with us, however, that if he should leave the field before the last of May, we would pay his expense home. His letter makes it clear that he left the field late in May (*United Christian Missionary Society Minutes, Volume 12, November 10, 1927*, p. 463).

Copies of the correspondence regarding the resignation of Mr. Morse and a statement concerning the aid given to him and his family in getting out of Burma were sent to the *Christian Standard*. However, no reply was ever received from the publication.

The Touchstone during 1926 discussed the controversy in the Gastambide Church of Manila. This congregation was claimed by the group following Leslie Wolfe and by those members who had remained loyal to the United Society Mission in the Philippines. A building had been constructed through a gift from Miss Cynthia Allen of Akron, Ohio, to the Society. Measures were taken for our Mission to hold this property. The Allens, too, were anxious that the church be held by the Society. During this controversy, the missionaries of the Society were spoken of as "modernist missionaries" and the statement was made that "Shylock demands his pound of flesh" (*Christian Standard*, March 12, 1927, p. 244).

The attitude of the Standard Publishing Company, through Robert E. Elmore, its editor of *The Touchstone*, was so critical in connection with our Philippine Mission that I am going to refer to some parts of it. One of the Filipinos, to whom Mr. Elmore had written, was disturbed by the nature of such methods and made the correspondence available to the Society's Mission in the Philippines. He had the identity of Mr. Elmore's signature on the letters notarized.

A number of letters were written by Mr. Elmore to Vidal Borromeo of Manila. These were legally accredited by a notary. They were written nearly a year before the Memphis Convention in November, 1926, and before the brotherhood's Commission to the Orient had reached the field.

These letters, written to Filipino members of the churches, contained attacks on the United Society, its missionaries in the Philippines, and on me. The letters referred to the Society as a "hierarchy," which term, to people converted from Roman Catholicism, tended to create extreme prejudice. In one letter,

Mr. Elmore stated that he was sending one hundred free copies of *The Spotlight,* which was the first name of the periodical afterwards called *The Touchstone,* adding that plenty of later copies would be available.

An undated letter was written in longhand by Mr. Elmore on both sides of a Standard Publishing Company letterhead to Messrs. Leon M. Bana and Vidal Borromeo of Manila. It stated that the Standard Publishing Company intended to spotlight the "betrayal" of the United Society. Mr. Elmore asked for the names of missionaries who had promoted "open membership." He wanted, too, documentary information, such as convention minutes and reports.

He added, in this letter, that he would have written to Mr. Wolfe except that his address was not immediately available. Nor, apparently, was the current brotherhood *Year Book,* containing names and addresses of all the missionaries. Mr. Elmore also stated that a new periodical, *The Spotlight,* would begin to expose those "denominationalizing" the brotherhood. A postscript requested any letters from Alexander Paul or myself among the secretarial group.

Another letter, addressed to Mr. Borromeo, declared that "loyal" churches of Manila and other parts of the Philippines would form an independent organization, free of United Society domination, if the Society did not enforce the resolution and recall "open-membership missionaries" as demanded by the Oklahoma City Convention of 1925. The gratuitous listing in this letter of several couples, serving as missionaries in the Philippines, was especially unfortunate.

A long, typed letter from Mr. Elmore, on stationery of the Standard Publishing Company and bearing his signature, to L. M. Bana of Manila was dated December 31, 1925. This letter stated that it was sent as a warning to the Filipino brethren. It was claimed that persons adhering to "modernism" could not generally be trusted. Such persons, it was alleged, would pretend friendship in order to further their plans. "Loyal" brethren, it was asserted, would not have any fellowship with such an ecclesiastical organization as the United Christian Missionary Society.

These are several samples of Mr. Elmore's letters to Filipino Christians. Mr. Elmore was then in the employ of the Standard Publishing Company.

Mr. Bana is still preaching in the Philippine Island churches that are cooperating with the missionary program maintained there by the United Society. He receives a small pension from the regular missionary budget of the Society for his long years of service.

During a missionary trip to the Philippines, shortly after the conclusion of World War II, E. K. Higdon, then an executive secretary in the United Society's Division of Foreign Missions, talked with both Mr. Bana and Mr. Borromeo. The Filipino churches and their members were severely tried during the difficult war years. They have been grateful for all that the Society has done and seeks to do for them in spite of inadequate funds.

I am reproducing on another page a sworn statement from Leon M. Bana, Filipino Christian, that he saw a check for several hundred dollars which Leslie Wolfe received from the Christian Restoration Association of Cincinnati, Ohio, before the Commission to the Orient had reached the Philippines on February 15, 1926. The statement explained that James DeForest Murch, then president of the Christian Restoration Association, wrote to Mr. Wolfe, saying that if Mr. Wolfe desired to be supported financially by that Association all he had to do was to cash the check. This Christian Restoration Association was closely connected with the Standard Publishing Company at that time, both in its organization (in 1925) and in membership of the governing board.

On March 19, 1927 (pp. 267 ff.), the *Standard* issued a call for a separate convention in Indianapolis the next October. This grew out of a Committee on Future Action, named at the Memphis Restoration Congress in November, 1926. An editorial in the issue of April 2, 1927 (p. 323) stated, "The brethren are tired of conventions that emphasize our differences over agencies and that spend their energies in watching the wheels go round." The Standard Publishing Company gave "the columns of the *Christian Standard* to the promotion of the meeting and has

printed the program booklet at no expense to the committee"
(*Christian Standard,* October 29, 1927, p. 837).

Thus began the sessions, not always annual, of the North
American Christian Convention which have continued ever
since. The divisive nature of this convention is indicated by
an editorial that appeared in the *Christian Standard* for May 15,
1937 (p. 416). It stated:

> The North American Christian Convention, as we understand it, is
> intended to be a unifying factor *among all those who believe in the
> unique character of Jesus Christ, the Son of God, and the unique char-
> acter of the Scriptures as divinely inspired and authoritative.* It cares
> nothing about unity with any one else.
>
> If that be divisive, make the most of it.

Sessions of the North American Christian Convention were
made permanent in 1950. In "An Appraisal of the North
American Convention," the *Christian Standard* of May 13, 1950
(p. 298), stated editorially:

> In an editorial in February, we voiced a criticism of the North Amer-
> ican Convention as we have observed it in the past several years. Our
> criticism centered around two points, first, that the convention is anemic
> in its program and message, and, second, that it is provincial in its or-
> ganization and outlook. . . . *The North American can and will go the
> way of the "International" when its sponsors fall prey to the same fallacy
> —that they and their admirers and followers constitute the "brother-
> hood."*
>
> . . . there seems to be a sincere effort to democratize control of the
> convention, and to bring a little system into the election of the continua-
> tion committee. (Incidentally, the convention voted to perpetuate it-
> self with annual sessions, and not to leave the spacing of meetings to
> the whims of the committee.)
>
> . . . The convention announced that it will distribute its own minis-
> terial relief offering, rather than turn it over to some other agency.

This reference to a convention offering for aged, disabled, and/
or destitute preachers was obviously a refusal to use the brotherhood's Pension Fund, the cooperative agency which functions in
this area of Christian concern.

Both the *Christian Standard* and the *Restoration Herald* have
been critical of the North American Convention during recent
years. Another example of this was contained in an editorial,

UNITED STATES OF AMERICA
PHILIPPINE ISLANDS:: SS
CITY OF MANILA.

Mr. Leon M. Baña, first being duly sworn, deposes and says:

That deponent is 39 years old, and a resident of Manila, P. I.

That sometime in the month of January, 1926, and at a time before the Commission sent to the Orient to investigate the case of Mr. Leslie Wolfe and to study conditions on the missions fields had arrived, the deponent was shown a check for approximately four hundred dollars (more or less) ($400.00) by the said Mr. Leslie Wolfe, said check having been sent the said Mr. Leslie Wolfe by the Restoration Association of Cincinnati, Ohio, U. S. A.

That Mr. Leslie Wolfe explained to the deponent that Mr. March of the Restoration Association had written to the said Mr. Leslie Wolfe that if the said Mr. Leslie Wolfe desired to be supported financially by the Restoration Movement, allthe said Mr. Leslie Wolfe needed to do to indicate that desire was to cash the check.

Further the deponent saith not.

Manila, P. I., October 12, 1926.

Subscribed and sworn to before me on the 12th day of October, 1926.

Affiant exhibited cedula No. *54571*, issued at Manila, the 5th day of January, 1926.

Book 4---- Page 34---- Dec 6----, 1926.

Notary public.

My commission expires December 31, 1926.

12/26

Courtesy, The United Christian Missionary Society

This affidavit certifies that Leon M. Bana, Filipino Christian, saw a check made out to Leslie Wolfe by the Christian Restoration Association of Cincinnati. This was before Mr. Wolfe's dismissal by the United Society.

"Provincialism Is Not Necessarily Geographical" (*Christian Standard,* May 19, 1951, p. 314), as follows:

We have felt for a number of years that the "North American" itself is quite limited in its outlook, particularly in regard to the personnel of its continuation committee. It is made up almost entirely of preachers, who succeed themselves with monotonous regularity. The continuation committee selects the nominating committee, which selects the continuation committee.

The opposition of the *Restoration Herald* to the North American Convention is expressed in succinct form thus (May, 1946, p. 2): "The Restoration Herald no more supports the North American convention than it does the International Convention, for the simple reason that the ring leaders of the former are accomplices of the ring leaders of the latter." Even more recently (September, 1950, p. 4), the *Restoration Herald* referred to the "quick decline and fall" of the North American Convention.

In the autumn of 1927, the united Church of Christ in China was formed. This had been discussed several years before in the China Convention of the Disciples' Mission, which approved the idea. The statement of the Mission was attacked by R. E. Elmore while the Foreign Christian Missionary Society was still in existence.

Alexander Paul, another secretary in the foreign department of the United Christian Missionary Society who was formerly one of the missionaries in China, was with me in the fall of 1927 on a missionary journey to the Orient. While in China we met with the committee which was working on the plans for the united Church of Christ in China. After hearing the discussion, we felt, as did our China missionaries, that it would be impossible for Disciples of Christ to join in the united church. This was because 1) churches in the union would be required to accept persons as regular church members who had not been immersed, 2) the organizational set-up was of a presbyterial order, and 3) provision was made for a committee, when necessary, to pass on the orthodoxy or heterodoxy of ministers in the united church.

Cheng Ching-Yi, moderator of the new united Church of Christ, told us in a conversation that the phases of the movement to which we objected had been pressed by the missionaries and the mission boards. He said, "We believe as the movement goes on and the Chinese themselves come into directive control of the united church, that these objectionable features can be eliminated."

Mr. and Mrs. Harry Schaefer began services as missionaries to India in 1913 under the Christian Woman's Board of Missions. Their second term was under the United Christian Missionary Society. They resigned from the Society while on furlough in 1927. They returned to India the next year as independent missionaries with the endorsement of the *Christian Standard*. Mr. Schaefer was well educated. He was graduated from The College of the Bible, Lexington, Ky.; received the M.A. degree from Butler College and studied at the College of Missions, and in September, 1920, had the B.D. degree conferred upon him by the University of Chicago Divinity School.

The Schaefer incident was an interesting one. He had not worked in accord with our India Mission, which was a strong organization with a large number of missionaries in Central India. He worked hard and was able, but did not get along satisfactorily with the numerous other missionaries who were organized into the India Christian Convention. He was the most liberal missionary among the Disciples in India with regard to church membership. He resented the visit of John T. Brown to India.

Mr. Schaefer advocated receiving unimmersed persons into the membership of one of our congregations in the railroad district near Bilaspur. This was where Christians of different denominations were working for the railroad. The church membership proposal of Mr. Schaefer was opposed by our India Mission and by R. A. Doan, a secretary of the United Society, while he was in India to survey the work for the mission board.

In addition, there had been some difficulties with regard to Mr. Schaefer's work. He had done much building for the Mission in Bilaspur and his construction work was excellent. However, he had undertaken the operation of a small furniture factory. This was an individual, private enterprise, against the rules of the Mission since no missionary was expected to engage in other work beyond his missionary labors.

Then there were other problems arising in connection with Mr. Schaefer's work because of his unwillingness to abide by the rules of the India Mission and the United Society.

Mr. Schaefer returned to the United States in September, 1926, for regular furlough. The India Mission was practically unanimous in not wanting him to return to any of the stations where missionaries were then located. He came to the United Society's headquarters, then in St. Louis, and talked the matter over. When informed that the Society could not send him back to India, against the advice of his fellow missionaries, he said that he would return as an independent missionary. He was asked not to locate in one of our own centers, but to take a new field where there would be no competition or controversy. He promised to do that.

In connection with the resignation of Mr. and Mrs. Schaefer, the actions of the United Society were explained in an information report from the foreign department (*United Christian Missionary Society Minutes, Volume 12, May 10, 1927,* p. 137), as follows:

The executive committee accepted the resignation of Mr. and Mrs. Harry Schaeffer, of India, in January. The adjustment of the salary question was left to the foreign department. A problem has arisen which the department wishes to present to the committee. In adjusting the matter, it was agreed that salary should be paid for one year following return from India, or until September 3 [1927], with the understanding that Mr. Schaeffer was to be in school and could not take other work. Mr. Schaeffer left school in February and began working for his own support as an independent missionary.

Although ordinarily the salary would only be continued for a part of the year, Mr. and Mrs. Schaeffer have recently lost a child and under the circumstances, the foreign department feels that the salary should be paid to September.

It was voted at that meeting of the Society's Executive Committee to continue payment of the Schaefers' salary until September (*United Christian Missionary Society Minutes, Volume 12, May 10, 1927,* pp. 100, 138).

When Mr. Schaefer returned to India in May, 1928, he went to Bilaspur, the place where he had worked before as a missionary of the United Society. Upon his return to India he widely publicized his work throughout the United States. He issued circulars with pictures in them. Some of these photos illustrated our work in India under the United Society. Yet there was nothing in the leaflets to indicate this.

A letter of protest was written to Mr. Schaefer about these actions of his. The letter cited his former attitude with regard to church membership in India, his difficulties with our India Mission, and reasons for the failure of the Society to send him back to India. No reply was ever received from him. A copy of this correspondence was sent to the *Christian Standard,* but no reply was ever received and no attention was paid to the correspondence in the paper's continued publicity in behalf of Mr. Schaefer and his independent missionary work. An illustration of the *Christian Standard* support for Mr. Schaefer was an editorial in its columns (November 3, 1934, p. 792), which stated:

> We strongly urge upon the brethren extra effort to provide the pledges by which this mission may be adequately supported. . . .
>
> It is a worthy work. They are striving to create self-supporting churches made up of natives capable of carrying on in their own strength. We ought to be generous enough to make it unnecessary for them to spend much of their time and money in appeals.

Mr. Schaefer died in Calcutta on April 19, 1946. Mrs. Schaefer has continued the missionary work with the aid of her daughter and son.

The College of Missions was moved from Indianapolis, Indiana, to Hartford, Connecticut, in 1928. This training school for new missionaries commissioned by the United Christian Missionary Society became affiliated with the Kennedy School of Missions of the Hartford Theological Seminary Foundation. The building it had occupied in the Irvington residential section of Indianapolis since 1910 had also served as headquarters for the Christian Woman's Board of Missions up to 1920 when the United Society began operations from St. Louis offices.

When the United Society established its headquarters in St. Louis, R. A. Long, who had given the Christian Board of Publication to the brotherhood, expressed a desire to provide a building for the Society's headquarters. However, business reverses made this impossible and the Society was paying high rental for its inadequate offices. When the College of Missions building in Indianapolis was vacated, it was offered to the

United Society for a headquarters. The Executive Committee of the Society voted approval of the offer in March, 1928, and the next month the Society's Board of Managers approved the move. These actions were reported by the *Christian Standard* after the International Convention which met in Columbus, Ohio, in April, 1928 (*Christian Standard*, May 5, 1928, pp. 424 ff.).

In its report of the Columbus sessions, the *Standard* report stated (May 5, 1928, p. 427):

A man asked how far Irvington, where the College of Missions is located, is from Indianapolis, what kind of a community it is, and if the streets are improved. This brought a hearty laugh from the Indianapolis people.

The actual removal of the world headquarters of the United Society from St. Louis to Indianapolis took place in August, 1928. The *Standard* had little comment concerning the move, but from then on the Missions Building address, 222 South Downey Avenue, became almost anathema to the periodical and its devoted followers. Missions Building now houses the headquarters of several other brotherhood agencies, as well as the staff of the United Society. A new wing became necessary and this was completed in 1947. The old library building of Butler College now forms an important service annex to Missions Building.

In the late summer and early autumn of 1928, the *Standard* promoted the second North American Christian Convention. It was held in Kansas City, Missouri, on October 10-14. The first release of the program appeared on the cover (p. 841) of the August 25, 1928, issue of the magazine.

Late in 1928 the *Standard* (December 1, 1928, p. 1217) published news of the establishment of the Pacific Bible Seminary in California. The first session was to begin in Los Angeles on January 3, 1929, it was announced. George P. Rutledge, former editor of the *Standard*, was announced as president and R. E. Elmore as dean. The periodical gave editorial endorsement to the new school (December 1, 1928, p. 1224).

As stated in the Introduction to this volume, 1929 was the year that Edwin R. Errett succeeded to the editorship of the

Christian Standard. His predecessor, Willard L. Mohorter, became secretary of the Standard Publishing Company at that time.

In the February 9, 1929, issue of the *Christian Standard* was an editorial entitled, " 'Disciples' Delegate Duties" (p. 128). It attacked the representation of our people in the Federal Council of Churches of Christ in America, now a part of the National Council of Churches. The men assailed were Finis S. Idleman, minister, and E. M. Bowman, layman, of the Central Church (now Park Avenue Christian Church) in New York City, and L. Ward McCreary, pastor of the Park Avenue Church of East Orange, New Jersey. The editorial referred to these men as belonging to the "open-membership cult" and they were labeled "ecclesiasticism worshipers." These expressions, to say the least, were unnecessarily harsh.

The moral backwash following World War I was on during this time and the United Society, like all other missionary boards, was suffering because of the shortage in offerings. On April 27, 1929 (p. 392), the *Standard* published an editorial, "Speaking of Luxuries," which was critical about the United Society and its debt. The editorial stated that the liability was due to "defiance of the historic position of the brotherhood" and added other accusations.

The International Convention that year was held in Seattle, Washington, August 8-14, 1929. F. W. Burnham, who had served ten years as the first president of the United Christian Missionary Society, was not re-elected. After he was chosen for another term of office in Columbus, Ohio, in April, 1928, the *Christian Standard* reported him as stating (May 5, 1928, p. 428): "I can give you this word of advice as to my own preference in the matter, and express the hope that when this next year is done you will relieve me from these responsibilities" as president.

Mr. Burnham had borne the heat and burden through a time of great controversy and through the years of delicate readjustment necessitated by the merger of so many organizations and so much personnel into one Society. He had experienced the turbulent Cincinnati, St. Louis, Winona Lake, Oklahoma City, and Memphis Conventions, among others, and had endeavored to harmonize our missionary interests, to launch the United

Society, to face the opponents and to carry on with integrity a world-wide program, to the leadership of which he had been chosen in 1919. No man in our fellowship ever had a more trying or more difficult post to fill.

In that Seattle Convention, W. A. Shullenberger, pastor of the Central Christian Church, Indianapolis, was elected president. He did not attend the convention and when informed of his election, he declined to serve. As the first vice-president of the United Society, I became the acting president upon the termination of President Burnham's service on December 31, 1929.

The location of the headquarters of the United Society was a significant factor in the opposition to Mr. Burnham's continuance as president of the organization. He was a foremost advocate of taking the headquarters of the Society to St. Louis when that issue was considered in 1920. However, after careful examination during the eight years in St. Louis, it had been found that the United Society had no legal status in Missouri, as a religious corporation, nor could it have under the provisions of the Missouri Constitution of that time. Meanwhile, the College of Missions building in Indianapolis had been vacated, as previously stated. This building was found to be adaptable for the Society's headquarters. Also, it was determined that the Indiana Constitution and laws were favorable to the operation and safeguarding of such a religious corporation as the United Society. Hence, both President Burnham and the Society's Board of Managers decided to make the proposed removal.

Actually, Mr. Burnham voluntarily resigned as president of the United Christian Missionary Society at the end of the calendar year 1929. The Society's Code of Regulations provided that the president should continue in office "for one year or until his successor is elected and qualified." Mr. Shullenberger declined to "qualify," after being officially notified of his election in Seattle. Therefore, Mr. Burnham was under authority to continue in office until, under a new regulation adopted in Seattle, the Board of Managers might elect somebody else.

At the conclusion of his service with the United Society, Mr. Burnham accepted a position in New York City under the direction of a joint commission representing the Federal Council of Churches and the American Council of the World Alliance for International Friendship Through the Churches. Mr. Burnham went to New York and served there for a brief time. He resigned against the protest of S. Parkes Cadman, chairman of the joint commission, to accept a call to the University Park Christian Church of Indianapolis. This new congregation was a merger of the North Park and University Churches. From Indianapolis, he was called in 1931 as pastor of historic Seventh Street Church of Richmond, Virginia. He continued there for fifteen years, resigning upon his seventy-fifth birthday in 1946, thereafter becoming pastor-emeritus in which capacity he served at the time of this writing.

On September 28, 1929, the *Christian Standard* published an editorial (p. 922), "Singularly Democratic," about the presidency of the United Society, in which it stated:

> Gossip runs over the brotherhood that Stephen J. Corey, vice-president, is to be considered president, and that his friends propose to make him president in fact. This would be quite appropriate in view of the fact that Mr. Corey stands for all those liberal policies on the mission field that have brought the Society to its present sorry plight.

Another, the third, North American Christian Convention, promoted by the *Christian Standard*, was held in Canton, Ohio, October 9-14, 1929. Reporting it in the issue of October 19, 1929, the paper stated that "the program made a powerful impact" (p. 985). A continuation committee was named by the convention to decide as to future meetings. One letter (p. 986) in this same issue stated, "No commission on harmony was needed at Canton."

An article, "Missionaries En Route to Tibet," in the October 19, 1929, issue of the *Standard* reported the return of J. Russell Morse as an independent missionary to the Tibetan border. He and his family sailed from Los Angeles, California, on August 9 for Atuntze, Yunnan, Chinese Tibet. In the article which Mr. Morse wrote, he stated that he was going out with a "highly qualified family" as recruits.

The recruits were Elias Stephen and Anna K. Simonhoff, former members of the Jewish faith. Mr. Simonhoff had received a degree from the Cincinnati Bible Seminary in June,

1928. Ralph L. Records, then dean of that school, stated that Mr. Simonhoff had studied in Petrograd for seven years, in Stockholm for two years, besides three years in the Chicago Theological Seminary, and one year in the Southern Baptist Seminary of Louisville, Kentucky. It was stated that Mr. Simonhoff had received several degrees.

Much praise was made in the article of the candidacy of Mr. Simonhoff as a volunteer for the mission field. It was announced that he would be the living link of the Mizpah Class of the First Christian Church, Long Beach, California. This church, under the ministry of George P. Taubman, had been an ardent supporter of the *Christian Standard* position and independent missionary work.

At the age of thirty-four years, Mr. Simonhoff was older than the usual first-term missionary. Thus one would expect difficulties in learning a foreign language although Mr. Morse claimed that his recruit could "preach fluently in five languages." Mr. Simonhoff likewise had a considerable family of three children which added to his risk in going out as a new missionary. His zeal was unquestioned. Without a mission board to back him, it was likely that he would be subjected to much handicap and embarrassment. Such proved to be the case.

The Simonhoff family sailed from Los Angeles on August 16, 1929, one week after the Morses had departed. The two families met in Hong Kong on September 21 (*Christian Standard,* January 18, 1930, p. 53). All finally reached Yunnanfu, a city in Southwest China, but a long way from near the Tibetan border where the Morses were going to resume missionary work. At Yunnanfu, apparently, there was a disagreement between Mr. Morse and Mr. Simonhoff and the latter was left there while the Morses continued their journey.

Mr. Simonhoff remained in Yunnanfu with his family, suffering privation for something like a year. He became an almoner for the Pentecostal Mission in Yunnanfu and was allowed to use one of that Mission's houses, which was not occupied, for his residence. The Pentecostal Mission also helped to supply the Simonhoff family with food.

Finally, a letter came in a roundabout way to the United Christian Missionary Society from a Pentecostal missionary in that Chinese city of Yunnanfu, a copy of which is before me as I write these lines. In this letter, Disciples of Christ were arraigned for not looking after their missionaries. He told of the dilemma which the Simonhoff family faced and how the Pentecostal Mission had befriended the family and kept its members from virtual starvation. The letter stated, in part:

. . . Simonhoffs came out here with Morses and were going up to Atuntze to start a work with them. But Bro. Simonhoff . . . refused to go farther than there. Consequently Morse had his (Bro. Simonhoff's) support cut off and now he must make his living as he can here in the city [Yunnanfu, Southwest China]. He has been teaching English, but pay is poor. The Pentecostal folks have been giving him his rent free in their house behind the chapel, but still with his wife and three children, he finds it hard to make ends meet. He is a Christian church man, and came out supported by the great church in Los Angeles, Taubman's, I think. . . .

He has been waiting for word from America for months and they will not even write him. It all arose out of misunderstanding between Bro. Morse and Bro. Simonhoff, and no doubt both of them were somewhat to blame for the mix up. However, unless help comes, I fear it will mean slow starvation for the Simonhoffs as they are really stranded here.

Immediately upon receipt of this letter, another one was written to the *Christian Standard*. The circumstances of this unfortunate incident were related and attention of the editor was called to the fact that the *Standard* had publicized the going of this man and his family to the mission field. At the same time the paper was called on to relieve Mr. Simonhoff from his impossible situation. A letter in reply was received from the editor stating that the *Christian Standard* had no responsibility for Mr. Simonhoff's going out or for his support, but that he was sent by the Long Beach, California, First Christian Church.

Upon receipt of the editor's letter, I wrote to George P. Taubman, pastor of the Long Beach Church. He, too, was told of the circumstances and urged to have the church do something for Mr. Simonhoff since that congregation was responsible for this independent missionary. Mr. Taubman answered that his church was not responsible, but that the Mizpah Bible Class had sent Mr. Simonhoff out and the matter would be presented to the class. Upon later inquiry, I discovered that the class had finally raised funds to send to Yunnanfu and bring the Simonhoff family home.

What occurred afterward in connection with Mr. Simonhoff, I do not know. This is but one incident of self-appointed missionaries going out independently without a responsible board back of them. This case was similar to the helplessness of Mr. Morse and his family when they were stranded in Northern Burma and received aid from the United Christian Missionary Society.

On October 26, 1929, the *Standard* published an editorial, "The Pension Fund and Autonomy" (p. 1018), which criticized this new brotherhood organization, as follows:

> . . . we favor the proposed Pension Fund . . . We are especially troubled that the trustees are not aware that they place the entire enterprise in jeopardy by recognizing those churches that practice "open membership" as truly churches of Christ. As a purely business measure, a withdrawal of recognition from these churches should, it seems, commend itself to business men about to appeal for eight million dollars.

In spite of this criticism, however, "Interest in Pension Fund Increases," stated the heading soon published over a column of news concerning the Pension Fund (November 30, 1929, p. 1145).

A two-page article by Leon L. Myers, later president of the Christian Restoration Association, appeared in the *Christian Standard* for November 30, 1929 (pp. 1132 f.). It was entitled, "Why the Associated Free Agencies Should Not Cooperate with the International Convention." Some of the phrases and statements freely used in the article included these: "The International Convention and the United Christian Missionary Society are identified so closely that the two are one and the same body," "entanglements of denominationalism . . . the demon which the Restoration movement has set itself to destroy," "the leadership of the United Society and the International Convention have always been untrue to the holy verities that have been the peculiar life of the Restoration movement," and "the infidel administration of Transylvania." The *Standard* in the same issue (p. 1139) editorially approved the statements of Mr. Myers, stating that his "incisive analysis . . . must command the respect of all."

The *Standard* of December 14, 1929 (p. 1189) announced that Robert E. Elmore was leaving the Pacific Bible Seminary to become the minister of the First Church, Phoenix, Arizona, on January 1, 1930. He remained in that pastorate until he returned to Cincinnati, Ohio, early in 1944, to continue his editorship of the *Restoration Herald* (*Christian Standard*, January 1, 1944, p. 8).

During 1930 the *Christian Standard* continued to use much space to publicize the Cincinnati Bible Seminary. The cover page of the issue of January 18 was headlined: "Cincinnati Bible Seminary Freed of Debt." The article stated that the school had 125 students for the ministry or other full-time Christian work. "Its directors and faculty have," the announcement stated, "adhered stedfastly and at personal sacrifice to their determination to establish a school of the Bible comparable to the old College of the Bible of [John W.] McGarvey's time."

Again, the developing Pension Fund was attacked by the *Christian Standard* for receiving support from open membership churches. "We believe the open-membership preachers and churches are not a part of the Restoration movement, and that they have no right in the pension plan," an editorial of May 10, 1930 (p. 448) stated. The same issue of the magazine featured an article by Peyton H. Canary, Jr., which was entitled, "Will the Pension Fund Finish Splitting the Brotherhood?"

The deficit of the United Christian Missionary Society in those depression years was often the subject of editorials in the *Standard*. Under the heading, "Why the Deficit Increases" (March 29, 1930, p. 306), the paper stated:

. . . there is something distinctly ungracious, if not dishonest, in the effort to lay the blame for the growing deficit of the United Society upon the supposed heartlessness or shortsightedness of the brethren at home . . .

The United Society deficit grows because the brethren do not trust the management of the United Society, and it is a libel on good people for the officers to lay it to any other cause.

Another approach of the *Standard* in commenting on the deficit was to attack one or more of the missionaries. An example

of this was an editorial, "The Higdons Return" in the issue of
July 12, 1930 (p. 670), in part, as follows:

> The total loss in receipts for general fund from sources of contribu-
> tions is $163,664.91, a loss of over 15 per cent.
>
> Naturally one searches for the reason for this astounding shrinkage.
> Even the present financial stringency does not explain a decrease of such
> proportions.
>
> One has not far to search . . .
>
> . . . among those going out . . . is none other than E. K. Higdon,
> the modernistic leader of the work in the Philippines, one of those whose
> teaching was so offensive that practically all the Filipino churches them-
> selves pulled away from the Mission, one who has repeatedly manifested
> the fact that he is not in sympathy with our position. This announce-
> ment of the intention of the Society to return Mr. Higdon to the field is
> a most illuminating commentary upon that shortage of contributions . . .
>
> That is the explanation for the decreasing contributions. That is
> the explanation for the rapidly mounting deficit. That is the explana-
> tion for the atrocity committed against all those missionaries being sent
> out to work under starvation budgets.

Note that the *Standard* failed to mention the fact that all mission boards had lost heavily in their offerings from the churches.
The Methodist Board, for example, had suffered far greater
proportionately than the United Christian Missionary Society
when the former had of necessity to return over 700 of its missionaries out of a total of 1,500. The United Society, under the
terrific financial losses, had dismissed nearly 100 of its foreign
missionaries out of a staff numbering 325.

As first vice-president (since July, 1927), I had been serving
during 1930 as acting president of the United Christian Missionary Society. It had been one of the most difficult years in
missionary history. Every effort had been made to stem the
tide of decrease in missionary contributions, but that had been
impossible.

I had never desired to be president of the Society. I had
been a foreign secretary for twenty-five years and felt that I
understood, somewhat, that type of work. I felt that somebody
else should be president and so informed the Executive Committee and the Board of Managers. However, during the International Convention in Washington, D. C., in October, 1930,
I was elected president over my own strong protest.

I had stated that I would not, under any consideration, accept the presidency unless some strong man should be chosen vice-president. I wanted a person with administrative experience and exceptional standing in the brotherhood, who would be a companion and help to bear the heavy load in the precarious times which we were facing.

With these qualifications in mind, I. J. Cahill, the popular and efficient secretary of the Ohio Christian Missionary Society, Cleveland, was chosen first vice-president. He had served for twenty years as the Ohio secretary after notable pastorates. He had been thoroughly tried through long experience, was highly respected and a man of deep devotion to the cause. It was a great comfort to all concerned and a blessing to the Society to have him as my intimate companion in the duties and responsibilities which fell upon the officers of the organization. He retired in 1936.

The *Christian Standard* published its first report of the Washington sessions on October 25. Referring to the United Society elections (p. 1023), it said, "In high glee the liberal element that backed Mr. Corey elected him and made a great demonstration over him and Mr. Cahill, insisting upon a speech from Mr. Cahill as well as from Mr. Corey." The November 1, 1930, issue of the *Standard* had an editorial analysis of the Washington Convention which used as a subhead "The Liberal Group Triumphant" in connection with comment on my election (p. 1050).

Thus, under the continuous attacks of the *Christian Standard*, the breach in the fellowship of the brotherhood of Disciples of Christ inevitably widened. The documented evidence of the magazine's constant publicity for such separate institutions as agencies, conventions, schools, missions, and summer camps is a significant marking of a separate church group. In view of this record of many years, an attack on W. T. Moore years ago is of interest in this connection.

W. E. Garrison briefly describes this event in his history of the Disciples entitled, *Religion Follows the Frontier* (pp. 266 f.). Commenting on it in his volume, *The Grounds of Divisions Among the Disciples of Christ*, A. T. DeGroot says (p. 187), "When the Disciples moved out into the larger Christian world, especially on the mission fields, they had to face new problems of inter-church relations."

The incident occurred in 1885 when the Foreign Christian Missionary Society conducted missionary work in England. Mr. Moore, serving under the Society, held the pastorate of the West London Tabernacle which had immersed and unimmersed members. During his ministry the church practiced only immersion and eventually nearly all of the old members were immersed. However, *The Apostolic Guide,* of Louisville, Kentucky, complained that Mr. Moore was "not representing the cause he was sent to represent." The *Christian Standard,* then edited by Isaac Errett, its first editor, vigorously defended Mr. Moore. Mr. Errett was then, and until his death in 1888, also the president of the Foreign Christian Missionary Society.

During this controversy the *Standard* published an editorial, "Concerning Mistakes" (July 25, 1885, p. 236), which stated:

The *Apostolic Guide* copies our article, and comments on it in an article filling two columns. We do not copy this, because much of it relates to questions which are not, at the present stage of inquiry, proper subjects of newspaper discussion. They involve charges against Bro. Moore's integrity which ought to be investigated by the Executive Committee of the Foreign Christian Missionary Society, and the Chairman of that Committee has invited the newspaper complainants to present their proofs, and to bring out all the "reserved forces" which they so mysteriously and threateningly speak of, that the Committee may be fully informed, and act in the light of all the testimony.

. . . the anti-society papers are already echoing, with delight, these wretched misrepresentations.

Another editorial in the *Standard* of August 15, 1885 (p. 260), said, "a newspaper brawl is more to their taste, and will suit their purposes better," and again, "let the *Guide* have all the honor it can claim for refusing to give to its readers a plain statement of undisputed facts."

Then, the issue of the *Standard* for August 22, 1885 (pp. 268 f.), had an editorial, "W. T. Moore's Position," which asserted:

This attempt to get up a new scare on the score of ecclesiastical authority, is as ridiculous as it is destitute of foundation. It is only another indication of the desperateness of a cause that requires a resort to such wretched misrepresentations.

All of which reads like a present-day defense of the policies and actions of the United Christian Missionary Society! The *Christian Standard*, under the editorship of Isaac Errett, *supported* the Foreign Christian Missionary Society and its missionary, Mr. Moore.

At the tenth annual meeting of the Foreign Christian Missionary Society, held in Cleveland, Ohio, October 21 and 22, 1885, this matter was considered. Isaac Errett and his son, Russell Errett (shortly afterward to become the chief owner and manager of the Standard Publishing Company) were in this meeting of the Society's Board of Managers. W. K. Pendleton was the presiding chairman and F. D. Power the secretary. On motion of General F. M. Drake the following resolution was adopted unanimously by those Disciples (*Proceedings* of the Foreign Christian Missionary Society, 1885, p. 16):

Resolved, That we, as a Board of Directors, do fully endorse the action of the Executive Committee in sustaining the London mission, and that notwithstanding the severe criticism of various newspapers in regard to said mission and Bro. Moore's labors, we hereby express our great satisfaction with the results which have been attained, and our confidence in and gratitude to Bro. Moore in his untiring and efficient labor.

In connection with the difficulties of adjusting missionary policies to the situation in foreign fields, it is of interest, also, to cite problems which arose in the independent missionary work enthusiastically supported by the *Christian Standard* in the Kimberley field of the South African Christian Mission to Negroes.

Before the United Christian Missionary Society was formed, Thomas Bambesi Kalane, a native of South Africa, came to the United States and studied at Wilberforce University, Xenia, Ohio. He then asked the Foreign Christian Missionary Society to send him as a missionary to his people in the Kimberley section. This was in 1917. The Society was already committed for more work than it could do in the great Belgian Congo field and, in addition, did not approve of Mr. Kalane.

Mr. Kalane had visited the Tabernacle Church, Columbus, Indiana, and interested the pastor, W. H. Book, in his hopes and dreams. The two men met first in 1913. Mr. Book then appealed in the *Standard* for educational funds for Mr. Kalane and the periodical, in the same issue, editorially endorsed the appeal: "There should be a quick response to this call" (*Christian Standard*, October 11, 1913, p. 1659). Mr. Kalane studied with Mr. Book and preached while collecting money for the projected South African work. The funds were banked by a Columbus committee. Mr. Kalane had studied at Wilberforce University for nine years before he met Mr. Book (*Christian Standard*, February 25, 1922, p. 3267).

Mr. Book sought to persuade the Foreign Christian Missionary Society to send Mr. Kalane to South Africa. But the Society steadfastly refused either to open a new field or to support Mr. Kalane. So the church at Columbus, which had withdrawn its support from the Society during the attack by the *Christian Standard* on Guy W. Sarvis (who went to China), undertook Mr. Kalane's support and sent him to South Africa as an independent missionary with the backing of the *Standard*. However, World War I had intervened and Mr. Kalane was unable to secure a passport for travel. Thus, he did not finally return to South Africa until late in 1920 when the war was over. He established a congregation at Kimberley of twenty-four members in February, 1921 (*Christian Standard*, June 29, 1940, p. 622; August 30, 1941, p. 906).

Mr. Kalane did a widely-heralded work among small, native churches in South Africa's Kimberley area, getting them to become Churches of Christ and reporting many additions to the membership. The *Christian Standard* was a strong advocate of this missionary program and raised funds for it for many years. When Mr. Kalane died, another native minister, Simon B. Sibenya, succeeded him. Then an appeal was made for an American white missionary to go to Kimberley.

The need of white supervision for the work with the South African natives had become necessary. W. H. Book wrote in the *Standard* (September 1, 1923, p. 1384) that the British Government did not permit a native person "to organize and carry on a work unless he is under the supervision of the white man. We were advised to comply with the conditions of the Government or Kalane must be deported."

O. E. Payne, elderly businessman of the University City Church, St. Louis, Missouri, was sent out independently in the summer of 1923 and supported by efforts of the *Christian Standard*. Mr. Payne died in May, 1925, while in that service and another appeal was made through the *Standard* for personnel. So C. B. Titus, a missionary who had been dismissed from our China Mission by the Foreign Christian Missionary Society, was sent to South Africa. He was then sixty-two years old. He was under contract with the "African Missionary Board in the Tabernacle Church of Christ" of Columbus, Indiana (*Christian Standard*, August 8, 1925, p. 17). However, on June 1, 1926, the Christian Restoration Association took the "money and good will of the Africa Christian Missionary Society" for the support of this missionary work (*Christian Standard*, August 30, 1941, p. 906).

In the autumn of 1927, Carl A. Roy Lewis and his wife went to South Africa to aid Mr. Titus. Mr. Lewis was a graduate of the Cincinnati Bible Seminary. The Lewises, who arrived in South Africa on October 28, 1927, had negotiated a five-year agreement with the Christian Restoration Association of Cincinnati for their missionary work. Mr. Lewis had not been at work with this Mission long when he discovered that many of the reported members of those churches had never been immersed. So, early in 1928, he resigned to take effect in May, 1929. This was because "open membership and infant dedication were practiced" (*Christian Standard*, March 15, 1930, p. 263). Mr. Lewis returned to the United States disillusioned and heart-broken. He publicized the whole matter in a pamphlet, *The Christian Restoration Association Self-Impeached*.

Not until the circulation of this pamphlet did the *Christian Standard* publish anything concerning the situation although Mr. Lewis had previously reported it to the magazine. The *Standard* report, "The Situation in the South African Mission to Negroes" (March 15, 1930, pp. 263 f.), included data from Mr. Lewis and the denial of his charges by the Christian Restoration Association. An editorial in the same issue (p. 258) labeled the charges "mistakes," stating, "the best of friends of the so-called 'independent agencies' have always been willing to admit that those agencies make mistakes" and "that mistakes have been made in the administration of the missionary work . . . in South Africa will be manifest."

Mr. Lewis visited the headquarters of the United Christian Missionary Society and related the whole story. He claimed that he had paid for his return trip to the United States, receiving inadequate financial assistance from those who had sent him and his wife out and publicized the South African Mission.

It is inconceivable that Mr. Payne and Mr. Titus did not know of this situation, even before Mr. Lewis arrived on the field. The case of the few native Christians in the Philippines and in China, whom the *Standard* accused of being improperly admitted into church membership, fades into insignificance in comparison with these independent irregularities in South Africa. It seems unlikely that Mr. Payne and Mr. Titus, who followed him as superintendent of the Mission in South Africa, did not reveal the situation promptly to the editor of the *Christian Standard*. Here, as in other instances, continuous attacks were made against the organized missionary work of the old, existing agencies while little was said about the so-called "mistakes" that were represented as committed by independent mission workers.

Chapter 6

DURING THE FINANCIAL DEPRESSION

During 1931 there seemed to be a calming of the waves of dissension within our brotherhood. The pressure of the financial depression and the consequent discouragement that faced the Christian cause throughout the United States and other parts of the world apparently had some effect upon everyone.

The Pension Fund of Disciples of Christ began full operation on April 1, 1931 (*Christian Standard,* April 11, 1931, p. 347). Headquarters had been established in downtown Indianapolis, Indiana. W. R. Warren, founding editor of *World Call,* international monthly magazine of the Disciples, served as executive vice-president. A. E. Cory was director and F. E. Smith the secretary.

This pension plan was for the ministers, missionaries, educators, and other employees of our churches and church-related institutions and organizations. It began with more than 2,000 individual members paying two and one-half per cent of their annual salaries and with more than 1,700 churches and organizations paying eight per cent of the salaries of employees who had enrolled in the system.

The *Christian Standard* of April 18, 1931 (pp. 386 f.), had an article by Leon L. Myers (later to become president of the Christian Restoration Association) entitled, "The Pension Fund a Menace to the Restoration Movement." In an editorial, "Will the Pension Fund Denominationalize Us?" in the same issue (pp. 390 f.), the *Standard* said, "We do not believe Mr. Myers has proved the points he claims to have proved." A rebuttal by Mr. Myers, under the same title as that used with his original article, appeared in the issue of May 9, 1931 (p. 463).

Joseph Keevil, then pastor at Marfa, Texas, was the first minister to die with the protection of the Pension Fund (*Chris-*

tian Standard, May 30, 1931, p. 538). In addition to engaging in pastoral work, Mr. Keevil had been a field representative of the Christian Restoration Association for seventeen months in 1927 and 1928 (*Restoration Herald,* October, 1928, p. 21; *Christian Standard,* June 20, 1931, p. 621).

Russell Errett, chief owner and general manager of the Standard Publishing Company since the death of his father, Isaac Errett, in 1888, died in Cincinnati on April 27, 1931, at the age of eighty-five years. The May 16, 1931, issue of the *Christian Standard* was dedicated to his memory. The future of the publishing house which he developed was emphasized in an editorial, "The Future of the Standard Publishing Company" (May 23, 1931, p. 514), as follows:

> Inasmuch as the late Russell Errett was known to be a majority stockholder in The Standard Publishing Company, there has naturally arisen in the minds of the friends of the cause some anxiety as to the effect his death will have upon the future of the institution he built up and controlled.
>
> They will be glad to know that in his will he made specific provision whereby the stock he held should pass into the hands of those in harmony with his policies. He very carefully summarized in the will the ideals for which the institution had been built up, and directed his executors so to dispose of his stock as to place it in the hands of persons who would carry out those ideals. . . .
>
> The brethren may look forward with confidence to the perpetuation of the institution as servant of the cause he loved.

The weekly issues of the *Christian Standard* since the death of Russell Errett reveal the continuous factual record of the way in which his policies have been perpetuated.

On June 13, 1931, the main editorial of the *Standard,* "Why the Lexington Meeting?" (p. 586) discussed the North American Christian Convention which met in Lexington, Kentucky, June 17-21. Sounding a warning against division, the paper said, "It will be nothing less than sectarian if we make of the North American Christian Convention the means of creating a faction or clique within the church."

This same editorial then pointed out that the need for the convention was 1) an emphasis on preaching, 2) fellowship founded upon loyalty to the Word of God rather than upon human institutions, 3) attention to ancient landmarks, and 4) time for a forward movement.

This convention was held in good spirit and in spite of the depression there were from 500 to 1,000 persons at the sessions, the *Standard* reported. Much was said at the meeting concerning problems of the depression. Editorially, the magazine said (June 27, 1931, p. 634) that, "We had in Lexington a splendid demonstration of the difference between the ecclesiastical mind and the Christian mind." This inferred, of course, that the convention exemplified the Christian mind in its spirit and outlook, that most of our Lexington ministers and churches who opposed the sessions manifested the ecclesiastical mind.

The 1931 International Convention met in Wichita, Kansas, on October 6-11. The attendance was smaller than usual because of the depression. The *Standard* of October 17, 1931 (p. 1011), recorded in sub-headings that the convention had "Small attendance, but splendid fellowship. No disposition to debate matters. Very little inspiration. No important changes in policy or personnel." The next week (October 24, 1931, p. 1035) the paper reported that the convention lacked "fire or enthusiasm which was noticeable in not only the business sessions . . . There was general complaint that the meetings were not inspiring."

The final report of the brotherhood's Commission on the Direction of Surveys was presented to the Wichita Convention. A thorough survey lasting several years had been made of the organized missionary, educational, and benevolent work of the Disciples. The report was presented to the convention by Raphael H. Miller, pastor of the Independence Boulevard Christian Church, Kansas City, Missouri, who was secretary of the Survey Committee. This report endorsed the recommendation of the foreign department of the United Christian Missionary Society that its missionaries should be withdrawn from Batang on the Tibetan border, as follows *(Final Report of The Commission for the Direction of Surveys to the International Convention of Disciples of Christ at Wichita, Kansas, October 6-11, 1931):*

The withdrawal from mission fields long occupied and others which have appealed to our loftiest sentiments through the labor and sacrifice of beloved ambassadors of Christ, seems like unwarranted retreat. But the clear mandate of Survey findings has been to centralize our efforts in favored fields and shorten our too far extended lines in order to make the most effective use of men and money. We cannot justify large expenditures for feeble results when there are so many opportunities for strategic advance and permanent advantage (p. 5).

In the Foreign Fields . . . we have withdrawn from Tibet (p. 12).

Commenting upon the Tibetan withdrawal, the *Standard* stated (October 17, 1931, p. 1012):

A large number of persons who do not approve of the step were not ready to join an open fight upon the Survey Report and the Society's action. The subject is not closed.

In a different vein, the report of the action by another editor, Willard E. Shelton, "High Lights of the Convention," in *The Christian-Evangelist* (October 15, 1931, p. 1371) said:

They [persons attending the Wichita sessions] did not like the withdrawal from Tibet . . . but they were willing to be convinced that those missionary executives who had given all their lives to the building of the Kingdom in foreign lands had not liked it any better, and had taken the step of withdrawal only when convinced of its necessity.

The United Society had experienced great difficulty in keeping missionaries on the Tibetan field. Since there was almost constant warfare on between the Tibetans and the Chinese, Batang, being in China and twelve miles from the border, was subject to numerous attacks. Our hospital had been riddled by artillery fire and the missionaries had been forced to move inside the walled city. The American State Department had repeatedly called me, as foreign secretary, to Washington and had scolded us severely for allowing missionaries, especially women and children, to remain at Batang or to return to the field.

Then, too, the United Society had been denied the possibility of opening a new station. This led to the congestion of a number of new missionaries and older ones in the small town of Batang. The many problems and the inability to do extension work beyond the station, because of dangers from warfare and Tibetan bandits, had made the work almost impossible. So it was decided to withdraw the missionaries.

This withdrawal, in 1931, from the Tibetan border did not mean that the work there was entirely abandoned. The United

Society still owns the property. There was a church there of considerable membership, a good Sunday school, church buildings, a native pastor, and a hospital with a native-trained assistant who was able to look after the dispensary. There was also a small orphanage and Christian literature had been written by Mrs. A. L. Shelton and printed in India for the Batang Mission.

The Society has maintained no missionaries at Batang in the more than twenty years since the withdrawal. The more recent developments concerning mission work in the Tibetan border area are explained in an information report made by the Division of Foreign Missions to the Board of Trustees of the United Christian Missionary Society, September 16 and 17, 1947 (*United Christian Missionary Society Minutes, Volume 26,* pp. 359 f.). This relates to the work of independent missionaries at Batang. The report follows:

In September 1940 the board of trustees approved an agreement to lease our properties in Batang to the Tibetan Christian Mission on certain conditions including our returning Mrs. Minnie Ogden to be associated with the mission. Because of the war the missionaries of the Tibetan Christian Mission were interned in the Philippines and none of them reached Batang. [Circumstances also prevented Mrs. Ogden's return.] Mr. Vernon Newland, the leader of the mission, has relieved us of any responsibility to lease the properties to him under the agreement. It is not his intention to return to Batang.

Mr. Edgar Nichols and his wife and family, assisted by two single women, have conducted work in Batang for the past few years. They have approached us for a lease of the properties there. Because of the fact that it is not our intention to reopen our work in Batang for financial and other reasons (the budget for Batang in 1923-24 was $26,561.50) the foreign division recommends an agreement to lease the properties as detailed under recommendation.

The United Society's trustees voted (p. 344) at that meeting to approve the recommendation which stipulated, among other things, that "Mr. Nichols and his group will be responsible for the upkeep of the properties, including all repairs, taxes, etc., The United Christian Missionary Society making no charges for the use of the properties."

The concluding article of the agreement stated that this understanding was "made in mutual good faith and each of the parties involved pledges himself or herself to be mutually helpful in attitude, word and deed." However, with the situation in China what it is in 1953, there are no missionaries at Batang.

The 1932 International Convention met in Indianapolis, October 12-16. Charles S. Medbury, pastor of the University Church, Des Moines, Iowa, had been elected president. He published a series of articles about the convention and its functions in the *Christian Standard*. One of them (May 7, 1932, p. 462) stressed the freedom of the convention, as follows:

The International Convention of Disciples of Christ aims to be just what its name implies. It is not a convention of the United Christian Missionary Society, nor of any missionary, educational or benevolent group among us. It is not the voice of "organized agencies." It is, rather, the gathering together, under the constitution referred to in former articles, of those who voluntarily assemble as Disciples of Christ, and to whom the affiliated units of the Convention report. . . .

Is there not footing here for men and women of all varied phases of thought among us today . . . if there are better ways, more fraternal, bigger spirited, or more efficient, than we have as yet found, let it be remembered that amendments are in order.

Mr. Medbury died suddenly on April 24, 1932, just after he had extended the Gospel invitation at the close of the Sunday morning worship service in the Des Moines church. Homer W. Carpenter, pastor of First Christian Church, Louisville, Kentucky, a vice-president of the convention, was chosen to preside at the Indianapolis sessions.

The year of 1933 was one of deep concern for the Christian cause. There was little controversy over issues in our brotherhood. The International Convention, which met in Pittsburgh, Pennsylvania, October 11-16, approved the recommendation that the National Benevolent Association and the Board of Church Extension should be separated from the United Christian Missionary Society. This had come to be a logical and reasonable procedure.

The Board of Ministerial Relief, which became a part of the United Christian Missionary Society shortly after the latter's organization, was the first function of the Society which wisdom and experience directed should be separated from the large agency. Consequently a reorganization in 1928 provided for the Board of Ministerial Relief to become the present Pension Fund of Disciples of Christ.

A Commission on Policies and Relationships of the United Christian Missionary Society had been appointed by its Executive Committee to study and report on both benevolence and church extension. W. F. Rothenburger, pastor of the Third Christian Church, Indianapolis, was chairman of the commission which submitted its recommendations in Pittsburgh.

As a part of the United Society the National Benevolent Association functioned as the benevolence department. This work consisted largely of separate homes for old people and for dependent children. They were managed locally and much of their maintenance funds was raised within the local areas. Often a local Community Chest shared in supporting a home. It was difficult to administer the benevolent work from a national headquarters.

The Board of Church Extension functioned within the United Society as the church erection department. It had formerly been essentially a missionary board. But it had accumulated permanent funds of about three million dollars for use in making loans to churches. In the early days these had been small loans to help weak churches start building houses of worship. This phase of the program decreased as the work grew and expanded. Many of the later loans were large. Many churches were helped in emergencies.

So the commission decided, and the Pittsburgh Convention approved the decision, that it would be better for the work of the United Christian Missionary Society to be confined to Christian missions at home and abroad and Christian education.

Often, for several years before the Pittsburgh action on separation of benevolence and church extension work from the United Society, the *Christian Standard* had criticized the continuation of these phases of work within the framework of the Society. In reporting the Pittsburgh Convention, Edwin R. Errett, editor of the *Standard,* wrote (October 28, 1933, p. 859) as follows:

One of the most amusing features of the Pittsburgh meeting was the effort on the part of the United Society friends to forestall any tendency on the part of any one to claim that the action of separating the Board of Church Extension and the National Benevolent Association was a surrender to the Society's enemies. It was earnestly urged that this was quite different, an action from within the Society. All right. Who cares? The important thing is that at last through self-criticism the proper change has been made.

After the separation of the boards, the Board of Church Extension established its national headquarters in Indianapolis, where the Pension Fund, too, maintains its own national offices. However, the Board of Church Extension continued at the Missions Building, headquarters also of the United Christian Missionary Society and other brotherhood organizations. The National Benevolent Association resumed its work in St. Louis, Missouri, where it had existed before the United Society was formed.

I addressed the 1934 Indiana Convention of Disciples of Christ on "Great Issues in Missions." The speech discussed some of the problems that were faced, especially in frontier work in America and on the foreign mission fields. The main points of the latter were:

1. The fact that missionaries had to go, not as in the old times, with strong prejudice against everything in the older religions which they found on the field, but they had to give credit for the good which they found and speak of Christianity as the fulfillment of it and the only religion that had redemption in it through a Savior. Also, that the missionaries should not attempt to take our own culture, in particular, to other lands, but leave the natives free to continue their own culture, where it was good, and make Indian Christians, and Chinese Christians, instead of American Christians on the field.

2. While missionaries were more necessary than ever, the natives should be pushed to the front, given leadership and responsibility, thus bringing the churches to self-support and self-direction. This meant that the missionaries had to stand behind and let the natives take the lead as they would become trained for leadership.

3. We should present, as far as possible, a solid front on the mission fields in Christian cooperation and plans of comity. We should have understandings with our neighbors, not giving up any of our convictions. But we should exercise, as a people who believe in Christian unity, every degree of Christian cooperation possible so that there would be no waste of time and

funds, and so that as many of the millions of unreached people as possible could be reached with the open Bible by every religious body.

4. We must go humbly, realizing our own inconsistencies, and seeing the need of our own redemption; not as a superior race, but as Christian brethren, with the common need of a Savior.

Edwin R. Errett, editor of the *Christian Standard*, was in that convention audience at Crawfordsville, Indiana. He requested a copy of the speech and one was sent to him. The address was published in the *Standard* of August 25, 1934 (pp. 583 ff.). Regarding the statements on cooperation and comity, Mr. Errett, in an editorial in the same issue, "What Does President Corey Mean?" (p. 580), stated:

In brief, it is altogether too clear that if President Corey's statement represents the United Society, that agency is committed to support of union movements into which it enters as one of the several denominations and to which it surrenders its Godgiven testimony as to the only divine program of Christian unity. It has no sense of any responsibility to testify for the New Testament faith and order.

In that editorial Mr. Errett failed to recognize that the places on mission fields where Disciples of Christ and our position are most appreciated and best understood are where we have entered into cooperative and comity efforts and have become better acquainted with our religious neighbors. Thus we have been able to give our testimony direct, instead of at long distance and in a controversial fashion. We have nothing to lose in cooperation. With our simple presentation of the Gospel and our plea for the unity of all Christians, we have much to gain. Genuine Christian cooperation is a steppingstone toward the larger unity, which is our goal.

It should be a matter of just pride that our missionaries have often been leaders in cooperative work with other church bodies. These consecrated workers have felt that since God was evidently cooperating with Presbyterians, Methodists, and Baptists, they, too, should do so. Then, they have felt that from the very nature of our plea for Christian unity, we would be remiss if we were not the first to press for every possible cooperation and they have never sacrificed their convictions in doing so.

During the 1934 International Convention in Des Moines, Iowa, October 16-21, I was re-elected president of the United Christian Missionary Society for another four-year term. The continuation of the depression and diminishing receipts of the Society made it impossible to maintain the world-wide work without increasing deficits.

It was at the Des Moines Convention that a significant recommendation of the United Society was approved. This provided for building the Society's annual budget on the basis of the actual income for the preceding year. This policy gradually enabled the Society to decrease the deficit which had grown so large during the years of general economic difficulty. The policy continues to govern the Society's budget and expenditures every year.

The indebtedness of the United Society was completely paid during the administration of Robert M. Hopkins, who was elected as my successor as president at the International Convention in Denver, Colorado, in 1938. The executive statement of Mr. Hopkins in the Society's twenty-second Annual Report (*1942 Year Book, Disciples of Christ,* p. 7) for the fiscal year ending June 30, 1942, declared:

It is with deep satisfaction we report that the debt in the general fund of the United Society has been paid in full. . . . This debt began to accumulate in 1920. It reached its peak of $1,126,952.34 in 1933. When the National Benevolent Association and the Board of Church Extension through mutual agreement withdrew from the United Society, each paid a portion of the debt. . . .

In order to avoid repeating such an accumulation of indebtedness, the budget is now based upon receipts, and must not exceed the total receipts of the preceding year.

The assets (net worth over direct liabilities) of the United Society on June 30, 1952, were $8,275,064.95. Total assets of the Society and the three old boards (American Christian Missionary Society, Foreign Christian Missionary Society, and Christian Woman's Board of Missions) amounted to $9,198,968.13 on the same date (*1952 Year Book, Disciples of Christ,* p. 150).

A plan of educational coordination was approved by the Des Moines Convention with "only one dissenting vote." It was prepared and presented by Roy G. Ross, religious educational secretary of the United Society, and Willard M. Wickizer, member of the Society's Executive Committee and pastor then at Maryville, Missouri (*The Christian-Evangelist,* October 25, 1934, p. 1386). These changes were reported in "Preaching and Tinkering" by the *Christian Standard* (October 27, 1934, p. 769), as follows:

The Board of Temperance and Social Welfare is discontinued and its functions transferred to the United Society. Most of the functions of the Board of Education are likewise transferred, though the Board continues as a conference of college presidents. This is a rather strange aftermath of the formation of the United Society and its partial dissolution by the separation of the National Benevolent Association and the Board of Church Extension a year ago. These smaller boards were not taken in at first. One of them wanted in. Now, with the others out, they are taken in, on the general plea that they are educational agencies, and all educational work should be consolidated. The principle question is whether the vigorous witness on social issues will not be lost in the larger cause.

Prior to the Des Moines Convention, after the proposals for educational coordination had been announced in the brotherhood press, the *Standard* had published an editorial, "The Lost Missionary Societies" (September 22, 1934, p. 664). In this, the paper stated, in conclusion, that, "There is something far more vital to be done about the United Society than any mere tampering with its organization."

The plan for Unified Promotion by the brotherhood agencies was approved by the Des Moines Convention with little opposition. It was reported by J. Edward Moseley in *The Christian-Evangelist* (October 25, 1934, p. 1388), as follows:

This unified plan of promotion, which it is tentatively planned to begin to operate on July 1, 1935, with a central office in Indianapolis, Indiana, is a trend toward the closest co-operative promotional effort ever undertaken by the Disciples of Christ. Joint promotion means that those boards, colleges, and organizations co-operating will work through a central office and seek to eliminate competition in securing funds and to develop more efficiency in securing and disseminating the funds for the various causes of the Brotherhood. . . .

At the time of approval by the convention the plan had been approved by seven national boards, twenty-three state societies, fifteen women's organizations, and five colleges. The National Benevolent Association and the Kansas State Society had disapproved.

The attack of the *Christian Standard* on this new cooperative venture of the Disciples was launched even before the plan had been approved by the convention. In an editorial, "Misgivings on Unified Promotion" (October 13, 1934, p. 5), the paper stated:

Our own conception is that, given a purpose to have a central collecting agency and to suppress competition, there could scarcely be a better plan. The difficulty lies in the purpose. As we have previously stated, we believe that there is a place for a genuine co-operation in promotion, but we can not see how a scheme to unite in gathering money can end in anything but misunderstanding, and even odium. The simple fact is that, while the United Society, as originally planned, has been breaking down, some leaders have been planning this new arrangement to effect a combination involving all state as well as national boards in what would appear as an official denominational trust.

Confronted with this statement, the record of Unified Promotion speaks for itself. It began operation in 1935, as planned, with C. O. Hawley, then as now, the executive director.

"The *Christian Standard,* Friend of Organized Work" was the title of an editorial in that periodical on February 2, 1935 (p. 102). Comment was made about the friendship and aid of Isaac Errett in the early years of the brotherhood's organized work. Then the paper was cited as an "ardent friend" of the Association for the Promotion of Christian Unity when it was established and as a generous promoter of the International Convention, among other agencies of the Disciples. It was pointed out that the magazine considered the Christian Restoration Association to be "in the same category . . . of organized work." Opposition to these agencies representing the organized work had arisen, it was stated, because of the "modernistic sympathies" of the boards. The editor also stated:

It was against modernism that the *Christian Standard* made its fight and it warned the boards against relations with modernism. If it is not such affiliation that has brought them to their present sorry plight, pray tell what is it? . . .

Any conception of "organized work" that means integration of churches into a convention or an organization, that is thereby made "official" is foreign to the New Testament and the genius of our people.

The editor also discussed, "Why the Christian Service Camps?" (*Christian Standard,* May 25, 1935, p. 496). The magazine helps to publicize and promote these camps among some of the youth of our brotherhood. The editorial said that the camps were justified by

> . . . the indoctrination to which they subject the young people. Most of the summer camps put on by the Religious Education Department of the United Society might just as well be the product of the Congregational Church or the Presbyterian Church, and some of them actually prepare the way for the seeds of modernism.

This editorial concession of being friendly to the organized work was always sufficiently qualified by the *Standard*.

Another 1935 editorial of the *Standard* (June 15, 1935, p. 567) discussed, "What's the Matter With the Brotherhood." The paper stated:

> Here is the fundamental difficulty in this brotherhood: A surreptitious development over a period of years, whereby a radical program is woven into an organization, and all the time loyalty is claimed and accusations of disloyalty hurled at the suspicious. Is it any wonder confidence has been shaken? Is it any wonder the advance of the older and larger agencies is at a standstill?
>
> A secondary factor in the situation is the organizational loyalty of the women. It is very well known that women are psychologically constituted so that they retain a loyalty to a person or an institution on an emotional basis, rather than on a rational one; a woman's loyalty to an erring son and unfaithful husband is a matter for admiration. When, however, this appears in church affairs it is perilous. When, in addition, it is given such opportunity as is provided by the chartering of auxiliaries in every congregation, we have the makings of peril to the independence of our ministry. That is precisely what has happened in this brotherhood. Certain leaders have presumed upon the loyalty and the admirable zeal of these good women to mislead them.

Since that editorial was published, Disciple women have become more closely unified than ever in the Christian Women's Fellowship. This organization is being eagerly embraced by the women in the younger churches of the mission lands, as well as in other countries.

Chapter 7

AN ATTEMPT AT MODERATION
WHICH FAILED

The eight years from 1936 to 1944 were not so critical as far as the *Christian Standard* was concerned. The editorials of Edwin R. Errett, then editor of the paper, were more conciliatory. As a member of the Commission on Restudy of the Disciples of Christ, he served with a group which was a cross-section of our brotherhood's thinking. In 1937 Mr. Errett was one of the Disciples attending the World Conference on Faith and Order in Edinburgh, Scotland. At that meeting he voted with the other delegates in approving the preliminary plans for the World Council of Churches.

Upon Mr. Errett's return to the United States he made some addresses regarding the world-wide movement to draw the various religious bodies together insofar as possible. He delivered an excellent and conciliatory message to the International Convention of 1937 in Columbus, Ohio ("The Faith of the Church in God," *The Christian-Evangelist,* November 11, 1937, pp. 1428 ff.; also in *International Convention,* 1937, pp. 63 ff.).

However, because of attacks accumulated in the *Christian Standard* through a long period of years, Edwin Errett's position was a most difficult one. Tides had been started flowing out across the brotherhood that could not be stopped. The hand of the past had to be recognized in the editorial and news columns of the periodical in order to keep faith with those persons who had been turned against all of our organized and cooperative work.

The Christian-Evangelist of November 28, 1935 (pp. 1546 f.) published an editorial entitled, "The Disciples and Their Sense of Mission." It called for a restudy of the Christian situation and the position of the Disciples in the light of the age in which

we were living.   This editorial urged that there should be a
changed emphasis for a changed age in terms of these "imperatives":   1) A new statement of ethics in a world facing the
horrors of war, the evils of poverty, the narrowness of creed,
and the discrimination against race; 2) the great necessity of
opposing with an affirmative Christian faith the new nationalistic religions that were rising all over the world; 3) the need
of a religion of faith in God and man being reborn; 4) the
recognition that Christianity is a way of life rather than an
emotional appeal to hit the sawdust trail; and 5) the need of
not so much turning our eyes backward for justification of parrotlike repetition of that which our pioneers preached with such
power for their age, but rather turning our eyes forward to discover our imperative in preaching that which meets the needs
of our own age.

This editorial was attacked by one which appeared in the
Christian Standard of January 4, 1936 (pp. 3 f.), under the title,
"And Still, Where Is the Distinctive Mission?"   Among other
things, it stated:

> The plea that all Christian people drop human creeds and human
> orders as tests of fellowship, in order to unite upon the New Testament
> platform is the distinctive message that we can proclaim and that no
> one else is proclaiming.

There was very little reference to the emphasis made by *The
Christian-Evangelist.*

On June 6, 1936 (p. 536), the *Standard* published a letter
from Robert E. Elmore and an answer to it.   Mr. Elmore had
attacked the organized work and especially the United Christion Missionary Society, quoting Mark Collis (then pastor of
Broadway Christian Church, Lexington, Kentucky) as having
said, "I want to see the United Society smashed."   Mr. Elmore
also quoted a former statement of Edwin Errett's, "I was not
bitterly opposed to the United Society at its inception.   Having, however, seen its workings, I detest it, I hate it."

Then Mr. Elmore said,

> As in 1926 so in 1936, I stand against the ecclesiasticism, rationalism,
> denominationalism and jesuitism of the organization which is making
> havoc of the once victorious and militant movement for New Testament
> Christianity.

In answering, Mr. Errett agreed in part, but disagreed with Mr. Elmore's strategy. The answer stated, in part:

In our judgment, the peril we always face is not merely the continued existence of "a United Society denomination," but the creation of an anti-United Society denomination, if you please . . . That would be in contravention of Mr. Elmore's definition of brotherhood.

For that reason the *Christian Standard* is following a policy of recognizing as brethren all who give evidence of being sincere believers in Christ as Lord and Saviour and seekers for New Testament Christianity, regardless of their position on the United Society. We refuse to make the United Society a test of fellowship.

However, the position of the *Christian Standard* since the death of Mr. Errett in January, 1944, does not bear this statement out. Opposition to the United Society increasingly has become a test of fellowship for Mr. Elmore and his publication, the *Restoration Herald,* as well as for the *Christian Standard.* In fact their later editorial statements indicate that all organizations and institutions affiliated with the International Convention of Disciples of Christ have been shut out from their circle of fellowship.

An editorial in the *Christian Standard* of October 10, 1936 (p. 980), mentioned the special fund raised to honor Dr. A. L. Shelton, martyred missionary to the Tibetan border. Obviously overlooking some circumstances that had to do with the Mission near the Tibetan border, the paper stated, "The failure to use the Shelton Memorial Fund for evangelistic advance in that dangerous region caused J. Russell Morse and his wife to withdraw from the United Society Mission in Batang."

As a matter of fact, the United Society handled the Shelton Memorial Fund with the greatest of care and it has been used, as far as possible, according to the original purpose. A part of the fund was used to send a group of new missionaries who were to occupy a new station which it had been hoped would be opened in the Tibetan border area. The remainder, $65,303.70, is held by the Society. Interest from this amount is used to train new missionaries. The trustees of the Society voted, at their meeting of May 15-17, 1950, "That the entire Shelton Memorial Fund be added to the $50,000.00 Shelton Memorial Endowment Fund for scholarships for missionary candidates" (*United Christian Missionary Society Minutes, Volume 28, May 15, 16, 17, 1950,* p. 17).

The reasons for the failure of the United Society to expand missionary work along the Tibetan border and the withdrawal from that field in 1931 have been discussed at length already in this volume.

"How Do We Affiliate?" was the title of an article in the *Christian Standard* of May 30, 1936 (p. 513), by S. S. Lappin, minister and former editor of the periodical. He stated:

> The "open membership" propaganda among churches of Christ has one leg and one only to stand on, and that? *Their contributions accepted by agencies considered to be official.* The brethren who give have choice of two courses: To fall in and thus seem to have fellowship with the sterile thing, or to repudiate the agencies that receive offerings from this source.

By this, no doubt, he meant that any congregation which had "guest" members, or recognized in any other way on the church roll those persons who had not been immersed, should be repudiated by all of our agencies. This is a sample of the "test of fellowship" which is raised again and again by the *Christian Standard* and many of its writers.

In the *Standard* for April 17, 1937 (p. 325), Mr. Lappin wrote again about church membership, stating:

> Such an act [receiving the unimmersed] is wholly unnecessary as a courtesy to our religious neighbors. Already they can do everything we ourselves do in a church and enjoy every privilege save one, the vote. They have place at our communion service if they choose to come. I have often had such folk in churches I serve, and have here in Central [Pittsburgh, Pennsylvania], not members of the church, but regular attendants and supporters of the cause.

This is, no doubt, the position held by the vast majority of our people. Yet these churches would not disfellowship a church with a different view as Mr. Lappin advocated.

At the 1937 International Convention in Columbus, Ohio, October 26-31, Charles Clayton Morrison, editor of *The Christian Century*, Chicago, delivered an address on, "The Church and the War System." The *Christian Standard* published the message under the title of, "Preparing the Church for the Next War" (November 20, 1937, pp. 1067 ff.). An editorial, "Even

If Mr. Morrison Is Wrong He Is Right" in the same issue (pp. 1063 f.) gave qualified praise to the speech, as follows:

> In publishing the brilliant, courageous and statesmanlike address of Charles Clayton Morrison before the Columbus Convention we do not, of course, intend to imply that we subscribe to all of his interpretation of the present world situation. Nevertheless, we would not publish it did it not in a remarkable degree give endorsement to a concept of the church and its proper service that we regard as of transcendent importance.

The years of 1937 and 1938 were rather peaceful years insofar as the *Christian Standard* was concerned.

It was during 1938 that the *Standard* opposed cooperation with the Community Church at Boulder Dam on the Colorado River in Arizona-Nevada (January 8, 1938, pp. 27 f.). The government had required that there be but one church in this temporary community of thousands of people who were building the dam. The United Society's Division of Home Missions made a contribution toward this effort to assist the religious development of the large number of people. A similar, cooperative plan had been followed in connection with comparable projects.

The June 18, 1938, issue of the *Christian Standard* (pp. 589 ff.) highlighted the so-called "loyal schools," publishing pictures of the graduates of most of these institutions. This group of schools at that time included the College of the Bible of Phillips University, the Pacific Bible Seminary, the Cincinnati Bible Seminary, the Manhattan Bible College, the College of Religion of Butler University, Northwest Christian College, and Johnson Bible College. The Minnesota Bible College and the Christian Normal Institute (now Kentucky Christian College) were mentioned, but no pictures of graduates were published.

It is interesting to note that sometime later both the College of the Bible of Phillips University and the School of Religion of Butler University were apparently dropped from the list of "loyal schools" by the *Christian Standard*. These two universities are affiliated with the Board of Higher Education of Disciples of Christ. The graduate seminaries of these two universities are now accredited by the American Association of Theological Schools. They are also active, sympathetic sup-

porters of the cooperative life of the brotherhood which has
been opposed by the *Christian Standard*. The periodical, by
proclaiming a selected group of schools as "loyal," thereby passes
judgment on the balance of our educational institutions as
"disloyal."

On July 31, 1938, my resignation as president of the United
Christian Missionary Society took effect. My retirement, in
keeping with the age-retirement policy of the Society, was draw-
ing near. I accepted a call to the presidency of The College of
the Bible, Lexington, Kentucky. Robert M. Hopkins, New
York City, succeeded me as president of the United Society.

At the International Convention which met in Denver, Colorado, October 16-21, certain organizational changes in the
brotherhood's program of higher education were approved. In
its report on this action, the *Christian Standard* claimed that
it disclosed "once more the folly of trying to manage everything
through one board." The paper reported the changes, as follows (November 26, 1938, p. 1151) :

> The effort to co-ordinate the work of higher education with the
> United Society, which was launched at Des Moines [in 1934], was de-
> clared a failure and the college executives resumed their independence,
> changing the title of their organizations [*sic*] from "College Association
> of Disciples of Christ" to "The Board of Higher Education of Disciples
> of Christ." Student work continues under the United Society. The
> plan was approved with no discussion.

There was little controversy during 1939, but constant emphasis on the "clique" of the Campbell Institute and the "domi-
nance" of this group in the leadership of brotherhood agencies.
The *Christian Standard* of March 25, 1939 (pp. 268 ff.) carried
a long article under the by-line of its editor, Edwin R. Errett,
with the title, "The Way to Peace." He stated that the difficulties with the International Convention, several of the national
agencies, many of the college leaders, and the curriculum of the
church schools all pointed to the "liberal" school of thought, a
"clique on the margin," centered in Chicago. So he suggested,
"Let us look, then, at the proportion in which members of the
Campbell Institute occupy controlling places in the boards."
Mr. Errett then listed a large representation of Institute members on convention programs, International Convention commit-

tees and commissions, and boards of the United Society, the Board of Higher Education, and the Association for the Promotion of Christian Unity. He added "that six of the last eight presidents" of the International Convention were members of "that clique," the Campbell Institute.

In connection with Mr. Errett's statements, it is of interest to note the names of those "eight presidents" of the International Convention of Disciples of Christ—which Mr. Errett did not do. They were: 1931 in Wichita, L. D. Anderson, pastor of First Christian Church, Fort Worth, Texas; 1932 in Indianapolis, Homer W. Carpenter, pastor of First Christian Church, Louisville, Kentucky; 1933 in Pittsburgh, George A. Campbell, pastor of Union Avenue Christian Church, St. Louis, Missouri; 1934 in Des Moines, W. F. Rothenburger, pastor of Third Christian Church, Indianapolis, Indiana; 1935 in San Antonio, D. W. Morehouse, president of Drake University, Des Moines, Iowa; 1936 in Kansas City, L. N. D. Wells, pastor of East Dallas Christian Church, Dallas, Texas; 1937 in Columbus, A. W. Fortune, pastor of Central Christian Church, Lexington, Kentucky, and 1938 in Denver, F. D. Kershner, dean of the Butler College of Religion, Indianapolis, Indiana.

It would be a little difficult for the casual reader to distinguish between the members and non-members of the Campbell Institute in this list of outstanding and recognized leaders of our fellowship. Those eight men listed certainly represent a fair cross-section of the brotherhood of Disciples of Christ.

On January 13, 1940 (pp. 27 f.), there was an editorial in the *Standard* on the Campbell Institute, which said:

> This clique subscribes to a general theory that places the seat of authority within the individual. It has nothing but contempt for what is called "external authority" and commands that come down to us from Jesus or from His authorized representatives, the apostles, are, of course, within the category of external authority. . . .
>
> Those of us who still believe in the Great Commission would do well to look at this clique as it is and, recognizing it for what it is, rid ourselves of the incubus before it completes the wreckage of every constructive work the churches of Christ possess.

These were very strong accusations indeed to hurl at the devoted Christian men who happen to be members of the Campbell Institute and who believe profoundly in the Great Commission and do no less than the *Standard* to put that commission into effect. Again, the magazine assumed the prerogative of judging individuals as to personal belief.

The International Convention met in Richmond, Virginia, in October, 1939, and in St. Louis, Missouri, in May, 1941. Because of the shift from an autumn to a spring date, no meeting of the International Convention was held in 1940. But the North American Christian Convention met on October 9-13, 1940, in Indianapolis; the *Standard* reported it (October 19, 1940, pp. 1053 ff.) as being "in every sense a triumph."

Carl S. Ledbetter, when receiving the Master of Arts degree from Butler University, wrote a thesis on "Open Membership in the Churches of Christ." This was printed in the *Christian Standard* in many issues, beginning August 31, 1940 (pp. 851 ff.) and concluding February 8, 1941 (pp. 137 ff.). It was, said Mr. Ledbetter, "somewhat abridged" and "somewhat revised" for publication. From his information he concluded that about 150 of our churches either had or did then practice open membership. These were listed in the *Christian Standard* of January 11, 1941 (pp. 33 f.) by Mr. Ledbetter.

Concerning Mr. Ledbetter's deductions, the *Standard* published an editorial, "All of One Piece" (November 16, 1940, p. 1161), which concluded this:

1. The open-membership theory is but a part of the general attitude that would discredit the whole authority of Jesus Christ.
2. The United Society educational leadership identifies itself with the sort of persons who promote open membership by employing them to create the curriculum materials for youth.

An editorial, "Facts and Opinions," in the *Christian Standard* of May 30, 1942, (p. 532) listed several of those who were to appear on the program of the Grand Rapids International Convention that summer as men holding "radical positions." Thus it judged the loyalty or disloyalty of others in the realm of doctrinal belief.

At the Grand Rapids, Michigan, International Convention, July 28—August 2, 1942, Clarence E. Lemmon, pastor of the First Christian Church, Columbia, Missouri, was elected president.

The convention report in the *Christian Standard* by its editor, Edwin R. Errett, was entitled, "A Convention of Hope" (August 8, 1942, p. 776 f.). It protested the election of Mr. Lemmon as not "fatal to better understanding, but it certainly gives no evidence of desire for such." In an editorial, "Hardly Adequate," the *Standard* of September 19, 1942 (p. 920) stated:

> The difficulty inheres not in the character of Mr. Lemmon. It inheres in the fact that he is one of those radicals who practice open membership and has been chosen to a key position and quite naturally conceives of the "general fellowship" to be served as including the radical speakers and the radical propaganda upon the same basis as the speakers and themes that adhere to the characteristic and fundamental principles of our movement. . . .
>
> It is, however, precisely that conception which we can not accept as a basis for our unity or a convention to which we can give endorsement.

The Columbia church is located adjacent to the University of Missouri and other higher educational institutions. The church had in 1928, by vote of the congregation, approved open membership and recognized some unimmersed people as members of the church. This was before Mr. Lemmon became the minister there. It seems to be quite a general custom of our churches in college and university centers to provide a temporary church home for Christian students of different denominations during their time away from their home churches by extending them the status of guest membership.

The *Christian Standard* continued to agitate the situation which arose as a result of Mr. Lemmon's election. The issue of September 19, 1942 (pp. 919 f.) also had an editorial, "Let Us Be Clear on This," which said:

> We are not trying to unite the conservatives with the radicals. The object of our endeavor and devotion is to develop a true unity among all the conservatives regardless of their agencies, their papers, their leadership and their previous affiliations. Such a unity we regard as the most important objective of the movement and the prerequisite of any effective service to the Christian world at large.

A postal card poll of our ministers in the autumn of 1942 was conducted by the *Christian Standard* under Mr. Errett's leadership. The poll was prompted by Mr. Lemmon's election at Grand Rapids and a news report that "this indicates that the brotherhood regards the practice of open membership as no

longer disqualifying a person for election to a key office in brotherhood agencies" (*Standard,* October 3, 1942, p. 968).

The ballot, a returnable postal card, contained the following
statement (*Standard,* October 3, 1942, p. 968):

YES	Do you approve the election of those who practice open
---	membership to key positions in the organizations offering serv-
NO	ice to the brotherhood?

An editorial, "It Is a Vote on the Interpretation," in the
Standard of October 10, 1942 (p. 1000) said:

We are not asking the brethren to vote upon the merits of Clarence
E. Lemmon. Nor are they asked to vote upon his abilities as a presiding officer or the probable course of his administration. Nor are they
asked to vote upon open membership.

The question put to them grows entirely out of the interpretation of
his election made by two radical newspaper men [Harold E. Fey and
Herbert L. Minard]. Our request for a vote upon it would never have
been made had it not been for that interpretation. We are conducting
no attack upon Mr. Lemmon, but frankly *we are conducting an attack
upon that radical interpretation of his election.*

The Christian-Evangelist strongly defended Mr. Lemmon in
an editorial (September 10, 1942, p. 991). This statement
pointed out that the *Standard* had drawn an unjustifiable conclusion that Mr. Lemmon's leadership as convention president
would be radical, intolerant, and an endorsement of open membership.

Apparently Mr. Errett, as editor of the *Christian Standard,* became so concerned with the complaints of his readers to this attack of the periodical that he decided to defend his actions. The
indignation that greeted this poll of our preachers had amazed
him, he wrote in an editorial statement, "So This Is Democracy?"
published in the *Standard* of October 17, 1942 (p. 1024).

This whole incident definitely illustrated that the *Christian
Standard* and its followers were not interested in unity with
their fellow-Christians *with whom they disagreed.* Rather, it
seemed to be then, and it has become even more so a decade
later, a question of uniformity according to theological dogmas
and interpretations proclaimed by the magazine.

The outcome of the postal card poll concerning Mr. Lemmon
was announced on the first editorial page of the *Christian Stand-*

is necessary is the conclusion on the part of one party or the other that they ought to break off their relations and make other arrangements. If this be done with due regard to ample notice, there is no reason to find fault or to impute dishonor.

Some preachers seem to assume that they have established some right to a pulpit when they have served in it for a time and that a congregation's request to break the arrangement is something of an insult. Nor have congregations been guiltless in this respect; a preacher's resignation is not necessarily a rebuke to the congregation, although some have been submitted in that spirit.

Those Quiz Programs

A NOVEL development in the North American Christian Convention is the introduction of what is termed by the Continuation Committee a "Quiz Hour."

As we understand this, it is designed to induce some careful thinking upon the application of some basic principles to the practical problems of our church life. Several leaders are to sit upon the platform and engage in a "panel" discussion of the principles and then the audience is to have the opportunity to "fire" questions at them from the floor (not to make speeches, however). It will be something like the "Town Hall."

The first of these "hours" will have to do with the nature of the church. For instance, Is the church "essentially, intentionally and constitutionally one," as "The Declaration and Address" of Thomas Campbell says it is? If so, what does this mean about "the practice of Christian unity"? What does it mean in terms of "open membership"? These questions may not come up, but they may.

In the third "Quiz Hour" the questions concerning agencies for missionary work and their relation to churches and questions about evangelistic meetings and "educational evangelism" may emerge.

In the second "Quiz Hour" we rather expect the elders who have recently come to life to give some expression to their concern for the nurture of the church.

Here is the possibility for something stimulating and practical.

Let Preachers Support Preaching

MINISTERS have been allowed some priority in the rationing of tires and gasoline. They have also been allowed exemption from draft for Army service.

This lays an obligation on the ministry that has already been on the conscience of many of them. They owe something to their fellows and their God in return for this consideration.

Fundamentally, the consideration grows not out of the thought that they are superior *persons*, but out of the thought that they have a superior *article* to dispense; that is, they have in the message of Jesus Christ something that will create and sustain the morale of men in such fashion as to make men capable of carrying the extra burden of these times effectively. The preachers are, therefore, under obligation to support preaching in a special degree. They are not only to give of their best in preaching but they are also to stimulate all church people to sustain preaching. They must lead all Christians to value and support preaching.

The forthcoming North American Christian Convention is particularly a preaching Convention. Those who attend will hear good preaching, their morale will be strengthened and they will become lovers of strong preaching.

It, therefore, becomes the duty of every preacher not only to do all he can to be present himself and thus fortify his own preaching ability, but also to stretch a point to get others there—his own members and members of other congregations. Even if this means that he must share his car with its precious rubber and gasoline, he will be but using that which is allotted him for support of preaching.

Builders of the Future

IT seems particularly appropriate that in this Ministry Number we should give particular emphasis to the gathering of camp leaders at Indianapolis. Twenty-five years from now the preachers telling how they happened to enter the ministry will have much to say of the Christian Service Camps.

The leaders of the Christian Service Camps will have a real get-together at the North American Christian Convention. It is scheduled for the Columbia Club on Friday at noon, and those in charge are particularly eager that all who belong to faculties of such camps shall be present.

"A Great Singing Convention"

THE following telegram from Ralph Pollock, leader of music in the North American Christian Convention, is of particular interest to the song evangelists, but all of us are profoundly concerned in the idea:

> Lowell, Ind., Sept. 28.—Attention singers. Plan to attend North American Convention. Singers' concerts will be part of program. The committee is desirous that we make this a great singing convention. Please write me you will attend. Two more added final service at Junction City, Ky. Closing two weeks here tonight; nine added. Field is continuously evangelistic. Marshall Weaver, pastor since December. Several from here will attend the North American Convention. We begin tomorrow Angola, Ind.; J. J. Whitehouse, minister. On to Indianapolis.— The Pollocks.

What better thing could a convention do to a people in the midst of the anxiety and gloom of world cataclysm than to put Christian songs in their hearts and send them out over the land singing the Christian faith?

We Are Asking the Ministers

COMMENTING upon the election of Clarence E. Lemmon to the presidency of the International Convention, Harold E. Fey said that this indicates that the brotherhood regards the practice of open membership as no longer disqualifying a person for election to a key office in brotherhood agencies.

We have already declared that we can not regard the action of the International Convention as an official action of the brotherhood. Nor do we consider that Convention's action as representative in kind. There is only one way by which to determine whether the action at Grand Rapids does mean what Mr. Fey says it means. That is to ask the brotherhood. But we know of no feasible method for polling all the brotherhood. The nearest test we do find feasible is to ask all the preachers, not on the basis that the preachers speak with any authority for the churches, but on the assumption that, in general, the sentiment of the preacher and of the congregation he serves will be apt to coincide.

It is necessary, of course, to use some list of the preachers for such a poll and, even though we recognize that the list in the Year Book is imperfect, it appears to be the one list that is free of duplications.

We have, therefore, in the past week sent to each preacher in that list a letter with a returnable postal-card ballot upon which has been printed the following:

YES	Do you approve the election of those who practice open membership to key positions in the organizations offering service to the brotherhood?
NO	

Of course, the editors have exerted themselves to make certain that the poll will be accurate and honest. No ballots will be counted if mailed after October 10. We shall report the results promptly.

We urge every minister to participate in order to make the poll truly representative.

This page is reproduced from the "Christian Standard" of October 3, 1942, p. 968. The editorial, lower right, discussed the postal-card ballot that the paper sponsored after the election of Dr. C. E. Lemmon as president of the International Convention.

ard for October 24, 1942 (p. 1047). Out of a total of 7,443 ballots mailed to the ministers of the brotherhood, the number returned totaled 3,708. Of those returned, 3,193 were efficacious votes, 697 of them being marked "yes" while 2,496 were marked "no." An editorial in this same issue denied that the magazine had any "hidden purpose" in conducting the poll.

Obviously, many of the ballots went into the wastebaskets of the preachers who received them. Many were returned with varied remarks, as might have been expected. The results were no more conclusive than a similar ballot would be if our ministers should be asked to vote on the qualifications of an editor of the *Standard* to be our sponsor in doctrinal tenets.

Another discussion of the *Christian Standard* during 1942 concerned the United Church of Christ in Japan which was brought about by Japanese authorities during World War II.

During the war the Japanese government exerted some pressure to effect a union of the Protestant bodies more rapidly. The Japanese government wished this representation of Protestant Christianity so that it would have a responsible body to deal with on religious matters. Our churches under the care of the United Society were included in the merger that was recognized by the war government of Japan. There was no interference with either doctrine or polity of the churches. Each religious body continued to conduct its work in its usual way.

Following the end of the war, a number of the church bodies felt that they should continue with at least this much of unity and cooperation. The united effort had proved to be fairly satisfactory during the war period. The United Society continued to share in the United Church, thus recognizing and encouraging what seemed to be a real step toward a possible ultimate union.

The United Society's Board of Managers met on May 4 and 5, 1943 in Missions Building, Indianapolis, and voted (*Christian Standard*, May 15, 1943, p. 433) :

That the board of managers approve the action taken by the board of trustees on March 10, 1943, relative to our policy for future work in Japan, as follows:

"That we affirm our determination to continue our fellowship with the Christian movement in Japan, that we authorize the department of

Oriental missions to express to the Japan section of the Committee on East Asia of the Foreign Missions Conference our interest in and sympathy with their suggestions to plan our future policy and program on a united basis, with the understanding that such plans will be brought back to the board of trustees for action."

This was published in connection with a report of that meeting of the Society's Board of Managers by Edwin R. Errett. The report was entitled, "United Society Frankly Commits Itself to Open Membership." An editorial, attacking the position of the Society, appeared in the same issue under the title, "The United Society Goes Sectarian" (p. 431). This editorial stated:

> What the United Society proposes to do is to proceed to plan for continuing work in Japan in co-operation with the denominations, and this co-operation looks toward some sort of support of or co-operation with the "Church of Christ in Japan." . . .
>
> The United Society writes Ichabod upon itself when it thus frankly declares that it has lost its unique reason for existence and descends to a sectarian plane of practice.

In a later editorial reference to this May, 1943, action of the United Society's Board of Managers regarding the United Church of Japan, the *Christian Standard* stated ("It Depends Upon the Missionaries," December 25, 1943, p. 1092) its position again, thus:

> . . . those who really believe in fundamental Christianity as do . . . [independent missionaries] are confident of going back and preaching and teaching true Christianity; those who are willing to pare down that message for a federal union of denominations, or for a social enterprise with Kagawa, or for political ventures with pagan shrines and emperor worship, believe that only a compromise with the government-sponsored "Church of Christ in Japan" will be possible. The latter is evidently the position of the leadership of the United Society, according to its May statement.

The individual churches in Japan are autonomous and self-directing. H. B. McCormick, then president of the United Society, accompanied by Virgil A. Sly, an executive secretary in the Society's Division of Foreign Missions, visited Japan and the Philippine Islands in 1950. In a subsequent report to the Oklahoma City International Convention of 1950, Mr. McCormick made it clear that the local freedom of the church suffers no interference whatsoever in the continuing program of the United

Church of Japan. Neither does the union affect the structure or the belief of a congregation. The local church determines its mode of worship, method of baptism, and observance of the Lord's Supper.

In his address, "Report on the Orient" (p. 5), Mr. McCormick stated:

Will the churches in the union be free to determine their own requirements for church membership? The answer in both countries is "Yes." In both the Philippines and Japan, in keeping with the assurances of local church autonomy, there is complete freedom for all church bodies in the union to retain their historic practices. Our churches in both countries continue to observe weekly communion and baptism by immersion. . . . Our national leaders in the Philippines stated, "We accept only, as members, those who have been immersed." In Japan our national leaders stated, "We receive into church membership those who after confession of faith are baptized by immersion."

The statements in the *Standard* editorial about paring down the message and about "political ventures with pagan shrines and emperor worship" failed to recognize that the United Christian Missionary Society has never stood for any such surrender.

It should be noted that many changes have taken place in Japan during recent years. The Emperor has renounced his assumed divine prerogative and in this renunciation Shinto worship has received a death blow. There has been much thinking and planning by the Japanese Christians. Toyohiko Kagawa and other leaders in Japan have been leading in a great advance in evangelism and in Christian cooperation. The reference by the *Standard* to Mr. Kagawa's "social enterprise," as though it had no connection with the Christian cause, was unfortunate.

In the *Christian Standard* for July 17, 1943 (pp. 629 ff.), P. H. Welshimer, pastor of the First Christian Church, Canton, Ohio, wrote about the issue confronting Disciples with regard to Christian unity. In an article entitled, "Unity Is Desirable; Restoration More So," he stated:

While unity is desirable, restoration of the church of the New Testament is more desirable, and in place of spending so much time in talking about unity we had better be about the business of having in every community, the restored church of the New Testament, and when we have that we will have unity, and we will never have it without it.

Sad to say this position has never gained us any unity. We have divided as a people once over the interpretation as to what the restoration of the New Testament Church was. We are now about to complete another division on the same issue. No other religious body has ever approached us for unity on this proposition and very likely no group ever will. On the other hand, we have never been able to approach any other church on this basis.

Mr. Welshimer has a large church in Canton, but it is doubtful if the congregations of that city are any closer to unity on the Restoration basis enunciated by him than they were fifty years ago when he began his ministry there. The opinions as to what the restoration of the New Testament church means are too numerous for "restoration" to be made our sole and only plea. Undoubtedly we will have to return to the original proposition of Thomas Campbell, one of our spiritual fathers, that the church of Christ on earth is "essentially, intentionally, and constitutionally one," if we make future progress toward Christian unity.

The "Call for Enlistment"

The *Christian Standard* of November 27, 1943, published "A Call for Enlistment" on its cover and following pages (pp. 1009 ff.). The "Call" concluded with the names of forty-nine preachers. The complete text of this "Call" and accompanying announcements follow in facsimile on succeeding pages.

The temporary Committee on Action, referred to in the "Call," consisted of eleven persons from the forty-nine signers of the manifesto. Burris Butler, then of Kokomo, Indiana, who shortly afterward joined the editorial staff of the *Standard,* was chairman. Fred Smith, Huntington, West Virginia, was secretary, and Lester Ford, Painesville, Ohio, treasurer. The other members' names are included in the reproduced pages that follow.

The endorsement of the "Call" by the *Christian Standard* was featured in the same issue (p. 1011). It should be noted in the reproduction of that page. The heading was, "Standard Endorses 'Call' and Prepares to Announce Supporting Program."

In connection with publication of the "Call," the paper also ran in the same issue a joint letter of endorsement with the signatures of P. H. Welshimer and W. R. Walker, two prominent ministers of the Committee on Action. Several amazing paragraphs deserve the reader's thoughtful attention.

This "Call for Enlistment" had the added significance in our brotherhood of being initially signed by a long list of ministers. However, after about three months, the *Christian Standard* apparently discontinued any reference in its columns to the "Call." No representative congregations answered the appeal. The published letters endorsing it came mostly from individuals.

The material in the *Standard* concerning this "Call" formed what seemed to be a blueprint of separation for the brotherhood of Disciples of Christ. One who knows a number of these brethren wonders why they permitted their names to be attached to such a statement. It was so unlike them to say such things. The joint letter accompanying the manifesto contained the most unfortunate phrases of all the material. It is difficult to reconcile the "Call" with the irenic spirit manifested in the editorial writing of Edwin R. Errett in the *Christian Standard* for several years preceding publication of the manifesto.

When the world is ablaze and Christianity itself is undergoing supreme tests, what does it mean in a religious body which came into being to promote the spirit of unity for which Christ prayed, for ministers to use a term like "fascistic" in describing attitudes of their brothers who may differ from them in opinions, but who believe that they are as loyal to Christ and his teachings as any other Christians?

The Christian-Evangelist published the "Call" as a matter of information for Disciples, but qualified it with an editorial in the same issue that was entitled, "This Is Divisive" (December 15, 1943, pp. 1211 f.). This editorial termed the "Call" a "dissentious document" and called the purposes "critical, negative and divisive."

Indeed, the "Call" was more than that. It was phrased with some of the most unfortunate words used in our vocabulary in 1943. Yet these were used by Christian brethren to accuse other Christians of their own fellowship!

CHRISTIAN STANDARD

PUBLISHED WEEKLY
SUBSCRIPTION, $2.00 PER ANNUM   **CINCINNATI, O., NOVEMBER 27, 1943**   OFFICES: EIGHTH AND CUTTER STS.
VOL. LXXIX—NO. 48

A CALL FOR ENLISTMENT

This "Call" is for all brethren the world over who are like-minded to volunteer to help in some or all of its objectives and for them to send their enlistment and their suggestions to the "Temporary Committee on Action"

Because we believe that in the present world crisis a new day of opportunity challenges the Christian world to proclaim the teaching and the way of life revealed in the New Testament Scriptures as the will of God for mankind;

Because we believe that in face of this approaching opportunity, the Christian world still needs the plea and the example that a brotherhood united on the one faith, one baptism, one God and Father of us all, came into being to demonstrate;

We call upon the brethren the world over

1. To discard a leadership which has misrepresented or minimized our plea and has sought in vain to make business corporations, not fellowship in doctrine and deeds, the bond of Christian fellowship.

2. To prepare to go forward by rallying the rank and file to a seeking out of a new and consecrated leadership which not only believes in our plea, but has sacrificed for it, to the end that the hosts may go forward proclaiming, in example as well as in word, the New Testament platform for Christian unity in Christ and not union on human expediencies. May we set congregations in order after the New Testament pattern. May we engage vitally in demonstrating the power of *Christian* education, *Christian* evangelism and *Christian* living, rather than human makeshift remedies for the uplifting of the world.

To this end we urge that the brethren the world over begin to plan together, with the help of all who put the authority of the Scriptures first, the simplest possible means of co-operating to carry out the following purposes:

1. To protect the brotherhood's testimony to the authority of the Christ and the New Testament doctrine and polity.

2. To protect a loyal ministry and loyal congregations from those who seek to divert them from faithfulness to the gospel.

3. To inspire a missionary zeal which will seek to plant churches everywhere faithful to the apostles' teaching, the breaking of bread and the prayers.

4. To extend and enrich the fellowship by restoring free, spontaneous, inspirational gatherings of the brethren in district, state or nation, to advance *Christian* education, *Christian* evangelism, *Christian* living.

5. To issue a literature for the aid of local forces in combating disloyalty and for the indoctrination and reconsecration to active service of the indifferent.

The preliminary plan is as simple as this: The signers of this call will select a group of eleven from their number to ask as a Temporary Committee for Action. This committee will be authorized to ask every loyal agency of publicity among us to endorse this call and give it widest possible circulation.

The call itself is for all brethren the world over who are like-minded to volunteer to help in some or all of the five objectives stated above and for them to send their enlistment and their suggestions to the Temporary Committee.

When the volunteer rolls are assembled, the Temporary Committee will arrange rallies where volunteers may

Courtesy, Library of The United Christian Missionary Society

The first page of "A Call for Enlistment" is reproduced here from the "Christian Standard" of November 27, 1943, p. 1009. The "Call" occupied most of three pages in this issue of the paper.

meet, where plans for leadership may be discussed and formulated until all who share in loyalty to the historic local Committees for Action appointed. position and plea of the brotherhood the world over have had opportunity to express their wills and join in forming final plans and leadership.

Permanent plans and permanent leadership will not be

Allison, Ben, Rising Sun, Ind.
Anglemyer, Shelney, Port Arthur, Tex.
BonDurant, George, Atlanta, Ga.
Book, Morris Butler, Orlando, Fla.
Boswell, Ira, Louisville, Ky.
Britton, Lawrence, Chester, W. Va.
Burns, James, Minneapolis, Minn.
Butler, Burris, Kokomo, Ind.
Canary, Peyton, Amarillo, Tex.
Dampier, Joe, Johnson City, Tenn.
Dance, W. Eric, Ft. Myers, Fla.
Dever, Lonnie, Erwin, Tenn.
Doty, C. L., Lawrenceville, Ill.
Dowdy, F. S., South Webster, O.
Dunn, C. V., Aurora, Mo.
Ellis, W. R., Toronto, O.
Ford, Lester, Painesville, O.

Foster, R. C., Cincinnati, O.
Hill, Joe, Covington, Ky.
Hossom, Harold, Erlanger, Ky.
Hoven, Ard, Cincinnati, O.
Hutchins, Howard, Wilkinson, Ind.
Lappin, S. S., Bedford, Ind.
Lillie, Robert, Calumet City, Ill.
McMillin, Don, Akron, O.
Morgan, Orval M., Lexington, Ky.
Mowrey, R., Terre Haute, Ind.
Musick, J. J., Elizabethton, Tenn.
Nickerson, Don, Barberton, O.
Perry, W. W., Cincinnati, O.
Poll, Harry, Cincinnati, O.
Rodgers, Stewart, Chicago, Ill.
Root, Clayton, Redlands, Calif.
Schaefer, Harry, Cincinnati, O.

Scott, Robert, Evansville, Ind.
Shaw, Roy R., San Jose, Calif.
Shockney, A. N., Portland, Ind.
Sparrow, O. T., Savannah, Ga.
Smith, Fred, Huntington, W. Va.
Smith, T. K., Columbus, Ind.
Strong, Homer, Long Beach, Calif.
Taylor, LaVerne, Carlisle, Ky.
Walker, W. R., Columbus, O.
Watts, R. A., San Bernardino, Calif.
Weaver, E. O., West Point, Ga.
Welshimer, P. H., Canton, O.
Whitehouse, J. J., Angola, Ind.
Williams, R. L., Longmont, Col.
Word, Archie, Portland, Ore.

Pursuant to the "Call," the committee of forty-nine has selected from its number a committee of eleven who will seek to enlist all who are in agreement with the announced objectives and prepare the way for a permanent committee and program to be chosen by all the brethren a year from now.

SEND YOUR ENLISTMENT TODAY TO THE COMMITTEE ON ACTION, BURRIS BUTLER, CHAIRMAN, 1030 S. BUCKEYE ST., KOKOMO, IND.

THE COMMITTEE OF ELEVEN

In accordance with the plan outlined in the "Call," each of the 49 signers voted for 11 of their number to serve on the temporary "Committee on Action." The following were chosen after agreement that the choice of the temporary committee would be restricted in area because of war-time travel conditions:

BURRIS BUTLER
LESTER FORD
R. C. FOSTER
ARD HOVEN
S. S. LAPPIN
P. H. WELSHIMER

ORVAL MORGAN
HARRY POLL
FRED SMITH
T. K. SMITH
W. R. WALKER

Eight of the eleven met in a preliminary meeting and organized for action. Because of imperative engagements in their local fields, S. S. Lappin, T. K. Smith and P. H. Welshimer were not present. The committee issued the following report:

SOUTH SIDE CHRISTIAN CHURCH
MARKLAND AVE. BETWEEN UNION ST. AND HOME AVE.
KOKOMO, INDIANA

RESIDENCE OF
BURRIS BUTLER, MINISTER
1030 S. BUCKEYE ST.

November 16, 1943.

THE CHRISTIAN STANDARD
Cincinnati, O.
Gentlemen:

Enclosed you will find a copy of "A Call for a Committee for Action," sponsored by nearly fifty loyal ministers and leaders of our brotherhood life. This "Call" is clear enough to be self-explanatory, and its immediate plan of operation is simple.

The forty-nine signers have chosen from among themselves eleven men (somewhat restricted in area for travel purposes) whom they have delegated to serve as a temporary committee to devise ways and means of action along the lines suggested. These eleven men have met and have organized, with Burris Butler, chairman; Fred Smith, secretary, and Lester Ford, treasurer. This is understood to be only a temporary arrangement until such a time as the brethren who voluntarily enlist themselves as in sympathy with these convictions and purposes shall have an opportunity to meet together and to plan a more permanent arrangement.

If you are in sympathy with these convictions and purposes, will you please give this "Call for Action" publicity through the pages of the CHRISTIAN STANDARD, and encourage loyal brethren to respond with their letters of enlistment and endorsement and with their suggestions as to possible procedures.

Incidentally, the election of a treasurer presupposes a treasury. We want to say as little as possible about money. We feel that the brethren will hail this move as long overdue and will support it with sufficient funds.

Sincerely yours,
Kokomo, Ind.   BURRIS BUTLER, Chairman.
1030 S. Buckeye St.

P. H. WELSHIMER AND W. R. WALKER WRITE JOINTLY ABOUT THE "CALL"

It expresses a conviction and a purpose.

The opening paragraphs state the conviction. We believe the present is a most opportune time to re-emphasize the plea for the restoration of the New Testament church as the only Scriptural (and therefore the only Christ-approved) basis for unity.

Unparalleled growth in numbers and spiritual power marked the first three-quarters of a century of our history. During the last two decades of the nineteenth century, membership in our churches increased 160 per cent.

It was an era in which New Testament Christianity

Courtesy, Library of The United Christian Missionary Society

This second page from the "Christian Standard" of November 27, 1943 (p. 1010), continues the material about the "Call for Enlistment." Names of signers and a "temporary" committee of eleven persons are shown.

was stressed by our preachers, congregations, missionary organizations and church publications.

We were united in a "fellowship" the like of which has seldom been experienced. We believe that happy condition can be restored if we of this generation return to the emphases and procedures of that earlier period.

The past few decades have been marked by other objectives on the part of some preachers, churches, organizations and periodicals. They seem to be more anxious to please the denominations than to maintain cordial relations between brethren in our own ranks. They think of union of organizations rather than of unity in the Spirit.

They look upon the kingdom of God as a religio-social state, subject to such mutations as human experience and expedience may deem proper.

The ideal they have in mind is fascistic. By centralizing control of church business enterprises, such as conventions, missionary organizations, educational institutions, publishing houses, etc., in interlocking directorates, they would dictate the programs of churches and control ministers by threats of ecclesiastical discipline. Whatever the motives which have led to the adoption of this ideology, the program is a distinct encroachment on the liberties which we have always insisted upon as within our Christian rights.

Some who pose as "authorized" leaders and representatives of the brotherhood are teaching and practicing open membership in the churches, exhibiting indifference as to the authority of the Scriptures, compromising with denominationalism and seeking control of all co-operative enterprises in the church. They are generating discord which threatens brotherhood unity. Unless these misrepresentatives of our plea and program are repudiated, we shall soon be in the same state religiously as the Axis powers find themselves politically. The tendency of organized Protestantism today is toward a totalitarian regime as intolerant and un-Scriptural as that of Rome. Our brotherhood should have no part in that.

The *purpose* is outlined in the later paragraphs of the "Call."

We feel certain that the items enumerated therein are such as you approve. If so, your co-operation in attaining them is sought.

P. H. Welshimer

W. R. Walker

Standard Endorses "Call" and Prepares to Announce Supporting Program

The directors of the Standard Publishing Company have studied the "Call," and have endorsed it with both resolution and instruction to the management to provide a supporting program. Our program and that of the Committee on Action may not always coincide in method, but they will be striving for a common objective—the defense and advancement of the authority and Lordship of the Christ.

The nature of this program as it affects the policy of the "Christian Standard" will be announced in some detail in the issue of this paper dated December 4. We, too, ask that our readers write the Committee on Action this week concerning their enlistment under the "Call," and write us next week concerning their reaction to our announcement of policy.

Disciples Divinity House Federates in Academic Group With Unitarians

By ALDIS L. WEBB

WITH the formation of the Federated Theological Faculty of the University of Chicago, the Disciples Divinity House became a part of a new academic arrangement in which four theological institutions have pooled their faculties to produce what has been described as "the largest Protestant theological faculty in America and one of the strongest in America."

The four schools—the University of Chicago Divinity School (Baptist), the Chicago Theological Seminary (Congregational), the Meadville Theological School (Unitarian) and the Disciples' Divinity House—plan to maintain their financial independence, their church affiliations and their corporate autonomy, but the students will have the instruction of the combined faculty, including thirty outstanding scholars from their respective denominations.

An inauguration and dedication service celebrating this academic event was held in Rockefeller Memorial Chapel of the University of Chicago, October 25. The speakers for the occasion were Robert W. Hutchins, president of the University of Chicago; Albert W. Palmer, of Chicago Theological Seminary, and Douglas Horton of the General Council of Congregational-Christian Churches. The services were preceded by an academic procession in which representatives from many academic and ecclesiastical institutions participated. The procession included the following:

Bethany College, Irvin E. Lunger.
Bible College of Missouri, Carl Agee.
Brite College of the Bible, Ellsworth Faris.
Butler University School of Religion, W. E. Garrison.
Christian Board of Publication, R. H. Miller.
Disciples Divinity School, Edward Scribner Ames.
Drake University, Charles C. Morrison.
Eureka College, L. W. H. Charnock.
Lynchburg College, R. B. Montgomery.
Pension Fund of Disciples of Christ, Paul G. Preston.
Transylvania College, Robert C. Lemon.
The United Christian Missionary Society, F. E. Davison.

Pres. Robert M. Hutchins, of the University, welcomed this closer relationship of these schools to the university and to each other in an address, "The Place of a Theological Education in a University." He stated: "We learn from these rules that theological knowledge has its roots in revelation, and we see that without revelation theology would not be distinguishable from other sciences and disciplines. But we learn, too, that theological knowledge grows and changes as much as all the rest of human knowledge. The Word of God is true. But since it is the Word of God, it is the most difficult of all things for us to understand. Although it in itself is always true, our interpretations of it are not necessarily true." Representatives of the four uniting faculties participated in the exercises.

Those familiar with the background of these four schools will appreciate how this federation has a good chance to work harmoniously. Several years back the Chicago University Divinity School was the storm center among Baptist Churches. The more conservative churches among the Baptists have turned their attention away from this liberal school and now send their students and support to the more conservative Northern Baptist Theological Seminary   [Continued on Eleventh Page]

Courtesy, Library of The United Christian Missionary Society

This is a facsimile of the last page of the "Call for Enlistment" from the "Christian Standard" of November 27, 1943, p. 1011. Note concluding paragraphs, top left, and endorsement at bottom.

Mention was made in the joint letter signed by Mr. Welshimer and Mr. Walker to "interlocking directorates." The letter ignored an action of the Grand Rapids International Convention on this matter "so that more Disciples could be used in the leadership of the agencies," and which was voted approval without dissent (*The Christian-Evangelist*, August 6, 1942, p. 870). The approved resolution of the convention stated:

We recommend that it be the future policy of the national boards reporting to the International Convention of Disciples of Christ to avoid interlocking directorates in the formation of the board of trustees, and that, where such a condition now exists, this policy become effective as rapidly as is consistent with wise business administration.

This recommendation about interlocking directorates was shortly afterward "accepted with approval" by the Board of Trustees of the United Christian Missionary Society. The twenty-fourth Annual Report of the Society, published in the *1944 Year Book, Disciples of Christ* (p. 8) stated:

The board of trustees after conference of representatives of seven agencies concerned has accepted with approval the advice embodied in the resolution adopted by the Grand Rapids Convention to avoid interlocking directorates among all brotherhood agencies reporting to the International Convention. It is the expressed desire of the board that in all future elections this principle shall be observed both in the selection of new members of the board and in reelections.

All of this material about a "Call" is an illustration of how far people will go under the influence of a magazine that is conducted by a publishing house, which has no board of trustees responsible to the brotherhood that it claims to represent and over which there are no checks or restraints. The paper's recurrent accusations and its psychology of repeated campaigns appealing for "loyalty" break down every sense of brotherly consideration. Again and again, instead of attempting to discuss matters temperately as though we were all adults and free, the *Christian Standard* has used unfortunate names for Christians with whom it disagrees to further its attacks and has issued accusing headlines about brotherhood leaders and organizations.

Following publication of the "Call," the *Standard* referred to the attitude of those attacked as "infidelity," a word that the magazine has used time and again for years when mentioning persons disagreeing with its positions. It is inexcusable, to say the least, for a Christian periodical to stigmatize another's spiritual reputation and especially when it is done by innuendo and generalities.

One week after the *Standard* published the "Call," an announcement appeared from the Executive Committee of the Standard Publishing Company, issued by Willard Mohorter, secretary (*Christian Standard*, December 4, 1943, p. 1033). It is reproduced exactly on the following pages. In part, it stated:

The management of The Standard Publishing Company desires to announce that beginning January 1 there will be a very definite change in the policy and character of the *Christian Standard*. Instead of continuing chiefly as a home paper of general religious information and instruction, we shall offer this journal as a rallying center for all who believe implicitly in the authority of Christ as revealed to us in the divinely inspired New Testament Scriptures. . . .

We shall devote the *Christian Standard* in the months to come to this issue which is as widespread as Christendom and which is today troubling every Bible-loving people: Will you follow the orders of Christ or the expediencies offered by ambitious men?

Thus the *Christian Standard* announced that it would continue spreading fear of "disloyalty" and of any ideas involving change from the accepted thought patterns of orthodoxy.

PUBLISHED WEEKLY
SUBSCRIPTION, $2.00 PER ANNUM

CINCINNATI, O., DECEMBER 4, 1943

OFFICES: EIGHTH AND CUTTER STS.
VOL. LXXIX—NO. 49

Dedicated to a Specific Service

In endorsement of the "Call" issued by the Temporary Committee on Action* the management of the Standard Publishing Company makes an important announcement

THE management of The Standard Publishing Company desires to announce that beginning January 1 there will be a very definite change in the policy and character of the CHRISTIAN STANDARD. Instead of continuing chiefly as a home paper of general religious information and instruction, we shall offer this journal as a rallying center for all who believe implicitly in the authority of Christ as revealed to us in the divinely inspired New Testament Scriptures.

It will become: First, a vigorous proclaimer and advocate of New Testament doctrine and life, and of the New Testament polity in which once we were a great united brotherhood.

Second, it will as vigorously protest every instance of the substitution of human expediency for the authority of Christ. It will help all who are like-minded to put a stop to misrepresentations of the historic position of our movement which is founded on His authority.

"Where the Book speaks," we shall not tolerate the substitution of expediency in the name of disciples of Christ to go unrebuked.

"Where the Book is silent," we shall champion the right of any Christian to uphold his own opinion in a Christian spirit.

We shall devote the CHRISTIAN STANDARD in the months to come to this issue which is as widespread as Christendom and which is today troubling every Bible-loving people: Will you follow the orders of Christ or the expediencies offered by ambitious men?

NOTABLE SERIES TO BEGIN JANUARY 1

First: New Testament Doctrine and Polity

The CHRISTIAN STANDARD will begin a weekly review of the historic position of disciples of Christ. The doctrine and polity on which our brotherhood came into being and was united as a brotherhood will be presented in systematic fashion, but in language for the comprehension of young as well as older Christians.

*See cover of the CHRISTIAN STANDARD for Nov. 27, 1943.

Herein will be summarized the body of truth based on the authority of Christ that we propose shall be aggressively advocated and as aggressively defended from misrepresentation.

Second: The Position of Infidelity

In this series from week to week we shall present a factual history of propaganda to substitute human expediency for the authority of Christ, especially in our brotherhood. How many organized agencies were enslaved and facts about some of many current abuses and misrepresentations of the New Testament position will be presented in brief, dispassionate form.

Third: Plans for Action

In this series from week to week we shall discuss practical plans for stopping misrepresentation of the plea, and emphasize the obligation of every believer in the authority of Christ to obey His orders as well as to defend them. With slight co-operation *we can stop misrepresentation*. Our biggest problem is to awaken the sleeping and to get about His business in an aggressive way.

And the News

Next will come news—and first, the news of the brethren who are with us wholeheartedly in a program to exalt above all human schemes the authority of the Christ. In marching ahead toward a common objective we need word from each other that   *Concluded on Third Page*

Courtesy, Library of The United Christian Missionary Society

The issue of December 4, 1943, beginning with this cover (p. 1033), was used by the "Christian Standard" to announce a radical change in policy.

December 4, 1943   **CHRISTIAN STANDARD**   (1035)   Page 3

What Paul says—very manifestly what he says—is that Christian love, which is the fruit of the Spirit, never wears out, as tongues, prophecies, special knowledge, etc., do fail or wear out. Paul says nothing whatever about love accomplishing all it attempts.

Think of the number of mothers who have poured out love upon wayward sons and daughters who went down into paths of worldliness. All to no avail. Think of others—wives, husbands, brothers, sisters, friends, ministers, etc.; for that matter, think of God and of Christ Himself spending love upon wayward and nonresponsive souls. Again and again such love has failed if we mean by failure the lack of the desired response.

Some day a great artist will paint a noble picture of the father of the prodigal son brooding with tears over the ring and the robe that represent the despised birthright of the dissolute youth in the far country. It is only the fact that the father's love could have failed of its object that lends piquancy to the story of that particular prodigal's return. Jesus never assured us that every prodigal would come back.

Let us carefully avoid the peril of the "proof text."

Sunday Afternoons

WRITING a letter to his home congregation, Virgil Elliott, on leave from Central Church, Pittsburgh, Pa., and serving as civilian chaplain of the Navy Radio Schools at Bedford and Hollidaysburg, Pa., commends Central for what it is doing for the Service boys in its area and goes on to make a pregnant suggestion to other preachers and congregations, as follows:

I am especially glad to see and know that Central Church is awake to the opportunities to be of help to the young men in that university district. Sunday afternoon is one of the hardest hours in the life of the average man in Service. These were the hours he used to enjoy with the friends he loved. I would say to the churches all over the land—OPEN YOUR DOORS FOR GOOD CHRISTIAN FELLOWSHIP TO THE MEN IN SERVICE ON SUNDAY AFTERNOON. Better the men should be entertained in the house of God in good fun with Christian people than to have them out on the streets or in some dive of iniquity.

If Sunday afternoon means so much to the boys by way of memories, does it not the more obligate us to build upon those wholesome memories the power of clean associations? Whatever it can do with other parts of the week, surely the church is in a position to utilize Sunday, and is it not obligated to prevent its property lying idle in that portion of that day?

A Queer Attachment

THERE are many good Christians who have a strange idea that loyalty to the Bible requires partiality to the King James Version and antagonism to every other translation.

There are reasons for antagonism toward certain modern translations and there are some particular points at which the American Revised Version could be more faithful to the original text; on the whole, however, the American Revised Version constitutes a more faithful representation in our present speech of what the divinely inspired writers really said than does any other version and especially than does the King James Version made in a speech three centuries old.

There is one phase of the matter, however, that causes the candid student of history many a smile. In giving himself to the promotion of circulation of the King James Version, the enthusiast, usually in blissful ignorance, promotes the circulation of as bold a falsehood as exists anywhere in all literature, for most copies of that version carry a panegyric of King James I of England that represents him as well-nigh a saint of generous spirit and remarkable integrity; whereas the truth is that James was an avaricious, scheming, niggardly and pusillanimous

character whom politics rather than his own hypocritical character made the champion of the Protestant cause. In their prejudice against the newer translation these good people scarcely have a moral right to devote themselves to circulation of such palpable falsehood and ought to be careful, whatever their preference, not to lay great claims to superior righteousness.

One Secretary Settles It

A NUMBER of the secretaries of state societies are to blame for the prevalence of "open membership" among the churches. In varied fashion they have tolerated it or given it recognition through programs or have failed to speak decisively against it at the opportune moment.

The following item at the head of the editorial column of the *Oregon Christian*, published by the Oregon State Board and other agencies of that area, and edited by the veteran C. F. Swander, would seem to permit no doubt as to where the secretary of that board stands, especially as he makes the matter rather emphatic by adding his signature and by emphasizing his readiness to answer the question "in the affirmative as well as negative":

ANSWERING A QUESTION

Some folks have been troubled about the state secretary. The question has been asked, "Does he stand for open membership?" (the practice of receiving members into the church without immersion). Unhesitatingly, unreservedly, unqualifiedly, unequivocally the state secretary says, "NO!" He is willing to answer it in the affirmative as well as negative, "I am against it." He has written against the practice and publicly spoken against it. It is a practice he condemns, no matter where practiced.—C. F. Swander, State Secretary.

The Brethren Are Answering India's Call

LAST week we received a report from Bro. A. B. Stockhoff about that first-mail response to the call of Harry Schaefer, Jr., for food for starving India. Brother Stockhoff challenged us with a call for $1,000 by December 1. This week he reports as of November 28 that the actual receipts have reached $728.

Manifestly, the brethren have taken up the appeal of Harry, Jr., and the challenge of Brother Stockhoff to reach $1,000 by December 1.

Address all gifts to A. B. Stockhoff, 402 E. Market St., Louisville, Ky. Designate it "for Famine Relief." He will receipt and forward regularly by cable. While you delay it, thousands are dying of starvation. Send all you can at once.

Dedicated to a Specific Service
Concluded from First Page

we may be drawn closer and know we are a mighty host able to possess the land in His name.

These come first in this time of paper shortage when we are under compulsion to reduce rather than increase the size of this paper.

We shall offer *The Lookout* and the *Bible Teacher and Leader* as adult publications of general service in the Bible-school field. We shall offer the *Christian Home Life* as a home and devotional magazine. But the CHRISTIAN STANDARD we shall devote to all who are interested in restoring the pattern of the New Testament church and a brotherhood built on acknowledgment of the authority of our Lord and Saviour.

THE EXECUTIVE COMMITTEE OF
THE STANDARD PUBLISHING CO.,
By WILLARD MOHORTER, Secretary.
Box 5. Sta. N, Cincinnati 3, O.

The concluding portion of the announcement of the Standard Publishing Co.'s change in policy for the "Christian Standard" is shown, lower right, in the issue of December 4, 1943, p. 1035.

Chapter 8

FINAL STEPS TOWARD DIVISION

Edwin R. Errett, editor of the *Christian Standard* since 1929, died on January 29, 1944. He had served the Standard Publishing Company for about thirty-two years. In 1912 he became office editor of the *Standard* and held that position until 1918. "From then until 1925 he served as a commentator and lesson writer for the Sunday-school publications of the company, and in 1925, was made editor-in-chief of those publications" (*Christian Standard,* April 6, 1946, p. 215).

His father, William Russell Errett (president of the Standard Publishing Company from 1923 "for about a decade") was a nephew of Isaac Errett and a cousin of Russell Errett (the manager of the Standard Publishing Company for so many years who had passed on in 1931). These facts about Edwin Errett's father were reported in the *Standard* of December 2, 1939 (p. 1152).

Following the death of Edwin Errett, the *Christian Standard* seemed to return to the attitudes expressed in *The Touchstone* under R. E. Elmore's editorship. This meant a revival of the attacks upon the brotherhood's organized work which were so manifest during the mid-twenties.

Some time after the death of Russell Errett in 1931, Harry Baird became treasurer of the Standard Publishing Company. Willard Mohorter had been named secretary in 1929, having been a member of the editorial staff of the *Christian Standard* since 1917 and editor of that periodical, 1922-29. Mr. Mohorter, member of our fellowship, had responsibility for matters concerning the brotherhood. W. R. Walker, minister of Columbus, Ohio, was named president, a position he still holds.

Before Edwin Errett's death in 1944, sharp differences had arisen within the company over the position of the *Christian*

Standard in matters affecting Disciples. Not long after this, James DeForest Murch, Aldis H. Webb, J. Vernon Jacobs, and others, left the company's employment.

It was quite noticeable during this time, too, that editorial attacks of the *Christian Standard* upon the cooperative life of the Disciples of Christ came frequently. The May 13, 1944, issue of the *Standard* announced (p. 306) that Burris Butler, a young minister of Kokomo, Indiana, was joining the staff as managing editor. The next year (*Christian Standard,* May 5, 1945, p. 274), Mr. Butler was promoted to the full editorship of the magazine. From the time that he joined the staff, accusations in the editorials seemed to increase. This was especially evident in the endorsement by the *Standard* of the attack of the "Committee of One Thousand" in 1946 and afterwards. This attack will be fully discussed in this chapter. The final culmination of the attacks by the *Standard* was the declaration, in 1950, that division had come among our people. This editorial pronouncement is to be discussed subsequently in these pages.

The September 16, 1944, issue of the *Standard* carried an editorial (p. 594) concerning statements by independent missionaries about their work. Mr. and Mrs. Luke D. Elliott, independent missionaries, then in Jamaica, had sent an "audited and notarized statement of money received and spent" for their work. The paper pointed out that "the Elliotts have set a good example to all independent missionaries who wish to use the columns of the *Christian Standard* for the solicitation of funds." The editorial further suggested:

. . . as a protection to our readers, any mission or agency desiring to use our columns for promotional purposes must (1) submit at least annually an audited statement of receipts and expenditures and (2) be ready to substantiate any claim made as to the work or its results.

It would be enlightening to know how far this wise proposition has been carried out. One of the many weaknesses of independent missions is the irresponsibility of those who have no duly-organized board back of them to which regular reports are made and without which there is no directive agency to check, not only their receipts and expenditures, but also the progress of the work they were sent out to do. Even though, as in the case of Mr. and Mrs. Elliott, a financial report is made to some editor, yet a newspaper is not constituted as a proper guide for such an enterprise and has no real facilities for the kind of auditing, both of finances and work, which distant missionary work requires.

Another angle of the support of independent missionaries was suggested in the June 25, 1949, issue of the *Standard*. An editorial, "Stabilize Missionary Support" (p. 410), stated:

It is comparatively easy for an enthusiastic preacher to cajole a church into taking on grudging support of a missionary, only to cut it off when the preacher goes to another place. World evangelism is too important to be at the mercy of petty whims and interim politics.

If the missionary is on the field under the auspices of a sponsoring committee, they should accept personal responsibility for seeing that he is adequately supported.

Yet how precarious is the support of even a sponsoring committee to meet the needs of a missionary who is in a faraway land!

"College of Bible Abandons the Plea" was the title of an editorial in the *Christian Standard* of August 4, 1945 (p. 482). This editorial was based on an article by T. Hassell Bowen, professor of Christian doctrine, for The College of the Bible *Bulletin* (July, 1945) of Lexington, Kentucky. In the article, Mr. Bowen had stated:

As a basis of that [Christian] union, Thomas Campbell announced the principle: "Where the Scriptures speak, we speak; and where the Scriptures are silent, we are silent." This gave rise to the plea for all churches to return to the Bible and to the "Ancient Order" of Christianity.

The results in part were disappointing. The sectarians did not accept the platform as expected and our fathers could not agree as to exactly what constituted the "Ancient Order" of the church. Furthermore, later scholarship discredited the idea of a fixed New Testament Church pattern and maintained that the early church was a development under the guidance of the Holy Spirit in the light of changing inward and outward conditions. The "Ancient Order" thus turned out to be like a river with its main stream and many tributaries, and not an architectural blueprint completed at Pentecost.

The *Christian Standard* then proceeded in its editorial to answer Mr. Bowen, stating, in part:

This is clearly a renunciation of the plea by the College of the Bible.
. . . .

Is it true that the results of the plea were disappointing? On the contrary. . . . It was not until in pulpits and Bible chairs dedicated to the plea when men began to repudiate the plea that "results were somewhat disappointing." The humanistic concept of the church as illustrated by the "stream and tributary" figure used by Mr. Bowen possesses the minds of the modernistic leaders of this movement away from the Restoration movement. . . .

In spite of the defection from the Restoration movement led by Chicago and Lexington, . . . there are many who continue to plead for Christian unity through the restoration of New Testament Christianity. . . . Within the past generation we have seen a rebirth of the movement in a number of new schools, like the Cincinnati Bible Seminary and others, who are . . . faithfully proclaiming that plea, and the results are not disappointing.

The *Standard* in this reply had stated, also, that John L. Davis, then executive secretary of the Board of Higher Education of Disciples of Christ, "continually derides the validity of 'restoration.'" The editorial then suggested that all of the educational institutions affiliated with the Board of Higher Education, having failed to protest the position of Mr. Davis, had likewise repudiated our plea.

The August 17, 1946 (p. 567) issue of the *Standard* had a list of the "loyal" Bible colleges. The list included the following institutions, with the dates of founding indicated: Alberta Bible College (1932), Calgary, Alberta, Canada; Atlanta Christian College (1925), Atlanta, Georgia; Cincinnati Bible Seminary (1924), Cincinnati, Ohio; Boise Bible College (1945), Boise, Idaho; Dakota Bible College (1942), Arlington, South Dakota; Eastern Christian Institute (1946), East Orange, New Jersey; Johnson Bible College (1893), Kimberlin Heights, Tennessee; Kentucky Christian College (1919), Grayson, Kentucky; Lincoln Bible Institute (1944), Lincoln, Illinois; Manhattan Bible College (1930), Manhattan, Kansas; Midwest Christian College (1946), Oklahoma City, Oklahoma; Minnesota Bible College (1913), Minneapolis, Minnesota; Nebraska Christian College (1944), Norfolk, Nebraska; Northwest Christian College (1934), Eugene, Oregon; Ozark Bible College (1942), Joplin, Missouri; Pacific Bible Seminary (1928), Long Beach, California; Restoration Bible College (1945), San Antonio, Texas; and San Jose Bible College (1932), San Jose, California.

Most, if not all, of these schools are still in existence, although several have changed their names. Eight of these Bible colleges, it will be noted, were established in the last decade. Others have been formed since the *Standard* published this list in 1946.

It is noticeable in this listing that the Butler School of Religion and the Bible College of Phillips University were omitted. Since Northwest Christian College became a member of the Board of Higher Education in 1951, it, too, will likely come under the ban of the *Christian Standard.*

"The Committee of One Thousand"

The International Convention of 1946 met in Columbus, Ohio, on August 6-11. It was the occasion for the launching of a severe attack against agencies and leaders of cooperative Disciples of Christ. The critics were self-styled, "The Committee of One Thousand." This group's attack was perpetrated through a full-page, paid, display advertisement in the *Ohio State Journal,* daily morning newspaper of Columbus, which ran in all editions of Wednesday, August 7, 1946.

Copies of the issue containing the advertisement were sold on the city's streets. Newsboys in front of the convention hall called attention to the attack as attendants entered or left the sessions. The accusations were rewritten by the Associated Press and other wire services so that the entire nation soon had reports of another lamentable division among Disciples. The complete text of the advertisement follows in facsimile from the *Christian Standard* where it was published in the issue of August 17, 1946 (pp. 562 f.).

The *Ohio State Journal* offered space to leaders of the convention for answering the paid advertising attack of the "Committee of One Thousand." However, this offer was not accepted. The early, green-paper edition of the *Journal* for Wednesday, August 7, 1946 (p. 2), in a separate news item at the end of the regular convention report, related the refusal, as follows:

Convention Ignores
"Open Letter"

Convention officials said yesterday they would ignore a challenge to debate made in "an open letter" by a group headed by Willis H. Meredith.

COMMITTEE OF ONE THOUSAND PRESENT THEIR PROTEST TO "INTERNATIONAL CONVENTION"

On pages 10 and 11 following, we reproduce an "Open Letter" from the Committee of One Thousand which appeared as a full-page statement in the *Ohio State Journal* (Columbus, O.), Wednesday, August 7.

We believe this document (along with the statement of this Committee which we reproduced in our August 3 issue) deserves the serious and careful consideration of Christians only everywhere. It represents the determined resolve of thousands of quiet Christians, who love the Word of God and who cherish their liberty in Christ, to resist further misrepresentation of their faith and practice.

These documents form another link in a series of warnings which through thirty years have been treated with scorn by the unethical group who falsely claim to represent a Bible-loving people.

According to the *Ohio State Journal* of August 7, the following is the convention leaders' reply to the warning of the multiplying thousands who are joining in declaring that they believe the Word and the New Testament way, and have commissioned no men to represent them:

CONVENTION IGNORES "OPEN LETTER"

Convention officials said yesterday they would ignore a challenge to debate made in "an open letter" by a group headed by Willis H. Meredith.

They said charges made against the convention had been successively made for years, that they will not be answered and no comment made at this time.

As the Columbus Convention actions again prove, the fact is that the convention leaders have no reply to make except to increase their defiance of their brethren and their God.

They have abandoned the Word of God as their rule of faith and practice.

They have accepted openly a denominational status for the sake of building ecclesiastical power.

They have misrepresented their brethren and have deceived their religious neighbors by false claims in order to gain place in denominational councils.

They have defied their God who said, "Not by might, nor by power, but by my Spirit, saith the Lord of Hosts."

THE ISSUE IS CLEAR AT LAST

Shall the brethren abandon the New Testament Scriptures as their rule of faith and practice?

That is the question every Christian only faces as the result of the betrayal of the cause by "International Convention" leaders.

Our fathers left denominationalism to proclaim the New Testament Scriptures as the only creed which needs no revision and to protest the Romish destruction of Christian liberty and the dependence upon might rather than right, which has always been an earmark of ecclesiasticism.

That we must return to a denominational status so that we may speak with authority in the Federal and World Councils of Churches is the decision of "International Convention" leaders. Without the right to do so, they have already presumed to speak for a people whom they do not represent.

The "International Convention" group is determined and set to carry with them into ecclesiasticism all whom they can dominate.

The great mass of the brethren who have paid a price for their liberty in Christ are taking their stand for the Word and for His Spirit. They are repudiating a false and self-appointed leadership to stand with all in the Christian world who put the Word and His Spirit before human loyalties. They are refusing to be a pawn in any political, worldly machine, be it Roman Catholic or Protestant.

The address of the Committee of One Thousand is Box 748, Jefferson City, Mo.

NOTE.—Due to the importance of the material on pages 10 and 11, which arrived in our offices as this issue of the "Standard" was in final stages of make-up, it was necessary for us to hold until next issue the fourth installment of James G. Van Buren's "The Conception of the Church Reflected in the New Testament."

FOR AUGUST 17, 1946

(561)   Page Nine

This page from the "Christian Standard," August 17, 1946 (p. 561), preceded a two-page reproduction of a page advertisement of the "Committee of 1,000" from a Columbus, Ohio, newspaper.

Copied from Wed., Aug. 7, 1946   OHIO STATE JOURNAL

AN OPEN LETTER!

Matthew 18: 16, 17.

But if he will not hear thee, then take with thee one or two more, that in the mouth of two or three witnesses, every word may be established.

If he shall neglect to hear them, tell it unto the Church: but if he neglect to hear the church, then let him be unto thee as a heathen man.—Words of Jesus.

—TO—

INTERNATIONAL CONVENTION DISCIPLES OF CHRIST
ITS SPONSORS AND DIRECTORS:

UNITED CHRISTIAN MISSIONARY SOCIETY, and CHRISTIAN BOARD OF PUBLICATION:

For many years faithful Christians have pleaded in vain with your groups to desist from your attacks upon the Bible as God's Holy Word. Such pleas were ignored.

Now in complete and detailed obedience to the mandate of the Saviour in Matt. 18: 16, 17, we issue this final urgent, and prayerful invitation, as we take the issue to the brethren.

We urge that, by definite and specific action of your convention, you publicly repudiate your men and your organizations which have attacked the authority of the Bible; that you adopt a declaration of faith and loyalty to God's Holy Word; and that you elect to office only leaders whose life records and pronouncements mark them as unflinching champions of the Book of books.

Only by such action can you repair the division in our ranks which your individual and collective attacks against the Bible have created.

Your offenses against the Christian Churches (Churches of Christ) are many and grievous. Among those which you should publicly confess and repent of, are the following:

YOUR FALSE PRETENSIONS of REPRESENTATIVE AUTHORITY

The International Convention of the Disciples of Christ has presumed to appoint members of the Federal Council of Churches of Christ in America on the numerical basis of the total membership of churches listed in the Year Book published by the International Convention. In view of the fact that the International Convention is a mass meeting of individuals, and does not, and cannot, have official standing, such appointments are a misrepresentation. Similarly fraudulent is the claim of the Christian Board of Publication to be the denominational publishing house of the "Disciples of Christ."

YOUR ATTACKS AGAINST BIBLE PECULIARLY ABHORRENT TO OUR CHURCHES

The motto of our movement has always been: "Where the Bible speaks, we speak; where the Bible is silent, we are silent." By your recent attacks on the Bible, you seem bent upon changing that motto to read: "Where the Bible speaks, it speaks falsely." When, in the early 19th century, Thomas and Alexander Campbell, all churches or sects, to lay aside their man-made creeds which divided them, and upon which no two could agree, and to accept the New Testament as the sole rule of faith and practice. 'On all interpretative controversies, complete freedom of opinion was guaranteed to all.'

CHRISTIAN STANDARD

Courtesy, Library of The United Christian Missionary Society

This is the first half of the page advertisement of the "Committee of 1,000" that appeared in a Columbus, Ohio, daily paper, August 7, 1946. This is here reproduced from the "Christian Standard," of August 17, 1946, p. 562.

Walter Scott, Barton Stone, Raccoon John Smith, and other leaders pioneered in our Restoration movement, they had no intention of founding another church or sect. They sought a common ground or basis, upon which all denominations could unite, as you well know. The result of their prayerful planning was an invitation to men of

From this sprang the aforementioned motto, making the Bible the very foundation of our brotherhood, and thus your attacks upon the Bible and your denial that it is God's Holy Word are more peculiarly abhorrent to our brotherhood than they could be to any other group.

YOU REPRESENT LESS THAN ONE PER CENT OF OUR BROTHERHOOD

As you well know, since and because of the attacks on the Holy Bible by leaders and literature of the above-named sponsors, you do not represent one per cent of our brotherhood. Easily could faithful neighboring churches send thousands of delegates into your convention on election day and take over. But that is not the Christian way. No effort will be made from the floor to have our suggestions accepted. In recent years, the trends of your conventions has been such that faithful Bible-loving Christians do not attend. Your action will be dominated, without interference, by those groups to whom this communication is addressed. In Christian love and prayer we send this final plea, as even now thousands of faithful brethren are carrying the news of the attacks against the Bible to the brotherhood. Thus, we have gone one step further even, toward peaceful solution than the admonition of the Saviour, as quoted above.

THE VITAL ISSUE WHICH YOU MUST DECIDE

The International Convention, the constituent agencies of the United Christian Missionary Society, and the Christian Board of Publication, once were among the honored institutions of our brotherhood. They were led by faithful Bible-loving Christians. They grew and prospered by the favor of God and the financial and moral support of our brethren.

If faithful Bible-loving Christians are forced to expose or destroy these agencies and to build others, it will be because your leaders have:

1. Repeatedly and persistently attacked the Bible as God's Word, and denied its truth.

2. Usurped authority over a brotherhood whose fundamental tenet is full and final authority of the Word of God administered through the local congregation.

3. Wasted our money in administrative expense and travel charged for roving "secretaries" whose work is largely occupied with church politics and the sale of printed matter which is not true to the Bible.

4. Completely divided our brotherhood by their attacks upon the Bible, so that hundreds of our churches will have nothing to do with their self-styled "organized effort."

FINALLY

If you refuse to heed this suggestion for a return to unity and loyalty to the Bible, which is the very foundation of our brotherhood, then we challenge you to designate a champion, such as Mr. Lemmon or Mr. Hopkins, or both, to set a date and place where they will publicly attack the Bible, as did the late Robert G. Ingersoll, with all the power and knowledge at their command. We will designate a spokesman who will publicly defend the Bible as God's Holy word, from the same forum.

Let the number and length of the addresses be such as Mr. Lemmon or Mr. Hopkins, or both, may choose. Let the discussion be advertised as an attack by your champion against the Bible. Let the newspapers and the radio chains be employed.

Too long have vital facts been kept from the brethren. Ninety per cent know nothing of the attacks against the Bible because thousands of our churches will not permit such literature on their premises, and members of other churches have not examined the subtle attacks upon the Scriptures, which features Anti-Bible literature.

In all good conscience, and with perfect candor, we desire to inform you that plans have been made to print 2,000,000 of the accompanying statements of fact, and to arrange for every member of every Christian Church (Church of Christ) to receive one. Copies of the folder, or statement of fact, which has been signed by thousands, and is now being distributed, are herewith attached.

Still cherishing the hope that your convention and its sponsors and directors will completely reverse its recent trends and return to the faith once for all delivered to the saints, we remain Loyal to His Word and Service.

THE COMMITTEE OF ONE THOUSAND

By Willis H. Meredith

Chairman of Executive Board

Courtesy, Library of The United Christian Missionary Society

The concluding portion of the page newspaper advertisement of the "Committee of 1,000," as it was reproduced in the "Christian Standard" of August 17, 1946, p. 563, is shown here.

They said charges made against the convention had been successively made for years, that they will not be answered and no comment made at this time.

As stated, this page advertisement from the *Ohio State Journal* was reprinted in its entirety in the *Christian Standard* of August 17, 1946 (pp. 562 f.). The page preceding the reproduced advertisement was headlined, "COMMITTEE OF ONE THOUSAND PRESENT THEIR PROTEST TO 'INTERNATIONAL CONVENTION'"—all in large, capital letters. A reproduction of this page follows, too.

The *Christian Standard* of August 31, 1946, gave most of two pages (pp. 595 f.) to a statement, "Missouri Committee of 1,000 Reports Phenomenal Growth," by Fred R. Barber, St. James, Missouri. The first of these two pages is duplicated on a succeeding page in facsimile. A boxed, featured statement on the first of these two pages bore the heading, "CHRISTIAN STANDARD Makes Contribution," which said, in part:

This committee and its action are not sponsored by the "Christian Standard." The phrasing used in the folder and the methods used in its distribution are not ours. Probably they are better than ours would be. But we believe these brethren are worthy of encouragement and support in carrying the facts directly to the Bible-loving people in the churches . . . .

While their efforts were confined to their own state, members of the committee financed their own work. . . . It is only fair that interested brethren from other states should give financial support.

The "Christian Standard" is forwarding a check for $100 to the Committee of One Thousand.

These endorsements of the "Committee of One Thousand" were upheld by an editorial, "Committee of 1,000 Deserves Support" which the *Standard* published in the issue of September 14, 1946 (p. 634). This editorial said:

The report on pages three and four from the "Committee of One Thousand" presents a cross section of the mail being received in their office. Brethren across the nation are responding to the call of the committee to arise and free the churches from those who attack the Bible under the guise of Christian teaching. While we want it plainly understood that this committee is not sponsored by the *Christian Standard*, we want it as well understood that we heartily endorse the announced objective of the committee; i.e., to carry to the people of the churches the

Missouri Committee of 1,000 Reports Phenomenal Growth

Deluge of requests for folders swamps overworked office force

Supporters Demand Enlargement of Committee's Scope and Activity

THE Committee of One Thousand was officially born July 1, 1946. Within less than two months it has become the fastest growing religious movement since Peter swung wide the doors of Christ's church at Pentecost. All are devout members of Missouri Christian churches or churches of Christ. Among the original members are some of the foremost "laymen" and ministers of the state.

Its original purpose was to expose the attacks against the Bible as God's Holy Word by the leaders and literature of the United Christian Missionary Society and the Christian Board of Publication—two organizations which were built and maintained by moral and financial support of Bible-loving Christians.

Its phenomenal growth and attendant developments already have forced a widening of the field to include other states, and even now are demanding that its original scope and purpose be broadened. Such decisions, of course, are for the future and the committee. The primary purpose, to place the now famous "folder," or statement of facts, in the hands of every member of every church will not be changed, because each of the thousands who have signed them pledged "our efforts, our resources, and our sacred honor" to that end.

GROWTH AMAZES COMMITTEE

Very definite and practical plans had been made and funds pledged to complete the plan in Missouri. The

Executive Board believed that all possible contingencies had been foreseen and provided for. Then came the deluge. Missouri Christians mailed folders to friends in other states. Then the CHRISTIAN STANDARD and the *Tri-State Christian*, published in Huntington, W. Va., reproduced the folder for the information of their readers. The effect was instant and overwhelming.

An office force, already staggering under the impact of Missouri demands and signatures, was buried under an avalanche of requests from sister states. From Washington to Florida, and from New England to Southern California they came pouring in.

NATION-WIDE SUPPORT

Next, the Executive Board delivered its "Open Letter" to the "International" convention at Columbus, with a challenge to debate the authority of the Bible in a public forum and over the radio, which the convention refused. The Associated Press sent the news of the challenge to fifteen hundred daily papers, with sixty million subscribers. Almost overnight the Missouri Committee of One Thousand awoke to the fact that its supporters and its responsibilities had become nation wide.

MISSOURI STILL FOOTING THE BILL

No request for folders or advice has been refused. The same Christian men and women who backed their faith with their money and their talents for the Missouri project have accepted the increased responsibility in the same spirit.

AS MOVE BECOMES NATIONAL, MORE FUNDS WILL BE NEEDED

Original pledges for printing, postage, office work, and supplies will have to be multiplied many times, but the faith of the committee is sublime. Convinced that God Himself is solidly behind this defense of His Holy Word, they have made commitments to see it through.

The national paper shortage posed a serious problem. A great Missouri printing house was commissioned to scour the market. Almost miraculously, it seemed, stocks of paper were found and bought so that printing of folders could proceed. A new supply of folders, over twice the number of the original printing, has come from the press, and they are being mailed as rapidly as possible.

CHRISTIAN STANDARD Makes Contribution

We are glad to present this story by Fred R. Barber, relating the progress of the Missouri Committee of One Thousand. Apparently this "grass roots" committee is proceeding on a sound premise: Give the people the facts and they will act on them.

This committee and its action are not sponsored by the "Christian Standard." The phrasing used in the folder and the methods used in its distribution are not ours. Probably they are better than ours would be. But we believe these brethren are worthy of encouragement and support in carrying the facts directly to the Bible-loving people in the

churches by means of their enlightening four-page folder.

While their efforts were confined to their own state, members of the committee financed their own work. If they are to furnish printed materials, the necessary office work, and postage to send folders into other states, it is only fair that interested brethren from other states should give financial support.

The "Christian Standard" is forwarding a check for $100 to the Committee of One Thousand. Your contribution can be mailed to Committee of One Thousand, Box 748, Jefferson City, Mo.

Courtesy, Library of The United Christian Missionary Society

This page from the "Christian Standard," August 31, 1946, p. 595, prominently displays at the bottom an appeal for the "Committee of 1,000." The magazine sent the "Committee" a check for $100.00.

story of the betrayal of the cause of Christ by self-styled "Brotherhood leaders" and their gross misrepresentation of the plea and the movement to restore New Testament Christianity.

The "report" referred to in the first sentence of the quote was by Lee Roy Schuler, minister, then of Moberly, Missouri, now of Eldora, Iowa.

One of the quotations above referred to a leaflet of the "Committee of One Thousand." Similar reference to the leaflet and/or statement of facts may be found, too, on the facsimile pages. This folder was published in facsimile by the *Christian Standard* (August 3, 1946, pp. 523 ff.) with the cover page of the magazine proclaiming, "Thousands Protest 'Organized' Infidelity." This cover page and the reproduction of the leaflet from that issue of the *Standard* follow in facsimile.

In addition to the material, similar to that in the Columbus advertisement, the folder, just above a place for endorsers to sign (shown in facsimile, too), had this pledge:

We will give no support, directly nor indirectly, to any religious group or institution which attacks the authenticity of the Bible as the revealed Word of God. We hereby solemnly pledge to each other, our efforts, our resources and our sacred honor, to the end that every member of every Church of Christ (Christian) shall receive the information herein contained. We also pledge renewed faith in, and support of, all of our missionary and evangelistic enterprises which are true to the Bible.

As indicated, the attack of the "Committee of One Thousand" was of such a character that the Columbus Convention did not answer and paid no official attention to it. That convention was attended by 3,100 Disciples of Christ who registered (*World Call,* September, 1946, p. 7), plus many others from the United States and Canada. Our conventions are mass meetings and any member of any congregation may attend the sessions. The program at Columbus was conducted in complete harmony.

During the convention, Gaines M. Cook, Cleveland, Ohio, for several years the state secretary of our brotherhood in Ohio, was elected as the first executive secretary of the International Convention which was authorized to start operating on a full-time basis for the first time in our history. Also, at the Columbus meeting, Harry B. McCormick, pastor at Lakewood, Ohio,

CHRISTIAN STANDARD

August 3, 1946

ISAAC ERRETT
Founder

DEVOTED TO THE RESTORATION OF PRIMITIVE CHRISTIANITY, ITS DOCTRINE, ITS ORDINANCES AND ITS FRUITS

Missouri Brethren Speak Out

Thousands Protest "Organized" Infidelity

"Grass Roots" Protest Movement Among Churches in Missouri Reaches
White Heat in Document Signed by Thousands Charging "Leaders" of
"Organized Work" with Infidelity. Christian Board and U.C.M.S. Named

THE common people need to be told, in language that any one can understand, that their children's souls are being poisoned in their own Sunday schools," said a prominent Missouri layman. "When they understand that," he continued earnestly, "they will arise in their wrath and throw the false teaching and the false teachers out of their churches. I didn't realize what was going on in the churches until I recently made an investigation of the Sunday-school literature being used in our church school. I have been too busy making a living. But now that I realize the situation, I intend to do something about it."

A "Grass Roots" Movement

This decision was the beginning of a movement in Missouri unique among our people. A strongly worded document was drawn up for circulation among the churches with the twofold purpose of informing the people of the churches and of obtaining signatures of members who are willing to devote time and influence to combat "modernism" and disloyalty to the revealed Word of God in both Christian Education and Missionary circles. Interesting enough this is not a preachers' movement, although preachers are co-operating in it. The CHRISTIAN STANDARD, usually alert to brotherhood developments, did not learn of it until it was well under way. It is a "grass roots" movement in the real sense of that phrase. A "layman" prominent in business circles drew up the document and is devoting his time and resources to its distribution. Another man, well known throughout the state, has furnished a car and driver. Others have made similar contributions.

Hopkins and Lemmon Named

The document being circulated among the church members is a strongly worded indictment of the Christian Board of Publication, St. Louis, Mo., and the United Christian Missionary Society, Indianapolis, Ind., on the charge that the Bible is attacked in their church literature,

and that missionary money is being used to teach that "the fundamental tenets of our church, as declared by Jesus and Peter and Paul, and reaffirmed by the Campbells, Scott, Stone, Smith, and other pioneer leaders, are all wrong." Proof is offered for the charges in quotations from the writings of "Organized Work" leaders. Robert Hopkins, president of the U. C. M. S., and Clarence E. Lemmon, president of the 1944 International Convention and staff-member of *Christian-Evangelist* and *World Call*, are specifically named.

Committee of One Thousand Formed

The closing statement of the folder is: "We will give no support, directly or indirectly, to any religious group or institution which attacks the authenticity of the Bible as the revealed Word of God. We herewith solemnly pledge to each other our efforts, our resources, and our sacred honor, to the end that every member of every church of Christ (Christian) shall receive the information herein contained. We also pledge renewed faith in, and support of, all of our missionary and evangelistic enterprises which are true to the Bible." Readers are urged to mail all signed folders to Committee of One Thousand, P. O. Box 748, Jefferson City, Mo. Apparently the anonymity of the "Committee of One Thousand" is rooted in the conviction that the justice of their cause is sufficient to receive a hearing and to achieve success without the added weight of "big" names.

No word has been received from the committee as to whether they propose to confine their activities to Missouri or to enlarge them to a nation-wide scale. The only hint is found in the final statement of the folder which pledges every signer to see to it that the information contained in the document is presented to "every member of every church of Christ (Christian)." It is probable that future activities of the Committee will depend on responses indicating interest in the movement outside of Missouri.

The complete text of the Missouri folder is carried in *fac simile* on pages three to six.

Courtesy, Library of The United Christian Missionary Society

The cover (p. 521) of the "Christian Standard" of August 3, 1946, was the periodical's first mention of the so-called "Committee of 1,000." The second and third paragraphs should be noted.

MISSOURI BRETHREN ACCUSE "DISCIPLE" ORGANIZATIONS

ATTACKS ON THE HOLY BIBLE BY CHRISTIAN BOARD OF PUBLICATION AND UNITED CHRISTIAN MISSIONARY SOCIETY LEADERS AND LITERATURE

Men Whose Salaries are Paid and Whose Very Bread is Bought by Faithful Bible-Loving Christians, Would Teach Christian Young People That the Sacred Book is Not the Word of God.

CHRISTIAN CHURCHES! CHURCHES OF CHRIST! DISCIPLES!

In deep sorrow and with profound regret, the undersigned, members, officers and ministers of more than 90 per cent of our brotherhood churches in Missouri, feel that our duty to God, to our children, and to ourselves, compels us to publish this information, and to make it available to all Christians.

Bible Attacked In Our Church Literature!

Men who deny the authenticity of the Bible as the divinely revealed Word of God, and who have departed, completely, from the historic position of our brotherhood, have obtained dominant positions, if not outright control, of two institutions, once highly esteemed in our churches.

These institutions are:

CHRISTIAN BOARD OF PUBLICATION, St. Louis, Mo., and
UNITED CHRISTIAN MISSIONARY SOCIETY, Indianapolis, Ind.

As a result, literature actually attacking the historical accuracy of the Bible, and denying, point blank, the statements of the Saviour, as reported in the Gospels, have been sent into our Sunday Schools by the *Christian Board of Publication,* to be taught to our children.

The *United Christian Missionary Society* is using our money to teach the heathen that the fundamental tenets of our church, as declared by Jesus and Peter and Paul and re-affirmed by the Campbells, Scott, Stone, Smith and other pioneer leaders, are all wrong. Emissaries of the *U.C.M.S.* are accepting into church membership, and promising salvation to those who refuse New Testament baptism, as practiced by the Apostles. This practice is called "Open Membership."

High officials of the *United Christian Missionary Society* also recommended literature for our Christian youth, which ridicules the miracles, as related in both the Old and New Testaments—and these officials include no less a personage than Robert M. Hopkins, president of the *U.C.M.S.*

COMPLETE PROOF OF ABOVE CHARGES

Many passages could be quoted from the officers, editors and literature of these two institutions, but space forbids. A number of the most glaring attacks are reproduced here in exact quotation for the information of fellow Christians. You, dear reader, will be astonished at the character of the assaults made upon the authenticity of God's Word by these, our so-called leaders, but the quotations are true, and will not be denied.

WE MUST ACT NOW!

The time for pleading and argument has passed. For several years, faithful leaders and preachers, moved by great tolerance and a desire to prevent division, have urged the leaders of the *United Christian Missionary Society* and the *Christian Board of Publication,* to stop their attacks upon the Bible as the revealed word of God. The attacks increased. Certain politico-religionists seemed determined to divide our brotherhood.

Hundreds of our Christian Churches will not use literature from these institutions because it is not "True to the Bible." Hundreds of churches do not contribute to the United Christian Missionary Society. Many of our greatest missionary projects and our most successful missionaries will not work under the "United Society." Truly, these attacks on the Bible have divided us.

Jesus taught us to "turn the other cheek," but this same Jesus resorted to great violence when duty required it. He scourged the politico-religious thieves from the temple. Such a duty now calls us to action. We have no alternative. Our stern duty, in defense of our faith and our children, compels us to render this verdict:

Duty Compels This Verdict

With a prayer in our hearts for a return to faith and loyalty by these two institutions, we are compelled to recommend to the hundreds of churches, of which we are contributing members, officers and ministers, that no support of any kind, moral or financial, shall be accorded to the *Christian Board of Publication,* or the *United Christian Missionary Society,* unless and until they have completely purged themselves of all enemies of the Bible. If, and when, the institutions herein discussed, shall publicly announce that their rolls have been purged of all enemies of the Bible as God's Holy Word (Pray God that it may be soon)—and that henceforth, no editors, officers, writers, speakers, missionaries or other representatives will be employed by them except those who are loyal to the Bible, then, and only then, will we be delighted to help them spread the glad tidings—the brotherhood.

Courtesy, Library of The United Christian Missionary Society

This is the first page of the leaflet issued by the "Committee of 1,000" and reproduced in the "Christian Standard" of August 3, 1946, p. 523.

FELLOW MISSOURIANS KNOW CLARENCE E. LEMMON

MOST OUTSPOKEN OF THOSE WHO DENY DIVINITY OF HOLY BIBLE IS C. E. LEMMON

LEMMON IS OFFICIALLY CONNECTED WITH CHRISTIAN BOARD OF PUBLICATION AND UNITED CHRISTIAN MISSIONARY SOCIETY

Official Organs of Both Carry His Name at Masthead in Every Issue

NO MAN COULD BE MORE TYPICAL SPOKESMAN FOR THE TWO ORGANIZATIONS

Lemmon's Attacks Published in Literature Sold to Sunday Schools for Instruction of Youth

One of the men who has been most outspoken and persistent in attacking the authenticity of the Bible is Mr. C. E. Lemmon.

More than any other living man, Mr. Lemmon is qualified to speak for the *Christian Board of Publication* and the *United Christian Missionary Society.* The Christian Evangelist is the official organ of the Christian Board of Publication. In every issue, the Christian Evangelist carries Mr. Lemmon's name at its masthead as one of its writers. The World Call is the official organ of the United Christian Missionary Society. In every issue World Call also carries the name of Mr. Lemmon at its masthead as one of its writers.

FORMER CONVENTION PRESIDENT

Both of the organizations, by their combined support, once elected Mr. Lemmon president of the International Convention of disciples of Christ.

So, when Mr. Lemmon attacks the authority of the Bible and disputes the clear statement of the Savior, he speaks with full approval of the "Christian Board of Publication" and the "United Christian Missionary Society". He has not been fired or repudiated. His name continues at the masthead of the propaganda organs of both organizations.

Now, what has Mr. Lemmon written about the Bible? Where was it published? For what purpose was it used?

The answers are that (1) it was published by the Christian Board of Publication and (2) sold to Sunday Schools to be (3) taught to teen age students and young people.

Mr. Lemmon Instructs Youth

And here are only a few of the things he wrote in our Sunday School literature as he tried to create the impression in the minds of our Sunday School boys and girls that the Bible is not the divinely revealed Word of God.

Webster Defines an Infidel

The most complete dictionary in the English language, Webster's New Unabridged, gives the following definition of an infidel:

"INFIDEL in modern popular usage, is a term of reproach for one who avowedly denies the tenets of Christianity and the truth of the Scriptures."

JESUS ENDORSES JONAH STORY; LEMMON DENIES IT

In Front Rank Magazine, published by the Christian Board of Publication, and sold to our Sunday Schools for use of young people, the following, written by Mr. Lemmon, appeared:

"Millions of men until recent times believed that portions of the Bible were equally valid as history. For example, the Book of Jonah tells the incredible story of the sea monster swallowing the prophet, and his living in the belly of the whale for three days and then being thrown upon the shore still living and able to preach repentance to the City of Nineveh. This was written by some Jewish author as a satire on the narrow outlook of a Jewish leader, who had to undergo a terrifying discipline before he was willing to preach to a foreign city."
—Front Rank Magazine.

We Must Choose Between Jesus and Lemmon

Jesus said: "Jonah was three days and three nights in the belly of the whale." Mr. Lemmon not only flatly repudiates the book of Jonah. He has no more respect for the Saviour of the world.

Lemmon Favors Evolution Over Genesis

Mr. Lemmon accepts the theory of the evolutionists in flat contradiction of God's declaration and the repeated declaration of Jesus and most of the Bible authors, that God created the world and the universe, including man.

In "Religious Helps", pages 35 and 39, Mr. Lemmon, our Sunday School literature editor, says:

"The evidence of scientific scholarship for this idea of the gradual development of man through natural processes, is so overwhelming that it cannot be successfully denied ....
Jonah is a fictional story, teaching the

---

universality of religion".—*C. E. Lemmon in "Lesson Helps".*

Lemmon Says Psalms, Ecclesiastes and Revelation are "Speculative"

Again "Rev." Lemmon wrote in "Front Rank" magazine—the magazine which carries the attacks on the Bible into the minds of our Sunday School children,—the following:

"Much of the material of the Bible is of a speculative nature. This is true of the Psalms, Ecclesiastes and Revelation."

What John and Paul, Inspired Apostles, Wrote About Traitors To God's Holy Word

"Now I beseech you, brethren, mark them that are causing the divisions and occasions of stumbling contrary to the doctrine which ye learned; and turn away from them. For they that are such serve not our Lord Christ, but their own belly; and by their smooth and fair speech they beguile the hearts of the innocent" (Rom. 16:17, 18).

"Whoever goeth onward and abideth not in the teaching of Christ, hath not God; he that abideth in the teaching, the same hath both the Father and the Son. If any one cometh unto you, and bringeth not this teaching, receive him not into your house, and give him no greeting; for he that giveth him greeting partaketh in his evil work" (2 John 9-11).

"I marvel that ye are so quickly removing from him that called you in the grace of Christ unto a different gospel; which is not another gospel; Only there are some that trouble you, and would pervert the gospel of Christ. But though we, or an angel from heaven, should preach unto you any gospel other than that which we preached unto you, let him be anathema."—Gal. 1: 6-8.

Courtesy, Library of The United Christian Missionary Society

The second page of the four-page leaflet of the "Committee of 1,000," reproduced in the "Christian Standard" of August 3, 1946, is duplicated here. This was p. 524 in the periodical.

HOPKINS' RECOMMENDATION OF FOSDICK RESENTED

PRESIDENT OF U. C. M. S. GIVES STRANGE ADVICE

SUGGESTS SHE FOLLOW H. E. FOSDICK IN TEACHING YOUTH OF MIRACLES

Fosdick Scoffs at Truth of Miracles

R. M. Hopkins is president of the United Christian Missionary Society. The United Christian Missionary Society, every year, receives approximately two million dollars from hundreds of churches. This money is contributed by thousands of "True to the Bible" Christians, most of whom will be surprised at what follows.

Miss Mabel Farmer is a teacher of young people of high school and college age at Hampton, Va. She is also president of a church "Circle" which contributed to the *United Christian Missionary Society*. Miss Farmer wrote a letter to President Hopkins, asking his suggestion for the best way to teach the miracles.

Dr. Hopkins answered by recommending that she consult a book written by Harry Emerson Fosdick.

President Hopkins Recommends Him

Here is what Fosdick believes and wrote and published in his book about the miracles:

"Joshua making the sun to stand still may be poetry, and the story of Jonah and the great fish may be a parable; the miraculous aspects of the plagues in Egypt and the magic fall of Jericho's walls may be legendary heightenings of historical events; the amazing tales of Elijah and Elisha may be largely folklore; and in the New Testament, finding a coin in a fish's mouth to pay the temple tax, or walking on water, or blasting a tree with a curse may be just such stories as have always been associated with an era of outstanding personalities and creative spiritual power. Certainly, I find some of the miracle narratives of Scripture historically incredible."

In addition to Mr. Lemmon, it is apparent that both Mr. Fosdick and his disciple, the president of the United Society, either have not read what Jesus said about Jonah being in the belly of the 'whale, or else that they do not believe, or care, what he said.

U.C.M.S. Teacher Quarterly

The United Christian Missionary Society has a curriculum committee, and publishes "Teachers' Quarterlies." To help prepare his lesson, the teacher of young people is urged in the "Senior Teachers Quarterly," to get the "Career and Significance of Jesus," written by W. B. Denny. The U.C.M.S. quarterly says: "It will inspire and definitely help

your teachers in the noble work which they are doing."

He "Knows" Gospels Are Not True

Here is what Mr. Denny believed and wrote and·published, and which might well have been written by Bob Ingersoll or Tom Paine:

"The attempt to take the gospels just as they stand is based on the assumption the gospels contain nothing but reliable history. Today, we know that assumption is not true."

U.C.M.S. RECOMMENDS HIM, TOO

Again, Mr. Denny says:

"In the gospels are a number of tales about the risen Jesus and his appearance in mysterious bodily form with strange new powers. Many people today feel that these stories are to be taken as stories that grew out of the devout imagination."

Christian Board's Bethany Literature Denies the Miracles

The "BETHANY" literature, published by the Christian Board of Publication and sold to Sunday Schools is sprinkled throughout, with proof that its authors and editors do not believe that the Bible is the word of God. A subtle effort, sometimes not so subtle, is apparent throughout this literature to destroy the faith of Sunday School pupils in the Bible as God's Holy Word. Hundreds of illustrations could be given. Here are just a few.

In "Senior Teachers Quarterly—Bethany Graded Lessons—Third Year," we find this subtle statement:

"None of the four Gospels or The Acts was written until after the death of Paul, Peter, James and John."

The writer lacked the courage to say so frankly, but what he said to Sunday School pupils, by sly inuendo, would make counterfeit and false, many of the books of the New Testament. The pupil would naturally wonder who could have written John's Gospel if it was not written until after his death.

The very same quarterly also contains this statement, published with the same sly attack on the authenticity of the New Testament and its authors.

"The last of the writings appearing in our New Testament was produced about A. D. 150."

If this statement were true, many of the New Testament books would have been written more than half a century after the death of the last Apostle, and much of the New Testament, with its inspired authorship, would be·a fake or a forgery.

SCIENCE PROVES BIBLE ACCURACY

Majority of Our Preachers, 90 Per Cent of Members Loyal. Don't Let Bible Enemies Mislead Our Children

Until 150 years ago, certain stories in the Bible seemed to be at variance with some ancient historians, and Christians accepted the Bible version on faith in God's word. Within the last century, millions of dollars have been spent and thousands of men have toiled under trained archaeologists in Bible·lands to get the facts. *The scientific record supports the sacred record.* Hundreds of specific, detailed proofs of Bible accuracy have awed the coldly calculating minds of world scientists with a new reverence for the sacred record as God caused it to be writtten. There is no possible excuse for the apostacy of certain so-called Christians.

In their attacks against the Bible·some writers have taken a more radical stand, even than did the late Robert G. Ingersoll, most famous infidel of modern times. Ingersoll's position was "I don't know."

Enemies of the Bible in our organizations have forced us to choose. Either we are Ingersoll Christians, or Bible Christians. Our churches·must be Ingersoll Churches of Christian Churches. Either we will cling to the Bible as the word of God, and as our sole creed for faith and practice—or we will embrace the doctrines of Lemmon, Fosdick, Hopkins and Ingersoll.

In each of the last 19 centuries, groups of radical men have attacked or ridiculed the Bible. They have flourished, waned, died, been forgotten, while the old Book rides new heights of popularity and acclaim. Seldom before, it is true, have men whose very bread was bought by Bible loving Christians, led the attacks, and so we commend the offenders to God's infinite mercy.

"THE TRUTH SHALL MAKE YOU FREE."

At least 90 per cent of our church members are loyal to the Bible. At least 80 per cent of them never heard of these attacks on the Bible. This folder which you are reading will correct that condition when placed in the hands of all church members. That is our goal. We invite your support and prayers.

The attacks against the Bible are inspired by a small group of selfish men, lusting for power, and bent upon division and control. They have used their official positions to punish our preachers who oppose them, and to reward those who accept their leadership.

Thousands of our preachers—a great majority—have stood faithful, courageous and true. If you find a preacher who is willing to defend, or apologize for enemies of the Bible, he probably has been

Courtesy, Library of The United Christian Missionary Society

Here is a facsimile of the third page of the leaflet broadcast across the brotherhood by the "Committee of 1,000." It is reproduced from the "Christian Standard" of August 3, 1946, p. 525.

COMMITTEE CALLS FOR ONE MILLION SIGNATURES

favored by them with a good pastorate, or honored with membership on one of their boards, bureaus, or committees.

SECTS GROW WHILE WE STAND STILL

No wonder we have been left far behind in membership growth by other churches. Read these admissions:

In World Call, of January 1944:

"While we have been gaining ministers, we have been losing churches at a corresponding rapid rate. In the twenty-three-year period ending in 1942, we lost 1,009 churches."

On Jan. 6, 1943 the Christian Evangelist:

"Disciples through the United Society have not opened a new foreign mission station since Wema, in the Belgian Congo, was begun in 1926. Paraguay, entered in 1918, was the last new field."

While the United Society was running into debt, recalling missionaries, selling mission property, and trying to save itself by an emergency million, other missionaries by the dozens on faith and faithfulness to the gospel have gone to new fields and baptized thousands.

THE REMEDY

A million signatures to this folder is the remedy. One tenth of that number will drive the enemies of the Holy Bible into headlong retreat. But we must not stop there. Every member signed, is our goal. With God's help, we will bind together our broken ranks and lead the Christian forces of the world back to faith, unity and loyalty with our reunited army. Fill as many folders as possible. Get signatures. He died for us. Let's work for Him. Write name and address plainly.

Mail all signed folders to

Committee of One Thousand
P O Box 748
Jefferson City, Mo.

"YE SHALL KNOW THE TRUTH AND THE TRUTH SHALL MAKE YOU FREE"—
Words of Jesus

We will give no support, directly, nor indirectly, to any religious group or institution which attacks the authenticity of the Bible as the revealed Word of God. We herewith solemnly pledge to each other, our efforts, our resources and our sacred honor, to the end that every member of every Church of Christ (Christian) shall receive the information herein contained. We also pledge renewed faith in, and support of, all of our missionary and evangelistic enterprises which are true to the Bible.

Name	Street Address or Rural Rt.	Post Office

Courtesy, Library of The United Christian Missionary Society

This is the last page of the leaflet produced by the "Committee of 1,000." It contained an appeal for signers, and a pledge. It appeared in the "Christian Standard," August 3, 1946, p. 526.

was chosen president of the United Christian Missionary Society to succeed Robert M. Hopkins who had reached the retirement age.

This propaganda of the "Committee of One Thousand" assumed that there was a group numbering at least one thousand persons. Yet the names of the committee were never revealed.

This attack, so enthusiastically endorsed by the *Christian Standard*, would hardly have been made during the editorship of Edwin R. Errett. The censure was similar to the earlier campaign of the Standard Publishing Company through *The Touchstone*, edited by Robert E. Elmore. This time, however, the International Convention and the Christian Board of Publication were included. The propagandists thus made accusations against responsible leaders of the Disciples of Christ and then challenged those accused to enter into a debate and themselves prove the accusations made against them!

This attack was maintained in the *Christian Standard* for several weeks. The "mailbag" of the "Committee of One Thousand" which was published contained many brief statements of support. The statements were seldom signed.

The *Christian Standard* of December 14, 1946, published nearly two pages (pp. 894 f.) about the "Committee of One Thousand" distributing circulars at four St. Louis, Missouri, churches. Three pictures were published showing the distribution among members of the Union Avenue Christian Church, following the conclusion of the Sunday morning worship on December 1, 1946. The report published resolutions of endorsement of the committee and its work which were voted that same Sunday by University City and Fourth Christian Churches of the St. Louis area. It was not pointed out, however, that prior to that particular Sunday these same two, small congregations had already been alienated from the brotherhood's cooperative program for years. Union Avenue and our other twelve churches there paid no attention to this propaganada barrage, except that Hampton Adams, minister of the Union Avenue Church, voiced his resentment and that of the church at such an approach.

The end of the "Committee of One Thousand" was noted in an unobtrusive news item that appeared in the columns of the

Restoration Herald for December, 1949 (p. 7). This item was as follows:

Committee of 1,000

Many letters of inquiry necessitate the following statement:

Since the death of Heber Nations [on March 11, 1948] and the withdrawal of Willis Meredith, founders and co-chairmen of the Missouri Committee of 1,000, the Committee as such is defunct.

Earlier, Mr. Meredith's notice of withdrawal from the committee appeared in the *Restoration Herald* (September, 1949, p. 7). It was, as follows:

A Card

Since the lamented passing of Heber Nations, my long time friend and fellow Christian, I have not been consulted, and have had no connection whatever with the Missouri Committee of One Thousand.

This Committee was brought into being at Rolla, Missouri, April 4, 1946, on the initiation of Heber Nations and those attending the Missouri Restoration Congress there. I served as Co-Chairman of the Committee with Brother Nations until his death, on March 11, 1948.

I am not now connected with this Committee of 1,000, nor shall be at any future time.

> Willis H. Meredith
> Poplar Bluff, Missouri
> August 15, 1949

Mr. Nations had resided at Jefferson City, Missouri, where the committee received its mail while it was in existence. Mr. Meredith is a resident of Poplar Bluff, Missouri. Both were laymen. Even yet, however, the propaganada of this committee is still distributed among our people and churches. Unfortunately, as is usually true with this type of material, it is accepted, often without hesitation, by persons who make no effort to learn the other side of the situation.

It is of interest in connection with the "Committee of One Thousand" that a small group in Kentucky attempted to use the committee's procedure. The Kentucky group was under the direction of Tibbs Maxey, graduate of the Cincinnati Bible Seminary and president of the College of the Scriptures (established in 1945), a school for Negroes in Louisville, Kentucky.

A leaflet was headlined, *The Committee of One Thousand in Kentucky*. Like the attack made at the Columbus Convention, names of the committee were not listed. The leaflet accused nearly every cooperative organization among the Disciples of Christ of "modernism," whatever that is. Included in the attack were the United Christian Missionary Society, the Kentucky Christian Missionary Society, Transylvania College, and The College of the Bible.

In this leaflet, partial statements from individuals were quoted, out of their context. Beyond that, interpretations of the quotations were introduced in headlines. Also, these critics even went so far as to use for their purpose some statements that had been made by Prof. E. E. Snoddy, long since gone to his reward, as well as those of the late A. W. Fortune, than whom there was no more beloved and trusted minister in our fellowship. In cautioning unwary Disciples about such interpretations, it must be emphasized, also, that the names of such a committee in Kentucky never have been produced.

During the autumn of 1946, while the *Christian Standard* was publicizing the "Committee of One Thousand," the magazine reported on the growth of Christian service camps. The article, appearing in the issue of September 28, 1946 (pp. 676 f.), stated that "1946 has been, in all respects, the most successful year in the history of the Christian Service Camp movement." A tabulation showed that there had been 158 camps during the summer of 1946 with an attendance of 14,220, that 1,236 persons became Christians at the camps, that there were 1,235 life recruits, and that 1,698 persons were on the faculty. These summer camps were set up and are conducted annually by persons opposing the summer conferences operating under auspices of the department of religious education of the United Christian Missionary Society.

"Stand Up and Be Counted"

Growing out of the propaganda of the "Committee of One Thousand," the *Christian Standard* started another campaign under the title, "Stand Up and Be Counted." It began with the publication, beginning on the cover page of the issue of June 7, 1947 (pp. 401 f.), of a detailed account of the controversy in the First Christian Church of Muskogee, Oklahoma. Under the ministry of C. W. Lipsey, the church had divided following a "controversy that had existed in the board of elders for some eighteen months."

The account in the *Standard,* headlined, "Muskogee Throws Off Shackles," stated that Mr. Lipsey had threatened to present his resignation as pastor unless the church changed its policy. The pastor's resignation stated, in part:

I want it thoroughly understood that my leaving is due to the policy and operation of the official board, the Bible school, and the missionary society. It is impossible for "two to walk together unless they be agreed." It is my conviction that no true church of Christ can be dictated to by human organizations, ecclesiastical groups, or any small group of people representing same, and yet be true to Jesus Christ. I am in total discord with the policies of the United Christian Missionary Society, the Federal Council of Churches of Christ in America, and the World Council of Churches. I am opposed to a "Super Protestant Church" dictated to by modernists as much as I am to a "Catholic Church" dictated to by a pope.

As matters reached a climax in the Muskogee church, the following resolution, presented by an elder, was adopted at a congregational meeting:

The elders and deacons of the First Christian Church, Muskogee, Okla., recognizing the need for a clear-cut statement of policy to guide this congregation do hereby resolve:

I. To support and promote only such missionary, educational, and benevolent work as proclaims the full gospel of Jesus Christ as revealed in the Scriptures.

II. Those who receive such support to be determined by the duly chosen leaders of the local congregation, without advice from outside the local church, unless solicited by these leaders.

III. No minister, missionary, or other worker shall be called to serve this congregation, in either the local church program, or otherwise, who is not in full accord with the foregoing resolution.

At a subsequent business meeting of the congregation with "some 500 to 600 people" attending, a statement of the church board enunciating rules of operation was approved and new board members elected. Mr. Lipsey, of course, announced that he would remain as minister of the congregation.

This same issue of the *Christian Standard* carried an editorial (p. 402) in extraordinarily large type for such comment. It was

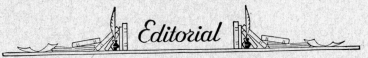

Editorial

Stand Up and Be Counted

WHEN a congregation like the First Christian Church, Muskogee, Okla., gives an overwhelming vote of endorsement to a faithful gospel preacher like C. W. Lipsey, and takes its stand as an undenominational New Testament church, that is news of the first order. We rejoice in giving to the brotherhood the story carried on page 1.

For many years an unfaithful leadership has tried to force denominationalism upon free churches of Christ. We have seen churches and preachers succumb rather than resist, lose their freedom in Christ, and with it their evangelistic zeal. Churches once great in their faith now stand as though stricken by the blight—fruitless and lifeless.

But an increasing number of congregations served by faithful ministers who refused to play the hireling, and by informed elders who were true to their trust, have thrown off the shackles of a sectarian leadership and have stood squarely on solid New Testament ground.

Scores, probably hundreds, of such churches have been reported singly in our columns as they took their stand. Thousands of others have stood their ground in silence.

Now we propose an "Honor Roll of the Faithful," of both congregations and ministers who have taken their stand and have refused to become a part of a denominational machine. Let us hear from you. Just a postcard or letter will do. Each week we shall carry a list of preachers and churches who send in their names. We may have carried your story previously in our pages. Let us hear from you anyway. You may have shunned publicity in the past. Let your name and example give courage to some one else.

By the time the returns are all in we are hoping to have presented a list of all ministers who are proud to stand as free men in Christ, and all congregations whose aim is to be undenominational New Testament churches.

Brethren have been demanding a listing separate from the "Disciples'" year book. Here it is. It is not a year book, of course. But it is a challenge to "stand up and be counted."

Brethren, let us hear from you!

Cast Off the Fetters!

DEPLORABLE are the religious conditions in our time which make it necessary for a church to adopt a resolution avowing its intention to be a church. Fundamentally, that is what is involved in such an action as that taken by First Church, Muskogee, Okla. Throughout the world local churches of Christ are in a life-and-death struggle in which their very nature is involved. They are forced to fight just for the right to be the church.

Under the influence of ecclesiastical pressure groups and self-glorifying leaders churches have become fundraising organizations, social clubs, protectors of vested interests, anything except what the Son of God intended for them to be. In every such group are persons who love the Lord, honor His Word, and try to serve Him. But they find little encouragement indeed in the "church" with which they are identified.

Here and there a church decides to be a church of Christ and determines to follow the pattern in the New Testament as its members follow their divine head. Glorious are the results that follow. Men learn the thrill that comes from breathing the air of freedom. The church delivered from lesser interests is able to devote its attention to its first task—bringing salvation to lost men through the power of the gospel.

Such deliverance can come about only as local congregations far and wide take action similar to that of First Church, Muskogee. Let brave men stand and serve notice that the church of Christ is "essentially, intentionally, and constitutionally" free from all overlordship except that of the Son of God Himself. Let the hands of the church be unshackled to serve the one Master. Let the feet of the church be unbound to follow the one leader. Let the church be the church! Yes, let it be the church of Christ!

As the truth made men free in the first century, the New Testament church advanced and the Word of God was multiplied. As men stood free in Christ in the nineteenth century, the Restoration movement grew and progressed. The lost world of our day desperately needs the glad news of redemption in Christ. Cast off the fetters.

BURRIS BUTLER, Editor; HOWARD E. KELLEY, Office Editor; HELEN LYONS, News Editor; W. R. WALKER, Editorial Counselor.

Volume LXXXIII. Number 23. The CHRISTIAN STANDARD, published weekly at 20 E. Central Parkway, Cincinnati 10, Ohio. Entered as second-class matter Jan. 31, 1880, at the post office at Cincinnati, O., under the Act of March 3, 1879. Printed in U. S. A. Address all communications to The Standard Publishing Company, Box 55, Sta. V, Cincinnati 10, Ohio. Subscription rates per year. United States, $2.50; Canada, $2.90; Foreign, $3.55. Single copy, 5 cents. Club rates: Five or more copies to one address, $1.75 per year or 45 cents per quarter; ten or more copies to separate addresses, $2.00 per year.

Courtesy, Library of The United Christian Missionary Society

The first announcement by the "Christian Standard" of its "Stand Up and Be Counted" campaign was made in this editorial of June 7, 1947, p. 402. Note the large type used for the appeal.

entitled, "Stand Up and Be Counted." This editorial page is reproduced in facsimile on a following page. The reader may note that the concluding portion of what seemed to be the same editorial was at the bottom of the same page, in smaller type, under the heading, "Cast Off the Fetters!" Other congregations were urged by the editorial to take similar action to that of the Muskogee church.

Following this appeal, the *Christian Standard* began publishing the names of the churches and ministers who wished to "Stand Up and Be Counted." The number that was listed each week was as follows:

Date	Page	Number of Churches Listed	Number of Pastors
June 21, 1947	434	20	34
June 28, 1947	451	38	46
July 5, 1947	467	43	44
July 12, 1947	483	30	41
July 19, 1947	499	26	39
July 26, 1947	515	33	36
Aug. 2, 1947	531	28	42
Aug. 9, 1947	551	20	31
Aug. 16, 1947	563	16	30
Sept. 6, 1947	615	28	44
Totals		282	387

Publication of the lists of churches and ministers in the "Honor Roll of the Faithful" in the *Standard* was discontinued with the issue of September 6, 1947. The total of less than three hundred churches and less than four hundred ministers must have been most disappointing for the magazine's editor. Those listed were thus only a small part of the approximately eight thousand churches and a like number of ministers of the Disciples of Christ in the United States and Canada.

The first list of the "Honor Roll of the Faithful" was published on the editorial page (p. 434) of the *Standard* for June 21, 1947. At the end of the list, the paper said:

We firmly believe there are hundreds of churches and preachers who wish to go on public record as undenominational. This listing provides that opportunity.

This list can be used as a basis of protests to the Federal Council and to every group that attempts to include free churches of Christ and gospel preachers in their denominational pretensions.

Only two of the larger churches which usually follow leadership of the *Christian Standard* were listed on the roll. They remained tabulated in the *1952 Year Book* of Disciples.

There were twenty churches listed in the first installment of the "Honor Roll" (*Christian Standard,* June 21, 1947, p. 434). A study of the gifts (or their lack) from those congregations to our organized work is revealing. According to the *Year Book* of Disciples (1946 and 1947), one church was not listed while six (1946) and three (1947) made no contributions to missionary causes (this figure fluctuates because many churches give one year but not another, due, usually, to indifference). Ten of the churches gave to Unified Promotion in 1946, eight in 1947; thirteen to benevolence in 1946, fourteen in 1947; six to the Crusade and/or Week of Compassion in 1947; one to the International Convention in 1947. Only the Women's Missionary Societies gave from two of the twenty churches.

In the *1951 Year Book,* three of the twenty churches were not listed; seven showed no missionary contributions. Of the other ten churches, five gave to some phase of the brotherhood's Crusade, nine for benevolence, and six (including one Women's Missionary Society only in one church) to Unified Promotion causes. One of the ten congregations contributed to every phase of cooperative work, including the International Convention! The *1952 Year Book* presents much the same picture.

After a careful study of the various published lists of churches, it seems doubtful that any church, or minister, was persuaded to change position by the "Stand Up and Be Counted" campaign of the *Standard.* Several, perhaps, had been alienated from organized brotherhood work for years.

The appeal to the churches and the ministers was to declare themselves as not belonging to a "denomination" and thus have their names listed on the "Honor Roll of the Faithful." The July 5, 1947, *Standard* (p. 467) put the appeal thus: "A list of congregations whose aim is to be undenominational New Testament churches, and of ministers who are proud to stand as free men in Christ."

A letter written by the editor of the *Standard*, Burris Butler, to a Kansas minister who questioned motives of the "Stand Up and Be Counted" campaign was published in the July 26, 1947, issue (p. 515). The letter was written in answer to the pastor's question, "Who Are the Faithful?" that had been asked in the bulletin of the West Side Christian Church, Wichita, O. Ray Burgess, minister. Mr. Butler wrote, in part:

> You seem to assume an attitude of suspicion toward the call to "stand up and be counted," as you say "I do not know what is really back of this movement." This suspicion in turn grows almost to the point of hostility as you prophesy, "but (I) think it will die as the 'call' did a few years ago."

> Let me assure you that what is "really back of this movement" is the intention to give every congregation and preacher who desires it an opportunity to go on public record as being no part of a "Disciples" denomination. This public statement on the part of free churches will serve as an anchor when the movement on the part of "Disciples" denominationalists to deprive churches of their property by court action becomes more prevalent than it is at present.

> . . . You speak of "the *drift* of our brotherhood toward the status of a denomination." This trend is more than a "drift." It is the result of an active conspiracy to denominationalize the Restoration movement. It is in opposition to this conspiracy and to save the faithful labors of 150 years that we call on the brethren to stand up and be counted.

Some resolutions, sent in by ministers, were published in the *Standard*. The following (June 28, 1947, p. 451), from Oren H. Whitton, minister of the Central Christian Church, Tampa, Florida, is typical: "Congregation passed by unanimous vote resolution declaring itself to be free from the dictates, wishes, and desires of any ecclesiastical body, missionary organization, or federal council." This was a striking expression, an excellent one for any church among the Disciples of Christ if occasion called for such a stand! The assumption, however, was that those not declaring themselves were disloyal!

One week the list of ministers' names published totaled forty-two (*Christian Standard*, August 2, 1947, p. 531). This was one of the largest of the weekly lists. The men listed as pastors of churches (nine did not appear to be) were shown in the *1947 Year Book* of Disciples of Christ with churches not contributing to any brotherhood causes, except for three. In these three churches only the Women's Missionary Societies made contributions to the causes represented by Unified Promotion.

As indicated, Mr. Lipsey, the minister, was responsible for the division of the First Christian Church of Muskogee. The larger part of the congregation followed him in his opposition to the United Society and other agencies and institutions of the Disciples, as well as the Federal and World Councils of Churches.

Mr. Lipsey soon resigned the Muskogee pastorate, however, going to the West Amarillo (Texas) Church in November, 1947. On August 1, 1949, he left Amarillo, it had been announced, to teach at Southern Christian College, a nonaccredited ministerial school, in San Antonio, Texas. (He had been educated at Randolph College, Cisco, Texas, now a defunct junior college of the Disciples, and at Pike's Peak Bible Seminary, a correspondence school which had conferred a doctor's degree upon him.) He died in Muskogee, September 1, 1949 (*Christian Standard*, September 17, 1949, p. 595; also *The Christian-Evangelist*, December 7, 1949, p. 1228).

In the election of new members of the church board at Muskogee First Church, many of the abler men there were not chosen because they did not agree with Mr. Lipsey's attitudes. These, and other members of the congregation, became discouraged and disgusted at the turn of events. They withdrew their membership from the First Christian Church and formed another congregation, Memorial Christian Church, which is supporting our cooperative work.

So another highly-propagandized campaign of the *Christian Standard*, purporting to call "scores, probably hundreds" of our churches to the enlistment and endeavoring to separate the "loyal" from the "disloyal" ended in frustration. Obviously, however, much damage is done by such unfortunate attacks. Many Disciples of Christ, not in touch with our cooperative work and reading only the publications of the Standard Publishing Company, have their minds prejudiced, many of them irrevocably, with distrust developed against their Christian brethren.

The *Christian Standard* of August 2, 1947 (p. 544), published the names and addresses of the brotherhood's "direct-support" missionaries. A summary of that list may be tabulated as follows:

Field	Missionaries on Field	Missionaries on Furlough	Recruits
ALASKA (Nine places)	25	4	0
BRAZIL (Rio de Janeiro)	0	0	2
BURMA (North Burma)	0	0	2
CHINA			
China Mission	0	0	4
Yunnan Chinese	2	0	2
COLOMBIA (Upper Andes)	0	0	2
GERMANY	0	0	4
HAWAII	6	0	2
HUNGARY	0	1	0
INDIA			
Central Provinces	3	1	0
Hamirpur District	5	0	0
Landour, United Prov.	5	0	2
ITALY			
Mediterranean Mission	3	0	2
JAMAICA	4	0	0
JAPAN			
Cunningham Mission	3	0	4
Kyushu Mission	0	1	0
Mabashi Mission	0	1	0
Osaka Mission	1	5	2
KOREA	0	4	0
MEXICO (Monterrey)	1	0	0
PHILIPPINE ISLANDS			
Cebu Mission	2	0	0
Philippine Mission	12	2	0
TIBETAN BORDER			
Batang	4	2	1
Tibetan-Lisuland	5	5	0
	81	26	29

In addition to the foreign missionaries, the paper listed twenty-nine workers in the United States, as follows: American Indian Evangelism, two; Allentown, Pennsylvania, two; Carson City, Nevada, one; French Acadian Mission, five; Japanese-American Evangelism, four; Jewish Evangelism (Christian Witness to Israel, New York), none; Mexican Evangelism, seven;

Mountain Evangelism, one agency, one worker, and an additional worker; Mountain Work and Choctaw Indian Evangelism, five; Negro Evangelism, one college and one committee; New York City Evangelism, two workers and a chapel.

Comparing this list with one which the *Standard* issued five months earlier (March 1, 1947, p. 160), several changes are evident. This August listing included the proposed Upper Andes Mission in Colombia, South America; the March listing omitted the Hawaii work and the mission at Landour, in the United Province of India. Then, within the United States, the March list omitted American Indian Evangelism and Mountain Work and Choctaw Indian Evangelism, both new pieces of work perhaps. The August list, however, omitted the independent benevolent work (in Boise, Idaho; St. Louis, Missouri, and Turner, Oregon) and a Hebrew Mission in Portland, Oregon, all of which were listed in March.

The March list contained names and addresses of fifty-two missionaries abroad, thirty-two on furlough, and thirty-nine recruits. The totals in these categories were quite different in the August listing, as a comparison with those totals indicates.

According to the August list, there were twenty-nine recruits for foreign service. These, of course, should not be counted as missionaries, for they had only expressed a desire to go out as missionaries. The *Missionary Handbook of Direct-Support Missionaries of The Churches of Christ, 1951* was checked to see how many of these missionary candidates reached the fields. This independent missionary directory showed that seventeen of the recruits reached the fields (two had returned to the United States because of illness and three were serving in different fields from the preferences listed in 1947). Of the twelve who were not in foreign missionary work, three were listed in the *1951 Year Book, Disciples of Christ* as students, four (counting the wives of the two pastors) were serving local churches as ministers, and the other five names were not shown in the volume.

It would be interesting, of course, to study the financial reports of the authenticated number of active missionaries, along with the audits of receipts and expenditures of these widely-scattered independent missions. W. E. Garrison and A. T.

DeGroot, in writing *The Disciples of Christ: A History,* received no answers to their requests for information about independent missions.

The *Christian Standard* of October 25, 1947 (pp. 743 f.), carried an article by Ralph R. Harter, an independent missionary in India, under the title, "Why I Could Not Be a U.C.M.S. Missionary." The following reasons were given: 1) "My supporters could not support me without supporting false prophets." In explaining this, he added: "Less than 35¢ of the original missionary dollar ever sees a missionary or a mission field." 2) "I am not a member of the denomination of which it is an agency." 3) The United Society's "comity agreements would limit the field of my evangelistic efforts." 4) Trustees of the United Society "purport to do the work of the Holy Spirit in sending out, recalling, and directing the movements of the missionaries."

A few facts should be examined in connection with Mr. Harter's arguments. The charge of "false prophets" is not worthy of discussion. The charge that "less than 35¢ of the original missionary dollar" aids the missionaries or the mission field is denied regularly. Independent workers often, however, charge that only ten cents of each missionary dollar ever gets to the fields!

Your Missionary Dollar is a leaflet issued annually by the United Society and available to anyone at any time on request. The 1950-51 leaflet showed that the Society's overhead (covering administration, service, and general expenses) totaled 15.4 per cent. The breakdown of the missionary dollar, based on the Society's annual, audited reports, indicated that 44.5 per cent went for foreign missions, 23 per cent for home missions, 15.4 per cent for Christian education, and minute percentages for men's work and audio-visual services. The 1951-52 leaflet, called *Headlines of Achievement,* shows that the United Society's overhead had decreased slightly last year to 14.47 per cent of each dollar.

By contrast, Garrison and DeGroot in *The Disciples of Christ: A History,* estimate that the financial overhead of independent missions approximates fifty per cent. They state (p. 509):

Thus the "overhead" of direct-support work apparently runs to at least half the funds received, not counting the cost of the missionary forwarding office maintained at Cincinnati. Eleven other forwarding offices were also listed [*Christian Standard,* March 1, 1947, p. 160], but doubtless these were maintained free of charge or with minor expense. Another example of the exorbitant overhead costs of independent work is found in the January, 1947, issue of the *Osaka News.* It reported nine foreign missionaries, either retired on pay or doing promotional work in America, and a solitary native representative in the field. For the closing three months of 1946 the home force reported spending $1,447.75 in America for promotion and $790.02 in "personal" and "living link" funds—while only $91.45 was sent abroad for work on the field. During those three months the $2,237.77 spent for costs in America succeeded in raising $2,325 additional for the mission funds— again an overhead cost of approximately 50 per cent.

Yet in the face of such factual overhead for independent missionary work, James B. Carr states in his book, *The Foreign Missionary Work of the Christian Church* (p. 96) that "there is no overhead expense" except for issuing and "mailing receipts and reports to the donors."

The lack of adequate and reliable financial reports of independent missionaries does not take into consideration the possible waste in other ways of missionary work not carefully guided by a responsible agency. The enormous waste of independent missions is very evident to the careful observer for these reasons: 1) Lack of careful selection of candidates, 2) delays in getting to the field of work, 3) absence of survey and group direction on the fields, 4) irregular time spent in the United States instead of on the field, 5) time used to promote and raise funds for the work, along with other factors in a self-directed, free-lance work, without a responsible guarantor to help supervise the mission.

Sponsoring committees of independent missions have real weaknesses. They were discussed in an editorial in the *Christian Standard* of May 24, 1947 (p. 370), which stated:

> But in too many cases such a committee is a figurehead whose chief function is to adorn the mission stationery. In such cases the committee rarely meets as a committee to consider mission problems or to receive reports. In one extreme case a large "committee" adorns a mission letterhead. Investigation has proved that many of the members of the committee did not know they were on it, few of them know anything about the work of the mission.

Mr. Harter's third point, a reference to limiting evangelistic effort through comity arrangements, is rather amusing. There is not a single comity agreement reached on a foreign field by our missionaries that has not enlarged rather than limited our field of effort. Disciples of Christ are in the Belgian Congo today because the American (Northern) Baptists reached an understanding with us when our two pioneer missionaries, Ellsworth Faris and Dr. Harry N. Biddle, recommended our purchase of the Bolenge station. Due to a lack of funds and workers, the Baptists let us have Bolenge, a remote station for them, and concentrated their efforts thereafter in the vast field of the Lower Congo. Disciples thus obtained a mission field with a population of 553,250 in it, all of one language, where we had a membership, in 1951, of 75,395 church members (*1952 Year Book, Disciples of Christ*, p. 153).

Then, in Paraguay, the Methodists withdrew and turned the field over to the Disciples. They felt that they had sufficient territory in other sections of South America. So today Paraguay is the sole mandate of the Disciples functioning there through the United Society; however, certain fundamentalist Protestants who do not observe comity are engaged in mission activities there, too. We are there thanks to an understanding with the Methodists.

Also, in the Philippine Islands our uncontested field was enlarged by comity arrangements with both Presbyterians and Methodists.

Moreover, in Mexico our field was enlarged many times by the comity agreement with both Methodists and Presbyterians.

The assumption that the Holy Spirit gives guidance to the independent missionary and not to those serving under the auspices of the United Society seems to be a rather presumptuous inference from the facts at hand. Perhaps the most unfortunate part of the matter is that Mr. Harter probably obtained his information in some "loyal" Bible college!

Disciple "Denominationalism"

The *Christian Standard* for February 14, 1948 (p. 107), published an editorial which opposed "A Crusade for a Christian World," a challenging cooperative program of Disciples democratically developed from the "grass roots." This movement sought to deepen spiritual understanding and to increase the regular giving of churches to the missionary, educational, and benevolent emphases of the brotherhood. The financial goal was $14,000,000 and developed from the basic needs of the participating agencies.

In the editorial, the paper said:

> To bring every local church into denominational bondage in every department of its activity is the objective. This highly financed and closely organized assault upon the freedom of the local church can be met only by Christians strong in the faith led by a ministry and eldership who are alert to these dangers. . . .
>
> It is a "Crusade for Control," a campaign of desperation to completely denominationalize the "Disciples" once and for all, and to insure the smooth and constant flow of funds from the captive churches into the denominational treasuries.

As the 1948 commencement season approached, the *Standard* published an editorial, "Bible Colleges and the Restoration Movement," in the issue of May 15, 1948 (p. 322). This discussed the purpose of the Bible colleges, seminaries, and institutes that were training ministers and other Christian workers to serve "undenominational" churches. The same issue carried a list of nineteen of the schools which reported an enrollment of about 2,300 students. In publishing the list, the editorial stated that the *Standard* was not "necessarily endorsing all their policies," and added:

> We have drawn the line at schools affiliated with the "Board of Higher Education of Disciples of Christ." To claim an undenominational position while actively working to build a denomination in fact seems to us, if not hypocritical, to be at least inconsistent.

This editorial statement indicated the reason for omitting some of the schools, formerly approved, from the list of schools endorsed by the *Christian Standard*.

Prior to the organizational meeting of the World Council of Churches in Amsterdam in the summer of 1948, the *Standard* ran an editorial entitled, "Amsterdam—Pentecost or Babel?" (June 5, 1948, p. 376). The paper stated:

> Extravagant claims of overenthusiastic propagandists often fall apart under the penetrating ray of careful analysis. Among these is the claim that the meeting of "the representatives of 135 communions from thirty-

nine countries" for the purpose of forming the "World Council of Churches" at Amsterdam, Holland, August 22 to September 4, will be a second Pentecost. . . . Is the meeting at Amsterdam to be a second Pentecost or a second Babel? . . .

We have had one Pentecost—no other is needed until the authority of the first is rescinded. The world has had one Babel and many repetitions of the spirit of Babel; another is not to be desired. The Babel-like confusions of the world will not be dissolved by a highly press-agented synthetic "second Pentecost." The unity essential to the world-wide acceptance of the Son of God will be found only in obedience to the revealed will and proclamation of the message of the Spirit of the Pentecost of Acts 2.

In an editorial, "Evidences of 'Disciples' Denominationalism," the *Standard* argued as follows (August 21, 1948, p. 552):

Shall we review the evidence that a well-organized denominational machinery exists, sponsored and operated by a clique of self-styled "Disciples," whose aim is to "rule or ruin" every local church of Christ or Christian church and every Christian preacher?

First of all, there is a *denominational convention,* the "International Convention of Disciples of Christ." However simon-pure its beginnings may have been, it now acts in a denominational capacity. Its office in Indianapolis is spoken of as "headquarters." Its full-time secretary has been labeled, "the voice of the Brotherhood." Its resolutions are heralded as representing the sentiment of 1,700,000 "Disciples." It proceeds to appoint representatives to such interdenominational groups as the "Federal Council of Churches of Christ in America," *on an interdenominational basis.* Its constituent agencies regard themselves as "the organized work of the Brotherhood," and both by inference and direct statement regard as "outside the Brotherhood" persons and churches who prefer to do Christian work through other channels.

Second, there is "Unified Promotion," a denominational device, if one ever existed, which has thrust itself upon the local church by outlining nearly so many "special days" for organizational promotion and money raising that little time is left for worship or evangelism or any other Christian activity by the local congregation.

The current *1947 Year Book, Disciples of Christ,* in use across the brotherhood when this editorial was printed, included (p. 167) the brotherhood's "Calendar of Special Days," which had been approved by our International Convention. This calendar listed five days for receiving special offerings in local churches for Christian concerns of the Disciples as expressed by the organized agencies. Several additional days or longer periods of time were suggested for local church use of educational emphases. These concerns included Christian education, evangelism, foreign missions, the Christian ministry, stewardship, and home missions. The statement of the *Christian Standard* "that little time is left for worship or evangelism" failed to recognize the facts.

This editorial expression continued as follows:

Third, there is the United Christian Missionary Society, a political organization gathering missionary funds from the churches and using the greater part of them for its own political and promotional benefit. The *World Call* is its propaganda journal. The departments of Religious Education, Missionary Education, Missionary Organizations, Financial Resources, are [*sic*] Men's Work almost entirely promotional in their activities and use every device of which they are capable to control local churches for their organization's benefit.

Through the Department of Home Missions, the U.C.M.S. has regimented and controlled the "State Secretaries" who have learned that they must "produce results" or seek other employment. The activities of the State Secretaries must be Number Four in our list of evidences that a deliberate effort is being made to build a "Disciples" denomination.

What the magazine failed to state, in connection with *World Call*, was that it is published not only by the United Christian Missionary Society, but by four other national boards of the Disciples: the Association for the Promotion of Christian Unity, the Board of Church Extension, the Board of Higher Education, and the National Benevolent Association. And the paper neglected to say anything about the numerous program functions of the United Society that are provided for our churches which use them or not as they choose.

This editorial concluded thus:

Fifth, there are the stereotyped state papers and state conventions.

And sixth, there is a deliberate assault upon the freedom of the ministry seen in the suggested ordination procedures sent out by the Department of Home Missions of the U.C.M.S. These recommendations include a denominational procedure of licensing, a denominational council, and a denominational service of ordination. In the procedure an oath of denominational loyalty is exacted from each ministerial candidate under the guise of "ministerial ethics." The end can be nothing less than an out-and-out denominational ministry.

And, most contemptible of all, this entire organizational set-up is geared to serve as the sales force of a private publishing concern which avoids paying its just share of taxes and postage by claiming that it is "the official denominational publishing house" of the "Disciples of Christ."

During the year of 1948 the *Christian Standard* seemed to repudiate all the state secretaries of the various state missionary societies. An editorial (May 22, 1948, p. 346) attempted to answer, "What Is a State Secretary?" A letter from John D. Zimmerman, then secretary of the Kansas Christian Missionary Society, was printed at the beginning of the editorial.

Mr. Zimmerman's letter had been written to a minister who had inquired about a pastorate in Kansas. In his reply, Mr. Zimmerman quite naturally asked about the preacher's "interest and attitude in missionary work" and stated that most Kansas churches were "co-operating with the brotherhood conventions and missionary agencies and with the Crusade." Mr. Zimmerman then added that these questions would be asked by the churches concerning the minister. Mr. Zimmerman also remarked that the church where this man ministered did not seem to be doing much for "our missionary program, at least not through our organized agencies."

The editorial in the *Standard* attacked Mr. Zimmerman's attitude and prerogative and then said:

This leads us to ask a question, "What is a 'state secretary'?" The answer is obvious from this "state secretary's" letter, quite evidently a routine piece of correspondence, he is the contact-man for the misrepresentative "Disciples" clique which is working diligently to denominationalize the brotherhood, to take captive or to persecute free ministers of Christ and to bind its will upon free churches of Christ. He may not be a modernist, but he is in league with modernists. He may be able to say with pious boldness that he does not advocate "open membership," but he is doing his part to betray the movement into the hands of the "open membership" crowd. For home consumption he may loudly insist that his "state society" is independent of the U.C.M.S., but his record proves his subserviency to the Indianapolis "headquarters."

Mr. Zimmerman's efforts to prevent independent pastors from going into the churches and changing their long-established missionary work and causing division are easily understood.

Another attack on state secretaries was made by the *Christian Standard* in an editorial, "Sectarianism in Oklahoma" (November 27, 1948, p. 794). The editorial quoted a report of Carl V. Covey, state secretary in Oklahoma, as follows:

"The spirit of co-operation is growing among our Oklahoma churches. Many so-called 'independent' and non-co-operative preachers have resigned, and more and more our churches are definitely stating, "We want a pastor who will co-operate with the brotherhood." This, we believe, is a wholesome attitude which is being expressed by the churches and tends to contribute to unity and progress."

Then the editorial in the *Standard* said:

Evidence is increasingly abundant that certain state secretaries no longer consider their work as being to serve the churches, but rather to lord it over the churches on behalf of certain vested interests which can not prosper or even exist without the offerings from the churches. These vested interests, failing to elicit adequate support on the merit of their work, have set about to get it by deliberately denominationalizing the brotherhood. This has necessitated propagandizing the local churches, and, in some cases, interfering in the affairs of the local church. "More and more" (to borrow a phrase), the secretaries of state missionary organizations have prostituted their jobs until they have become little more than "finger men" for the national organizations.

One only has to sit in a conference of the devoted, state missionary executives, as I often have, to discover how free they are from dictation by anyone! They are the servants of the churches in their own states, functioning under the direction of their state conventions and the democratically-chosen state missionary boards of leading Chistian ministers and lay people.

Of course, the state secretaries are always anxious to maintain the missionary integrity of the churches which have long supported the established work of the Disciples. Such churches do not desire the disturbing influence of independent ministers, who, if not observed, would enter these pulpits and create havoc. For the faithfulness of the state secretaries to the churches, the *Christian Standard* presumed to label them with the underworld name of "finger men"!

In a series of sixteen articles in the *Christian Standard* (beginning September 4, 1948, pp. 588 f. and concluding December 18, 1948, pp. 841 f.), Mrs. C. E. Stark of La Plata, Missouri, discussed "the deliberate trend toward liberalism and denominationalism seen in certain literature offered for use in Christian education" (December 11, 1948, p. 827). Her findings were about educational materials created by the Curriculum Committee of the United Society's Division of Christian Education and those published by the Christian Board of Publication. There was reference, also, to the "even more odious denominational material recommended by" writers of the Christian Board (September 4, 1948, p. 586).

An editorial appeared in the *Standard* of September 4, 1948, which carried the first article by Mrs. Stark. "Are You Responsible?" the editorial inquired, in the use of Christian Board materials, thus:

For aiding and abetting the modernistic clique in their long-range program to gain control of agencies through which to promulgate their humanistic teachings?

For helping to misrepresent the plea and the people of the Restoration movement by financing such misrepresentations through "missionary" and "Crusade" offerings?

The "Bible-centered" materials of the Standard Publishing Company were featured in connection with these articles. This was done in a bold-faced box entitled, "The Issue," which ran with each of Mrs. Stark's articles. This promotional blurb, also marked and reproduced, in facsimile, on a following page, stated:

THE ISSUE

Christian Board of Publication Sunday-school literature teaches that the wisest human experience (its writers being the judge) is the source of authority in religion.

Standard Publishing Company literature teaches that the Bible is the inspired Word of God and that the Bible (not human opinion) is the final authority in faith and practice for all Christians.

If you do not believe that the Bible is God's Word, you may be satisfied with literature based on human opinions.

If you are a Bible-honoring Christian, you will label such literature as you would other poison and protect your children from it.

The above is an astounding statement, issued by a large, Christian publishing house against a brotherhood-owned publishing house which now reports to the International Convention of Disciples of Christ.

One Hope

By MRS. C. E. STARK

La Plata, Mo.

First of a series of revealing articles showing how certain literature offered for "Christian" education would undermine the divine authority of the Bible

THE Bible is the Word of God. Its first division, the Old Testament, tells how God put the first two people in an ideal setting and gave them one simple rule to keep. They were promised punishment if they broke the rule. Adam and Eve learned that God meant what He said, because when they disobeyed, God put them out into a world where they could expect toil, pain, and death. He no longer walked and talked with them. For thousands of years, they and their descendants knew God only in some indirect way, and the obedient, thoughtful ones hoped for a way to be reconciled to God. The New Testament tells of the Redeemer who was finally sent to reveal God to men and to save all who will accept Him.

Christians serve this living Saviour, who promises that they, too, may have everlasting life if they believe and obey Him. This promise is known to us through the Bible. Our only hope comes through belief in this Book. If we believe what the Bible says about Christ and His promises, then we must believe what the Bible says about itself. Time after time the Book claims that it is given by inspiration of God. Brief examples are given here: "For the prophecy came not in old time by the will of man: but holy men of God spake as they were moved by the Holy Spirit" (2 Peter 1:21); also, "All scripture is given by inspiration of God, and is profitable for doctrine, for reproof, for correction, for instruction in righteousness: that the man of God may be perfect, throughly furnished unto all good works" (2 Timothy 3:16, 17).

Being given by God, who is all-wise, the Bible was true and perfect when it was written, is true today, and will always be true. "Heaven and earth shall pass away," Jesus said, "but my words shall not pass away" (Matthew 24:35).

One would suppose that a book making such wonderful promises would be the most carefully taught of all books, that every person who has heard of the Book would be searching it continually, would be earnestly contending for the faith that it teaches, and would be showing that he loves the Saviour by keeping His commandments. But even from the beginning it was not so.

Before the New Testament was completely written, some were teaching wrong doctrine. The apostle Paul had spent much time with the church at Ephesus, preaching, teaching, and doing mighty works that the Christians might be strong in the faith. When he said good-by to the elders of the Ephesian church, he warned them in this way, "For I know this, that after my departing shall grievous wolves enter in among you, not sparing the flock. Also of your own selves shall men arise, speaking perverse things, to draw away disciples after them. Therefore watch, and remember, that by the space of three years I ceased not to warn every one night and day with tears" (Acts 20:29-31).

Peter also warned Christians, "But there were false prophets also among the people, even as there shall be false teachers among you, who privily shall bring in damnable heresies, even denying the Lord that bought them, and bring upon themselves swift destruction. And many shall follow their pernicious ways; by reason of whom the way of truth shall be evil spoken of" (2 Peter 2:1, 2).

Soon after the church was established, false teachers crept in. They called them-

THE ISSUE

Christian Board of Publication Sunday-school literature teaches that the wisest human experience (its writers being the judge) is the source of authority in religion.

Standard Publishing Company literature teaches that the Bible is the inspired Word of God and that the Bible (not human opinion) is the final authority in faith and practice for all Christians.

If you do not believe that the Bible is God's Word, you may be satisfied with literature based on human opinions.

If you are a Bible-honoring Christian, you will label such literature as you would other poison and protect your children from it.

selves Christians, but taught another gospel. Their trick of taking part of the Bible and denying part of it deceived many. To this day we are so easily deceived that it takes a considerable jolt to awaken us. But when we once catch one of the wolves without his mask of sheep's clothing, it is an interesting experience. It sharpens our spiritual eyes and makes it easier to round up the destructive gang.

Remember that the psalmist said, "Thy word is true" (Psalm 119:160). But here is a book that does not agree with that. We are going to quote at length from a book that is widely recommended by writers of one certain line of church-school literature, offered as a help for teachers of young people in the Bible school. The book is "The Career and Significance of Jesus," by W. B. Denny. In discussing the miracles of the Bible, he says:

"One [point] is that we can not take for granted that the story is true just because it is in the Bible. To say that would make the Bible itself a miracle, and then *that* miracle would have to be *proved* before we could reasonably accept it. But the view that the Bible is a miraculously perfect book can not be proved, and in the judgment of almost all trained minds, has been definitely disproved. The writers of the Bible could, and did, sometimes forget facts, and mistake their own fancies for facts, or err in their judgment, or exaggerate because of their very earnestness. . . . When they were amazed at the greatness of Jesus, when they wanted to express their boundless admiration and reverence for Him, the one most natural way for them to do so was to exaggerate (unconsciously, of course) His simple and natural deeds into wonderful and supernatural tales." [Emphases and parentheses are Denny's.] (Denny, *The Career and Significance of Jesus*," copyright, 1933, *The Ronald Press Co.*, pp. 155, 156. Used by permission.)

Much more of the same kind of thing is written there. The book does not take into account that Jesus promised the disciples that He would send the Holy Spirit to guide them into all truth (John 14:26; 15:26; 16:13). According to the Bible, the Holy Spirit came on the day of Pentecost and fulfilled that promise (Acts 2).

Reading again from Mr. Denny's book:

"Modern scholarship has shown conclusively that the method of harmonizing [the Gospels] is not satisfactory. The method is based on the assumption that the Gospels contain noth-

ing but reliable history. Today we know that this assumption is not true." (*Ibid.*, p. 5. Used by permission.)

In these quotations notice the indefinite use of "trained minds" and "modern scholarship."

Reading further, we find mention of the different Gospel accounts. He is speaking of Mark believing in Jesus as the Jewish Messiah, an apocalyptic Messiah. He writes:

"These leanings of Mark must be kept in mind when studying his Gospel, for there are reasons for believing that they go considerably beyond what Jesus actually believed and taught about himself." (*Ibid.*, p. 22. Used by permission.)

Next, it is explained that Luke "compiled his Gospel out of earlier written Gospels." Then:

"The Gospel according to Matthew was constructed in the same general manner as the Gospel according to Luke. . . . It was not written by the apostle Matthew; how it came to be attributed to him (early in the second century) is not clearly known." (*Ibid.*, p. 23. Used by permission.)

Turning a page, we read concerning sources for a reliable biography of Jesus:

"Modern scholars, almost without exception, recognise that this Gospel [John] can not be used as an historical source with the same confidence that we feel toward Mark and the 'Teaching Source'." (*Ibid.*, pp. 24, 25. Used by permission.)

These quotations are only a few sentences to show what is said about the Bible itself. Later, we will read examples of what is said about Jesus and God. There are 466 pages in this book. We have carefully read it that we might choose from it passages that show you the meaning that the author intends to give throughout the book.

You will see that it has been said that a story is not true just because it is in the Bible, that the apostle Matthew did not write the Book of Matthew, that Mark is not a reliable reporter, that Luke did not write from firsthand information, and that the Gospel of John is of little historical value. In the foreword of the book the purpose is said to be this:

"At the same time, nearly one-third of the book is devoted to the study of the religious significance of Jesus, so that it is also an introductory course on the meaning of the Christian religion." (*Ibid.*, p. xi. Used by permission.)

Thus, the book, "The Career and Significance of Jesus," claims to explain the Christian religion, and at the same time it would count as untrue the only book that can explain Christianity. On what could we base our faith if not in Christ as the Bible reveals Him? Whom could we trust to judge what part of the Scripture we would believe and the part we would disregard? "Of your own selves shall men arise speaking perverse things to draw away disciples after them." You may think that this is an odd kind of reading for Bible-school teachers. The passage quoted and many more like them will prove to you that there are two different kinds of religion going under the name of Christianity. One believes the Bible as it is written; the other looks at the Bible as a

CHRISTIAN STANDARD

This page is a facsimile from the "Christian Standard" of September 4, 1948, p. 588. Note the boxed feature at the top of the page, in boldface type, headed, "The Issue."

Sensing the need for understanding and unity among the Disciples of Christ, the 1934 International Convention, meeting in Des Moines, Iowa, authorized the appointment of the Commission on Restudy of the Disciples of Christ. The group that was named consisted of outstanding, representative leaders of the brotherhood. The following-named persons served on the commission during all or part of its existence. Those whose names are starred in this list were members when the group concluded its long deliberations:

*Edward Scribner Ames, *L. D. Anderson, H. C. Armstrong, *Eugene C. Beach, *R. M. Bell, *George Walker Buckner, Jr., *F. W. Burnham, George A. Campbell, *Homer W. Carpenter, *C. M. Chilton, *Abram E. Cory, *J. H. Dampier, *Virgil L. Elliott, *Stephen J. England, Edwin R. Errett, A. W. Fortune, Graham Frank, *Winfred Ernest Garrison, *Henry G. Harmon, *Claude E. Hill, Edgar DeWitt Jones, *Frederick D. Kershner, *Hugh B. Kilgour, *Clarence E. Lemmon, *Raphael Harwood Miller, Orval M. Morgan, *Charles Clayton Morrison, *James DeForest Murch, *William F. Rothenburger, M. E. Sadler, *Orman L. Shelton, Willard E. Shelton, *G. Gerald Sias, *T. K. Smith, George H. Stewart, *W. E. Sweeney, *Robert S. Tuck, *Dean E. Walker, L. N. D. Wells, *P. H. Welshimer, and *J. J. Whitehouse.

The attitude of the *Christian Standard* toward the Commission on Restudy was typical of its position on any cooperative undertaking among the Disciples of Christ. An editorial in the periodical for April 3, 1948 (p. 220), stated:

Actually, the Commission on Restudy is an ineffective discussion group composed of men who hold varying shades of belief and disbelief. Its very existence is an attempt to perpetuate the fallacious assumption that believers and unbelievers can be joined together in a "Brotherhood."

The commission deliberated for more than a decade on the "origin, history, slogans, methods, successes and failures" of the Disciples of Christ, as charged by the Des Moines Convention in 1934. A comprehensive report of the findings, summarizing present problems of our brotherhood, was approved by the San Francisco International Convention of 1948. The text of that significant study, except for the four introductory paragraphs, follows (*1948 Year Book, Disciples of Christ*, pp. 120 ff.) :

Our Present Problems

The Commission would record its judgment that the most immediate problems requiring our attention in order to the preservation and development of our unity may be reduced to the following statements:

Our first major problem is to distinguish carefully the nature of our agreements and differences.

We are forced to recognize in the analyses of 1946 and 1947, that our differences deal with matters of basic importance. The differences lie in the realm of history, of theology, of application of principles to the problems of the church, of methods in labor and cooperation. The agreements are in the area of fact, of faith, and of doctrine. The differences touch only the periphery of the Christian life, but the agreements are at its center.

We hold that the divisive differences are obstacles to be overcome, while our agreements are foundations on which to build. These agreements speak of the person of Jesus Christ, confession of whom as Son of God, Lord and Saviour, is the sole affirmation of faith necessary to the fellowship of Christians; of the definitive place which the New Testament holds in our personal religious lives and in the work of the Church; of the Church itself as Christ's body, making a reality on earth of the fellowship of those who are Christ's; of the unfinished business before the Church in the persons of those who have not heard or have not heeded the Gospel of Christ; and of the absolute necessity of unity among Christians as a condition to the answer to Christ's prayer that the world may believe. These matters of agreement are neither few nor trivial. They lie at the center of the faith that constitutes us a people, and a people of God.

Our second major problem is to discover, maintain and enjoy fellowship.

The discord, hatred and bitterness which evidences the alienation of this age from God, the desolation of this present world, would seem to be warning enough that God abandons to their destruction those who live in strife. We would, therefore, that our brethren seize quickly upon whatever fellowship we may have, that by cultivation we may enrich it; and that under the healing rays of the light of Christ it may be purified; so that we may exemplify the reconciled community of him whose ministry was the breaking of the walls of partition among men.

Fellowship among Christians is based on the relation they sustain to Christ. It is, therefore, personal, not organizational; religious—personal commitment to Christ—not theological; moral, not legal. The sole element of constraint is the love of Christ. Nothing must be permitted to obscure this high view of fellowship. At the same time, we may rightly appropriate all practical means of expressing this fellowship. Among such means we may note the various agencies for Christian work; direct participation by the local church in work beyond its own community; and attempts to make Christianity "one community" in fact, such as the "ecumenical movement." Each such activity may be interpreted on a sub-personal level, and so be evil; each may express an extension to personality, and so be Christian.

Our third major problem lies in educating our people to the realization, intellectually and practically, of the nature of our movement.

We cannot think of our brotherhood as a sect, but think of it rather as a demonstration of that unity to which Christ has called his whole Church. The historic distinctiveness of our people is not of our will, but has been made necessary in order that we may appropriate unto salvation the instruments of Christ's appointment for his Church. To these appointments, of belief, of ordinance, of doctrine, of policy, we lay no exclusive claim. Within these appointments we seek the unity of his Church and the salvation of men.

When we plead for the unity of the Church, it is not alone unity for unity's sake; when we plead for the Good Confession of Christ as the sole creedal requirement, it is not merely for the abolition of human creeds; but this plea for unity in faith is in order that Christ may be unobscured and that the world may believe in him, and be saved.

We are therefore persuaded that at no time has the demand been more imperative than now for a demonstration of the sufficiency and catholicity of the New Testament Church as the divine agent in human redemption.

We Therefore Sound a Call to All Disciples

That we sink into oblivion the particularisms which divide us as a people, and rally ourselves to a supreme and common effort for the realization of Christian unity, beginning each one with himself. Let each examine himself in the light of his relationship to Christ, as the center of that unity. Let each examine himself in respect to the teachings of the New Testament in his personal and corporate life. Let each one hear again the Gospel, and judge again his attitudes and sentiments, his programs and procedures, his thoughts and deeds—whether these things flow from the preaching of Christ and him crucified. Let us be no less concerned that our cooperative life shall relate itself to these same standards. Let each agency and congregation examine its stewardship, and so form and declare its policies and activities that all may rejoice in their manifest loyalty to the spirit and mandate of Christ's New Covenant.

That we evaluate our differences by treating them for what they really are, opinions which are subjects for free and open discussion, and which all are free to accept or to reject, answering only to Christ. To make these divergences from our central agreements more than this is to fall into the sin of sectarianism, and by overvaluing, actually devalue the silences of the Bible wherein we find liberty.

That we rise to a new sense of our mission to the Church and our mission to the world, noting their essential interdependence; for only if the Churches hear our Lord's prayer for unity may we expect the world to believe. Let us remember the holy purpose calling our movement into existence—the nations must wait in ignorance and destruction for Christians to unite. How can we today, standing under the impending world tragedy, do less than throw ourselves unreservedly into the one divinely commissioned business of the Church—and, using whatever means and methods may commend themselves to our Christian intelligence, seek to reach all this generation's unreached with the Gospel of our blessed Lord: We mean not alone the first proclamation of the Gospel to those who have not heard—but the continued preaching to those who have not heeded. We would reach with the Gospel those in the Church "who having ears, hear not"; we would reach the architects of our social order; we would reach all the people in all affairs, that they may all pass under the judgment of the Gospel. Let us not be preoccupied with the dangers of disunity, but lift our eyes from the deadly concern we have for our particularistic preferences, and take to a desperate world the Gospel of its redemption! We live in this hour as men on borrowed time. Can we expend it, under God, on less than the most urgent work? Cannot we as a people point the way by our agreements to the unity of a Church resurgent, consecrated only to the Gospel of reconciliation with God through Christ Jesus, furnished in the grace of God with power to win the whole world? To do less, as we judge, is to forfeit our heritage as Disciples; nay, is to be found false stewards of the mystery of the faith.

In a time of sectarian strife, we were called into being as a people to bear witness to the unity of the Church without which its divine task could not be accomplished. Now again in a critical time of confusion we see the Church recognizing the impotency of division and seeking the power of unity. The Church will hear us now, and be restored to her might, if we but give clear voice to that plea to "unite for the conversion of the world." This is the dynamic of our mission.

We close with a fervent prayer, that God may grant us the grace of his Providence, that our concern for lost men may so burden our souls that we shall find no rest until the Church is united for the world's redemption, through the Gospel of Jesus Christ as proclaimed in the New Testament.

The 1949 International Convention, which met in Cincinnati, dismissed the Commission on Restudy with "high commendation and appreciation" (*1949 Year Book, Disciples of Christ*, p. 18). A Restudy Extension Committee was authorized by the 1949 Cincinnati Convention "to give guidance in planning and fostering study and discussion groups, and implementing such plans and methods as promise the greatest good to our brotherhood" (*1949 Year Book, Disciples of Christ*, p. 124). This committee consists of ten persons, all of whom served formerly on the original commission. The final report in 1949 of the commission also called for the appointment of a Commission on Christian Doctrine, but the *1952 Year Book* contains no directory of such a group.

The 1949 International Convention met in historic Music Hall, Cincinnati, on October 25-30. It celebrated the centennial of our first national convention and of the American Christian Missionary Society's founding. The Society subsequently became a part of the United Christian Missionary Society when it was formed. The convention registration totaled 8,300, making it the "largest convention of Disciples in forty years," according to Ronald E. Osborn's report in *World Call* (December, 1949, p. 24). The Standard Publishing Company did not ignore this convention in its home city of Cincinnati. It conducted a competitive rally in the Emery Auditorium of Cincinnati, simultaneously with the convention, at which Standard literature was promoted. Many of the International Convention attendants found a promotional booklet of the Standard Publishing Company under the doors of their hotel rooms.

Some months after the next International Convention, held in Oklahoma City, October 9-15, 1950, the *Christian Standard* announced that it was withholding support from the Christian Missionary Fellowship.

This was a new organization formed by some supporters of independent missionary work. The group applied to the International Convention in Oklahoma City for membership, but was refused (*1950 Year Book, Disciples of Christ*, p. 35). The editorial in the *Standard* (May 5, 1951, p. 282) stated:

From the information at hand we have drawn the following conclusions:

1. The Christian Missionary Fellowship is organized as a missionary society. That any group of brethren has a right to organize such a society is a principle for which the *Standard* has always consistently contended. That it is wise or expedient for such a society to be organized at this juncture we deny. In view of the successful growth of independent missions during the past twenty years, the formation of such an organization is entirely unnecessary.

Our experience with earlier missionary societies leads us to withhold our support and endorsement from this agency which has within it all the seeds of evil inherent in such organizations.

2. Already this infant agency has shown itself to be enamored by power and organization. It endeavored unsuccessfully in October to become a reporting agency of the "International Convention." Thus it indicated its acceptance of the misrepresentative claims of that convention to be in some way official. The convention turned down the request on the ground that the work to be undertaken by the new organization is already being done by the U.C.M.S. . . .

3. We have no quarrel with any who wish to support this organization, or any other. We believe in Christian freedom, and endeavor to practice it for ourselves and toward others.

But we have committed ourselves definitely to the cause of New Testament Christianity. Our news pages are open to those missionaries who are dependent upon God and their faith in Him, rather than in the might and power of missionary organizations.

This statement was entirely in keeping with the repeated declarations of the *Christian Standard* in recent years. It has consistently maintained its stand for free-lance independence in all missionary, educational, and evangelistic work instead of any cooperative guidance.

In the issue of June 11, 1949, the *Christian Standard* again opposed the World Council of Churches (p. 378). It quoted from a pamphlet by Chester A. Tulga, secretary of the Conservative Baptist Fellowship, Chicago, as follows:

1. The World Council of Churches is not an answer to the prayer of Jesus for the unity of true believers, but the fulfillment of the dark prophecies of the New Testament that in the latter days men will depart from the faith.

2. The World Council of Churches has no authoritative doctrinal basis that makes it unmistakably evangelical or guarantees that it will be evangelical in membership.

3. The trends toward a superchurch are implicit in the World Council even though such intention is explicitly disavowed.

4. The World Council will attempt to express its own compromises with the faith through interdenominational agencies in every community and through the denominational program of every member denomination.

5. The World Council in equating Capitalism and Communism became a force for the propagation of world socialism and must be recognized as the religious front for world socialism, which they erroneously call the "Kingdom of God."

6. The atmosphere in which the World Council was born was not an atmosphere of penitence and intercession, but rather the spirit of festivity

and ecclesiastical manipulation. It was not another Pentecost because it was not the kind of gathering that the Holy Spirit could bless.

7. The organization of the World Council marks the end of the historic Protestant protest against Romish doctrines and practices and ushers in a period of apostate non-Roman catholicism.

8. Membership in the World Council of Churches is a betrayal of the faith of historic Christianity and a departure from the testimony of historic Protestantism, and consents to that form of ecclesiastical union which counts adherence to historic Christianity a secondary thing. This is contrary to the teachings of the Scriptures and believers can have no fellowship with it.

The editorial in the *Standard* then stated:

From our viewpoint, in addition to the indictments made by Mr. Tulga against the World Council, we would add the following:

1. The World Council presents a pattern for the church different from and foreign to the New Testament pattern. While its leaders say out of one side of their mouths that it is not a church, but merely a council, out of the other side they insist that it is nothing less than "the ecumenical church." And no more than a casual survey is needed to see that its pattern is not the church of the New Testament.

2. The World Council recognizes and is organized upon the basis of the validity of denominationalism. It is not a movement of like-minded individual Christians. It purports to be a body made up of official representatives of denominational bodies.

3. Any claim on the part of the "Disciples" members of the World Council to represent anybody but themselves is false and misleading. This misrepresentation is of a piece with "Disciples" membership in the Federal Council; with the comity arrangements; and with the Christian Board membership in the interdenominational Publishers' Association.

In all of these remarks the *Christian Standard* overlooked entirely the natural progress of the various Protestant bodies toward unity. The paper harked back to the situation at the beginning of our movement nearly 150 years ago when the passion of our fathers for Christian unity was considered to be an arch heresy. What was then deemed heresy has now become almost the orthodox of the greater part of Protestantism. We must not ignore the contemporary movement toward unity that is sweeping the Christian world and in which Christian leaders openly declare the shame of disunity. Neither can we retreat from it because it is coming in a different way than our fathers thought possible. Our early leaders were prophets of many of the urges toward unity that have already been realized; they were not dogmatic separatists who would deep-freeze themselves from these surging tendencies if they were here today.

It is interesting to note the early longing for unity with the Baptists on the part of Isaac Errett, first editor of the *Christian Standard*. In the second issue of the magazine (April 14, 1866, p. 12), there was a lengthy editorial on, "Union With the Baptists." It was a dignified, irenic statement of the situation at that time and a plea that the two bodies find a way to unite. He began the editorial thus:

We published, in our first number, some very cheering facts, indicative of a strong desire, in certain localities, for union between the Baptists and Disciples. In other quarters, there are strong symptoms of the same desire. We have long known that many among our Baptist brethren had allowed the bitter prejudices of former times to wear away, and were privately longing and praying for the "set time to favor Zion," by a union of the two most powerful branches of the family of immersionists in our country. . . . On our part, the desire has been constant; and our actions have been in harmony with our wishes. We have never held the Baptists away from us. Our pulpits have always been open to them. We have freely co-operated with them in every good work, when we could meet them on common ground; as in the A. & F. Bible Society, the Am. Bible Union, etc. . . . However wide our differences on speculative and even on some practical points, we have ever been willing to hold all these in abeyance, and fraternize with them as holding the one Lord, the one Faith, and the one Baptism. The generation which initiated the heated strife between us has passed away. A new generation, with altered sympathies, is now on the stage. The spirit of the age is different. The proclivities of this time are certainly less sectarian —in many cases are strongly towards the union of all the followers of Christ. If union on a large scale is ever to be realized, we may naturally expect it to commence among those who are next-door neighbors. . . .

It seems to us, therefore, that the following points need to be reached:

1. An agreement to drop all names of the church not authorized in the holy Scriptures.

2. An agreement to abandon all human articles of faith as tests of fellowship.

3. An agreement to drop all theorizings in the pulpit, and to preach Jesus Christ and him crucified, and to proclaim aloud to all the world, "He that believeth and is baptized shall be saved."

4. And for the rest, to forget the alienations of the past; cultivate forbearance, peace, and good-will for the future; and abandon all occasions of controversy for the sake of carrying on a vigorous war for the overthrow of sectarianism.

What criteria for present-day unity with the American (Northern) Baptists from that noble lover of unity, Isaac Errett! Since that date, more than eighty-five years ago, what changes in attitude have come in the Christian world, what a longing for unity has arisen! What open-minded Disciple or American Baptist would disagree with such a platform for conference and study about union? Can any person imagine that Isaac Errett, if among the living in our world, would not rejoice to serve on the Commission on Baptist-Disciple Relations which has been considering union? What a contrast between the welcoming approach of Isaac Errett in the *Christian Standard* of 1866 and the studied aloofness and opposition of that paper today!

The movement toward Christian unity has been greatly influenced by new understandings. Among these is the conclusion of scholars that the New Testament does not reveal an absolute blueprint for the detailed organization of the local church, but rather that Christianity in its beginning was a fluid movement adaptable to changing conditions and needs. There have been decidedly new attitudes in the stream of Christian history, influenced by new conditions in the world. Our fathers could not foresee these things. If they could have done so, however, most of them would have rejoiced in them. By the same token, we of today cannot shut our eyes to these encouraging facts.

The World Council of Churches is not Christian union, and does not claim to be, but it is a significant and promising cooperative movement of Christians. It is entirely advisory with no control whatever over the churches as anyone who reads its statements and literature may see. The understandings plainly delineate the inalienable rights of the churches. Each church has retained the right to ratify or disapprove any utterance or action of the World Council.

The significant decision of Disciples of Christ to affiliate with the World Council of Churches was taken in the 1938 International Convention in Denver, Colorado. This unanimous action was referred to by *The Christian-Evangelist* (October 27, 1938, p. 1176) in an editorial review, written by J. Edward Moseley, one of the editors at that time, as follows:

The high point of the Denver convention came Tuesday afternoon, October 18, at 3:15 o'clock when one thousand Disciples of Christ stood and voiced their united approval of the basis upon which the World Council of Churches of Christ is being formed. It was a dramatic hour, the actual vote having been preceded by a moving plea from Graham Frank, who was our representative and that of the Congregationalists at Utrecht, Holland, last May when a proposed constitution for the council was drafted.

In the words of Mr. Frank, Disciples are "both disposed and qualified" to participate in the council. There was a thrill in voting on this matter. The action came as the first item of business on Tuesday afternoon, thus making other matters that came up later anticlimactic.

No more significant action in voicing our plea of Christian unity has ever been taken. It was a fitting climax to the Denver International Convention, which strengthened our Christian faith in the future possibilities of advancing the Kingdom of God, and deepened the realization that we can dwell together in unity, whatever may be the issues upon which we disagree.

Edwin R. Errett reviewed the Denver Convention action regarding the approval of the World Council of Churches in the *Christian Standard* of October 29, 1938 (p. 1053). His endorsement was expressed thus:

. . . One of the most important actions of the convention was the declaration of its willingness to relate itself to the World Council of Churches whose constitution was drafted at Utrecht, Holland, last May. Unfortunately the representative of the Federal Council of Churches of Christ was given the honor of presenting the matter so that some brethren acquired a prejudice, but the situation was saved chiefly by the messages of Graham Frank (I say messages, because Brother Frank made one of the greatest addresses of the convention on this matter before the Committee on Recommendations, and it was largely because of this that he was called upon to make another address before the convention assembly when this matter was made the first item of business).

There are, in my judgment, some important changes to be made in the constitution, and when our delegates go to the first meeting of the World Council they should be instructed; but those changes can not be made now, and I think the council itself a good thing with an emphasis both upon independence and catholicity that is in harmony with our own position and will promote true Christian unity.

Like all actions of our International Convention which affect the churches, this expression made in Denver in 1938 revealed the deep longings of Disciples of Christ for unity. How eagerly we grasped the opportunity to join in a forward movement to practice unity and thus prove the sincerity of our eloquent advocacy of it!

Certainly the World Council of Churches is not a means of ecclesiastical association, or control, but of interchurch relationship that is as free as the air we breathe.

The attitude of the *Christian Standard* toward interchurch relationship was set forth, again, in an editorial, "Centralization" (November 11, 1950, p. 714). Discussing the organization of the National Council of the Churches of Christ in the United States of America, the journal said:

> Let no one be deceived by the pretense that this Council is nothing more than a "co-operative service agency." Disciples of Christ are particularly in a position to be wary of "service agencies" acting in a purely "advisory" capacity. At the present moment, local churches are being attacked in the courts by agency partisans on the ground that non-support of the U.C.M.S., the state societies, and similar organizations constitutes a departure from the "doctrines, tenets, and beliefs" of disciples of Christ, and therefore forfeits their rights to use of their church buildings. . . .
>
> Just what will be the bounds of arrogance on the part of this new combination of "service agencies" time alone will reveal. But we have a hint in the reckless claims of the constituent agencies.
>
> In our opinion, with the formation of this ecclesiastical monstrosity and what will be its parent body, the World Council of Churches, the Reformation has been set back several hundred years.

Such charges need not be answered here again. What a striking contrast is this editorial judgment with that of Mr. Errett's spirit and attitude regarding the World Council of Churches in 1938 in Denver.

Chapter 9

THE LOGICAL OUTCOME

Several detailed quotations from the pages of the *Christian Standard* during recent years were cited toward the end of the Introduction to this volume (pp. 12 f.). These pointed out that in the judgment of the periodical, the "whole coterie of institutions" affiliated with the International Convention of Disciples of Christ, having "abandoned the plea, and forsaken the movement," they are, therefore, "no longer *of* the Restoration movement."

Differences among Disciples of Christ, the *Christian Standard* admitted, are due to a "fundamental contradiction in theology and philosophy." The "old agencies," the journal contended, cannot be reformed "from their apostasy," since they have "set themselves to destroy the plea that ostensibly they were meant to forward and defend."

So the editorial decree of excommunication was issued and the *Christian Standard* has presumed to draw a dividing line in our brotherhood. It has staked itself and its "loyal" followers off while deliberately and finally placing all who disagree with its policies outside the corral! Thus has this periodical separated itself from the great host of our cooperative churches and from the Disciples of Christ who wish to advance. The paper has tied itself to a literalistic interpretation of the motto, "Where the Scriptures speak, we speak; where the Scriptures are silent, we are silent," in a way quite as legalistic as the attitude of the "anti-organ" Churches of Christ (listed separately from their brethren, the Disciples of Christ, in the United States Religious Census since 1906).

The "anti-organ" separatists could not find anything in the New Testament with regard to instrumental music, missionary societies, or Sunday school literature. So, they repudiated all of these "unscriptural" devices. Now, the modern separatists of the brotherhood find the International Convention, the United Society, the state missionary societies, the Board of Higher Education and its affiliated institutions and agencies, the Association for the Promotion of Christian Unity, along with the National and World Councils of Churches just as "unscriptural" and so all have been repudiated.

The *Christian Standard* has published its material so long, with regard to Disciples who do not keep step with it, that the periodical has reached the logical outcome of fifty years of attack and controversy. Accusing headlines and other materials have been used steadily to label all Disciples disagreeing with its positions.

The magazine has left no room, as pioneer Disciples did, for fellowship together of liberal, medial, and conservative. Indeed, it has interpreted its proclaimed fundamentalist position with such inflexible rigidity that it has made fellowship and open-minded discussion difficult with any who differ in the least with the paper's point of view and policies. The *Standard* has been instrumental in building up a group of churches and affiliated institutions which has become as exclusive a denomination as could be imagined and in which fellow Christians supporting our cooperative, organized work are unwelcome. What a tragic departure from the days of Thomas Campbell, Barton W. Stone, and the progressive founding editor of the *Christian Standard*, Isaac Errett.

This sort of technique which the magazine has so often used, for so many years, has been most unfortunate. In the religious world it is especially so considered. One of the distressing outcomes of this movement, largely developed through the influence of the *Christian Standard* and the *Restoration Herald*, is the widespread and constant attempt to turn Christian churches from their long connection with the cooperative life of our brotherhood of Disciples of Christ to the independent, non-cooperative group.

Preachers from conservative Bible-training schools, like the Cincinnati Bible Seminary, have developed enthusiasm for this sort of procedure. They are for the most part sincere and earnest young preachers. Lacking familiarity with our brother-

hood's cooperative institutions and procedure, they fail to identify themselves with our organized fellowship and fail to welcome those persons supporting it. Consequently, they consider
that they are helping to save the "Restoration" movement by
disrupting our long-established churches and turning them away
from what they term the "sect" or "denomination" of the Disciples.

Many times, after getting into our pulpits, these preachers
attack the United Society or our colleges, perhaps even individuals, using very freely the terms "disloyal," "apostate," and "infidel" against all those whom they oppose. Many people in these
churches, with no personal knowledge of those attacked, often
get the idea that the persons and institutions and agencies mentioned compose a group of "heretics" bent on destruction of our
churches!

Some of the independent ministerial schools attempt to avoid
the issue officially by sending out student preachers with a neutral
viewpoint as between the cooperative and non-cooperative work
of the brotherhood of Disciples. However, there are usually
professors on the faculties of these schools who are strongly non-
cooperative and they are nearly always aggressive. The result
is that many of the students leave these schools with a similar
non-cooperative attitude and many of them are actively antagonistic to our cooperative life.

Apparently, these students are not only kept isolated from
our great cooperative life and fellowship, but they are really in-
sulated as well, through lack of any association outside of their
own group and because of the constant negative and denuncia-
tory influences. Thus they go out and avoid the claims of cooperative fellowship advanced by the progressive congregations
of Disciples.

An example of what often happens occurred in the 1950
county convention of Disciples at Frankfort, Kentucky when a
graduate of the Cincinnati Bible Seminary was given a place on
the program. He was to speak on religious education, but took
advantage of the courtesy of the convention to attack the cooperative brotherhood work. He was, of course, called to task
by the level-headed leaders of the convention. This showed,

however, the teaching and influence to which many of these young ministers have been subjected.

There are also many instances where young preachers so trained have been called to churches and getting the confidence of the members as soon as possible, they have inaugurated an antagonistic program against the long-held missionary and educational programs of the churches. They have circulated materials tending to arouse suspicion, even using literature issued during the 1920s as well as that of the 1940s and 1950s; have broken up women's missionary societies, and, where possible, have turned the whole missionary and educational interests of the congregations from the cooperative to the independent procedure. Where they could not attain this result, they have succeeded in dividing churches that were once harmonious.

There are cases where members of the churches have rebelled against the attempt to reverse the long-held teachings and practices and take over the organization and property dedicated for years to the principles and practices of cooperative Disciples of Christ. Court actions by churches or members are to be regretted. Yet when Christian convictions are at stake and just rights are involved which legal precedent protects, court proceedings are a last resort in order to defend inviolate rights.

The church at Eldora, Iowa, is involved in a case where members of long standing in the congregation recently refused to submit to the actions of the minister in his attempt to take over the church property. The congregation has been connected with the Disciples of Christ from its beginning. The case was taken to the District Court of the State of Iowa by twelve plaintiffs, members of the church until expelled by the non-cooperative group. The action was taken against the Eldora minister and the non-cooperative official board of elders, deacons, and trustees.

After a careful hearing, a judgment and a decree were entered, sustaining the members who did not wish the church removed from the cooperative Disciple fellowship.

The pastor, Lee Roy Schuler, a graduate of the Cincinnati Bible Seminary, went to Eldora in 1947. He began by attacking the Disciple agencies with which the church had been identified through the years, declaring that they were "sinful."

Then he and his followers expelled from the local church every member (including a former pastor, A. L. Ragsdale) protesting Mr. Schuler's position. This was done after an attempt to change the articles of incorporation of the congregation.

The verbatim findings and decree of Judge Sherwood A. Clock, issued at Hampton, Iowa, on August 23, 1951, were published as a supplement to *The Christian News,* monthly paper of Iowa Disciples, for September, 1951. This publication is issued by the Iowa Christian Missionary Society whose executive secretary, Loren E. Lair, is editor. The following quotations are from the typed court's opinion in this Eldora case:

No other conclusion can be drawn from the evidence other than that Schuler has by these acts lead many of his flock into a fixed and determined departure from the established customs of this church. While each Christian Church is an independent body, it appears without dispute that it has been the immemorial custom for the Christian Church to affiliate in state and national organizations and that this church did seek the aid of these organizations in carrying out their work and activities in their local church. . . . That the Eldora Church did, as has been stated from the very beginning, take part in the sectional, state and national activities and that these activities became by custom a very part of the church at Eldora and a part of the denominational beliefs of the church. A departure from this custom coupled with other facts as disclosed in this case can have no other result than to take this church into a new and different denomination [pp. 4, 5]. . . .

The Court further finds that the defendants by their new By-laws have set additional conditions as to the right of admission into the church by adding

1. Confession of belief in the Virgin Birth;
2. Acceptance of "Full and complete authority of Christ as so examined and accepted by the pastor" before the name can be added to the church roll.

From the evidence in this case the Christian Church is a church that never has had any published or adopted creed of faith other than "No creed but Christ." Here these defendants publish and declare what they determine as their interpretation of the creed with additions that have never been accepted by the church and which are directly against the teachings of the church since its organization. By so doing they are taking away the right of individual interpretation of the Scriptures, that being one of the very basic principles of the faith of the Christian Church [p. 6]. . . .

While it may be correctly said that the church had a right to pass these by-laws as a part of their independent right to govern their own affairs, yet when considered with all of the other facts as a whole, the passing of these by-laws were but a part of the plan to take over this church and to change its very structure [p. 6].

. . . one cannot help but conclude from the entire picture as presented that the defendants if they succeed would become a part of a movement headed by the Christian Benevolent Association [a group in St. Louis, Missouri, publicized by the *Christian Standard,* and aligned with the "independent" forces of the Disciples of Christ] [p. 9].

The defendants know or should know that the history of every religious denomination shows that no church can live alone—the fellowship with other churches is not only helpful to the churches but to the individuals as well and that it is absolutely necessary if the denomination is going to carry out the very teaching of the church—and further in order to run the material business of the church that the churches must be affiliated together as a group and to do so there must be a state and national organization [p. 9].

. . . This Court is not quarreling with the defendant Schuler. He has a right to his beliefs which the Court believes are sincere, but under the law he cannot take over a church and mold it over to his beliefs. He has a right to his beliefs, but if his beliefs are as shown by the evidence in this case fundamentally contrary to the beliefs of the Christian Church let him seek out a flock of fellow believers and establish a church founded on his beliefs. The Court must and does find that the plaintiffs have proven their case and that they are entitled to the relief demanded [p. 10].

As a part of the court's decision, it was "ordered, adjudged and decreed":

That the Court does hereby establish and enforce an ecclesiastical trust in and to all of the property both personal and real of the Church of Christ at Eldora, Iowa, in these plaintiffs and those members who have been true to the original teachings and practices of the Church of Christ at Eldora, Iowa, [p. 11].

The defendants in the Eldora case appealed the District Court decision to the Iowa Supreme Court. In an opinion handed down on November 11, 1952, the Supreme Court partly affirmed and partly reversed the action of the lower court (*The Christian-Evangelist,* December 17, 1952, p. 1236; January 21, 1953, p. 60).

When a church is congregationally governed, the Supreme Court affirmed, it is not subject to historic beliefs and practices. Therefore, withdrawal of cooperation from Disciple agencies by the defendants does not mean departure from the "fundamental faith" of Disciples of Christ. On the other hand, the Court ruled that the 1949 Articles under which some members were expelled were invalid and thus upheld the District Court in reinstating those members.

The Supreme Court added that the proceedings of the Eldora church, after Mr. Schuler became pastor, did not minimize the difficulties already existing in the congregation. "There can be no doubt of his responsibility for the changes," the Court's opinion asserted.

The Plaintiffs appealed to the Iowa Supreme Court for a rehearing and a reversal of the decision of November 11, 1952. Their petition charged that the defendants won a majority vote of the Eldora congregation and then proceeded to change the group's basic beliefs and practices. The Supreme Court refused the rehearing and thus reaffirmed its unprecedented ruling that the many changes in the historic beliefs and practices of the Eldora church were of little consequence because the congregation is governed by local autonomy.

Another case concerned the First Christian Church of Pontiac, Illinois, in 1949. There, a pastor led the congregation to adopt a new constitution and attempted to take away the right of the church to carry on its doctrines, tenets, and activities as previously held and practiced. The Circuit Court at Pontiac found on May 3, 1949, that the pastor, Herbert W. Hill, and others of the congregation, had violated the doctrines and tenets of the Christian Churches (Disciples of Christ) held throughout the years by the founders of this New Testament congregation. The conclusion of the court was that Mr. Hill and his followers had by their actions "broken away from the church" (Christian Church of Pontiac) and "therefore lost and forfeited all rights, title, and interest in and to the properties of the plaintiff" (Christian Church of Pontiac).

The implication of such a court decree is that the property and organization of an established church cannot be used to change the long, continuing doctrines and practices of that established congregation, if any part of the group is opposed to such changes from the original beliefs and practices.

Another example of what is currently happening may be found in connection with the First Christian Church of Salem, Illinois, which until recent years has been in full accord with the cooperative forces of the Disciples. Under the leadership of dissident ministers from independent schools who have opposed the regular practices of the congregation in its cooperative work, the church expelled the Women's Missionary Society from the building and locked the doors against it. The church board and congregation were led, also, by these ministers to adopt a constitution for the church which contains a creedal statement. This is a procedure as opposite and detrimental to the position and traditions of Disciples of Christ as accepting the Nicene Creed or the Westminster Confession of Faith would be. The divisive, creedal formulae (Articles of Faith), adopted at Salem, follow:

This Church believes and teaches the following:

THE TRINITY:

The triune God, Father, Son and Holy Spirit; co-eternal in being, co-identical in nature, co-equal in power and glory, having the same attributes and perfections.

VERBAL INSPIRATION:

The verbal inspiration and plenary authority of both Old and New Testaments, inerrant in the original writings, infallible, and God breathed.

TOTAL DEPRAVITY:

The depravity and lost condition of all men by nature, and of himself utterly unable to remedy his lost condition.

PERSONALITY OF SATAN:

That Satan is a Person, the author of sin, and the cause of the fall; that he is the open and declared enemy of God and man; and that he shall be eternally punished in the Lake of Fire.

VIRGIN BIRTH:

The virgin birth and deity of Jesus Christ eternally. His sinless humanity. His substitutionary death, His bodily resurrection, His present intercession at the right hand of God, and His personal coming again to rule and reign on the earth.

SALVATION:

Salvation is the gift of God by grace, received by personal faith in the Lord Jesus Christ, whose precious blood was shed on Calvary for the forgiveness of our sins, and baptism by immersion.

BLOOD ATONEMENT:

The shed blood of Jesus Christ the only atonement for sins.

RESURRECTION:

The bodily resurrection and Lordship of Jesus.

THE ETERNAL STATE:

The bodily resurrection of all men, the saved believers to eternal bliss in heaven, and the eternal punishment in hell of all who have rejected Christ as Savior.

SEPARATION:

That all believers should live in such a manner as not to bring reproach upon their Savior and Lord; and, that separation from all religious apostasy, all worldly and sinful pleasures, practices and associations is commanded by God.

MISSIONS:

The obligation of all believers to witness by life and by word to the truths of Holy Scripture, and to seek to proclaim the Gospel to all mankind as the absolute command of God to evangelize all nations.

SECOND COMING OF CHRIST:

The personal, premillennial, and imminent return of our Lord Jesus Christ.

The cooperative group of the Salem church went into the Circuit Court of Marion County, Illinois, at Salem for a delayed hearing on February 4, 1952. They sought to protect the congregation from the separatists who had taken control. While lawsuits by congregations or members are regrettable, yet the people loyal to the history of the congregation at Salem felt that this was the only way to preserve the inherent rights of the congregation. In the summer of 1953 the Circuit Court Judge dismissed the complaint and a counter claim for "want of equity."

Disciples of Christ may well take note of the widespread processes by which the independent and separatist ministers and groups infiltrate into and disrupt churches. Such disruption is happening, or has already happened, in church after church in many states, including California, Illinois, Indiana, Iowa, Ohio, Texas, Virginia, and West Virginia, among others. In such cases, cooperative groups or churches of Disciples which win court decisions *should remain firmly together* after the court decree has been issued. Otherwise the church property may remain in control of separatists. This has happened.

Aside from the "heresy" attacks that many of these separatist preachers make upon individuals, agencies, and institutions, they repeatedly state that money given through the United Christian Missionary Society is largely wasted and that missionaries who have given their all and gone out to devote their lives in strange and difficult lands in the name of Christ cannot be trusted! What unfortunate statements!

The independent and separatist forces never have been willing to face the fact that carefully-organized work, properly directed, is always far less expensive than independent, free-lance missions. Independent missions are frequently carried on without proper guidance and often left largely to the judgment of self-appointed, unguided, and many times, poorly-trained and inexperienced individuals. This is especially true in the extremely difficult and complex work of foreign missions when one has to face a strange language; an age-long, alien religion; and a culture quite different from our own in circumstances which test the most careful and rigid selection, training, and adaptation of the missionary.

One who has been connected with the missionary life of the brotherhood of Disciples of Christ as long as I have, can testify to the devotion of our consecrated missionaries, hundreds of them, in distant lands, in spite of increasing opposition from the independent forces.

The Use of Labels

The attacks of the *Christian Standard* on persons and organizations have just about exhausted the list of labels that could be used in its propaganda. One of the first was "German rationalism." Then came "destructive critic," "propagandist," "cult," "coterie," "clique," "disloyal," "modernist," "apostate," "infidel," "vested interest," "machine," "ecclesiasticism," "bureaucrats," "finger men," and other terms.

During recent years, the term "modernist" has been the chief stock-in-trade of the *Standard* for anyone who might differ with it on a controversial issue. Thus the minds of persons who are uninformed or confused or susceptible, in the face of the repetitious use of this label, form an image of someone or something most undesirable, to say the least. The background, or circumstances, do not seem to be considered by the periodical when the term is used. Always, with regard to the accused, the matter is apparently either all white, if approved, or all black if disapproved.

The inconsistency of the use of the term "modernist" seems apparent. It is a kind of general appellation for every attitude which is contrary to that approved by the *Christian Standard*. Apparently, the paper would define modernism as, "God is an idea in the human heart." That is, humanism over against any supernatural conception of religion or any acceptance of Jesus Christ as the divine Son of God.

So, as indicated, the periodical accuses anyone deviating from its position with digression from commonly accepted religious truth. For instance, a person may be extremely conservative in his doctrinal viewpoint, but if he recognizes the church membership of an unimmersed Christian, then he becomes a "modernist" to the *Christian Standard* with all of the assumed, dangerous implications of the word. Yet the magazine does not stop there. If a person or an organization even recognizes another church or person as belonging to our fellowship, after accepting an unimmersed person, then that person or organization is tagged "modernist."

The sad fact is that this soon starts the cry of "disloyal," "modernist," "apostate," and "infidel," not only in the *Christian Standard*, but it becomes the hue and cry of students and graduates of numerous Bible colleges recognized by the magazine.

Extreme attitudes always bring a reflex in the opposite direction. The reaction from the accusations of the *Standard* has constantly opened the eyes of people to a broader liberality and freedom in religion. Perhaps the chief consolation to be gained from these attacks is the help provided in awakening Disciples of Christ to a more vigorous, open-minded cooperative attitude.

What a change has come since the early days of the *Christian Standard* when differences developed between Benjamin Franklin, another of our early editors, and Isaac Errett. The former stood for the individualistic, legalistic, and noncooperative group while the latter, then editor of the *Standard,* contended for the organized missionary societies and the necessary cooperation with which to conduct the work of the brotherhood. About the only point at which the present position of the *Standard* seems

to be at variance with the separatist view of Benjamin Franklin
and his followers is on the matter of instrumental music in
church services.   And added to this now is a use of terms of
which Benjamin Franklin was never guilty in the hottest de-
bates with Isaac Errett and the open-minded, progressive *Christian Standard* of that period!

In the *Christian Baptist* of 1826 (p. 199), Alexander Campbell, the editor, wrote as follows:

> The people every where have an insatiable appetite for sound doc-
> trine.   They eat whole sermons after sermons, and run after this and
> that preacher for sound doctrine, and are as hungry as before. . . . It
> would be of infinite more importance to the religious community and to
> the rising generation, if, from the teacher's chair, in the church, and in
> every christian family, less was said about this sound doctrine, and the
> time occupied therein devoted to recommending, enforcing, and prac-
> tising that "holiness without which no man shall see the Lord."

The *Standard* has alienated many Disciples who hold a sincere conservative theological position and who have longed for
a brotherhood periodical that would sincerely represent their
position without calling those disagreeing "disloyal."   There are
many such Disciples and they do not want our brotherhood to
divide again.

Some of these persons, because they have participated in International Convention programs or had a part in other cooperative undertakings of the Disciples, have been criticized
by the *Christian Standard* and the *Restoration Herald*.   These
publications have even come to the point of strictures on the
independent North American Christian Convention because it
has tried to keep its programs non-controversial.   These numerous Disciples are confused and do not know which way to turn
now since the *Standard*, which once had so much influence with
them, absolutely repudiates the International Convention and
the entire cooperative, organized life, state and national, of the
Disciples of Christ.

Christians do not usually go to court to sue for libel, even
under great provocation.   However, when it is remembered that
a Christian minister's reputation is his only negotiable asset and
his most sacred possession, one wonders how much he should

take without recourse to secular law for protection and redress. Yet, sad to say, there is no common Christian level for adequate reply.

One of our younger, trusted, and able state secretaries, Loren E. Lair of Des Moines, backed by his own board, the Iowa Christian Missionary Society, resorted to legal action. In March, 1952, his $50,000 libel suit against Robert E. Elmore, editor of the *Restoration Herald*, and the Christian Restoration Association as publisher, was heard by a jury in the Federal Court in Des Moines. Mr. Lair charged that he was defamed by Mr. Elmore's writings. The jury returned a verdict for the defendant. Mr. Lair appealed that decision to the United States Circuit Court of Appeals on January 16, 1953.

A cover page editorial in the *Christian Standard* of July 29, 1950 (p. 465), was entitled, "A Program on Which All Can Unite," that is, New Testament evangelism. This page is reproduced in facsimile on a following page. After an opening sentence in capital letters, the editorial began thus:

> . . . too much effort is dissipated by little petty quarrels over trifles that have nothing to do with saving souls or making the world a better place. By this time, we ought to know that there are many things on which we will never all agree—like which convention is best to attend, which missionary is most deserving of support, which school is best in which to be educated, or whether the second coming of Christ is pre- or post- or a-millennial, or whether we should remarry divorced people, or call our congregation "Church of Christ" or "Christian Church," or whether the use of tobacco is a venal or a mortal sin.
>
> *But all of us, who follow Christ, can unite on the one thing that matters most:* A PROGRAM OF SOUL-WINNING AND EVANGELISM THAT WILL BUILD THE KINGDOM OF GOD BY BUILDING THE LOCAL CHURCH.

Exactly what the *Standard* meant by "A Program on Which All Can Unite" is somewhat uncertain. An editorial statement over the name of W. R. Walker, editorial counselor of the magazine and president of the Standard Publishing Company, had appeared just four weeks previously under the title, "Somebody Is Thinking Confusedly: Who?" (July 1, 1950, p. 410). Referring at the beginning to an editorial in another brother-

DEVOTED TO THE RESTORATION OF PRIMITIVE CHRISTIANITY, ITS DOCTRINE, ITS ORDINANCES AND ITS FRUITS

CHRISTIAN STANDARD

Vol. LXXXVI   Cincinnati, O., July 29, 1950   No. 30

A Program on Which All Can Unite

[An Editorial]

AREN'T WE ALL TIRED OF FIGHTING AND CONTROVERSY OVER ISSUES THAT WON'T MATTER ANYWAY ONE HUNDRED YEARS FROM NOW!

Certainly there are many things that do matter—like contending for the faith, for instance. But too much effort is dissipated by little petty quarrels over trifles that have nothing to do with saving souls or making the world a better place. By this time, we ought to know that there are many things on which we will never all agree—like which convention is best to attend, which missionary is most deserving of support, which school is best in which to be educated, or whether the second coming of Christ is pre- or post- or a-millennial, or whether we should remarry divorced people, or call our congregation "Church of Christ" or "Christian Church," or whether the use of tobacco is a venal or a mortal sin.

But all of us, who follow Christ, can unite on the one thing that matters most: A PROGRAM OF SOUL-WINNING AND EVANGELISM THAT WILL BUILD THE KINGDOM OF GOD BY BUILDING THE LOCAL CHURCH.

Whatever our personal convictions may be on many questions of opinion, we are already committed to a ministry of building the church of Jesus Christ by winning sinners to Christ and edifying the saints in Christ.

So, why not unite in a campaign to DO MORE EFFICIENTLY WHAT WE ARE ALREADY TRYING TO DO IN THE LOCAL CHURCH?

Is there a conscientious preacher, or elder, or deacon, or Bible-school officer or teacher who would not like to see in his local church:

Attendance doubled at all services?

More workers enlisted and trained?

More souls won to Christ than you have had in years?

Giving doubled?

WE BELIEVE IT CAN BE DONE—WE KNOW IT HAS BEEN DONE IN SOME PLACES—AND WE OFFER THE SERVICES OF THE CHRISTIAN STANDARD FOR THAT PURPOSE

FROM NOW ON

The CHRISTIAN STANDARD IS PLEDGED TO DO EVERYTHING IN ITS POWER TO PROMOTE NEW TESTAMENT EVANGELISM IN OUR PAGES.

Yes, we have tried to promote and support New Testament evangelism in the past. But now we intend to devote the greater part of our space to the direct promotion of a program of evangelism in the local church that will do all the things we spoke of above: double attendance, enlist workers, win souls, double giving.

Yes, we are devoted to the "Restoration of primitive Christianity, its doctrine, its ordinances, and its fruits." But the phase of primitive Christianity that is in greatest need of being restored right now is EVANGELISM.

ARE YOU INTERESTED?

ARE YOU WITH US?

CAN WE ALL GET TOGETHER IN A SIMULTANEOUS PROGRAM OF NEW TESTAMENT EVANGELISM THAT WILL MAKE THE WORLD SIT UP AND TAKE NOTICE?

If your answer is YES, sit down right now and write us a letter or postal card and say so, or, better still, send us a telegram! Let us have the evidence that our conviction in this matter is right, and that we can make a concerted and united attack on the citadel of Satan and bring captives to the feet of King Jesus.

Courtesy, Disciples of Christ Historical Society

The numerous cooperative forces of the Disciples of Christ have been virtually ignored by the "Christian Standard" since this editorial announcement appeared, July 29, 1950, on the cover (p. 465).

hood publication on, "Maintaining Unity and Diversity," the statement by Mr. Walker on the editorial page of the *Standard* said:

> The editorial also pleads for "Disciples" to stay together. This prompts more questions. Who are "Disciples"? Only those who belong to the "Disciples" denomination? If so, the editor has little cause for worry. They will stay together under the leadership of those who believe in ecclesiastical union and control. . . .
>
> In just what are those "Disciples" "united"? In support of certain ecclesiastical machinery.

On the part of the *Christian Standard,* undoubtedly, the plea for unity is to its own group whom it claims to be loyal "Restorationists," and whom it has cut off, editorially, from all cooperative forces connected in any way with the International Convention of Disciples of Christ. After spending fifty years in creating a distinct division among Disciples of Christ, the paper now appeals for unity among its own group and suddenly stops controversy in its own pages.

After a careful study of the controversial issues involved in the attitude of the *Christian Standard,* and the consequent division which is apparent among us, it would seem that the greatest difficulty lies in matters of opinion. Our theological differences are no greater than those experienced by the Methodists or the Congregationalists. Yet they have held together in a rather solid and effectual unity. The difficulty with the Disciples seems to lie in the fact that the International Convention, the state conventions, the United Christian Missionary Society, the Board of Higher Education and its affiliated institutions have come to be an issue and a test of fellowship insofar as many of those not supporting these agencies are concerned. Thus, comparable issues which by the Campbells, Barton W. Stone, and Isaac Errett were conceded as matters of opinion, have now become, through the attacks of the *Christian Standard,* tests of comradeship and brotherhood.

Alexander Campbell wrote in the *Millennial Harbinger* of February, 1845 (p. 51), about "Our Position to American Slavery." Referring to the division in the churches over that controversial issue, he said: "We are the only religious community in the civilized world whose principles (unless we abandon them) can preserve us from such an unfortunate predicament."

One is also reminded of an early controversy arising over the fact that one of the pioneer preachers of our movement, Aylette Raines, was a Universalist. He joined the Disciples, but still held to his belief in the ultimate salvation of the race. He was strongly attacked by some of the brethren because of his supposed heresy. Thomas Campbell, however, championed him as follows (*Early History of The Disciples in the Western Reserve, Ohio,* by A. S. Hayden, p. 168) :

> The devil has brought this question into this association [Mahoning, Warren, Ohio, in 1828] to sow discord among brethren. Bro. Raines and I have been much together for the last several months, and we have mutually unbosomed ourselves to each other. I am a Calvinist, and he a Restorationist [that is, one of a faction among the Universalists]; and, although I am a Calvinist, I would put my right arm into the fire and have it burnt off before I would raise my arm against him.

Thomas Campbell was philosophically a Calvinist, he stated, which few Disciples are today, yet we revere Thomas Campbell as one of our four outstanding spiritual "founding fathers."

How strange it seems that a Christian people who escaped division over the slavery issue before and during the Civil War, not to mention other issues—all of which were treated with extreme tolerance as a matter of opinion—should now be divided over the issues chronicled in this volume! So, after nearly fifty years of controversy, we have come to the consequent aftermath of unbrotherliness—a sad division in the "house of unity."

That which is desperately needed now, among Disciples of Christ, is consideration and confidence to establish a solid front. We need to eliminate name-calling and substitute brotherliness. We need every conservative, every liberal, and everyone who may occupy middle ground—every sincere leader who puts the Lordship of Jesus Christ and his supremacy over the human soul first. There are enough sinister tides running against Christianity itself in the world to compel unity among us and to discourage every effort to bring distrust into a great Christian family of believers. It is especially tragic when unnecessary division comes to a group like the Disciples of Christ, whose reason for existence is the unity of Christ's followers!

It is not inconsistent that there be a conservative group among us which resists any change and a liberal group which pushes forward to change with impatience. The inconsistency lies in the fact that those of one group judge the opinions and actions of another and vice versa. This has led to isolation on the part of each group with differences being grossly exaggerated. The great mass of Disciple preachers and churches occupy a medial position and have proceeded cooperatively and democratically to create and develop our present organized work.

We could have and should have remained united if we had followed the appeal of P. H. Welshimer, minister of Canton, Ohio, to "disagree without being disagreeable," or better yet, if we had adopted the slogan of the Chinese delegation at the Jerusalem Missionary Conference of 1928: "We have agreed to differ, we have resolved to love, we have united to serve." But such Christian exhortations have not been followed and schism has resulted.

Two Alternatives for Disciples

Two alternatives appear possible for Disciples of Christ in the face of the present situation within the brotherhood:

1. There is the exclusive concept that we have instituted the church with inerrancy after the New Testament pattern, that this is the absolute norm at which unity for the Christian world can be attained, and that this consummation will be achieved only when the other religious bodies come to accept the position held by the Disciples of Christ. This alternative of aloofness from and opposition to Christian cooperation is advocated by the *Christian Standard*, the *Restoration Herald*, and their supporting "independent" constituency.

2. Then, there is the positive plea for Christian unity on a non-dogmatic, New Testament basis with religious democracy which is strengthened by freedom of thought and scriptural interpretation. This alternative bears witness in the spirit of Christ and of longing that all who believe in him may be one. It implies, of course, our consistent and sincere participation in the ecumenical work of Protestantism on a world level. *The*

Christian-Evangelist, World Call, and the agencies of the co-operative forces of the Disciples follow this second alternative.

The group upholding the first alternative would contend that we must present the counsel of absolutism and perfection to the rest of the Christian world until all others yield to our plea and position as we conceive it. Such exclusiveness, in isolation, has nothing to be gained.

The second group, while convinced that it adheres to the significant essentials and spirit of the "founding fathers" of the Disciples, to the best of its ability, has realistic misgivings from our experience in unity. This group is convinced that Disciples do not necessarily know all that may be known about unity. These Disciples of this second category assume that the best way to approach unity is to proceed as far as possible with the co-operative Christian movements and in them give our witness and testimony to the noble simplicities of the New Testament ideals which we hold.

In fact one of the strongest appeals for entering and encouraging cooperative movements of Christians is the opportunity provided to bear our witness for unity. It is a sobering fact that Disciples of Christ are better understood and more appreciated in the mission fields of the Belgian Congo, Latin America, the Philippines, China, Japan, and India than here in the United States and Canada.

In these mission fields our missionaries and native, national Christians have been leaders in launching into cooperative work with other Christians. This has given the Disciples of Christ the close, friendly relationship which is so much more convincing and effective than critical and antagonistic aloofness. Disciples in the United States and Canada, however, are rapidly advancing in their cooperative outlook to the attitude assumed for so long by the missionaries.

Those Disciples who follow the first alternative would place their hope in isolation and criticism from afar off; those who follow the second would place their hope in cooperative fellowship and witnessing.

Since "Restorationism" has not always emphasized the spirit and has become for so many a hard and fast mould, it would seem better to return to the simple belief of the movement at its beginning. This was that the acceptance of Christ as Lord and Saviour was the great common denominator for unity and that any attempt at forced uniformity in matters of organization and development is, in reality, a departure from the spirit of the New Testament.

A great difficulty lies in the fact that the *Christian Standard* seems to leave no middle ground for consideration and eventual unity among ourselves. I cannot believe, however, that a large number of the more conservative yet considerate Disciples of Christ will go along to complete separatism. Surely there is a middle ground which makes possible cooperation in the great objectives toward unity.

I do not believe that this conservative group will follow the *Christian Standard* in absolutely and finally withdrawing from our whole organized, cooperative life as a brotherhood—the International Convention, the United Christian Missionary Society, and our numerous other cooperative functions. The lack of response to the repeated "disloyalty" appeals of the *Standard* and the longing of Disciples for Christian unity adds to this conviction. Surely the cohesive principle of unity that we have preached for nearly 150 years should keep the great body of Disciples of Christ from fragmentation and denial of the plea which brought us into existence.

J. H. Garrison, editor of *The Christian-Evangelist* for many years, was a contemporary, friend, and fellow advocate of progressive attitudes and policies with Isaac Errett, the first editor of the *Christian Standard*. On his page, "The Easy Chair," in *The Christian-Evangelist* (April 11, 1929, p. 480), Mr. Garrison, then eighty-seven years of age, wrote the following challenging statement:

Are we Disciples, who started out a century ago to plead for Christian union, losing our zeal for this holy cause, or are we losing confidence in ourselves as fit instruments of our Lord for promoting it? ... *What changes or modifications in the way of addition or subtraction, are demanded among the Disciples to make their plea more efficient, either in its substance or in the manner of its presentation to the world?* The religious world today is very different from what it was a century ago. Science has given us a different conception of nature and the universe. Biblical criticism has changed for most of us, our view of the Bible, making it not a less, but a more valuable book for the student of religion. This increase in light is evident in every department of human knowledge. Is it possible that all these changes do not require any readjustment in the matter and method of a plea for unity inaugurated more than a century ago? But if so, what? Is there any question before us more important than that?

Since Mr. Garrison wrote that, there has developed the great ecumenical urge of the Protestant bodies for cooperation and unity manifest now in both the National Council of Churches and the World Council of Churches.

Is it not true, however, that a religious movement like the Disciples of Christ becomes stultified when there is insistence that all opinions adhere to one point of view? When that happens does it not cease to be a movement and become a crystallized sect? By thus limiting its outlook and freedom, such a group closes its window shutters to new light from without, dims its light from within, thereby freezing itself into dogmatic conformity.

There is a place in Christendom for the Disciples of Christ as never before with the progressive membership of our churches advancing with the spiritual and cultural tides of the times and keeping a high place in all the truly cooperative and ecumenical enterprises to which the churches are turning with increased fervor.

Our future as a great unity movement certainly does not lie in narrow separatism among ourselves or in aloofness from interchurch fellowship in the name and cause of Christ. It rather lies, as Mr. Garrison indicated, in re-thinking our position, re-marking our path, and maintaining our faith and a place of leadership and influence in the significant ecumenical movement for the healing of the broken body of Jesus Christ.

Chapter 10

THE COOPERATIVE WORK
CONTINUES TO GROW

Any question as to the present status of the brotherhood of Disciples of Christ may be answered by a glance at the impressive and encouraging growth of our cooperative work. This picture may help the concerned reader to overcome any sense of ambiguousness developed from reading the previous pages.

Only a few highlights can be cited about the major agencies of the Disciples of Christ. These have been secured from their annual reports and other sources to indicate the growth in their outreach and the increase in financial support by churches of the brotherhood. This growth occurred, of course, in spite of fifty years of continuous attack on most of the organized, cooperative work.

A steady development of the agencies is especially noticeable since 1920. That was the year when the United Christian Missionary Society was launched and the opposition of the *Christian Standard* and other antagonists became more intense. Comparisons do not portray the whole story and are impossible in many instances because of the changing scene. However, they do afford a basis for some observations on the present status of the undertakings of the brotherhood.

The type of work done in many areas has changed greatly since the establishment of the United Society. A number of services has been withdrawn, but other phases of the work have been strengthened. Increasingly, the emphasis has been on quality rather than quantity. Rather than to begin additional work, here and there, the Society's policy has been to develop existing program and activity for a more effective Christian witness. All of the present foreign fields are far from being fully occupied.

The past one third of a century has witnessed an increase in the national church membership on the foreign mission fields of more than 300 per cent. The total membership on the foreign fields in 1920 was 22,381. By 1950, in 281 churches, the membership totaled 100,122. In 1920 there were 3,200 baptisms of new converts in the foreign missions compared with 7,022 in 1950 (*First Annual Report of the United Christian Missionary Society,* October 1, 1920–June 30, 1921, p. 43; *1952 Year Book, Disciples of Christ,* p. 153).

In 1920 there were 266 foreign missionaries serving under the United Society. The number later increased, only to be sharply decreased during the depression years. This, of course, necessitated the withdrawal of missionaries from several fields and decreased the number on all other fields. By 1952 the number of missionaries had slowly climbed back to 224 in spite of postwar inflation and the increasing need for an expanding evangelistic, educational, and medical outreach everywhere. This number represents active missionaries only and does not include any candidates, or volunteers, as recruits are designated. Yet with fewer missionaries, a much larger program is now being carried out on all of the fields. This has been possible because of the ever-increasing effectiveness of the developing national leadership in the indigenous church. The following figures reveal the extent of the growth of the work on the foreign fields:

1920		1950
196	Organized Churches	281
976	Regular Meeting Places	1,495
3,200	New Members by Baptism	7,022
22,381	Total Membership	100,122
1,368	National Workers	2,391
119	Schools (Not Union)	341
11,602	Pupils	17,365
100	Ministerial Students	201
30	Hospitals and Dispensaries	38
276,472	Medical Treatments	665,713

These and other interesting comparative figures may be studied in the *1921 Year Book, Disciples of Christ* (pp. 49 f.) and in the latest *1952 Year Book, Disciples of Christ* (p. 153). It should be remembered that no figures on the missionary work in China are included in the 1950 tabulation. This temporary withdrawal was caused by the political situation in China.

Much more time and money are now necessary to prepare missionary personnel for the arduous tasks of foreign service. The young people dedicated to such Christian ministry must go through a careful screening process for work under the United Christian Missionary Society. Years of specialized training are necessary. They must be prepared for the constantly changing situation on the foreign fields that means yielding more and more responsibility to the national church membership on the mission fields. Only through complete identification with the people among whom he lives and works will the modern missionary achieve unhindered fellowship with the indigenous, younger church.

At the present time, the United Society maintains mission work in eleven foreign fields, not including China. When the political situation in China forced the withdrawal of all missionaries from the successful work there, the Society joined with the British Churches of Christ in a joint missionary endeavor in their established work in Thailand. In 1946, the Society began to preserve and strengthen the scattered remains of the independent missionary venture of the 1920s in South Africa. As was explained in a previous chapter, the United Society withdrew from work in Tibet in the 1930s.

The number of "link" relationships for the support of foreign missionaries has increased, too, since 1920. In that year there were 327 such churches (*First Annual Report of the United Christian Missionary Society,* October 1, 1920–June 30, 1921, p. 150). In 1952 there were 511 such relationships maintained by both churches and individuals. The Society now seeks to provide for each missionary's support by providing three link supports at $1,000 each annually for every missionary (*1952 Year Book, Disciples of Christ,* p. 143).

Cooperation in Christian missions and education, both at home and abroad, continues to be fundamental with the United Society. The basic policy is to engage in such work in every instance where a project done together may be more effective. A. Dale Fiers, president of the United Society, endorsed the commitment to comity on behalf of the Society thus (*Leaven,* February, 1952, p. 1): "We believe in the practice of comity and we are thoroughly committed to it as a working policy in our missionary program."

Work done cooperatively by the United Society now includes participation in united Christian councils, evangelism, language schools for missionaries, schools for nationals, printing presses for Christian literature, leper colonies, seminaries, bookstores, and medical institutions.

The United Society has supported Robert Tobias as the representative of the Disciples of Christ on the staff of the World Council of Churches in Geneva for several years. He has made a significant contribution to the Society's ecumenical ministry as a member of the staff of the Council's department of interchurch aid and service to refugees.

In addition, an increasingly effective ecumenical witness is maintained by the United Society through sharing in the comprehensive program of the National Council of Churches of Christ in the U.S.A. This is done through both staff participation and financial support. A large number of the Society's employed and voluntary personnel are among the scores of Disciples' representatives serving through the National Council. These Disciple names cover nearly eight impressive pages in the *1952 Year Book, Disciples of Christ* (pp. 221-228).

Disciples who are currently staff members of the National Council are, for the most part, former employees of the United Society. The number includes Roy G. Ross, recently chosen general secretary of the Council and Wilbur C. Parry, associate administrative secretary. Others are: Jesse M. Bader, Richard E. Lentz, Raymond F. McLain, Mr. and Mrs. Emory Ross, Miss Helen F. Spaulding, and James L. Stoner.

Mrs. James D. Wyker of Columbia, Missouri, has rendered outstanding service as a Christian leader as the chairman of the General Department of United Church Women of the National Council of Churches. This department deserves much credit, for instance, in helping to send Mrs. Rosa Page Welch, of Chicago, around the world in 1952-53 as an "Ambassador of Good-will." An accomplished singer, she has helped to dispel erroneous ideas spread abroad about the ill treatment of Negroes in the United States. The United Society had a share in making it possible for Mrs. Welch to win friends abroad. She has climbed many stairs since her student days at the Southern Christian Institute, a junior college under sponsorship of the United Society at Edwards, Mississippi.

At the time of the organization of the United Christian Missionary Society, about twenty schools and community centers were maintained by the board in the United States. There are now only six such institutions under control of the Society. This looks like retrenchment. Yet with changing times and needs, some of the services formerly rendered by these institutions have been assumed by local community or government agencies. Other programs were discontinued when the needs were finally met. Some became self-supporting. The present home mission institutions have been greatly strengthened. The case of Jarvis Christian College of Hawkins, Texas, will illustrate.

In 1920, Jarvis was an elementary and high school for Negroes with an annual budget of $41,000. Now it is a four-year, senior college, accredited by the Southern Association of Secondary Schools and Colleges. Scholastic recognition is now given to Jarvis graduates by accredited colleges and universities. The college must continue to maintain high standards in order to remain on the approved list of the accrediting agency. The current yearly budget of Jarvis now totals $205,983.80. In 1920 the total staff numbered twenty-one persons. Now the faculty alone totals twenty-six. Under the continued supervision of the United Society, Jarvis is today pioneering in a significant program of fundamental education.

Space prohibits indicating detailed ways in which the United Society's program of church development, evangelism, work with Spanish-Americans, town and country churches, urban churches, and mission congregations is constantly being strengthened.

A brief tabulation from three sources will indicate some of the increased effectiveness of the Christian educational program of the United Society (*Eleventh Annual Report of the United Christian Missionary Society*, July 1, 1930, to June 30, 1931, p.

83; *1921 Year Book, Disciples of Christ,* pp. 134 f. and 140-142;
1952 Year Book, Disciples of Christ, pp. 166, 167, 169) :

1920		1952
6	Summer Camps, Conferences	295
391	Student Enrollment	20,270
60	Faculty	2,847
25	Religious Ed. Field Staff	55
3	Student Centers	124

These figures do not include comparable projects on the foreign fields that are conducted by the United Society staff. Also,
space prohibits details of the widespread program of student
work, vacation church schools, Bible chairs, world fellowship
meets, etc. In addition, there is now a comprehensive program
of social and missionary education which informs and inspires
concerned Christians. Channels are varied for applying Christian teachings to the world's pressing social problems.

Alan Dale Fiers became president of the United Christian
Missionary Society in 1951. He is the youngest person ever to
hold this responsible position. He, of course, had no part in
any of the controversies which involved the preceding presidents of the Society with the *Christian Standard* and other opponents. He is a graduate of Bethany (W. Va.) College and
the Yale University Divinity School. He came to the Society
from the pastorate of the Euclid Avenue Christian Church of
Cleveland, Ohio. He has just recently returned from his first
world journey which was made for observation and study of the
missionary work in the Belgian Congo, India, Thailand, and
Japan.

In 1953, the United Society is a proved brotherhood instru-
ment for the most efficient outreach of local churches. Disciples
of Christ chose it as a medium for more effective work in missions
and education. Some 2,200 volunteers now compose numerous
committees and other groups that guide and assist the Society's
comprehensive programs. The churches continue to show increased liberality in answering appeals to support the Society,
thus enabling it to help meet the world's needs. On June 30,
1952, the Society had a net worth of $8,275,064.95, the largest
in its long and useful history (*1952 Year Book, Disciples of
Christ,* p. 149).

The International Convention of Disciples of Christ is the out-growth of our first General Convention, formed in 1849 with Alexander Campbell as the first president. It has been attacked by the *Christian Standard* for many years. The present organization, representing our churches in both the United States and Canada, dates from 1917. Its strength and popularity have increased through the years. Assemblies that are mass meetings meet regularly, in most cases every year, in various American cities. All persons who attend and pay the registration fee are entitled to vote.

The convention receives and expresses itself on the reports of its affiliated agencies. Action is advisory yet it carries much weight because of the quality of its leadership, as well as the large attendance and wide representation of those present. The annual agency reports are usually audited and notarized, as recommended by the convention. These reports and all resolutions are carefully studied by a Committee on Recommendations of about 200 members, democratically chosen by the various state and area conventions of the Disciples. The convention programs provide stimulating information, inspiration, and fellowship.

Since 1946, the International Convention has maintained a full-time headquarters office in downtown Indianapolis. It compiles the annual *Year Book of Disciples of Christ*. Gaines M. Cook has been the executive secretary since 1946. Outstanding Disciples are honored with the presidency of the convention. A total of 1,443 congregations underwrote the budget for the year ending on June 30, 1952. This represented 202 new contributing churches for that fiscal year (*1952 Year Book, Disciples of Christ*, p. 44).

Other Representative Brotherhood Agencies

Unified Promotion, like most of the other responsible brotherhood agencies, while voluntarily set up, is legally incorporated. It is the medium by which local churches and state and national agencies cooperate to promote interest in and giving to various brotherhood causes.

Growing out of increased competition for the same missionary dollar, Unified Promotion began to function in 1935 with fifty-three participating boards. It has always tried to emphasize cooperation, the spirit of which is an indispensable part of the brotherhood heritage.

The receipts of Unified Promotion are distributed among the cooperating agencies and institutions. Distribution of the funds is now moving away from a percentage plan to allocations on the basis of an agency's needs and in consideration of the needs of other agencies. Those needs are carefully studied by the Commission on Brotherhood Finance which consists of fifteen representative Disciples. The receipts of Unified Promotion have grown from $876,377.90 (*1936 Year Book, Disciples of Christ*, p. 114) in 1935-36 to $2,867,895.71 (*1952 Year Book, Disciples of Christ*, p. 182) in 1951-52. The number of contributing churches, varying from year to year, last year numbered 4,094 (*1952 Year Book, Disciples of Christ*, p. 184).

C. O. Hawley, executive secretary, has directed the work of Unified Promotion since it was launched in 1935. The annual chairmanship of the governing Board of Directors rotates among laymen, women, and ministers.

The Association for the Promotion of Christian Unity dates from 1910 when Peter Ainslie called his fellow Disciples to a new dedication to Christian unity. The board seeks to cultivate Christian unity and to stimulate a growing ecumenical fellowship through literature and conferences. The work is conducted on a voluntary basis by the officers and twenty-five commissioners, elected for three-year terms.

The Association is making its greatest contribution now by increasing the concern among the churches of the brotherhood for a more effective ecumenical witness. This is manifesting itself in contributions to the National Council of Churches from an increasing number of our congregations. Such gifts for the year 1951-52 amounted to $22,046.98. The World Council of Churches received, for the same period, gifts of $9,826.62 from a lesser number of churches (*1952 Year Book, Disciples of Christ*, pp. 780 ff.). These gifts do not include amounts received for specific phases of ecumenical work from the Week of Compassion gifts.

The Board of Church Extension exists to assist our churches in the planning and financing of church buildings and parsonages. Its loans are both interest-bearing and interest-free. Architectural guidance is provided, along with assistance in fund-raising and dedications. As of December 31, 1952, the Annual Report of the Board indicates there were 849 loans in force with balances of $6,537,360.46. (Highlights of the report appear in the *1953 Blue Book* and will with more detail, subsequently, in the *1953 Year Book, Disciples of Christ.*) Since 1932, not a loan has been made by the Board upon which a dollar of either interest or principal was lost. This experience proves that churches are excellent financial risks.

A number of the loans are with conservative congregations which support missions independently but are not thereby disfellowshiped. In 1952, a total of 176 interest-bearing loans amounting to $2,192,104.69 were closed. In addition, there were thirty-one interest-free loans issued for $102,525.00. These figures contrast sharply with the smaller ones of 1921-22, when sixty-six churches received loans totaling $462,580.00 (*1921 Year Book, Disciples of Christ,* pp. 105 ff.).

During 1952, a total of 567 congregations were assisted with services of the Bureau of Architecture of this Board of Church Extension. As of December 31, 1952, 215 organizations and fifty-three individuals had $2,367,324.58 on deposit as interest-bearing, trust funds. Interest of $62,423.20 was earned by these depositors during the year. Through such deposits everybody gains and more churches are assisted with loans.

Total gross assets of the Board of Church Extension are currently at an all-time high with a total of $7,021,355.96. During the five-year period ending December 31, 1952, there was a total gain in the Board's permanent funds of $1,221,449.05. Interest receipts and loan principal repayments in 1952 reached all-time highs.

The Board of Higher Education and the institutions and agencies affiliated with it have likewise progressed during these years of controversy. While there was a brotherhood association of colleges in 1914, the present Board of Higher Education was organized in 1938. The board membership represents lay personnel, ministers, and executive heads of member institutions and agencies. The Board exists as a medium of two-way communication on the national level between our churches and educational institutions and agencies.

The thirty-four affiliated member agencies and institutions all cooperate voluntarily in the Board of Higher Education. This group consists of colleges and universities, and seminaries, most of which are fully accredited. In addition, there are a number of Bible chairs and foundations connected with universities. These are all in the framework of the cooperative life of the brotherhood.

A few statistics suggest some of the impressive growth of these institutions, in spite of continuous criticism and attack (*1921 Year Book, Disciples of Christ*, pp. 217, 223; *1922 Year Book, Disciples of Christ*, p. 39; *1952 Year Book, Disciples of Christ*, p. 22):

1921		1952
9,561	Students	26,304
933	Ministerial Students	2,243
?	Faculty	1,184
$ 159,873.70	Gifts from Churches	$ 625,131.76
$15,602,490.00	Total Assets	$71,281,015.75

The list of the thirty-four institutions and agencies that are affiliated with the Board of Higher Education of Disciples of Christ is an outstanding one. Names, founding dates, and locations of these institutions and agencies follow:

Founded	Name Location
1780	Transylvania College, Lexington, Ky.
1840	Bethany College, Bethany, W. Va.
1849	Midway Junior College, Midway, Ky.
1850	Hiram College, Hiram, Ohio
1851	Christian College, Columbia, Mo.
1853	Culver-Stockton College, Canton, Mo.
1855	Butler University, Indianapolis, Ind.
1855	Eureka College, Eureka, Ill.
1861	Chapman College, Los Angeles, Calif.
1865	The College of the Bible, Lexington, Ky.
1873	Texas Christian University, Ft. Worth, Tex.
1875	Southern Christian Institute, Edwards, Miss.
1881	Drake University, Des Moines, Iowa
1889	Cotner College, Lincoln, Neb.
1890	William Woods College, Fulton, Mo.

Founded	Name Location
1894	Disciples Divinity House of The University of Chicago, Chicago, Ill.
1895	Northwest Christian College, Eugene, Ore.
1896	Bible College of Missouri, Columbia, Mo.
1901	Kansas Bible Chair, Lawrence, Kan.
1902	Atlantic Christian College, Wilson, N. C.
1903	Lynchburg College, Lynchburg, Va.
1906	Phillips University, Enid, Okla.
1909	Drury School of Religion, Springfield, Mo.
1910	Indiana School of Religion, Bloomington, Ind.
1912	Jarvis Christian College, Hawkins, Tex.
1916	Illinois Disciples Foundation, Champaign, Ill.
1920	Overdale College, Birmingham, England (Associate Member)
1922	Oklahoma Christian Foundation, Norman, Okla.
1924	Butler School of Religion, Indianapolis, Ind.
1927	Bible College of New Zealand, Dunedin, N. Z. (Associate Member)
1928	Disciples Foundation, Vanderbilt University, Nashville, Tenn.
1929	College of the Churches of Christ of Canada, Toronto, Ont.
1930	Student Centers Foundation, Ames, Iowa
1949	Christian College of Georgia, Athens, Ga.

The Christian Board of Publication of St. Louis came into existence in 1911 when a broad charter was received from the State of Missouri for the cooperative, brotherhood publishing concern. It operates under a self-perpetuating directorate of thirteen prominent Disciples of Christ. It succeeded the Christian Publishing Company, purchased in 1909 by R. A. Long, Kansas City businessman, from J. H. Garrison and other stockholders. Mr. Long's original investment for the stock totaled $129,000. Subsequent gifts over a period of twenty years by Mr. Long brought the total of his contribution to $404,307.95.

Mr. Long's investment in the Christian Board has now increased more than four times. Gross assets, as of December 31, 1952, amounted to $2,465,378.35. The capital and surplus now total $1,527,798.23, which includes the R. A. Long gift of $404,-307.95, and earned surplus of $1,123,490.28. Gifts distributed to the missionary and educational agencies of the Disciples during the years by the Christian Board have amounted to $1,000,-041.91. The funds distributed among the brotherhood causes amounted to more than $50,000 annually over a period of several years. As a member of the International Convention, regular reports are made to it by the Christian Board.

The Christian Board of Publication is the only publishing house of the Disciples of Christ which is owned and maintained by them in their own behalf. No dividends are ever paid to private interests. The charter under which the Christian Board operates explicitly states that:

> . . . net income and surplus, if any, accruing to the association and not needed for the expenses or extension of the business, shall be by the Board of Directors, from time to time, turned over to and paid into the treasury of some one or more of the missionary, benevolent, church extension, educational societies, or other agencies of the Christian churches (Disciples of Christ).

This provision for the distribution among brotherhood agencies of any income that is surplus earnings is in sharp contrast to the Standard Publishing Company of Cincinnati, recently offered for sale through a New York stock firm for $6,000,000.

The annual business of the Christian Board of Publication, employing 250 people, now totals approximately $2,500,000. Net sales in 1920 amounted to only $456,990.70. Job printing accounts for about one-third of the total volume of annual business. Church school sales explain an additional $1,000,000 plus. *The Christian-Evangelist,* weekly journal of information, interpretation, and inspiration, now has the largest circulation of its ninety-year history. Every single department of the publishing house is showing an increase in volume of business. This explains why an adjacent building has been purchased recently by the Christian Board for minimum expansion. Remodeling of the structure now proceeds.

The National Benevolent Association of the Christian Church developed from humble beginnings in St. Louis in 1886. It has the increasing support of both independent and progressive churches. More than 25,000 persons have received Christian care in its homes since 1887 when the N. B. A. was chartered as the brotherhood's administrative agent for benevolence.

In 1920 there were six homes for children and six for the aged. These served a minimum of 467 children and 125 old people every day in the year (*1921 Year Book, Disciples of Christ,* pp. 121 f.). There are now seven homes for children and eight for the aged. These served 1,387 persons (941 children, 416 aged men and women) in 1951-52 (*1952 Year Book, Disciples of Christ,* p. 101). Three new homes have been received into the expanding fellowship of the N. B. A. since the end of World War II. Additions have been made to most of the other homes, too, in the postwar years.

The first benevolence report, after the N. B. A. became a constituent part of the United Christian Missionary Society in 1920, shows an expenditure of $218,006.86 (*1921 Year Book, Disciples of Christ,* pp. 183 f.). The contributions from the churches for the year ending June 30, 1952, totaled $788,155.09 (*1952 Year Book, Disciples of Christ,* p. 101). More than one-half of this amount is received annually in generous Christmas offerings. The N. B. A. has been separated from the United Society since 1933.

The Pension Fund of Disciples of Christ serves the brotherhood's ministers, missionaries, evangelists, chaplains, educators, state and national executives, and some lay personnel of the churches and agencies. Coverage, gradually being broadened, provides benefits for total and permanent disability, old age retirement, and death.

The Pension Fund began operation in 1931. Its assets have increased from $1,185,408.35 that year (*1932 Year Book, Disciples of Christ,* p. 142) to $13,513,910.49 at the end of 1951 (*1952 Year Book, Disciples of Christ,* p. 114). Beneficiaries have already received about $6,000,000 during the existence of the plan. As of June 30, 1952, there were 4,354 active members, supported by 4,756 church or organizational accounts (*1952 Year Book, Disciples of Christ,* p. 112). The more conservative ministers and churches are constantly encouraged to accept all of the Pension Fund's provisions. A number have already done so.

World Call became the international magazine of the Disciples of Christ in 1919 after a merger of five journals. It is now published by five of the major, national boards. In 1921-22, the average monthly circulation was 57,375 (*1922 Year Book, Dis-*

ciples of Christ, p. 35), while in 1951-52 it was 62,001 (*1952 Year Book, Disciples of Christ,* p. 198). The magazine's peak postwar circulation was slightly more than 75,000, an all-time high of paid circulation for this journal. It is published without any subsidies from any source. All of the major causes of the cooperative life and activity of the Disciples are regularly represented in the columns of *World Call.*

The National Association of State Secretaries is a fellowship organization, mutually advisory, for executives of the state and area missionary organizations of the Disciples. During the last third of a century, the programs of all of the state boards have expanded in terms of personnel, evangelistic outreach, additional program services, and aid to local churches. Many of the state offices are now housed in their own buildings.

There were forty-one state secretaries in 1922 (*1922 Year Book, Disciples of Christ,* p. 55). The latest, *1952 Year Book, Disciples of Christ* (p. 98) shows that there are 52 secretaries, 14 evangelists, 35½ office helpers, and 120 mission pastors. During the fiscal year ending June 30, 1952, a total of 3,372 churches were assisted. The staff members received 2,587 new members (including 1,206 by baptism) into the churches, delivered 4,911 sermons and addresses, organized 20 new churches, wrote more than 100,000 letters and postals, distributed more than one million pieces of literature (including state periodicals), and traveled more than one million miles.

This far-reaching program was carried out, strange as it may seem, with receipts of $852, 971.51. In addition, $33,553.94 was added to the permanent funds of the various state boards. Several of the larger states received more than $40,000 each during the year and two had budgets of more than $100,000 each.

A statistical survey of the membership and financial stewardship of the Disciples across the years would reveal growth. However, many weak churches have unfortunately faded away and thousands of members are relatively unknown factors on far too many church rolls. The latest, *1952 Year Book, Disciples of Christ,* continues to include the incomplete statistics of the non-cooperative, conservative, and independent churches of the brotherhood. The total resident and nonresident membership in 7,931 congregations in the United States and Canada now numbers 1,824,062 (*1952 Year Book, Disciples of Christ*, p. 792). Because of the inclusiveness of such figures, therefore, no comparisons of membership statistics, drawn from this source across the last third of a century or more, would have any meaning concerning the growth of the cooperative work of the Disciples.

These paragraphs indicate some of the highlights of the recent impressive growth of the cooperative agencies of the organized work of the Disciples of Christ. This steady and encouraging advance has been made in the face of repeated attacks through journals representing certain of the independent forces of the brotherhood. The agencies discussed in this chapter represent the major causes of concern among cooperative Disciples. There are several other boards, representing growing aspects of brotherhood work, that are affiliated with the International Convention of Disciples of Christ. However, these are younger organizations for the most part and have not been subjected to the unrelenting opposition that the major boards have long endured. So, in spite of fifty years of criticism and attack, the cooperative life and activities of the Disciples of Christ have grown steadily and significantly.

The future offers the brotherhood of Disciples of Christ promising potentialities for development. It is not the first time, nor is it likely to be the last, that the brotherhood has been confronted with seemingly insurmountable obstacles. Fully realizing that by its very nature Christianity demands the impossible, we move forward resolved that in all things the will to be one may be paramount with all who are willingly enlisted as Disciples of Christ "that they may be one."

EPILOGUE

Developing through the half century of strife recorded in this volume, there have finally emerged fundamental differences in viewpoint which are quite real today among Disciples of Christ. "How Do We Differ?" was discussed in the Eureka (Ill.) College *Bulletin* of July, 1949, and the material here was largely adapted from that statement. In the main, this divergence is portrayed by those persons who support the organized, cooperative agencies and those persons who fail to support these agencies. The differences in viewpoint would seem to exist in the following areas of Christian concern:

Christian Unity

Those supporting the agencies: Believing that traditional creeds and ecclesiastical authority are obstacles to Christian unity, this larger group of Disciples has sought to attain unity by any means not out of harmony with the spiritual truth revealed in the New Testament. This unity is approached by cooperation and fellowship with other Christian bodies within which they seek to make a distinctive witness of our movement, but with an open mind toward all possible avenues of unity. This group does not consider that the motto, "Where the Scriptures speak, we speak; where the Scriptures are silent, we are silent" affords an adequate criterion for unity among ourselves or other religious bodies. The early church was a spiritual movement, this group contends, hardly affording an absolute blueprint in details of church polity. These convictions have led the main stream of our cooperating churches and leaders to be interested in cooperative work with other religious bodies on the mission fields and at home. This has led to interest and participation in the developing ecumenical movement, currently expressing itself in the National and World Councils of Churches with all of their multiple outreach in behalf of the needy peoples.

276

Those not supporting the agencies: Believing that traditional creeds and ecclesiastical authority are obstacles to Christian unity, this group of Disciples holds to the conviction that the only way to achieve unity is through the restoration of a particular New Testament pattern of the church.   The group, also, apparently believes that the crystallized pattern of our more conservative brethren has already attained the absolute New Testament norm and needs no further reconsideration.   These convictions have led to the assumption that cooperation or fellowship with denominations is unscriptural, is to be avoided, and that the only way to achieve Christian unity is to win all Christians and churches to what is presumed to be the restored New Testament pattern in its primitive form.   This has developed into the philosophy of "Restoration" as over against any cooperation as one of the paths towards possible unity.

Interchurch Cooperation

Those supporting the agencies: Believing that the cause of Christian unity is advanced by interchurch cooperation, therefore, Disciples should not only cooperate, but take the lead in such work.   Thus in local worship services, daily vacation Bible schools, the exchange of pulpit speakers, as well as in national and international associations, representing most of the major Protestant bodies, we should participate.   Especially is this true in the mission fields where union educational institutions, union hospitals, union seminaries, union printing presses, and comity agreements for the better occupation of vast fields are gladly entered into, thus demonstrating the spirit of unity.   In fact, one of the strong features in the cooperative program of those supporting the agencies is this friendly working together with other Christians and other churches in meeting common human and spiritual needs.   This is considered one of the best avenues in which to bear witness to the plea of the Disciples for unity.

Those not supporting the agencies: Believing that interchurch work on a state, national, and international level is, relatively speaking, a recognition of denominationalism, such activity is generally opposed as unwise.   Believing, too, in the "open field," this group is opposed to all comity understandings with other

Christian groups at home and abroad, as to territory or work, asserting that this procedure becomes a limitation of freedom and a recognition of a denominational status and is, therefore, contradictory to Restoration principles.

Church Organization and Work

Those supporting the agencies: Believing that since the New Testament does not provide a completed, hard and fast structural organization, in all of its details, this group asserts that the church is consequently left free to adapt forms of organization and cooperation necessary for the realistic needs and conditions of these times.   This belief thus resulted in recognized missionary societies and conventions with the set-up and advisory organization needed to provide for direction, consultation, inspiration, auditing, and review of the work conducted cooperatively. Such organizations conducting programs, democratically approved in our conventions, make reports regularly of that work to those assemblies.   The missionary societies and other boards with the responsibility of selecting, sending out and securing the support of missionaries are responsible to the churches for properly guiding the work.

Those not supporting the agencies: Believing that the New Testament provides a sufficient, unified pattern of organization, this group declares that any further administrative cooperation is unnecessary and unscriptural.   Therefore, it is insisted that the local church affords an adequate organized criterion and that representative, advisory conventions, with societies reporting to them, form an "ecclesiastical" and dangerous system, which is unscriptural.   Any convention, it is maintained, should be held only for preaching, indoctrination, and fellowship, aside from rallies of "protest."   Furthermore, it is declared that all missionary and educational work should be "independent" and with "direct-support"; any agencies considered necessary should be "free agencies," without any convention oversight—only that provided by the local congregations.   In addition, it is asserted, that missionaries should not be subject to selection, training, and support through cooperative organizations, but be independent, self-directed, and directly-supported by churches and interested individuals.

Church Membership

Those supporting the agencies: All these churches practice only immersion as baptism and the great majority accept only immersed believers into church membership. Yet they grant the right of congregational autonomy to those churches which maintain that they are practicing Christian unity by welcoming into membership recognized Christians who have not been immersed and who do not make this action a test of fellowship.

Those not supporting the agencies: These churches accept only immersed believers as members and while they fully recognize unimmersed people as Christians and commune with them in the open-to-all-Christians observance of the Lord's Supper, yet they contend that "open membership" churches and ministers are alien to the Restoration movement and should be disfellowshipped and not recognized as belonging to the Disciples of Christ; furthermore, that contributions from "open membership" churches should not be accepted by any agency of this fellowship.

Ministerial Education

Those supporting the agencies: They hold that ministers, like the early fathers of the movement, should be educated according to the best of approved standards, comparable with those of other professions and other religious bodies, and where possible should have an accredited college education as well as specialized training for the ministry itself. This has led to the establishment of colleges, universities, Bible colleges, and seminaries with scholastic standards on a par with similar institutions of other religious bodies and which are recognized as maintaining scholarly standards with the educational norms of our state educational systems.

Those not supporting the agencies: They hold that the training of the Christian ministry should be in schools which specialize almost exclusively in the teaching of the Christian faith, particularly from the viewpoint of the Restoration movement. Such schools provide a short-cut to the ministry with a limited approach. It is not considered necessary for such schools to be accredited by state educational authorities or regional academic associations. This has led, in recent years, to the founding of a number of schools, under "Restoration" auspices, of lower scholastic standards and almost entirely devoted to the training of ministers and other Christian workers.

*   *   *   *   *   *

The above outline of differences in viewpoint among the Disciples of Christ, although not always so sharply defined, indicates the areas of diverse judgment.   However, it would seem that not even these rather radical differences of view and policy necessitate a real division among the Disciples of Christ so long as they are not made tests of fellowship and if honest disagreements are not heralded by certain periodicals as "disloyalty," "apostasy," and "infidelity."

It is not likely that Disciples of Christ will ever agree on what constitutes the essentials of the Christian faith.   Perhaps our historic slogan should reflect our actual experience and be phrased realistically thus:

> In the things on which we agree, unity;
> In the things on which we do not agree, liberty;
> In all things, the will to be one.

BIBLIOGRAPHY

Books

Brown, John Thomas, compiler, *Churches of Christ in the United States, Australasia, England and Canada.* Louisville: John P. Morton & Co., 1904, xv + 683 pp.

— and Edwin William Thornton, editors, *Who's Who in Churches of Christ,* Biographical Sketches and Portraits of Ministers and Other Leaders. Cincinnati: Standard Publishing Co., 1929. 299 pp.

Campbell, Alexander, *Debate on the Evidences of Christianity.* Alexander Campbell's Works. Vol. II. Cincinnati: Bosworth, Chase & Hall, 1871. 465 pp.

Carr, James B., *The Foreign Missionary Work of the Christian Church.* St. Louis: John S. Swift Co., 1946. viii + 169 pp.

Centennial Convention Report. One hundredth anniversary of the Disciples of Christ, Pittsburg, October 11-19, 1909. Cincinnati: Standard Publishing Co., n. d. 618 pp.

DeGroot, Alfred Thomas, *The Grounds of Division Among the Disciples of Christ.* Chicago: Privately printed, 1940. 228 pp.

Garrison, James Harvey, editor, *The Reformation of the Nineteenth Century.* St. Louis: Christian Publishing Co., 1901. 514 pp.

Garrison, Winfred Ernest, *Religion Follows the Frontier,* a History of the Disciples of Christ. New York: Harper & Brothers, 1931. xiv + 317 pp.

— and Alfred Thomas DeGroot, *The Disciples of Christ: A History.* St. Louis: Christian Board of Publication, 1948. 592 pp.

Harrison, Ida Withers, *History of the Christian Woman's Board of Missions* (1874-1919). 3rd ed.? Lexington, Kentucky: Privately printed, 1920. 210 pp.

Hayden, Amos Sutton, *Early History of The Disciples in the Western Reserve, Ohio.* Cincinnati: Chase & Hall, 1875. 476 pp.

Moore, William Thomas, *A Comprehensive History of the Disciples of Christ.* New York: Fleming H. Revell Co., 1909. xiv + 830 pp.

Morro, William Charles, *"Brother McGarvey,"* the Life of President J. W. McGarvey of The College of the Bible, Lexington, Kentucky. St. Louis: Bethany Press, 1940. 266 pp.

Spencer, Claude Elbert, compiler, *An Author Catalog of Disciples of Christ and Related Religious Groups.* Canton, Missouri: Disciples of Christ Historical Society, 1946. 367 pp.

—, compiler, *Periodicals of the Disciples of Christ and Related Religious Groups.* Canton, Missouri: Disciples of Christ Historical Society, 1943. 145 pp.

Stevenson, Dwight Eshelman, *Walter Scott, Voice of the Golden Oracle.* St. Louis: Christian Board of Publication, 1946. 240 pp.

Warren, William Robinson, *The Life and Labors of Archibald McLean.* St. Louis: Bethany Press, published for United Christian Missionary Society, 1923. 399 pp.

—, editor, *Survey of Service.* St. Louis: Christian Board of Publication, 1928. 723 pp.

Official Documents, Minutes, and Reports

Blue Book, 1953. Annual Report for 1952, Board of Church Extension of Disciples of Christ. Indianapolis: Board of Church Extension, 1953. 12 pp.

Constitution and By-Laws of the United Christian Missionary Society. Revised ed. Indianapolis: United Christian Missionary Society, September 1, 1929. 12 pp.

Depositions of Robert E. Elmore . . . and Jewell Bishop . . . in Cincinnati, Ohio, . . . April 17, 1951. In case of Loren E. Lair, Plaintiff, vs. The Christian Restoration Association and Robert E. Elmore, Defendants. In the District Court of the United States for the Southern District of Iowa, Central Division. 84 pp., typed.

Eldora, Iowa, Church of Christ. Equity No. 52-299, Judgment and Decree, In the District Court of the State of Iowa, In and for Hardin County, Issued at Hampton, Iowa, on August 23, 1951. 12 pp., typed.

Eleventh Annual Report of the United Christian Missionary Society. July 1, 1930, to June 30, 1931. Indianapolis: United Christian Missionary Society, 1931. 122 pp.

Facts About the Visit of John T. Brown to Some of the Mission Fields and Answers to His Statements in the Christian Standard. St. Louis: The Executive Committee of the United Christian Missionary Society, 1924. 32 pp.

Final Report of The Commission for the Direction of Surveys to the International Convention of Disciples of Christ at Wichita, Kansas, October 6-11, 1931. Indianapolis?; n. p., 1931. 31 pp.

First Annual Report of the United Christian Missionary Society. October 1, 1920–June 30, 1921. St. Louis: United Christian Missionary Society, 1921. 237 pp.

Foreign Christian Missionary Society Executive Committee Minutes. January, 1915–November, 1919; December, 1919–October, 1936. Unpublished.

Foreign Missionary Manual of The United Christian Missionary Society (Disciples of Christ). St. Louis: n. p., 1924. 24 pp. Indianapolis: n. p., 1946. 43 pp.

Headlines of Achievement (formerly *Your Missionary Dollar*). Indianapolis: United Christian Missionary Society, 1952. 8 pp.

International Convention, Disciples of Christ, Columbus, Ohio, October 26-31, 1937. [Edited by J. Edward Moseley.] St. Louis: Christian Board of Publication, 1938. 407 pp.

McCormick, Harry B., *"Report On the Orient."* (Speech on October 12 at Oklahoma City International Convention, Disciples of Christ, October 9-15, 1950.) 1950, mimeographed. [13 pp.]

Minute Books and Records, Advisory Committee, Philippine Christian Institute. (Mission of the United Christian Missionary Society, Disciples of Christ.) February, 1920, to August, 1927. Unpublished.

Minutes of International Convention of Disciples of Christ, Memphis, Tennessee, November 11-17, 1926. Typed. 97 pp.

Proceedings of the Foreign Christian Missionary Society, 1885. Cincinnati: Foreign Christian Missionary Society, 1885?. [52 pp.]

Report of the Commission on Restudy of the Disciples of Christ. Authorized by the International Convention of the Disciples of Christ, San Francisco, 1948. 29 pp.

Report of the Commission to the Orient, Together With the Executive Committee's Charge to the Commission. St. Louis: United Christian Missionary Society, July 15, 1926. 40 pp.

Second Annual Report of the United Christian Missionary Society. July 1, 1921–June 30, 1922. St. Louis: United Christian Missionary Society, 1922. 253 pp.

Statement of the Executive Committee of the United Christian Missionary Society, Together With the Latest Report of the China Mission and All the Missionaries in China. St. Louis: Accepted by the Board of Managers and by the United Christian Missionary Society in the International Convention, Disciples of Christ, of 1922, and reprinted in 1924. 16 pp.

United Christian Missionary Society Minutes. Volumes 9 and 10 (1926), 12 (1927), 26 (1947), and 28 (1950). Unpublished.

Year Book, Disciples of Christ:
1921, 1922. St. Louis: United Christian Missionary Society.
1932. Indianapolis: United Christian Missionary Society.
1936, 1942, 1944, 1946. Indianapolis: Year Book Publication Committee.
1947, 1949, 1950, 1951, 1952. Indianapolis: International Convention of Disciples of Christ.

Your Missionary Dollar. Indianapolis: United Christian Missionary Society, 1951. 4 pp.

Pamphlets and Leaflets

Brown, John Thomas, *The U.C.M.S. Self-Impeached,* A Review of Evidence of Public Record Which the Executive Committee of the U.C.M.S. Must Face. Cincinnati: Standard Publishing Co., 1924? 47 pp.

Church, Samuel Harden, *Religious Progress in America.* Pittsburg: Roy P. Morris, 1910. 42 pp.

Committee of One Thousand. *Attacks on the Holy Bible by Christian Board of Publication and United Christian Missionary Society Leaders and Literature.* Jefferson City, Missouri, 1946. 4 pp.

Committee of One Thousand of Kentucky. *Attention Kentucky Churches!* Louisville, Kentucky, 1946? 4 pp.

Elmore, Robert E., *Should the United Christian Missionary Society Be Dissolved?* Los Angeles: W. S. Humphries, 1926? 31 pp.

Errett, Isaac, *Our Position.* Cincinnati: American Christian Missionary Society, n. d. 32 pp.

Hanson, Robert Edward and Eleanor Wolfe Hanson, *History of Philippine Mission Churches of Christ.* (Reprinted from *Christian Standard* of November 5, 12, 19, 26, 1949). Cincinnati: Standard Publishing Co., 1950. 16 pp.

Henry, David H., editor, *Missionary Handbook of Direct-Support Missionaries of The Churches of Christ.* Eugene, Oregon: Henry Printing Co., 1951. 22 pp.; 1952. 32 pp.

McLean, Archibald, *Debarred From the Standard!* Cincinnati: n. p., 1907. 16 pp.

Stark, Mrs. C. E., *One Hope.* Cincinnati: Standard Publishing Co., 1949. 86 pp.

Periodicals

Christian Baptist, Bethany, Va. Alexander Campbell, editor. Monthly. 1826, 1828.

Christian-Evangelist, The, St. Louis, Mo. Lin D. Cartwright, editor. Weekly. 1894, 1902, 1912, 1926, 1929, 1931, 1935, 1935, 1937, 1938, 1939, 1942, 1943, 1949, 1952, 1953.

Christian News, The, Des Moines, Ia. Loren E. Lair, editor. Monthly. Supplement to September, 1951.

Christian Standard, Cincinnati, O. Burris Butler, editor. Weekly. 1866, 1867, 1868, 1870, 1874, 1885, 1902, 1905, 1906, 1907, 1909-1914, 1916-1951.

Christian Weekly, The, Louisville, Ky. 1905.

College of the Bible Bulletin, The, Lexington, Ky. Bi-monthly. July, 1945.

College of the Bible Quarterly Bulletin, The, Lexington, Ky. May, 1917.

Discipliana, Nashville, Tenn. Claude E. Spencer, editor. Quarterly. April, 1944; October, 1948.

Eureka College *Bulletin,* Eureka, Ill. Monthly. July, 1949.

Gospel Advocate, Nashville, Tenn. B. C. Goodpasture, editor. Weekly. 1935.

Leaven, Indianapolis, Ind. Louise Moseley, editor. Monthly, except July and August. February, 1952.

Millennial Harbinger, Bethany, W. Va. Alexander Campbell and others, editors. Monthly. 1834, 1842, 1845.

Ohio State Journal, Columbus, O. Daily. August 7, 1946.

Quarterly Bulletin of the Campbell Institute, The, Chicago, Ill. 1903, 1905. See, also, *The Scroll.*

Restoration Herald, The, Cincinnati, O. Robert E. Elmore, Editor. Monthly. 1928, 1939, 1946, 1949, 1950, 1951.

Scroll, The, Chicago, Ill. Monthly. 1906. See, also, *The Quarterly Bulletin of the Campbell Institute.*

South African Christian, Cape Town, South Africa. Carroll C. Roberts, editor. Monthly. 1928.

South African Sentinel, The, Johannesburg, South Africa. Basil Holt, editor. Quarterly. 1946-1952.

Spotlight, The, Cincinnati, O. Robert E. Elmore, editor. Monthly. September, 1925. See, also, *The Touchstone.*

Touchstone, The, Cincinnati, O. Robert E. Elmore, editor. Monthly. 1925, 1926. See, also, *The Spotlight.*

World Call, Indianapolis, Ind. George Walker Buckner, Jr., editor. Monthly, except August. 1919, 1920, 1922, 1925, 1926, 1946, 1949.

INDEX